State-building and National Militaries in Postcolonial West Africa

WESTERN AFRICA SERIES

State-building and National Militaries in Postcolonial West Africa

Decolonizing the Means of Coercion, 1958–1974

Riina Turtio

 JAMES CURREY

James Currey
is an imprint of
Boydell & Brewer Ltd
PO Box 9, Woodbridge
Suffolk IP12 3DF (GB)
www.jamescurrey.com
and of
Boydell & Brewer Inc.
668 Mt Hope Avenue
Rochester, NY 14620–2731 (US)
www.boydellandbrewer.com

First published 2023

The publisher has no responsibility for the continued existence or
accuracy of URLs for external or third-party internet websites referred
to in this book, and does not guarantee that any content on such
websites is, or will remain, accurate or appropriate

A catalogue record for this book is available from the British Library

ISBN 978-1-84701-342-2 (James Currey paperback)

The open access version of this publication was funded by the
Swiss National Science Foundation

This publication is printed on acid-free paper

Language editor: Kimberly Storr

Contents

Illustrations

Map

Figures

Tables

Full credit details are provided in the captions to the images in the text. The author and publisher are grateful to all the institutions and individuals for permission to reproduce the materials in which they hold copyright. Every effort has been made to trace the copyright holders; apologies are offered for any omission, and the publisher will be pleased to add any necessary acknowledgement in subsequent editions.

Abbreviations

AAOF	Archives de l'Afrique Occidentale Française (Archives of French West Africa)
ADCI	Archives Diplomatiques, Côte d'Ivoire (Diplomatic Archives, Côte d'Ivoire)
AND	Archives Diplomatiques, Côte d'Ivoire
ANB	Centre National des Archives du Burkina Faso (National Archives Centre of Burkina Faso)
ANG	Archives Nationales de Guinée (National Archives of Guinea)
ANN	Archives Nationales du Niger (National Archives of Niger)
AOF	Afrique Occidentale Française (French West Africa)
CADC	Centre des Archives Diplomatiques de La Courneuve (La Courneuve Diplomatic Archives Centre)
CADN	Centre des Archives Diplomatiques de Nantes (Nantes Diplomatic Archives Centre)
CER	Centre d'exploitation du renseignement (Intelligence Exploitation Centre)
CFA	West African Franc
CGRDS	Central General Records of the Department of State
CIA	Central Intelligence Agency
CMLN	Comité Militaire de Libération Nationale (Military Committee of National Liberation)
CMS	Conseil Mitaire Suprême (Supreme Military Council)
DAM	Direction des Affaires Africaines et Malgaches (Directorate of African and Malagasy Affairs)
FF	French Franc

FFAN	Fonds Foccart, Archives Nationales (Foccart Collection, National Archives)
FLNG	Front de Libération Nationale de la Guinée (Front for the National Liberation of Guinea)
FRUS	Foreign Relations of the United States
FWA	French West Africa
GDP	Gross Domestic Product
GGI	Good Governamce Indicator
GNI	Gross National Income
MAE	Ministère des Affaires Etrangères (Ministry of Foreign Affairs)
MF	Malian Franc
NARA	National Archives and Records Administration
ODA	Official Development Assistance
OPEC	Organization of the Petroleum Exporting Countries
PAIGC	Parti africain pour l'indépendance de la Guinée et du Cap-Vert (African Party for the Independence of Guinea and Cape Verde)
PDCI	Parti démocratique de Côte d'Ivoire (Democratic Party of Côte d'Ivoire)
PDG	Parti démocratique de Guinée (Democratic Party of Guinea)
PPP	Purchasing Power Parity
SAM	Secrétaire général de l'Élysée aux affaires africaines et malgaches (General Secretary for African and Malagasy Affairs)
SDECE	Service de Documentation Extérieure et de Contre-Espionnage (External Documentation and Counter-Espionage Service)
SGDN	Secrétariat général de la défense nationale (General Secretariat for National Defence)
SHD	Service Historique de la Défense (Defence Historical Service)
SIPRI	Stockholm International Peace Research Institute

UDV   Union Démocratique Voltaïque (Voltaic Democratic Union)

US-RDA   Union soudanaise-Rassemblement démocratique africain (Sudanese Union-African Democratic Rally)

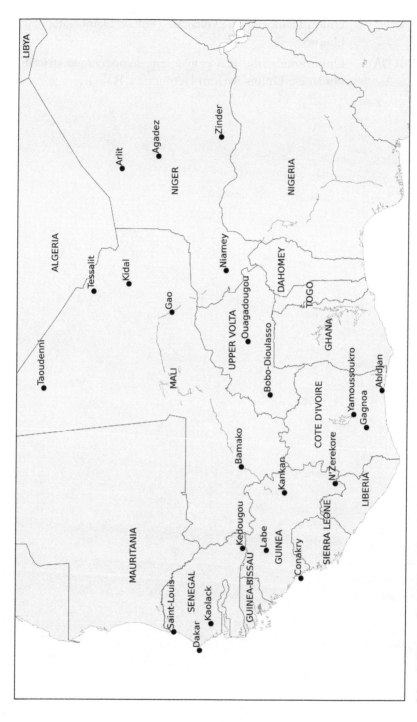

Map 1. Francophone West Africa in 1960.

1
Introduction

What can the development of national militaries in francophone West Africa in the 1960s and 1970s tell us about decolonization and state-building? How was the development of national militaries and political systems in the region influenced by foreign assistance and colonial state structures? These are the two central questions asked in this book. The answers it puts forth emphasize the decision-making powers of African political elites while acknowledging the limitations imposed by their need for external expertise and resources, as well as the profound impact of foreign military assistance on the shape of national armies and political systems in francophone West Africa.

To provide context to the analysis that follows, this chapter discusses the wave of decolonization that took place in the region just as the Cold War intensified, before outlining the approach taken to this research and the structure of the book. The formation of national armed forces in Africa was impacted both by the process of decolonizing (and state-building) and by the polarity of international relations at this time, but few studies have examined these influences in a comparative framework, as this book seeks to do. Thus, it is necessary to return to October 1958, when Guinea gained its independence, and became the first country in French West Africa to abandon the French Community.

Peaceful Decolonization and the Cold War

In 1958, Sekou Touré, president of newly independent Guinea, called on French troops to withdraw, nationalized French-owned companies, and refused to recognize loans taken during the colonial period. Fearful that Guinea would provide a model for its other colonies, the French government adopted a hostile position towards the nationalist leader and urged French allies to deny assistance to his nascent administration (see Chapter 2). Indeed, French president Charles de Gaulle believed the socialist government of Guinea could be brought down in a matter of months through an economic blockade.[1] The Guinean government turned to communist countries for economic and military assistance and received so much military aid from Czechoslovakia that the French intelligence services began to worry that it could be used to support rebel movements in neighbouring countries.

According to Maurice Robert, French intelligence actors participated in multiple covert efforts to depose the Guinean president. These included falsifying Guinean currency and arming Guinean dissidents at the Senegalese border,[2] although, available archival evidence refers only to the embarrassment of the Senegalese government when a weapons cache was found near the border of Senegal in 1960[3]. Touré survived these attempts to remove him from power largely due to economic and intelligence assistance from the communist bloc. However, in 1961, after the election of President Kennedy, the United States also began providing economic assistance to Guinea. Compared to his predecessor, Kennedy gave less weight to the opinions of the French, and generally felt the Cold War would be won or lost in Africa.[4] His support even swayed Touré to take the American side during the Cuban Missile Crisis and deny Soviet planes the option of refuelling in Conakry, on their way to re-equipping Cuba.[5]

Cold War superpowers were deeply interested in Guinea because it was (and still is) home to one of the world's largest reserves of bauxite – a mineral used in aluminium manufacturing. French investments in bauxite

---

1   Maurice Robert, *'Ministre' de l'Afrique: Entretiens avec André Renault* (Paris: Seuil, 2004), p. 107.
2   Ibid., pp. 103–9. Also see: Jacques Foccart, *Foccart Parle: Entretiens avec Philippe Gaillard*, vol. 1 (Paris: Fayard, 1997), pp. 175 and 214; Chargé d'affaires, French Embassy Conakry, 'Situation intérieure Guinée', 28 May 1960, 5AGF/1637, Fonds Foccart, Archives Nationales (FFAN); External Documentation and Counter-Espionage Service (SDECE), 'Guinée: Le complot contre le régime', 9 May 1960, 5AGF/1637, FFAN.
3   French Ministry of Foreign Affairs, Directorate for Africa-Levant, 'Guinée', 2 July 1960; Chargé d'affaires, French Embassy Conakry, 'Situation intérieure Guinée', 28 May 1960.
4   Philip E. Muehlenbeck, *Betting on the Africans: John F. Kennedy's Courting of African Nationalist Leaders* (New York: Oxford University Press, 2012); Robert B. Rakove, *Kennedy, Johnson, and the Nonaligned World* (Cambridge University Press, 2012).
5   US Embassy Conakry to Department of State, 'Bi-weekly no. 7', 15 July 1963, POLGUIN, 770b, Box 3922, Central General Records of the Department of State (CGRDS), National Archives and Records Administration (NARA); US Embassy Conakry to Department of State, 'Bi-weekly no. 8', 22 July 1963, POLGUIN, 770b, Box 3922, CGRDS, NARA; Thomas Cassidy, US Embassy Conakry, 'Sino-Soviet Bloc Political-Economic Relationships with Guinea', 18 July 1963, POLGUIN, Box 2257, CGRDS, NARA.

mining made 'losing' Guinea economically painful, which helps explain French hostility towards American involvement in the country. However, the nature of this involvement was fluid and relations between Guinea and the US deteriorated quickly after Kennedy's assassination in 1963, and also because of the continuing war in Vietnam and the US alliance with former colonial powers Portugal, Belgium, France, and Great Britain. Hence, Touré's decision-making cannot be explained solely as a pragmatic effort to maximize foreign assistance, as pan-Africanism also influenced his strategic perspective, just as it did for leaders in neighbouring Ghana.[6]

Military coups against the socialist presidents of Ghana and Mali made Touré intensely suspicious of both Western powers and his own national armed forces. Increasingly, he viewed the Soviet Union as a key partner in providing military equipment, training, and technical assistance to Guinean forces, and the US as a source of economic assistance and investment. Walking this Cold War tightrope provided several African governments with external resources but also generated instability, and in many cases exacerbated leaders' paranoia. In Guinea, many influential Guineans with foreign connections were arrested and executed for alleged links to plans to overthrow the government. These included prominent individuals involved in the development of the Guinean national armed forces, such as the first Guinean minister of defence, Fodéba Keïta.

In 1959, Keïta took primary responsibility for organizing the Guinean security and armed forces (see Chapter 5) and developed good relations with American and West German officials through military cooperation projects. It remains unclear whether he participated in an attempted coup against Touré. The notes of Vasili Mikrohin, a Soviet intelligence official, suggest that the Soviet Union fabricated evidence to cast suspicions on American activities in Guinea,[7] and Keïta's own communications to American officials indicate that he suspected he was subject to something of this sort.[8] Nonetheless, Keïta was arrested and executed in 1969, on charges that he was behind a military coup plot.[9]

---

6   Frank Gerits, '"When the Bull Elephants Fight": Kwame Nkrumah, Non-Alignment, and Pan-Africanism as an Interventionist Ideology in the Global Cold War (1957–66)', *International History Review* 37, no. 5 (2015), pp. 951–69.

7   Vasili Mitrokhin and Christopher Andrew, *The World Was Going Our Way: The KGB and the Battle for the Third World* (Basic Books, 2005), pp. 437–9.

8   Pierre Graham, US Embassy Conakry, to Department of State, 12 March 1965, POLGUIN 1964–1966, Box 2260, CGRDS, NARA.

9   Evidence of Keïta's guilt or innocence is inconclusive, but French intelligence reports do suggest that Deputy Chief of Staff of the Guinean Army Kaman Diaby had

There is similar mystery surrounding a Portuguese-led attack on the Guinean capital in November 1970, as the goal and identity of the planners are disputed to this day. At the time, Guinea was cooperating with Cuba to support the anti-colonial movement in neighbouring Guinea-Bissau and had taken Portuguese prisoners. The obvious purpose of the Portuguese-led attack was to liberate these prisoners from detention in Conakry; but whether the intention was also to kill both President Touré and the leader of Guinea-Bissau's anti-colonialist movement is a matter of debate. Touré also accused France and West Germany of involvement in devising the attack (see Chapters 2 and 5), and the confessions of Guineans who were arrested – which were published in the newspaper *Horoya* in 1971 – along with an internal memo, suggest that this was the case.[10] However, an American report claimed Touré had emphasized the role of foreigners in the attack to divert attention from internal dysfunction and dissatisfaction in Guinea.[11]

Either way, the poor response of Guinean forces to the attack raised Touré's suspicions that the army had collaborated with the attackers.[12] Army Chief of Staff Noumandian Keïta and a number of other soldiers were executed for their alleged participation, and a subsequent purge within the army rid the forces of many influential soldiers with ties to France or past service in the French military. We may never know exactly what happened in November 1970, but this example and others like it demonstrate the considerable impact of the Cold War on the development of the national armed forces and the political system in Guinea, as well as other countries in francophone West Africa.

The Soviet Union did have a significant influence on the development of the Malian armed forces, for the government in Mali received most of its military equipment from the Soviet Union, both before and after the military coup in 1968. In fact, the value of Soviet arms transfers to Mali and Guinea surpassed the value of French military transfers to other francophone

declared support for a coup against Touré. See Ministry of Armed Forces, SDECE, 'Guinée-Sénégal-Côte d'Ivoire', 29 July 1966, 5AGF/1647, FFAN.

10 Presidency of the Republic of Guinea, State Secretariat for National Defence, 'Élément de renseignement sur la production agricole dans l'armée', 17 November 1971, 3N1, Archives Nationales de Guinée (ANG); Mamadi Keïta, Cabinet Minister, Presidency of the Republic of Guinea, 'Rapport sur les méfaits des agents de la 5eme colonne', 18 November 1971, 3N1, ANG.

11 US Embassy Conakry to Department of State, 'Fifth column in Guinea', 20 July 1970, POLGUIN 1970–1973, Box 2340, CGRDS, NARA.

12 US Embassy Conakry to Department of State, 'Policy Planning Paper', 6 July 1971, POLGUIN 1970–1973, Box 2341, CGRDS, NARA.

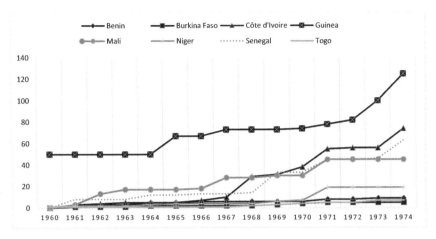

Figure 1. The cumulative value of arms transfers to francophone West Africa, 1960–1974 (Source: SIPRI arms transfers database, https://www.sipri.org/databases/armstransfers, accessed 27.12.2021).

West African countries (see Figure 1). Guinea and Mali voted most often with the Soviet Union in the United Nations General Assembly, a level of diplomatic support that it did not enjoy from other regional countries receiving its military aid (see Figure 2). Despite this, the role of the Soviet Union in the development of postcolonial states and the diplomatic support it gained through military and intelligence cooperation has often been underestimated.[13]

In general, the concept of socialism was popular among the leaders of newly independent countries, as capitalism was associated with colonialism. Touré thus made opposition to colonialism and imperialism a centrepiece of his foreign policy, and he was not alone in so doing. In fact, the diplomatic support that newly independent countries provided each other revolutionized international relations in the 1960s.[14] In addition to the Cold War, colonial structures also influenced the building of national militaries. Even in Guinea and Mali, national armed forces were initially formed from

13 Guia Migani, 'Sekou Touré et la contestation de l'ordre colonial en Afrique sub-Saharienne, 1958–1963', *Monde(s)* 2, no. 2 (2012), pp. 257–73; Elizabeth Schmidt, *Foreign Intervention in Africa: From the Cold War to the War on Terror* (Cambridge University Press, 2013).

14 Matthew Connelly, *A Diplomatic Revolution: Algeria's Fight for Independence and the Origins of the Post-Cold War Era* (New York: Oxford University Press, 2002).

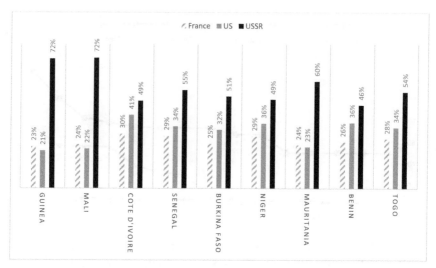

Figure 2. Voting similarities at the UN General Assembly, 1960–1974 (Source: UN votes: https://digitallibrary.un.org and https://dataverse.harvard.edu/dataset, published 03.02.2009, accessed 12.4.2020).

soldiers transferred from the French military, who were then deployed to bases left empty by the French departure.

In other francophone West African countries, continuities from the colonial period were even more striking. Their governments remained aligned with France after independence, and their armies continued to be trained and equipped by France (see Chapters 2 and 3). In fact, five of these governments – Senegal, Côte d'Ivoire, Dahomey, Mauritania, and Niger – had explicitly requested that French military bases be maintained on their territories. Hence, decolonization in West Africa did not always mean the withdrawal of France. The strategic importance of this region meant that successive French governments invested significant resources in maintaining influence in former French colonies. To that end, military cooperation and close interpersonal relationships between African and French decision-makers were crucial.[15]

The person who was largely responsible for realizing France's Africa policy from 1960 to 1974 was Jacques Foccart, the General Secretary for

---

15 Jean-Pierre Bat, *Le syndrome Foccart: la politique française en Afrique, de 1959 à nos jours* (Paris: Gallimard, 2012), pp. 81, 137–9, 152–8, 216, and 248–54; Tony Chafer, *The End of Empire in French West Africa: France's successful decolonization?* (Oxford: Berg, 2002).

African Affairs, who used both French intelligence networks and personal relationships with African presidents to protect French interests. French officials like Foccart also perceived themselves as defending the former colonies against any 'foreign interference'. However, the France's power to dictate the policy decisions of African governments is sometimes overestimated.[16] As examples in this book will demonstrate, there were limits to French influence, and African politicians and soldiers alike made decisions that French officials neither wanted nor expected.

Ultimately, the decisions made by African governments demonstrate that African political and military elites have played the most important role in developing African political systems and national armed forces. Even in Senegal and Côte d'Ivoire – the two countries most strategically and economically important to France, and the recipients of the greatest amount of French military and economic assistance – those policies formulated by the executive most strongly shaped the development of national forces. While a French military presence and considerable French aid may have helped assure stability in Senegal and Côte d'Ivoire, similar assistance did not shield other African presidents from military coups.

In 1974, Niger became the fifth of the nine francophone West African countries to undergo a coup when its former colonial soldiers removed Hamani Diori, the country's first president.[17] Diori had been an important ally of France until relations between the two countries soured after he attempted to negotiate a better price for his country's uranium. At the same time, Diori's domestic legitimacy was undermined by accusations of corruption, brought nakedly to bear by a famine that afflicted much of the population. The corruption of civilian governments has been linked to the tendency of soldiers to carry out coups,[18] if only because it provides a convenient excuse,[19] and in Niger, it did so for the Chief of Staff of the Nigerien Armed Forces, Seyni Kountché. On the Easter weekend of 1974, following the death of French president Georges Pompidou, Kountché assumed power and ousted the civilian government. In interviews, Nigerien

16 Robin Luckham, 'French Militarism in Africa', *Review of African Political Economy* 2, no. 5 (1982), pp. 55–84; Guy Martin, 'Continuity and Change in Franco-African Relations', *Journal of Modern African Studies* 33, no. 1 (1995), pp. 1–20.
17 Togo and Dahomey experienced coups in 1963, and Upper Volta in 1966, before Mali in 1968.
18 Tendi Blessing-Miles, 'Transnationalism, Contingency and Loyalty in African Liberation Armies: The Case of ZANU's 1974–1975 Nhari Mutiny', *Journal of Southern African Studies* 43, no. 1 (2017), pp. 143–59.
19 Paul Nugent, *Africa Since Independence* (New York: Palgrave Macmillan, 2004).

soldiers said they had calculated that Pompidou's death would catch the French off guard. On top of this, the absence of French technical assistants over the holiday weekend had presented a good opportunity for avoiding detection.

Although France had a military base in Niger and a military cooperation agreement with Diori, French forces did not intervene to stop Kountché.[20] This lack of response led to suspicions that France was behind the coup, as it presented an opportunity for assuring access to Nigerien uranium. However, France did not seem to gain from Diori's political demise. In fact, when negotiations on Nigerien uranium restarted, Kountché won the right to sell some of Niger's uranium to whomever he wished.[21] The Nigerien military also requested that French forces withdraw, and that military cooperation with West Germany and the US be strengthened, which increased the material resources available to Nigerien forces.

Nigerien soldiers justified the coup by highlighting the corruption of the civilian government, especially its failure to help Nigeriens suffering from drought and famine. It was indeed the unpopularity of the civilian government that facilitated the coup.[22] As one Nigerien gendarme explained: 'Everyone was tired of Diori, even his ministers. Even Sani Siddo, who was one of Diori's fidèles, was among the plotters.'[23] Siddo, who had been the head of Diori's presidential guard, was arrested soon after the coup, along with some of his alleged co-conspirators, as Kountché centralized power to himself.[24]

Despite promises to the contrary, the military coup and increased uranium production in Niger had little positive impact on the wellbeing of ordinary Nigeriens. In 1974, when Kountché came to power, Niger had the highest child mortality rate in Africa, and it had roughly the same rate thirteen years later when he died in office. Nor did his death mark the end of the military's political role in Niger – most presidents before the millennium had started their careers in the armed forces – and Nigerien soldiers would again carry out coups in 1996, 1999, and 2010. In the post-Cold War years,

[20] Klaas van Walraven, '"Opération Somme": La *French Connection* et le coup d'état de Seyni Kountché au Niger en avril 1974', *Politique africaine* 134, no. 2 (2014), pp.133–54.
[21] Gabrielle Hecht, *Being Nuclear: Africans and the Global Uranium Trade* (MIT Press, 2012), pp. 100–3.
[22] Interviews in Niamey, May 2019.
[23] Ibid.
[24] Ambassador Paul-Henri Gaschignard, 'Situation intérieure', 24 September 1974, 478PO1–94, Centre des Archives Diplomatiques de Nantes (CADN) and 'Situation intérieure', 3 July 1974, 478PO1–94, CADN.

the external response to coups did become less permissive and scholars have argued that pressure to democratize made following formal procedures more important.[25] Nevertheless, many francophone West African countries continue to see soldiers playing a political role.

After the 1978 military coup in Mauritania, only three francophone West African countries remained in the hands of civilian presidents. Senegal's Léopold Senghor would be the only one of the first francophone West African presidents to leave office voluntarily, when he transferred power to a hand-picked successor in 1980. In Guinea and Côte d'Ivoire, military coups did take place, but not until after the deaths of their first presidents. These histories reveal the central role of soldiers in the development of state institutions and political systems in the region, and also make clear that environmental conditions, international politics, and colonial history also shaped the structure of state institutions. Even so, more attention should be given to the agency exerted in the decisions and actions of African elites and citizens in determining the futures of their countries, and this study attempts to do that by analysing the decisions of francophone West African governments.

Armed Forces and State-building: The Development of National Militaries in West Africa

The nine countries analysed herein were all part of French West Africa – *Afrique occidentale française* – and shared similar colonial structures. However, upon independence, the new governments took different turns regarding economic, foreign, and defence policy. This study focuses on four key themes: the autonomy, sovereignty, legitimacy, and governance. First, the degree to which African governments were autonomous in making defence-related decisions is considered, as well as the impact of foreign military assistance on national armed forces and political systems. Second, the effectiveness of these governments in maintaining sovereign control over their populations and territories is explored, in order to uncover factors that have influenced the development of national military capacities. Third, the question of how these governments dealt with colonial coercive structures and legacies of colonial violence is examined. In other words, how did they seek to legitimize their rule, their use of force, and institutions of coercion? Finally, the ways in

---

25 Daniel Posner and Daniel Young, 'The Institutionalization of Political Power in Africa', *Journal of Democracy* 18, no. 3 (2007), pp. 126–40.

which different governance strategies have impacted militaries and societies as a whole in these countries is analysed.

Each of the countries that once made up French West Africa – Côte d'Ivoire, Dahomey (now Benin), Guinea, Mali, Mauritania, Niger, Senegal, Upper Volta (now Burkina Faso), and Togo – are discussed in this text. To better understand the impact of foreign assistance, the analysis considers six of these in pairs, based on their relationship to international powers: the two countries that received military assistance from communist states (Guinea and Mali); the two countries most closely allied with France (Côte d'Ivoire and Senegal); and the two countries that remained close to France but received the least French economic and military assistance (Upper Volta and Niger). The decisions of these governments from 1958, when Guinea gained independence, until 1974 are analysed.

In 1973, all nine francophone West African governments experienced a profound shift, as did many others around the world. As oil-importing countries, they had to absorb the rising costs of energy, and the 1973 oil crisis reduced the resources available for public spending.[26] This had an impact on militaries and shaped diplomacy. For example, as the price of oil increased, so did the influence of the Gulf, leading most African countries to cut their diplomatic ties to Israel. In 1974, French foreign policy also changed, when Valéry Giscard d'Estaing became president and Jacques Foccart was no longer the French General Secretary for African Affairs.[27]

Foccart's role had been so dominant that jealousies and suspicions swirled around him within French diplomatic circles. In fact, in 1971, a French diplomat complained to his American colleague that Foccart was 'more powerful than ever' after the death of de Gaulle. When Foccart had disagreements with the Foreign Ministry, he would 'resolve' the dispute by announcing that he had talked with the president, who had come to a (Foccart's) decision. 'Whether he has really talked to Pompidou, no one knows, but nobody dares to question him', said one French official.[28] As this research focuses on African rather than French decision-making, it cannot provide a final judgement on Foccart's role. However, at least in the case of Sékou Touré, it seems that de Gaulle overrode the Foccart's efforts

---

26 Nicolas van de Walle, *African Economies and the Politics of Permanent Crisis, 1979–1999* (Edinburgh: Cambridge University Press, 2001), p. 3.
27 Bat, *Le syndrome Foccart*, pp. 337–86.
28 US Embassy Paris, 'Memorandum of conversation: Michel van Grevenynghe, Deputy Chief of Staff to Yvon Bourges', 26 April 1971, POL AFR–FR 1970–1973, Box 2034, CGRDS, NARA.

to reconcile the two presidents. From the perspective of African leaders, Foccart was key to facilitating their contact with the French executive, even if French ambassadors also played an important role in some countries, as in Côte d'Ivoire.

By centring the outlook and decision-making of African governments in building their national militaries, and the impact of those decisions on state-building, this book acknowledges that the development of national armed and security forces is essential to understanding state formation, since coercion and statehood are linked. To a large extent, statehood is a function of the power to make decisions about the rules that regulate human interactions, and the capacity to enforce them. This places the means of coercion at the heart of what a state *is*, as coercion is necessary not only to enforce the rules but also to sometimes decide who makes them. A monopoly on the legitimate use of force is thus seen to characterize the state,[29] as it allows rulers to control the land and population within a certain territory.

Colonial states were based on foreign dominance, but their recourse to violence was limited after the initial conquest, and the capacities of their administrators to enforce formal rules established in the metropole were marginal. Therefore, at independence, few African countries had the administrative capacity to govern their territories.[30] In many cases, colonial empires had constructed minimal administrative structures,[31] as the prevailing view was that colonies should be fiscally self-sufficient.[32] As a consequence, newly independent countries faced the enormous tasks of building both state institutions and administrative structures.

Extending the reach of state control only makes sense, however, if a state has sufficient economic or coercive resources at its disposal, and if control over territory provides resources to the central government. In the process of decolonization, the power to define the rules, and the means to enforce them, was transferred to local populations but colonial structures would continue to provide the basis for state institutions, as changing them would have required resources and technical expertise that most nascent countries

---

29 Max Weber, *Theory of Social and Economic Organization* (New York: Free Press, 1964), pp. 325–66.
30 Frederick Cooper, *Colonialism in Question: Theory, Knowledge, History* (Berkeley: University of California Press, 2005), p. 157; Patrick Chabal and Jean-Pascal Daloz, *Africa Works: Disorder as Political Instrument* (Oxford: James Currey, 1999), p.12.
31 Cooper, *Colonialism in Question*, p. 157; Chabal and Daloz, *Africa Works*, p. 12.
32 Crawford Young, *The African Colonial State in Comparative Perspective* (London: Yale University Press, 1994), p. 97.

lacked. Hence, statehood is not only about making rules and enforcing them, but also about resources. How a state attains and uses resources, and how they are allocated, forms the basis for all state institutions, including its armed forces. Thus, the building of national militaries occurs in dialogue with the development of political systems.

The tendency of soldiers to assume political roles and overthrow colonial and postcolonial civilian governments reflected weaknesses in the structures of political participation and taxation in those governments. Social spending in the colonial state was kept to a minimum and was mainly allocated to Europeans on the premise that colonies should pay for themselves.[33] The few educational opportunities available to colonized Africans were usually situated in capital cities, which created or maintained huge social disparities. After independence, weak systems of taxation and deficient social spending persisted. There had also been a stark rise in overall spending after the Second World War, mainly due to increasing social demands. As the colonies had yet to generate additional revenues, this led to large budget deficits that carried over into the postcolonial period and were covered by external assistance or credit.[34]

The role of foreign resources, structures, and expertise differentiate state formation in Africa from the same process in Europe, where the administrative capacities were developed as a by-product of the rulers' need to attain the men, arms, and finances with which to wage war.[35] In francophone West Africa, state formation as a consequence of decolonization was largely peaceful, but armed forces still played important roles in the development of postcolonial states. Indeed, in former French colonies and in West Africa – where military coups and military rule are both common – the actors making decisions about state-building have often been soldiers.[36] In fact, by 1980, more than half of the countries

33 Leigh Gardner, *Taxing Colonial Africa: The Political Economy of British Imperialism* (Oxford University Press, 2012).

34 Denis Cogneau, Yannick Dupraz, and Sandrine Mesplé-Somps, 'African states and development in historical perspective: Colonial public finances in British and French West Africa', *PSE Working Papers*, No. 2018–27, 2018.

35 Charles Tilly, *Coercion, Capital and European States, AD 990–1990* (Oxford: Blackwell, 1997).

36 Pat McGowan and Thomas H. Johnson, 'African Military Coups d'Etat and Underdevelopment: A Quantitative Historical Analysis', *Journal of Modern African Studies* 22, no. 4 (1984), pp. 633–66; Patrick J. McGowan 'African military coups d'état, 1956–2001: frequency, trends and distribution', *Journal of Modern African Studies* 41, no. 3 (2003), pp. 339–70.

in Africa had experienced a military coup, a chain of events that started with the military takeover in Togo in 1963.[37]

These coups demonstrated the weaknesses of centralized political systems and concentrated power, although foreign military and economic assistance often contributed to the consolidation of power and resources, as it allowed governments to monopolize the means of coercion or attain sufficient economic resources to remain in power, even with limited internal support. Towards the end of the Cold War, it became increasingly evident that state-building efforts in many parts of Africa had not been altogether successful, at least if measured by indicators of economic development or political stability. The failures were most obvious in the security sector: instead of providing security, national militaries and police were among the main sources of insecurity.[38]

State security apparatuses in Africa were – and are – weakened by a lack of supervision, the abuse of public resources and democratic control, and impunity for serious crimes and human rights violations. Few plans and activities to support state-building and the restructuring of security establishments in Africa, often with Western assistance, have achieved the desired results. The question is why – one reason that has been suggested is that post-independence elites have had few incentives to institutionalize their rule or build effective state institutions, preferring centralized rule based on patrimonial ties.[39]

Cold War competition increased the economic and military resources available to African governments and militaries, but also had destructive consequences on postcolonial states in Cold War conflict zones.[40] Military assistance may have been granted by Cold War powers to authoritarian rulers on the basis of factors such as a state's stability or political alliances,[41]

37   Nugent, *Africa Since Independence*, p. 204; Samuel Decalo, *Coups and Army Rule in Africa* (London: Yale University Press, 1976), p. 6.
38   Dominique Bangoura, 'L'état et la sécurité', *Politique Africaine* 61 (1996), p. 39; Robin Luckham, 'The Military, Militarization and Democratization in Africa: A Survey of Literature', *African Studies Review* 37, no. 2 (1994), p. 22.
39   William Reno, *Warlord Politics and African States* (London: Lynne Rienner Publishers, 1998), p. 22; Chabal and Daloz, *Africa Works*, pp. 13–15; Jeffrey Herbst, *States and Power in Africa: Comparative Lessons in Authority and Control* (Princeton University Press, 2000), pp. 85, 225, and 253–4.
40   Odd Arne Westad, *The Global Cold War: Third World Interventions and the Making of Our Times* (Cambridge University Press, 2006).
41   Christopher Clapham, *Africa and the International System* (Cambridge University Press, 1996), pp. 80–96 and 137–8; Cooper, *Africa since 1940: The Past of the Present* (Cambridge University Press, 2002), pp. 159–60.

but the availability of foreign military and economic assistance contributed to strategies of extraversion among African elites more broadly. In other words, these elites were focused on mobilizing resources from the external environment instead of relying on citizens for support.[42]

Previous scholarship on the history of francophone West Africa has overlooked the impact of foreign military assistance or Cold War competition on state-building.[43] Foreign resources were, however, more readily available during state-building processes in the region precisely because decolonization coincided with intense Cold War competition. The priority given to foreign assistance by African presidents shrank their domestic bases of support, making their overthrow more tempting to local challengers. At the same time, foreign military aid contributed to the ability of state coercive capacities to extend the strength of political institutions. The centralization of power and the concentration of resources to a few individuals often made soldiers the only actors capable of challenging the government. With wealth and opportunity beyond their reach, ordinary citizens had little reason to object when soldiers claimed to be protecting them from corrupt politicians.

Military coups made foreign actors more eager to provide military assistance in order to build strong relations with African military elites. Even so, foreign human and material resources did not always increase national military capacities. Indeed, civilian governments feared building strong armed forces that could pose the risk of a military coup. Moreover, military rule often decreased the military effectiveness of national forces. When leading officers were engaged in state governance, indiscipline and internal infighting became more common.

Sources and Methodology

The role of soldiers in the development of postcolonial states in Africa extended beyond their engagement through national armed forces to the rest of society. This was true even in the few West African states that did not experience military coups or military rule. However, only a few studies have analysed the development of African armed forces from a comparative historical perspective, primarily due to difficulties in accessing information, as archival sources on national militaries have not been available. Meanwhile,

---

[42] Jean-Francois Bayart, 'Africa in the World: A History of Extraversion', *African Affairs* 99 (2000), pp. 217–67.
[43] Patrick Manning, *Francophone Sub-Saharan Africa, 1880–1985* (Cambridge University Press, 1988).

research based mainly on interviews limits the perspective and number of case studies, statistical analyses of large numbers of states restrain the analysis to a few parameters and increase the likelihood of missing significant factors, and single case studies often concentrate on technical aspects of the military and rely on interviews and secondary sources, which are cited in the footnotes in each chapter. Comparative analysis is thus key to understanding the impact of foreign military assistance and presence, particularly in the rare cases where it did *not* contribute to a weak military or authoritarian rule. For instance, the history of Senegal provides examples of factors that contributed to its successful civilian control and the institutionalization of its army. Analysing multiple case studies, alongside archival research, interviews, and quantitative databases, can help illuminate which factors have most significantly influenced the building of national militaries.

Studying the development of armed forces through quantitative data does have its drawbacks. Numerical data for postcolonial African states, for example, is often unreliable or incomplete.[44] Nor do numbers tell the whole story regarding the development of national militaries or postcolonial states. Even if the data is accurate, the estimated numerical strength of an army or the military spending of a state does not indicate its military capabilities, or whether soldiers have adequate equipment and training. Similarly, the value of an arms transfer does not speak to whether military equipment is operational, or whether the technical expertise and budgetary allocations are in place to use and maintain it. Whilst the military expenditures of a state might well reflect the priority given to soldiers in a society, they do not necessarily imply the capacity of a government to control its population and territory, particularly if the bulk of military resources are used to pay officer salaries, rather than maintain equipment properly and train soldiers.

Insufficient and incorrect data will always limit our understanding of the development of national armed forces. Nonetheless, this research addresses and attempts to mitigate this challenge by incorporating documents from French, American, Senegalese, Guinean, Nigerien, Ivorian, and Burkinabe archives. French military, diplomatic, and presidential archives offer the most complete information on the development of armed forces in francophone West Africa. Guinea and Mali aside, French technical assistants worked within the national armed forces of these countries, and thus provided fairly accurate information about them. Of course, there is a considerable risk of

---

44 Morten Jerven, *Poor Numbers: How We Are Misled by African Development Statistics and What to Do about It* (Cornell University Press, 2013).

bias in relying on French analyses of African armed forces, which is why material found in French archives has been cross-referenced with diplomatic reports from US officials. These archival documents are complemented by interviews with Ivorian, Burkinabe, Nigerien, and Senegalese soldiers, as well as quantitative data from the World Bank and the Stockholm International Peace Research Institute (SIPRI). Nonetheless, there remain many uncertainties and unanswered questions. Hopefully, these can be answered in the future, in interviews with African political and military elites and through the declassification of military, intelligence, and diplomatic archives.

Objectives and Structure of the Book

The primary objective of this book is to provide new insights into the way colonial structures, foreign actors, and foreign resources influenced the development of postcolonial African states. It seeks to encourage students and researchers to find innovative ways of combining archival research, interviews, and quantitative evidence in studying history, state institutions, and development. A secondary objective is to persuade both students and scholars of the need to take a more comprehensive view of state institutions. The development of armed forces is integrally linked to political and economic systems, for example, and should not be analysed separately from other state structures. Taking a wider perspective on the development of state institutions also means accounting for both endogenous and exogenous factors.

Through the lens of military aid, this study emphasizes the importance and limits of foreign influence in Africa. Foreign military assistance or foreign interventions in Africa can evoke controversial associations and popular conspiracies about neo-colonial control over African raw materials in exchange for military backing of dictators. Evidence supporting such theories does not appear in this book, which instead makes a case for acknowledging the power of African decision-makers in their asymmetrical bilateral relations with foreign powers. By analysing the personal role of African presidents while recognizing the environment in which they operated and were shaped, this book offers some nuance. Comparative historical research on state institutions can allow us to understand both the structural and individual limits to their development, and can also highlight the potential for change.

This book aims to contribute new subtleties to the ways the first presidents of francophone West Africa are viewed, each of whom is a controversial figure in their own country. For some, these presidents are national heroes, while for others, they are brutal dictators or colonialist collaborators. As the former head of a country can be seen as the cause of exclusion, suffering, and national or personal misfortune, family and personal histories often determine how an individual remembers a president.

Here, an attempt has been made to avoid examining military aid or authoritarian rulers through the moral dichotomy of good and evil. The purpose is to analyse the interests and motivations that impact and explain human behaviour, which often combine oppositional drivers such as self-interest and altruism. These interests and motivations do not imply impact, especially in an unpredictable world where humans frequently miscalculate the situation. In fact, this book challenges the basis of most conspiracy theories by providing evidence of just how *badly* those in power have predicted the future or the consequences of their actions.

Finally, this book seeks to inform decision-makers and citizens in countries receiving and granting military assistance. The case studies it presents demonstrate, for instance, that countries granting military aid have had little control over how it was used. Hence, such countries should carefully evaluate whether their objectives can be achieved in a given context, and whether those objectives are shared by the receiving government, in which case military assistance may have fewer adverse and unexpected effects. These case studies also show how real or imagined competition between different actors can increase the likelihood of miscalculations when decisions are made quickly and without proper information-gathering, sharing, and analysis. This calls for better coordination of assistance both with other granting countries and local actors. The cases in this book also make it clear that when granting countries focus solely on maintaining or increasing their influence, protecting their economic interests, and attending to their immediate security concerns, it often results in adverse long-term impacts. This was true in francophone West African countries, where the centralization of power and resources often led to instability.

The history of francophone West Africa highlights many of the pitfalls of relying on foreign assistance, which commonly undermines a government's legitimacy and narrows the base of support for its leaders. In other words, it is a risky strategy. The option to blame foreign actors for domestic shortcomings may effectively gather popular support, but it can also make a government appear powerless and weak. While external resources can help members of the political elite buy local support, those resources can quickly be shifted to a competitor, as examples in this book will illustrate. Thus, receiving governments may find it useful to undertake a realistic analysis of any partner country. Ultimately, most successful development strategies in our interconnected world require international cooperation, and the case studies presented in this book suggest that African governments should not assume they are predetermined victims in international interactions. All decision-making is limited by structural and political factors, but the different decisions made by African presidents demonstrate that alternatives do exist and can be exercised. This means that current and future African policymakers have the power to shape a different future for their countries, and for the continent, if they focus more on building institutions and less on building a personal following, and form governments that rely more on citizens and less on foreign backing and resources.

The four thematic aspects of statehood – autonomy, sovereignty, legitimacy, and governance – reflect the transformation of a colony to an independent state that occurs in the process of decolonization. Importantly, this transformation not only implies a change in status, but also concrete expectations about what independence brings, namely, a new state that enacts policies of its own choosing and has sovereignty and effective control over the population and territory within its borders. Furthermore, the principle of self-determination – which paved the way for decolonization and independence in Africa – presumes that governments in independent states have a relationship with their subjects, that rulers and institutions in these states are considered legitimate by a majority of the population, and that citizens should participate in decision-making through political institutions and processes.

The perceived failures of African state-building can likewise be described in relation to autonomy, sovereignty, legitimacy, and governance. Autonomy was challenged by the importance of external actors and resources in African policy decisions and state development. Moreover, the availability of this external assistance reduced the incentives for governments to ensure sovereign control over their territory and population. The provision of infra-structure and services by states was uneven, and the weak control exerted by central governments became more visible when challenged by non-state armed groups. Legitimacy was undermined by this reliance on exogenous actors and resources, as well as the weaknesses of endogenous structures. National armed forces also faced issues of legitimacy, related in part to the colonial roots of these institutions, and also to the way they were used to dispose of opposition and silence dissenting voices in what often became one-party states. On top of this, the centralization of power and resources into just a few hands created problems in governing the armed forces, most clearly demonstrated by the regularity of military coups and military rule during the decades following independence.

The following chapter, on autonomy, examines the degree to which francophone West African governments were able to make their own defence-related decisions. It argues that these governments had more room to manoeuvre in their relations with external actors than previously thought. Indeed, case studies reveal how skilfully some African presidents used the desires and fears of foreign partners to maximize foreign assistance and increase their personal power. Chapter three, on sovereignty, analyses the decisions of francophone West African governments in developing national military capacities in order to increase government control over their populations and territories. Colonial security structures were not designed or well-adapted to guarantee the territorial integrity of these independent states, nor to provide security for their citizens, and many nascent African governments encountered difficulties in trying to alter colonial coercive structures. The lack of resources and expertise was the biggest obstacle, but on top of this, incentives to build a strong and institutionalized military were reduced by the availability of foreign assistance, the frequency of military coups, and the existence of few external threats. The fourth chapter, on legitimacy, describes the transition from colonial security systems to national militaries, and efforts by African governments to address the difficult legacies of colonial coercive structures. Chapter five looks at how national militaries in francophone West Africa were governed, particularly how centralized political systems based on personal ties influenced the development of national armed forces.

2

Autonomy: Foreign Assistance and African Decision-making

Decolonization and state-building took place in West Africa against the backdrop of the Cold War, and saw African decision-makers draw ideological and economic inspiration for their own nations from competing socialist and capitalist countries.[1] This international competition also increased the willingness of foreign actors to provide assistance to African governments, which afforded them some influence over African decision-making. However, foreign assistance to African governments increased the centralization of political power and resources, giving African presidents little incentive to share this power and these resources with potential challengers.[2] This chapter focuses on the ways foreign actors pressured African governments to adopt specific decisions, highlighting the strategies used by African presidents to take advantage of foreign ambitions in order to mobilize resources from the external environment.

Questions about the impact of foreign influence on African decision-making are important because they relate to ongoing debates about *what went wrong* with African economic, political, and social development. The failings of African state institutions can be blamed on foreign intervention, on the legacy of European colonialism, or neo-colonialism, or on the recklessness of Cold War states that offered self-serving aid to authoritarian leaders.[3] However, this book focuses on the agency of African officials by analysing their decisions and actions, and this chapter shows that leaders in the nine francophone West African governments made very different decisions at independence. For example, despite sharing the same colonial structures – all having been part of French West Africa – newly independent Guinea, Mali, and Upper Volta asked French troops to leave, while Niger, Côte d'Ivoire, Mauritania, and Senegal all insisted these troops remain.

---

1   Westad, *The Global Cold War.*
2   Reno, *Warlord Politics and African States*; Chabal and Daloz, *Africa Works.*
3   Schmidt, *Foreign Intervention in Africa: From the Cold War to the War on Terror.*

The varied strategies of these West African countries regarding alignment with Cold War powers and with France demonstrate that political power was indeed transferred to local governments upon independence, and that African leaders made decisions foreign allies did not want or predict. Still, the role of African *citizens* in national decision-making remained limited. Charles Tilly has suggested that this is because the means of coercion were provided by external powers. He has noted that European state institutions were formed over time as a by-product of efforts by rulers to acquire the means to wage wars, whereas in Africa, these institutions were simply imported from Europe. The internal state-building process that took place in Europe also forced European rulers to negotiate with citizens on the role of state institutions because they depended on the economic contribution of their populations.[4] In Africa, however, rulers could largely dismiss popular opinion, as both the means of coercion and the resources to sustain regimes were provided from the outside. Postcolonial states where popular support for leaders was low were prone to instability, and while African states received military equipment from external powers and were dependent on foreign technical assistance to operate and maintain that equipment, African national militaries were made up of African soldiers – who could and did influence the decisions of African governments.

Research on precolonial state formation in Africa underscores the fact that state-building processes have long been determined by the ease with which the means of coercion can be monopolized. In the precolonial era, the arrival of technologically superior weapons from Europe, which could not be manufactured locally, allowed the means of coercion to be monopolized by smaller numbers of people. Trade with Europeans in slaves and firearms incentivized African rulers to capture populations and extend their reach over larger territories. This made them dependent on access to European weapons, the very same technology European powers would use to establish colonial empires.[5] The minimalist administrative structures of European colonies in Africa could not have functioned without African partners and, like postcolonial states, colonial states were formed and maintained by the cooperation of external actors with local elites.[6]

---

4   Tilly, *Coercion, Capital and European States, AD 990–1990*, pp. 14–15, 195–6, 199–200, and 206–8.

5   Jack Goody, *Technology, Tradition and the State in Africa* (London: Hutchinson, 1980); Richard Reid, *Warfare in African History* (Cambridge University Press, 2012).

6   Cooper, 'Possibility and Constraint: African Independence in Historical Perspective', *Journal of African History* 49, no. 2 (2008), pp. 167–96, see 171 and 176; Bayart, 'Africa in the World', pp. 220–2 and 248–9.

Historical continuities can be seen both in the strategies of extraversion used by African elites – which were aimed at mobilizing the utmost resources possible from the international environment – and in their role as colonial and postcolonial gatekeepers, who had little capacity to control people and territory but effectively extracted resources and power from the flow of goods to the outside world.[7] These continuities can be attributed to the fact that creating and maintaining the capacity of a state to control territory and populations is expensive, never mind the cost of legitimizing that state control and its appropriation of resources, such as by building infrastructure and providing services. Rather than appropriating resources by directly taxing the population, which was often poor and geographically dispersed, African governments attained most of their resources through foreign aid or international trade tariffs. As long as these resources were available, it was unnecessary for leaders to achieve and maintain control over the whole territory of a state, assuming they controlled the capital city. Hence, African governments had few inducements to institutionalize their rule or build effective state institutions.[8]

Cold War notions about national sovereignty, and weak institutions, meant that gaining control of main administrative offices was all it took to obtain the power to sign contracts with foreign partners.[9] As examples in this book demonstrate, only small circles of elites benefitted from the status quo in many postcolonial states, and general populations thus had little reason to support their governments. This allowed a few individuals with connections and resources to easily reverse government decisions, which is why African presidents tended to keep such a close eye on the politicians responsible for national armed and security forces, as well as the military elite. The possibility of a coup constantly hung in the air, incentivizing foreign powers to develop close relations with military leadership through assistance schemes.

This reliance on this foreign assistance increased the likelihood of personal rule and centralized power in African governments.[10] External economic aid helped African rulers meet the demands of one part of their population,

7   Cooper, 'Possibility and Constraint', pp.186–7; Bayart, *The State in Africa: The Politics of the Belly* (New York: Longman, 1993) pp. 20–1.
8   Reno, *Warlord Politics and African States*, p. 22; Chabal and Daloz, *Africa Works*, pp. 13–15.
9   Reno, *Warlord Politics and African States*; Clapham, *Africa and the International System* (Cambridge University Press, 1996).
10   Reno, *Warlord Politics and African States*, p. 22; Chabal and Daloz, *Africa Works*, pp. 13–15.

while outside military assistance allowed them to silence others. The focus of this chapter – the autonomy of African governments – is reflected in the contrasting decisions made by francophone West African countries in this context. It is clear that foreign actors did not dictate African defence policy, and cases presented below will show that African political and military elites acted in ways that in fact ran counter to the interests of foreign partners.

Other recent research has similarly emphasized African agency in international relations,[11] although it has accentuated to whom and to what extent the actions of African leaders mattered. The anchor of this chapter is not agency, but *autonomy*. In other words, how independent were African governments in making decisions? How freely could they formulate their defence policies? What strategies or factors increased their autonomy or limited their freedom of action? How did foreign powers seek to influence the development of African militaries? To analyse the influence of Cold War powers and the former colonial power on the defence policies of francophone West African governments, these countries were sorted into three pairs based on their international allegiances: Mali and Guinea, which received military assistance from communist states; Senegal and Côte d'Ivoire, which were of great economic and strategic important to France; and Upper Volta (Burkina Faso) and Niger, which – together with Mauritania, Togo, and Dahomey – attracted the lowest levels of foreign assistance.

The autonomy of governments in Guinea and Mali vis-à-vis their foreign partners, including the former colonial power, was marked by them turning to the Soviet Union for military assistance. As the next section details, the governments of both states sought to limit their dependence on the Soviet Union, but the military assistance it provided gave Moscow considerable political influence; more than France or the US achieved through economic assistance. Meanwhile, the Senegalese and Ivorian governments, both of which maintained their alignment with France, exerted their autonomy in ways that helped both countries avoid military coups. The strategic importance of Senegal and the economic importance of Côte d'Ivoire led France to allocate most of its economic and military assistance to these countries, and to maintain a French military presence. France was also keen to limit the political, economic, and military influence of other foreign powers in Senegal and Côte d'Ivoire, which increased the negotiating power

---

11 Obert Hodzi, 'China and Africa: economic growth and a non-transformative political elite', *Journal of Contemporary African Studies* 36, no. 2 (2018), pp. 191–206; Andy Deroche, 'Asserting African Agency: Kenneth Kaunda and the USA, 1964–1980' *Diplomatic History* 40, no. 5 (2016); Gerits, '"When the Bull Elephants Fight"', pp. 951–69.

of these states with France. The autonomy of the remaining francophone West African countries, which were less strategically and economically important to France, was weakened by their minimal receipt of military and economic assistance. These countries had to build their armies with few resources, and most experienced multiple military coups.

The Pros and Cons of Neutralism: The Reliance of Guinea and Mali on the Soviet Union

France is often seen as a neo-colonial actor in its former colonies, and its recent intervention in Mali has been presented in this light. However, from 1960 to 1990, it was the Soviet Union that played the most important role in building both the Guinean and Malian national militaries, which were armed almost exclusively with Soviet weapons. In fact, the value of Soviet arms transfers to Mali and Guinea surpassed those of France to other francophone West African countries (see Figure 1).

The alignment of Mali and Guinea with the communist bloc was reflected in their voting at the United Nations General Assembly, as more than 70% of the time they cast their ballot with the Soviet Union (see Figure 2). Any French influence on Guinean and Malian policies was limited, as both presidents – Guinea's Sékou Touré and Mali's Mobibo Keïta – had distanced themselves from France after independence. When other Western countries refused to offer them any significant military assistance, the two presidents had turned to communist leaders. Initially, Touré and Keïta took great care to mitigate Soviet influence by, for example, continuing to solicit military assistance from the West in order to 'preserve their neutralism' and maximize foreign aid. Nevertheless, by the 1970s, the Soviet Union had taken firm control of the Guinean and Malian militaries, even though Western countries dominated their economic spheres.

At the time, Guinea was more reliant on US investment and economic aid, while Mali was still receiving close to one-third of its economic assistance from France, which meant that Malian relations with France were better than Guinea's. France sought in vain to alter the nationalist policies of newly independent Guinea through diplomatic, economic, and covert means, as tensions rose over the Guinean refusal to recognize loans taken during the colonial period and the nationalization of French companies. Guinea was also obligated to pay damages to France, meaning that French aid to Guinea was negative throughout the 1970s (see Figure 3). Guinea's mineral wealth attracted foreign powers from both sides of the Cold War and generated

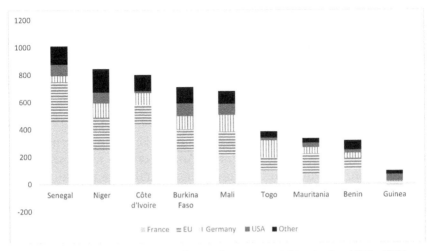

Figure 3. Economic assistance to francophone West Africa in the 1970s (US$ million) (Source: World Bank DataBank, https://databank.worldbank.org/home. aspx, accessed 21.5.2022)

friction between them, and in many ways, Guinea's independence and its foreign policy exposed the limits of French power.

Western countries, including France, learned a key lesson from Guinean independence and sought to safeguard amicable relations with the nascent Malian government, despite its socialist orientation. French officials were also less hostile towards American activities in Mali, where French companies were not subject to the disputes or damages they suffered in Guinea. After independence, France remained Mali's main trade partner and as well as its most important source of economic assistance. This was true even after the 1968 military coup. Military coups elsewhere made Western governments seek to maintain good relations with Malian and Guinean soldiers by offering them limited equipment and training.

In both Guinea and Mali, this foreign assistance often had undesired outcomes. US and West German military cooperation programmes ended in the arrest and executions of Guinean soldiers who had worked with American and German officers, and when the Malian government received weapons from Israel, Israeli officials were largely in the dark as to their final destination. The minimal military equipment (and economic assistance) received by the Guinean and Malian governments from Western actors did little to increase the influence of these countries, for the quantity of weapons provided by the Soviet Union and China far outweighed Western contributions. In fact, Soviet aid exceeded the needs of Guinea and Mali, both of which had more guns than soldiers, raising the question of who was using these weapons and for what purpose.

Fears grew in the West that weapons intended for Guinea and Mali might be used to support rebel forces in neighbouring states. Guinea was particularly active in assisting and hosting anti-colonial actors, which helped foster a sense of common purpose in the region but complicated Guinean relations with Western countries. Training provided by communist militaries also ensured that a young generation of African officers felt closer to the Soviet Union, allowing Moscow to increase its influence in both Guinea and Mali by the early 1970s, when many older officers had either been arrested or had retired. Differences in how soldiers were trained also made it difficult to develop troop cohesion, a problem that continued into the new millennium.[12]

The presence of foreign actors with a variety of objectives contributed to instability in these two countries and generated tensions within their governments and militaries. In Mali, the dissatisfaction of Malian soldiers with foreign assistance was a factor in the 1968 military coup, and in Guinea, the military also eventually assumed power, after the death of President Touré in 1984. Though the relations of both countries with France improved after their respective coups, the demise of their socialist leaders had little impact on the assistance provided by China and the Soviet Union, reflecting how easily foreign assistance could be transferred from one government to the next. It was the Soviets who were most effective in gaining political influence from these relationships, though. In order to understand how Moscow won more influence in Guinea through military aid than Western states did through economic aid, it is useful to consider how defence-related decisions made by the Guinean government were impacted by the external environment. This included hostile actions by the French, anticolonial movements, and, of course, the availability of Soviet military assistance.

Neutralism in Sékou Touré's Guinea

The defence policy of President Touré was a product of realist calculations of threats and opportunities facing Guinea combined with idealist notions of national sovereignty and Third World liberation. He advocated a 'positive

---

12   Dorothée Thiènot, 'Le blues de l'armée malienne', *Le Monde diplomatique*, May 2013, p. 13.

neutralism', grounded in the acknowledgement that 'the world is co-owned by all nations and peoples and that only relationships of absolute equality can generate equity, harmony and the progress of universal society.' As he explained it:

> Positive neutralism in its negative aspect rejects determinism condi-
> tioned by the attitude of France, the USSR, China, Great Britain or
> the United States. Positive neutralism asserts that international issues
> do not concern only the United States, France or the USSR, China
> or any other powerful country, that the world is not theirs, that they
> are not alone to take responsibility over it.[13]

In newly independent states such as Guinea, foreign actors influenced the building of national militaries in two opposing ways – by offering aid or by posing a threat. Foreign states did both in Guinea, at one time providing military assistance, and at another conspiring against the government. This was certainly true of the Soviet Union, the US, and West Germany. Meanwhile, President Touré had to balance two opposing sides in his government – those advocating pro-Soviet policies and those seeking a closer relationship with the West.

The abrupt changes he made to foreign policy would suggest that Guinean decision-making was not dictated from outside. In many ways, the Guinean position can be seen as a reflection of the strategies of extra-version used by the country's elite, who exploited Cold War competition to obtain maximum foreign assistance and do away with domestic opposi-tion.[14] However, the argument can also be made that Touré's commitment to positive neutralism and African nationalism safeguarded Guinean national sovereignty while successfully attracting the external resources needed to build state institutions. After all, compared to every other francophone West African country, Guinea took a significantly different route to independence and its aftermath.

Guinea was the only unit of French West Africa that refused to join the French Community in a popular vote in September 1958, opting instead for immediate independence. Both French and US intelligence reports

---

13 Sékou Touré, *L'Afrique et la révolution* (Paris: Présence Africaine, 1977), p. 178.
14 SDECE, 'Note: situation de Guinée', 24 April 1959, 5AGF/555, FFAN; The High Commissioner representing the President of the French Community in Dakar to President of the Community, General Secretariat, 25 May 1960, 5AGF/1637, FFAN; Abdoulaye Diallo, *Sékou Touré 1957–1961: Mythe et réalités d'un héros* (Paris: Harmattan, 2008), p. 90; Boubacar Yacine Diallo, *La Guinée, un demi-siècle de politique (1945–2008)* (Paris: Harmattan, 2011), p. 161.

described Sékou Touré as a nationalist and pan–Africanist who had protected his reputation by avoiding an overreliance on Soviet support.[15] In other words, even though Touré had begun his political career in the labour movement, his country was not predestined to join the socialist camp. This point was raised by French diplomatic, military, and intelligence officials when they met on 9 October 1958 to discuss how to respond to Guinean independence.[16] They contended that the worst thing France could do was to withdraw from the country completely, thereby leaving a vacuum for communist countries to fill. They recommended further that France not take a hostile position towards Guinea, partly because they thought the Guineans had only a small chance of success and partly because significant French interests were at risk.[17] Indeed, France had considerable investments in Guinean bauxite mining and some 3,000–3,500 French nationals in the country. Even so, France was unwilling to give substantial assistance to Guinea, fearing this would send the wrong message to other French colonies and encourage them to secede.[18]

Despite the opinions of French officials that France had nothing to gain from delaying the recognition of Guinean statehood or its membership of the United Nations,[19] the French government reacted to Guinean independence with hostility, engaging in economic, diplomatic, and covert actions meant to damage Touré.[20] France's external intelligence service, the

15 French Intelligence Service, 'Problèmes de défense soulèves par l'indépendance de la Guinée', 18 January 1959, GR9Q5122, Service Historique de la Défense (SHD); James Loeb, US Embassy Conakry, to Department of State, 'Year with Sékou Touré', 8 September 1964, USGUIN 1964–1966, Box 2258, CGRDS, NARA, and 'US policy assessment', 26 January 1966, POLGUIN 1964–1966, Box 2256, CGRDS, NARA.

16 French Intelligence Service, 'Problèmes de défense soulèves par l'indépendance de la Guinée', 18 January 1959, GR9Q5122, SHD.

17 General Fourquet, Head of the 5th Division of the Defence Staff, to the Head of the French Intelligence Service, 'Au sujet de réunion de 9 October 1958 AMDN/PSY – Note sur la politique française vis-à-vis de la Guinée', 13 October 1958, GR5Q22, SHD.

18 Director General of the SDECE to Fourquet, Head of the 5th Division of the Defence Staff, 'Note au sujet de la Conférence de Travail du 13 August 1958', 21 October 1958, GR5Q22, SHD; Fourquet, 'Au sujet de réunion de 9 October 1958 AMDN/PSY – Note sur la politique française vis-à-vis de la Guinée,' 13 October 1958.

19 André Lewin, *Ahmed Sékou Touré (1922–1984): Président de la Guinée de 1958 à 1984*, vol. 3 (Paris: Harmattan, 2010), Chapter 34.

20 National Defence General Staff, Intelligence Division, 'Le problème Guinéen', 17 April 1959, GR9Q5122, SHD; Francis Hure, Chargé d'affaires, to the Minister of

SDECE, insisted that Touré's early career and previous actions placed him firmly on the side of the Soviets.[21] Their suspicions must have increased when, soon after independence, French officials, teachers, doctors, and technical assistance personnel in Guinea were largely replaced by individuals from Czechoslovakia, Yugoslavia, and East Germany.[22] The SDECE proposed that any public sympathy shown by France to newly-independent Guinea should not preclude the use of the 'most radical means' to ensure the country remained in the French sphere of influence.[23] A 1959 intelligence report emphasized that the threat Guinea posed to France, to the French Community, and to Western interests generally, had to be contained and eliminated, although any direct action was considered too risky.[24]

In truth, the personal distaste of French president Charles de Gaulle for his Guinean counterpart was the main reason for French hostility towards Guinea. In August 1958, when de Gaulle toured French West Africa to promote the French Community, Touré gave a speech that so deeply offended the French president that he became convinced the Guinean nationalist leader was a radical communist who could not be trusted.[25] In his speech, Touré had announced that Guinea preferred 'freedom in poverty to wealth in slavery'.

Multiple letters written by Touré to de Gaulle, as well as other Guinean sources, testify to the efforts of Guinea to 'normalize its relations' with France and secure French assistance.[26] President de Gaulle refused to reply to Touré's letters and demanded that no assistance be allocated to the

---

Foreign Affairs, 'Situation économique de la Guinée', 31 March 1959, 5AGF/1638, FFAN; Robert, *'Ministre' de l'Afrique,* pp. 103–9; Foccart, *Foccart Parle,* pp. 175 and 214; Chargé d'affaires, French Embassy Conakry, 'Situation intérieure Guinée', 28 May 1960; SDECE, 'Guinée: Le complot contre le régime', 9 May 1960.

21 Director General of the SDECE to Fourquet, 'Note au sujet de la conférence de travail du 13 August 1958', 21 October 1958.

22 French Intelligence Service, 'Problèmes de défense soulèves par l'indépendance de la Guinée', 18 January 1959; National Defence General Staff, Intelligence Division, 'La pénétration communiste en république de Guinée', 12 April 1960, GR9Q5122, SHD; Presidency of the Community, 'Note à l'attention de monsieur le secrétaire général – experts étrangères en Guinée', 22 December 1960, 5AGF/1637, FFAN.

23 Director General of the SDECE to Fourquet, 'Note au sujet de la conférence de travail du 13 August 1958', 21 October 1958.

24 National Defence General Staff, Intelligence Division, 'Le problème Guinéen', 17 April 1959.

25 Foccart, *Foccart Parle,* pp. 165–6 and 214.

26 Nabi Ibrahima Youla, *Grande figure africaine de Guinée: Entretiens avec Djibril Kassomba Camara* (Guinée: Harmattan, 2012), Chapter 3.

Guinean government.[27] France also tried to prevent, or at least postpone, Guinean membership of the United Nations. In 1962, several years after independence, de Gaulle still refused to meet a Guinean delegation and insisted that no member of the French government do so either, writing that it was 'never' the time to 'give in to Sékou Touré's Guinea'.[28]

After Guinean independence, France ceased its trade with Guinea and cut off all assistance. De Gaulle believed that such an economic blockade would topple Touré's regime in two or three months. This did not happen, not even with French intelligence services also working to weaken the Guinean government, including falsifying Guinean currency in order to destroy the already suffering economy, and by training and arming Guinean dissidents close to the Senegalese border.[29] French officials later admitted that Guinean neighbours Côte d'Ivoire and Senegal were also implicated in efforts to depose Touré.[30] In one incident, for example, in May 1960, an arms cache was discovered near the Senegalese border. This heightened Touré's sense of urgency to consolidate his own security forces, and more resources were allocated to this purpose.[31] This was easier said than done, as many of the troops who participated in operations against Touré were Guineans who had served in the French army,[32] thus he could not be sure that those soldiers who had transferred into the Guinean military would remain loyal to him.

Nevertheless, external threats dictated that Touré develop a strong, well-equipped army. Upon Guinean independence, the French had withdrawn all military equipment that could be transported and destroyed the rest. In October 1958, when Guinea sent a request for military assistance to the

---

27 General Secretary for the Community and African Affairs to General de Gaulle, note dated 4 November 1963, 5AGF/558, FFAN; Charles de Gaulle, 'Note pour monsieur Foccart', 31 March 1962, 5AGF/558, FFAN.

28 General de Gaulle, note dated 2 April 1962, 5AGF/558, FFAN.

29 Robert, *'Ministre' de l'Afrique*, pp. 103–9; Foccart, *Foccart Parle*, pp. 175 and 214; Chargé d'affaires, French Embassy Conakry, 'Situation intérieure Guinée', 28 May 1960; SDECE, 'Guinée: Le complot contre le régime', 9 May 1960.

30 Robert, *'Ministre' de l'Afrique*, pp. 103–9; Foccart, *Foccart Parle*, pp.175 and 214; Pierre Graham, US Embassy Conakry, to Department of State, 'Current position and future prospects of the Touré regime', 14 April 1966, USGUIN 1964–1966, 462, Box 2259, CGRDS, NARA.

31 French Ministry of Foreign Affairs, Directorate for Africa-Levant, 'Guinée', 2 July 1960; Chargé d'affaires, French Embassy Conakry, 'Situation intérieure Guinée', 28 May 1960.

32 Robert, *'Ministre' de l'Afrique*, pp. 103–9; Foccart, *Foccart Parle*, p. 175; SDECE, 'Guinée: Le complot contre le régime', 9 May 1960.

US through Liberia, it was ignored by US officials,[33] even though they were aware that Guinean soldiers had no uniforms, and the police and gendarmerie had no rifles or shells.[34] Hence, Touré turned elsewhere, and in March 1959, a shipment of 265 tonnes of weapons and 150 tonnes of munitions arrived in Conakry from Czechoslovakia.[35] The arms had been manufactured by the Soviet Union but were shipped from Czechoslovakia so as to preserve Touré's neutralist stance.[36] French intelligence assessed that the weapons received by Guinea exceeded the country's needs, and determined they were bound, at least in part, for 'subversive' forces in neighbouring countries.[37] According to a French military intelligence report, the thirty Czechoslovakian technicians and instructors also arrived, and trainings were proposed for Guinean military personnel in Czechoslovakia.[38]

Most specialized personnel in the Guinean army, and all Guinean pilots, were trained in Yugoslavia or the Soviet Union.[39] Between 1960 and 1963, Guinea received additional military equipment, direct from the Soviets.[40] This included 22,000 personal weapons, sixty-five heavy machine guns, thirty mortars of all calibres, fifty-four anti-tank or anti-aircraft canons, and seventy-five tanks.[41] The shipments ended due to the Guinean

33 John Howard Morrow, *First American Ambassador to Guinea, 1959–1961* (New Brunswick, NJ: Rutgers University, 1968), Chapter IV; US Embassy Conakry to Department of State, 13 May 1959, 770b 1955–1959, Box 3651, CGRDS, NARA.

34 US Embassy Conakry to Department of State, 13 May 1959.

35 National Defence General Staff, Intelligence Division, 'La pénétration communiste en république de Guinée', 12 April 1960.

36 Curt F. Beck, 'Czechoslovakia's Penetration of Africa, 1955–1962', *World Politics* 15, no. 3 (1963), pp. 403–16.

37 Robert, *'Ministre' de l'Afrique*, p. 103. Also see documents in File GR9Q5122 in the Service Historique de la Défense (SHD) and File 5AGF/1638 in the Foccart Collection of the Archives Nationales (FFAN).

38 National Defence General Staff, Intelligence Division, 'Fiche sur la Guinée', 7 April 1959, GR9Q5122, SHD; Office of Overseas Studies, 'Transmission de renseignements: République de Guinée', 29 April 1959, 5AGF/555, FFAN; Robert *'Ministre' de l'Afrique*, pp. 103–4.

39 See documents in File 5AGF/1639, FFAN; File GR9Q5122, SHD; and File DEFGUIN, Box 1550, CGRDS, NARA.

40 General Secretary for African and Malagasy Affairs, 'Situation de l'armée nationale de Guinée', 11 September 1962, 5AGF/1639, FFAN; Presidency of the Republic, Special Staff, 'Aide militaire des pays de l'est à la Guinée', 6 November 1963, 5AGF/558, FFAN.

41 Presidency of the Republic, Special Staff, 'Aide militaire des pays de l'est à la Guinée', 6 November 1963; Supreme Commander of the Armed Forces in the AOF-Togo Defence Zone, 'Guinée, forces armes et de sécurité 1961', GRH151, SHD; US Embassy Conakry to Department of State, 'Guinean military expenditures and purchases',

rapprochement with the US, but Guinea would receive more weapons from the Soviet Union after it severed diplomatic relations with France in 1966.[42] In addition to military assistance, the Soviet Union hoped to influence Guinea's economic sphere, particularly through multiple agricultural and industrial projects. It also extended a considerable line of credit in 1959 – an estimated US$ 56.5 million[43] – and offered its petrol to Guinea at advantageous prices.[44]

French officials calculated in 1959 that eastern bloc assistance to Guinea was already higher than the assistance they had allocated to their former colonies. They worried that this volume of aid would make Guinea's 'neutralist' stance attractive to other African countries, even with the failures of the Guinean economy.[45] Estimates by US officials put Soviet bloc assistance to Guinea between 1958 and 1963 at some US$ 125 million.[46] In 1971, a French report indicated that of the US$ 708 million spent by the Soviet Union in sub-Saharan African countries between 1959 and 1971, nearly 25% had gone to Guinea.[47]

---

20 February 1969, DEFGUIN 1967–1969, Box 1550, CGRDS, NARA; Thomas Cassidy, 'Sino-Soviet Bloc Political-Economic Relationships with Guinea', 18 July 1963; Graham, US Embassy Conakry, to State Department, 'Guinean military strength: Personnel and weapons', 19 April 1966, DEFGUIN 1964–1966, Box 1649, CGRDS, NARA.

42 Ministry of Armed Forces, SDECE, 'Aide militaire soviétique à la Guinée', 6 June 1966, 5AGF/1647, FFAN; Cassidy, 'Sino-Soviet Bloc Political-Economic Relationships with Guinea', 18 July 1963; John Kizler, US Embassy Conakry, to Department of State, 'Bi-weekly no. 37', 18 November 1965, POLGUIN 1964–1966, Box 2256, CGRDS, NARA.

43 See documents in File GR9Q5122, SHD; and Files 51QONT/34 and 51QO/52, CADC.

44 National Defence General Staff, Intelligence Division, 'La pénétration communiste en république de Guinée', 12 April 1960, and 'Pénétration soviétique en Guinée', 1 March 1968, GR9Q5122, SHD; Ministry of National Defence, SDECE, 'URSS–Guinée relations économique, étude communiquée par les services allemands', 13 April 1971, 51QONT/34, CADC; Minister of Foreign Affairs, 'Aide étrangère à la Guinée', 20 October 1962, 51QO/52, CADC; Cassidy, 'Sino-Soviet Bloc Political-Economic Relationships with Guinea', 18 July 1963.

45 Hure, 'Situation économique de la Guinée', 31 March 1959; National Defence General Staff, Intelligence Division, 'Prestige africaine de la Guinée', 12 October 1959, GR9Q5122, SHD.

46 Cassidy, US Embassy Conakry, to Department of State, 'Five years of Guinean independence: an assessment', 1 October 1963, POLGUIN, Box 2257, CGRDS, NARA.

47 Ministry of National Defence, SDECE, 'URSS–Guinée relations économique, étude communiquée par les services allemands', 13 April 1971.

In the early 1960s, Touré continued to remain careful to avoid becoming entirely reliant on the socialist bloc, going so far as to expel the Soviet Ambassador, Daniel Solod, in December 1961 on the basis of his involvement in the 'teachers plot'.[48] The French ambassador at the time noted that, even if Solod had committed some 'imprudent acts', he would not have been expelled had Soviet aid in Guinea been more effective.[49] In fact, this action was related to the failures of communist economic policies in the country and the 'negative effects USSR ideological influence had on Guinean national unity'.[50] The conciliatory attitude of Soviet officials following Solod's expulsion exposed Guinea's importance to the Soviet strategy in Africa, and the US took note.[51] By then, French and American officials were speculating that the considerable resources invested by communist countries in Guinea were an indicator that the Soviet Union sought to make Guinea their showcase partner in sub-Saharan Africa.[52]

Western observers blamed the Soviet Union's failure to make Guinea an attractive economic model for developing countries on its inefficient aid, political interference, racism, and arrogance.[53] A French report from 1962 quoted a Guinean official, who described the disillusionment that had developed among Guineans vis-à-vis Soviet aid:

> … several myths have been unmasked. We have learned that the selflessness of states that help others is a myth. French capitalists often lied to us, but we knew when they were lying to us. The Eastern

---

48   Lewin, *Ahmed Sékou Touré (1922–1984)*, vol. 4, Chapter 49.

49   Telegram, French Embassy Conakry to Directorate of African and Malagasy Affairs, Paris, 26 January 1962, 5AGF/1639, FFAN.

50   Ibid.

51   Attwood, US Embassy Conakry, to Department of State, 'Factors which may produce subversion, violent disturbance and lead to disorder', 14 June 1962, 770b.02/1-160–770b.13/1-462, Box 1944, CGRDS, NARA.

52   National Defence General Staff, Intelligence Division, 'La pénétration communiste en république de Guinée', 12 April 1960; Cassidy, 'Sino-Soviet Bloc Political-Economic Relationships with Guinea', 18 July 1963; William Brubeck, Executive Secretary, 'Memorandum for George Bundy, the White House: President's meeting with Special Envoy from Guinean President Sékou Touré', 30 April 1963, POLGUIN, Box 2257, CGRDS, NARA.

53   Foccart, *Foccart Parle*, p. 176; Robert, *'Ministre' de l'Afrique*, pp. 105–7. Also see documents in File POLGUIN 1963, Box 2257, CGRDS, NARA; File USGUIN, Box 2254, CGRDS, NARA; File POLGUIN 1963, Box 2240, CGRDS, NARA; and Files 5AGF/1637, 5AGF/1638, 5AGF/1640, and 5AGF/558, FFAN.

officials deceived us even more, but we didn't know they could lie to us. We let ourselves be bound by agreements we couldn't get out of.[54]

Economic failures were the primary reason Guinea actively sought assistance from the US and West Germany between 1961 and 1963.[55] Touré had already found success with his strategy of maximizing aid from both sides of the Iron Curtain, when he presented West Germany with something of a test in March 1960.[56] Rumours had reached Conakry that East Germany had presented its credentials before the Guinean ambassador in Moscow, and because West Germany had a policy of not providing aid to any country that established diplomatic ties to East Germany, it threatened to withdraw from Guinea.[57] In response, Touré officially denied that diplomatic representation on an ambassadorial level had been agreed with East Germany.[58] The results were positive, as both East and West Germany ended up providing aid to Guinea.[59] In fact, according to World Bank data, West German aid to Guinea in the 1960s totalled about US$ 23 million (see Figure 4). The US, which at first refused to allocate aid to Guinea due to the request of its ally France, provided US$ 24 million in aid in 1963 alone.

President Eisenhower's administration had not granted any meaningful assistance to newly independent Guinea because the US Department of State during Eisenhower's presidency was heavily influenced by the European Bureau – that is, French opinion – regarding US actions in Africa.[60] The first American ambassador to Guinea, John Morrow, noted in his memoirs

---

54 Jean Mialet, 'Note à l'attention de Monsieur le président de la république, président de la communauté: situation de la Guinée', 23 March 1962, AG/5F/1640, FFAN.

55 Lewin, 'La Guinée et les deux Allemagnes', *Guerres mondiales et conflits contemporains* 210, no. 2 (2003), pp. 77–99.

56 Gareth M. Winrow, *The foreign policy of the GDR in Africa* (Cambridge University Press, 2009), p. 63.

57 Morrow, *First American Ambassador to Guinea*, Chapter XIII.

58 Winrow, *The foreign policy of the GDR in Africa*, p. 63.

59 Lewin, 'La Guinée et les deux Allemagnes'; Telegram, French Embassy Conakry to Directorate of African and Malagasy Affairs, 7 November 1959, 51QO/3, CADC; The High Commissioner representing the President of the Community to the Prime Minister, 'Notes techniques de renseignements', 16 May 1960, 5AGF/1637, FFAN; National Defence General Staff, Intelligence Division, 'La pénétration communiste en république de Guinée', 12 April 1960; Telegram, François Seydoux, French Embassy Bonn to Ministry of Foreign Affairs, 9 July 1962, 51QO/36, CADC; National Defence General Staff, Intelligence Division, 'Fiche sur la Guinée', 7 April 1959.

60 Morrow, *First American Ambassador to Guinea*, Chapter XII. This is also discussed by Muehlenbeck in *Betting on the Africans* and Rakove in *Kennedy, Johnson, and the Nonaligned World*.

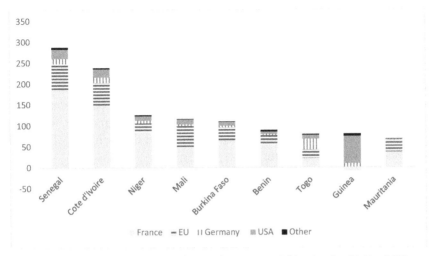

Figure 4. Economic assistance to francophone West Africa in the 1960s (US$ million) (Source: World Bank DataBank, https://databank.worldbank.org/home. aspx, accessed 21.5.2022).

that Guinea–US relations suffered from the late US recognition of Guinea, as well as the fact that he, Morrow, only reached Conakry nearly a year after Guinean independence. In fact, America's refusal to send economic and military aid was so resolute that when Touré requested English teachers, the US sent just one for a country of more than three million inhabitants. Even after he visited the US in October 1959, Touré received no promises of aid.[61] However, in 1961, when President Kennedy was elected, US policy towards Africa took a turn, away from the French.[62]

William Atwood, who Kennedy appointed as Morrow's successor, described the attitude of the Eisenhower State Department as 'beyond the pale' and explained that the Kennedy administration wanted to 'find out if [the Guineans] are neutralist, and bring them around, to give them a little aid, and to show them that what we do is more practical than what the Soviets do. Never mind what the French think.'[63] Kennedy believed the Cold War would be won or lost in Africa, and he was not only active but somewhat

61 Morrow, *First American Ambassador in Guinea*, chapters II and VI.
62 Muehlenbeck, 'Kennedy and Touré: A Success in Personal Diplomacy', *Diplomacy and Statecraft* 19, no. 1 (2008), pp. 69–95.
63 Attwood, remarks in Dayton Mak and Charles Stuart Kennedy, *American Ambassadors in a Troubled World: Interviews with Senior Diplomats* (Praeger, 1992), p. 85.

successful in convincing African presidents of benign US intentions. Unlike the State Department he inherited, which thought Guinea was lost to the communist bloc, Kennedy was of the view that Touré took his reputation as a pan–Africanist leader too seriously to become a Soviet stooge.[64] Touré was thus invited to visit the White House, where a significant aid package was negotiated, with the US promising funding for the construction of a dam on the Konkoume River, an English language programme, food aid, training for Guinean administrative personnel, and the inclusion of Guinea as a Peace Corps destination.[65]

Kennedy's efforts paid off during the Cuban Missile Crisis, when Touré backed the US and denied Soviet planes the option to refuel in Conakry, en route to Cuba.[66] This came as an unpleasant surprise to the Soviets, who had assisted Guinea in building the airport in Conakry.[67] Communist countries responded by reducing their assistance to Guinea, claiming it had been misused and had not produced the expected results due to Guinean administrative inefficiencies.[68] A Soviet diplomat complained to his Western

[64] Muehlenbeck, 'Kennedy and Touré'. These views were also repeated later in Loeb, 'Year with Sékou Touré', 8 September 1964; Loeb, 'US policy assessment', 26 January 1966; and Brubeck, 'Memorandum for George Bundy, the White House: President's meeting with Special Envoy from Guinean President Sékou Touré', 30 April 1963.

[65] Telegram, US Department of State to Embassy in Guinea, 24 June 1961, 770b.5-MSP/6-161, CGRDS, NARA; US Secretary of State Rusk to President Kennedy, 'Memorandum', 1 July 1961, 770b.5-MSP/7-161, CGRDS, NARA; Telegram, US Department of State to Embassy in Guinea, 13 September 1962, 770b.11/9-1362, CGRDS, NARA; 'U.S. Economic Assistance Program in Guinea', Background Paper Prepared in the Agency for International Development, 4 October 1962, Department of State Conference Files, Lot 65 D 533, CF 2173; Jean Mialet, General Secretariat for African and Malagasy Affairs, 'Note à l'attention de Monsieur le Secrétaire Général', 18 October 1961, 5AGF/1638, FFAN; M. Boulmer, 'Note à l'attention de monsieur le président de la république, président de la communauté. Bilan de l'aide des états unis à la Guinée', 20 August 1962, 5AGF/1639, FFAN.

[66] US Embassy Conakry to Department of State, 'Bi-weekly no. 7', 15 July 1963, and 'Bi-weekly no. 8', 22 July 1963; Cassidy, 'Sino-Soviet Bloc Political-Economic Relationships with Guinea', 18 July 1963; Loeb, 'US policy assessment', 26 January 1966.

[67] Muehlenbeck, 'Kennedy and Touré'.

[68] US Department of State, 'Memorandum of conversation: General situation in Guinea – Yves Eichenberger, President of Bauxites du Midi; Tom Covel, Washington representative of Aluminum Limited Canada; Henry Tasca, Deputy Assistant Secretary', 6 February 1963, POLGUIN, Box 3922 CGRDS, NARA; Cassidy, 'Sino-Soviet Bloc Political-Economic Relationships with Guinea', 18 July 1963, and 'Five years of Guinean independence: an assessment', 1 October 1963.

colleagues that the Guineans were ungrateful, calling them 'impossible to work with'. For their part, Guinean officials openly criticized communist assistance.[69]

Despite this mutual dissatisfaction, US officials estimated it was unlikely the bloc would 'be supplanted completely' in Guinea, as Touré was well aware that the absence of bloc competition would reduce assistance from the West.[70] From the US perspective, the main challenge was not 'Soviet economic domination' (because 'the Soviets are not that generous'), but Guinea's maintenance of policies reflecting an 'early Soviet development pattern', which were incompatible with US objectives in Guinea.[71] The Kennedy administration had envisaged Touré as a useful ally because of his pan-Africanist credentials,[72] yet US policies in Congo and South Africa, and towards Portuguese colonialism, created endless friction.[73]

It was the US alliance with France that was especially harmful, however, as the French were 'trying to insert a pro-French regime' in Guinea,[74] and French officials were openly hostile to US activities in the country.[75] A 1959 US Embassy report noted that 'France wanted revenge and to show Africa that Guinea could not run itself'.[76] It was the opinion of French officials that American assistance was helping Touré remain in power and that Touré's

69 Attwood, 'Factors which may produce subversion, violent disturbance and lead to disorder', 14 June 1962; Cassidy, 'Sino-Soviet Bloc Political-Economic Relationships with Guinea', 18 July 1963; Cassidy, US Embassy Conakry, to State Department, 'Guinean Dissatisfaction with Soviet Union', 13 September 1963, POLGUIN, Box 2240, CGRDS, NARA.

70 Cassidy, 'Sino-Soviet Bloc Political-Economic Relationships with Guinea', 18 July 1963.

71 US Embassy Conakry to Department of State, 'Guinea's International Policy as of September 20, 1965: An appraisal by Ambassador Loeb on the Day of his departure', 22 September 1965, POLGUIN 1964–1966, Box 2256, CGRDS, NARA.

72 Cassidy, US Embassy Conakry, to Department of State, 'Implications of recent Touré correspondence to the president', 20 June 1963, USGUIN, Box 2254, CGRDS, NARA; Loeb, US Embassy Conakry, to Department of State, 'Year-end assessment', 29 December 1964, POLGUIN 1964–1966, Box 2256, CGRDS, NARA; Loeb, 'Year with Sékou Touré', 8 September 1964.

73 Cassidy, 'Sino-Soviet Bloc Political-Economic Relationships with Guinea', 18 July 1963.

74 Ibid.

75 Cassidy, 'Five years of Guinean independence: an assessment', 1 October 1963; Graham, US Embassy Conakry, to Department of State, 'Impact on Franco-American relations of increased American activities in Guinea', 24 February 1964, POLGUIN 1964–1966, Box 2261, CGRDS, NARA.

76 US Embassy Conakry to Department of State, 13 May 1959.

'positive neutralism' was only profitable so long as it was not adopted by too many other countries.[77] US officials also recognized that Touré had grown dependent on their assistance.[78] In 1967, the US ambassador wrote that 'the fundamental question' in US–Guinea relations had long been 'to what extent the US wished to assist the Touré regime and whether by granting aid the US was in fact helping Touré stay in power.'[79]

The Kennedy administration had viewed its assistance to Guinea as a means of keeping a popular African nationalist from becoming reliant on Soviet aid.[80] It had acknowledged Touré's authoritarian tendencies,[81] but it was only in the 1970s that the 'tyranny' experienced under his regime was officially noted.[82] By that time, Touré's policies and frequent verbal attacks on the US had led officials to question whether their strategy in Guinea was the right one. However, they saw no realistic alternative to Touré,[83] especially if they were to safeguard US economic interests in the country, particularly in bauxite mining. US officials also continued to insist that their assistance was necessary to help reduce Guinean dependence on the Soviets.[84]

Granting military assistance to Guinea was also seen as a way to build relations with the Guinean military elite and to obtain intelligence. West

77 Hure, 'Situation économique de la Guinée', 31 March 1959; Jean-Pierre Hadengue, General Secretariat for African and Malagasy Affairs, 'Note: à l'attention de monsieur le président de la communauté: Déclaration de Sékou Touré sur l'aide reçue par la Guinée', 5 December 1960, 5AGF/1637, FFAN; French Embassy in the US to the Directorate for Africa–Levant, 'Relations entre les états unis et la Guinée', 17 November 1971, 51QONT/34, CADC.

78 Loeb, 'US policy assessment', 26 January 1966.

79 Robinson McIlvaine, US Embassy Conakry, to Department of State, 'United States–Guineans relations: where do they stand?' 2 June 1967, POLGUIN 1967–1969, Box 2165, CGRDS, NARA.

80 Loeb, 'Year with Sékou Touré', 8 September 1964; Loeb, US Embassy Conakry, to Department of State, 'Another Guinean crisis', 15 June 1965, USGUIN 1964–1966, Box 2258, CGRDS, NARA, 'Year-end assessment', 29 December 1964, and 'US policy assessment', 26 January 1966; Dean Rusk to US Mission in Geneva, 'Guinean National Liberation Front', 22 November 1967, POLGUIN 1967–1969, Box 2164, CGRDS, NARA.

81 See documents in File USGUIN 1963, Box 2254 and File POLGUIN 1964–1966, Box 2256, CGRDS, NARA.

82 See documents in File POLGUIN 1970–1973, Boxes 2341 and 2259, CGRDS, NARA.

83 See documents in File POLGUIN 1964–1966, Boxes 2256 and 2261; File POLGUIN 1967–1969, Boxes 2164 and 2165; and File USGUIN 1964–1966, Boxes 2258 and 2259, CGRDS, NARA.

84 Loeb, 'US policy assessment', 26 January 1966.

Germany had started assisting the Guinean army with the construction of a road in 1963,[85] and its mission actively shared information with France and the US.[86] When Guinean officials, satisfied with the German programme, requested heavier equipment from the US,[87] the US embassy in Conakry's response was favourable. They hoped American support would diminish the influence of the Soviet bloc on the Guinean army and expose Guinean military officials to US influence.[88] Nevertheless, the State Department and Pentagon hesitated. Their main concern was how African governments which were 'friendlier' to the US would perceive the assistance, but were also apprehensive about a multi-million dollar US-funded programme being implemented by technicians and officers trained in Czechoslovakia and the Soviet Union.[89] To convince the Pentagon to allocate the funding, the US Assistant Secretary for African Affairs argued that 'the object of this particular program in Guinea is less to assist the Guineans than to protect our own interest there'. He noted that:

85 US Embassy Conakry to Department of State, 'West German military mission visits Guinea', 29 March 1963, 770b, Box 3724, CGRDS, NARA. The construction project reportedly cost US$ 2 million, covered by a loan repayable over 15 years, with 2% annual interest. See US Embassy Conakry to Department of State, 'Bi-weekly no. 7', 15 July 1963.

86 McIlvaine, US Embassy Conakry, to Department of State, 7 June 1967, DEFGUIN 1967–1969, Box 1550, CGRDS, NARA; US Embassy Conakry to Department of State, 16 December 1966, DEFGUIN 1964–1966, Box 1649, CGRDS, NARA; Kizler, US Embassy Conakry, to Department of State, 'Fire destroys arms at army camp Alpha Yaya', 22 April 1966, DEFGUIN 1964–1966, Box 1649, CGRDS, NARA; Graham, US Embassy Conakry, to Rusk, 'Guinean military preparedness', 18 March 1966, DEFGUIN 1964–1966, Box 1649, CGRDS, NARA.

87 See documents in File DEFGUIN 1963, Box 3724; File USGUIN 1963, Box 2254; and File USGUIN 1964–1966, Box 1755, CGRDS, NARA.

88 Attwood, US Embassy Conakry, to Department of State, 'US civic action assistance to Guinea', 20 February 1963, USGUIN, Box 2254, CGRDS, NARA; US Embassy Conakry to Department of State, 'Information needed for assessment of new civic action program proposals for African countries', 19 June 1964, DEFGUIN 1964–1966, Box 1649, CGRDS, NARA; Loeb, US Embassy Conakry, to Department of State, 'Guinean request for military assistance', 10 March 1964, USGUIN 1964–1966, Box 1755, CGRDS, NARA; Loeb, US Embassy Conakry, to State Department, 11 June 1964, DEFGUIN 1964–1966, Box 1649, CGRDS, NARA.

89 Rusk, US Department of State, to Embassy Conakry, 'Civic action assistance to Guinea', 1 February 1963, USGUIN, Box 2254, CGRDS, NARA; Wayne Fredericks, Acting Assistant US Secretary for African Affairs, to John McNaughton, Assistant Secretary for Defense for International Security Affairs, Pentagon, 30 December 1964, USGUIN 1964–1966, Box 1755, CGRDS, NARA.

the size of [the US] political and economic commitment in Guinea and the need to protect it through exercise of influence on the military and acquisition of intelligence concerning it places a high priority on establishment of a military program as promptly as possible.[90]

The US government took two years to make up its mind.[91] Touré also hesitated, concerned with how an American military presence would be perceived by other African countries.[92] Finally, though, in November 1965, a US military engineering team arrived in Conakry.[93] Despite initial successes,[94] the programme experienced setbacks linked to technical issues and the Guinean political climate.[95] American soldiers reported difficulties working alongside Guinean soldiers with had negative attitudes towards the US.[96] American officials did start to build friendly relations with key actors in control of Guinean security structures, such as Defence Minister Fodéba Keïta – who the US ambassador referred to as 'the second most powerful man in Guinea'[97] – and Deputy Chief of Staff of the Armed Forces Kaman Diaby.[98] Diaby in particular was considered by the US to be central to any potential coup, because 'to do anything the armed forces would need Diaby's consent'.[99] When Diaby and Keïta were later accused of involvement in an attempted coup, suspicion thus extended to the US as well.[100]

The US terminated its military assistance programme in Guinea in 1967, as did the West Germans (although they continued to work in Guinean

90 Fredericks to McNaughton, 30 December 1964.
91 See documents in File USGUIN 1964–1966, Box 1755, CGRDS, NARA.
92 US Embassy Conakry to Department of State, 1 March 1965, USGUIN 1964–1966, Box 1755, CGRDS, NARA.
93 Kizler, US Embassy Conakry, to Department of State, 'US military aid program in Guinea', 3 November 1965, USGUIN 1964–1966, Box 1755, CGRDS, NARA, and 'Bi-weekly no. 35', 21 October 1965, POLGUIN 1964–1966, Box 2256, CGRDS, NARA.
94 Loeb, US Embassy Conakry, to Department of State, 9 April 1965, USGUIN 1964–1966, Box 1755, CGRDS, NARA.
95 US Embassy Conakry to Department of State, 13 March 1967, POLGUIN 1967–1969, Box 2163, CGRDS, NARA.
96 US Embassy Conakry to Department of State, 24 November 1966, USGUIN 1964–1966, Box 1755, CGRDS, NARA.
97 Loeb, US Embassy Conakry, to Department of State, 'Series of Annoyances', 20 May 1965, POLGUIN 1964–1966, Box 2256, CGRDS, NARA.
98 See documents in File DEFGUIN 1964–1966, Box 1649 and File USGUIN 1964–1966, Boxes 1755 and 2259, CGRDS, NARA.
99 Graham, 'Current position and future prospects of the Touré regime', 14 April 1966.
100 US Embassy Conakry to Department of State, 'Bi-weekly no. 7', 15 April 1969.

military factories).[101] Relations between the US and Guinea had deteriorated largely due to American policies towards Portuguese colonies, South Africa, and Rhodesia.[102] However, the military coup against Touré's most important ally, Kwame Nkrumah, was the cause of the most serious tensions, as Touré believed the US was complicit.[103] According to French reports, Guinea's worsening relations with Western powers renewed Soviet interest in Guinea, and more Soviet military assistance to the country was negotiated.[104]

In 1965, Touré received multiple warnings from informants that the US was conspiring against him, but Defence Minister Keïta did not find the allegations convincing.[105] Keïta even suggested to US officials that the Americans could 'get the CIA involved in this affair … [to] find out the real origin of these reports.'[106] In all likelihood, he assumed Soviet agents were fabricating evidence against the US. He did not give the French the same benefit of the doubt. Touré accused the French ambassador of attacks against him and severed diplomatic ties to France in November 1965,[107] and from 1965 to 1975, Italy was the designated facilitator of French relations to Guinea. French officials, dissatisfied with the volume of information they received from the Italians throughout this arrangement, often turned to the French director of the bauxite mining company FRIA for reports on Guinean events and to negotiate with Guinean officials.

101 See documents in File POLGUIN 1967–1969, Box 2163 and File POLGUIN 1964–1966, Boxes 1755 and 2256, CGRDS, NARA.

102 Terence Todman, US Embassy Conakry, to Department of State, 'Policy analysis and Resources Allocation (PARA) paper for Guinea', 31 May 1973, POLGUIN 1970–1973, Box 2341, CGRDS, NARA.

103 See documents in File 5AGF/1647, FFAN and File USGUIN 1964–1966, Boxes 2259 and 2260, CGRDS, NARA.

104 General Sécretariat for African and Malagasy Affairs, 'Note à l'attention de monsieur le président de la république: contact entre la Russie soviétique et la Guinée', 14 March 1966, 5AGF/1647, FFAN; Ministry of Armed Forces, SDECE, 'Aide militaire soviétique à la Guinée', 6 June 1966.

105 Philippe Koenig, Ambassador of France in Guinea, to Minister of Foreign Affairs Maurice Couve de Murville, 6 March 1965, 5AGF1644, FFAN; Ministry of Armed Forces, Joint Command Dakar, 'Naufrage navire guinéo-portugais', 26 September 1965, 5AGF/1644, FFAN.

106 Graham, US Embassy Conakry, to Department of State, 12 March 1965.

107 Foccart to President de Gaulle, 'Expulsion de l'ambassadeur de France de Conakry', 19 November 1965, 5A GF/558, FFAN; General Secretariat for African and Malagasy Affairs, 'Note à l'attention du président de la république', 16 November 1965, 5AGF/558, FFAN.

The year after Touré broke diplomatic ties with France, the *Front de libération nationale de la Guinée* (FLNG) would call for his violent overthrow. This organized opposition movement was established in Paris, Côte d'Ivoire, and Senegal.[108] Guinean opposition actors frequently contacted French officials seeking financial and military support to oust Touré,[109] but French authorities forbid any direct contact with FLNG members and carefully monitored the organization's activities.[110] The US took a similar stance, instructing US diplomatic staff to avoid any contact with the organization, warning them to avoid expressing 'any comments which might conceivably be interpreted as constituting even tacit US approval'. US officials did not consider the FLNG an alternative to Touré, referring to it as an 'ineffective opposition group' challenged by 'internal dissensions and personal rivalries', and noting that it had 'no organization within Guinea'.[111] The suspicion that FLNG had been 'penetrated by Touré's agents' was another reason for caution.[112]

A military coup was also unlikely to change Guinean foreign policy, as soldiers who had been trained in communist countries increasingly held senior military positions. In June 1970, a Guinean source informed Foccart's office that the only way to depose Touré would be through a diversion at the borders, which would require significant French material and financial assistance.[113] US officials also felt that a military coup in Guinea would not

---

108 Ministry of Armed Forces, SDECE, 'Projet d'action du front libération national de la Guinée', 23 November 1967, 5AG/1646, FFAN; Ministry of Interior, Directorate of General Intelligence, 'L'opposition Guinée France', 2 December 1966, 5AG/1646, FFAN; Ministry of Armed Forces, SDECE, 'Guinée-Sénégal-Côte d'Ivoire', 29 July 1966; Dean Rusk to US Mission in Geneva, 'Guinean National Liberation Front', 22 November 1967.

109 Jean Lagarde, Ambassador of France in Senegal, to Minister of Foreign Affairs Couve de Murville, 'La Guinée nouvelles manière vue par un sénégalais', 1 December 1964, 5AGF/1644, FFAN; Ministry of Armed Forces, SDECE, 'Guinée-Sénégal-Côte d'Ivoire', 29 July 1966.

110 General Secretariat for African and Malagasy Affairs, 'Note à l'attention monsieur Plantey', 5 April 1966, 5AG/1646, FFAN.

111 Rusk to US Mission in Geneva, 'Guinean National Liberation Front', 22 November 1967. In 1967, the FLNG argued it had significant support in the Guinean army, gendarmerie, and police, which would help it carry out a military coup. See Williams, US Embassy Accra, to Department of State, 'Purported plans for coup in Guinea', 17 July 1967, POLGUIN 1967–1969, Box 2165, CGRDS, NARA.

112 Rusk to US Mission in Geneva, 'Guinean National Liberation Front', 22 November 1967.

113 General Secretariat for African and Malagasy Affairs, 'Note à l'attention de M. René Journiac: relations avec la Guinée', 10 June 1970, 5AGF/1648, FFAN.

advance their interests, advising in a 1966 report that the sympathies of soldiers were 'unknown and [their] political experience non-existent'.[114] The Americans, who believed a potential coup in Guinea would be carried out with the assistance of Côte d'Ivoire and France, expected any incoming government would thus 'owe its existence to [Ivorian president] Houphouët-Boigny or the French' and would most likely adopt an anti-US position.[115]

Touré is thought to have had fairly thorough knowledge of the hostile intentions of Guinean opposition actors, and of their collusion with French, Ivorian, and Senegalese officials.[116] Yet it was not only activities of the 'East' and 'West' and their proxies that influenced Guinea's foreign policies, or the development of its armed forces. Events in Africa, from wars of liberation to military coups, had a significant impact on the Guinean approach to defence. Touré watched as other pan-Africanist leaders were ousted by the military – first Lumumba in Congo in 1961, then Kwame Nkrumah in Ghana in 1966, then Modibo Keïta in Mali in 1968. The coup against the Ghanaian president made an especially strong impression on Touré, who grew even more suspicious of his own army.[117] His confidence was shaken further by the military coup in neighbouring Mali just two years later.[118] Not long afterwards, thirteen Guinean soldiers were sentenced to death, and twenty-seven to forced labour, for allegedly planning to assassinate Touré.[119]

Of all the events that had taken place in West Africa, the anti-colonial conflict in Guinea-Bissau may well have had the most significant impact on Touré's decision-making. The Parti africain pour l'indépendance de la Guinée et du Cap-Vert (PAIGC), which began an armed rebellion against the Portuguese administration in 1961, later established its headquarters in Conakry. In 1964, Cuba started providing PAIGC with medical and military

114 Graham, 'Current position and future prospects of the Touré regime', 14 April 1966.
115 Ibid.; Albert Sherer, US Embassy Conakry, to Department of State, 'Prospects of Sékou Touré's regime', 11 October 1971, POLGUIN 1970–1973, Box 2340, CGRDS, NARA.
116 Graham, 'Current position and future prospects of the Touré regime' 14 April 1966.
117 Lewin, *Ahmed Sékou Touré (1922–1984)*, vol. 5, pp. 177–90.
118 General Secretariat for National Defence, Intelligence Exploitation Centre, 'La situation en République de Guinée à la suite du coup d'état militaire au Mali', 26 January 1969, GR9Q5122, SHD; Lewin, *Ahmed Sékou Touré (1922–1984)*, vol. 5, pp. 177–90 and 251–70; Bob Melone, US Embassy Conakry, to Department of State, 'Stirrings in the Guinean army', 17 December 1968; Thomas Hughes, Director of the Bureau of Intelligence and Research, US Department of State, 'Guinea: Touré Demilitarizes the Military', 16 January 1969, DEFGUIN 1967–1969, Box 1550, CGRDS, NARA.
119 Lewin, *Ahmed Sékou Touré (1922–1984)*, vol. 5, Chapter 64.

assistance and training, and though Touré took the US side in the Cuban Missile Crisis, the anti-colonialist struggle in Guinea-Bissau nevertheless brought Guinea closer to Cuba. By 1967, Cuba had started training militia forces in Guinea.[120]

American reports suggest that much of the military aid the Soviets sent to Guinea from 1967 to 1969 was redirected to PAIGC,[121] which controlled key parts of Guinea-Bissau by 1968. This led Portugal to attack Conakry on 22 November 1970,[122] primarily to free Portuguese prisoners being held there. However, the operation was also said to be aimed at assassinating both Touré and Amílcar Cabral, leader of PAIGC, and the Portuguese-led forces consisted of members of the Guinean opposition and soldiers from Guinea-Bissau.[123] Some FLNG members who participated in the attack had previously served in the French army.[124]

The operation had succeeded to the extent that the Portuguese prisoners were freed, with most managing to escape the country, but neither Touré nor Cabral were assassinated. While the Guinean opposition hoped it would gain more internal support for toppling Touré, the population had remained passive.[125], and the sluggish performance of the Guinean national armed forces in response to the attack in Conakry gave Touré reason to suspect they had collaborated with the attackers.[126] Portugal denied its connection to the

---

[120] Ministry of Armed Forces, SDECE, 'Guinée-Cuba: stage de formation de la milice à Cuba', 5 January 1968, 5AGF/1647, FFAN; General Secretariat for National Defence, Intelligence Division, 'La Guinée du Président Sékou Touré: Annexe G – Les forces armées guinéennes et l'assistance militaire soviétique, chinoise et cubaine', 3 June 1977, GR9Q5122, SHD; US Embassy Conakry to Department of State, 'Bi-weekly no. 8', 24 April 1967, POLGUIN 1967–1969, Box 2163, CGRDS, NARA, and 'Bi-weekly no. 17', 15 August 1967, POLGUIN 1967–1969, Box 2163, CGRDS, NARA.

[121] McIlvaine, US Embassy Conakry, to State Department, 'Miscellaneous military intelligence', 2 April 1968, DEFGUIN 1967–1969, Box 1550, CGRDS, NARA.

[122] Piero Gleijeses, *Conflicting Missions: Havana, Washington, and Africa, 1959–1976* (University of North Carolina Press, 2002), pp. 185–214; Intelligence Exploitation Centre, 'Les événements de Guinée et leur développements diplomatiques', April 1971, GR9Q5122, SHD.

[123] 'Un rescapé des geôles de Sékou Touré', *Jeune Afrique*, 18 May 1971; Intelligence Exploitation Centre, 'Les événements de Guinée et leur développements diplomatiques', April 1971.

[124] Diefenbacher, Ministry of Interior Director of International Police Technical Cooperation Services, to Jacques Foccart, 'Note concernant les activités au Sénégal d'opposants au régime de Sékou Touré', 22 July 1970, 5AGF/1648, FFAN.

[125] See documents in File FNGUIN 1970–1973, Boxes 891 and 2341, CGRDS, NARA.

[126] US Embassy Conakry to Department of State, 'Policy Planning Paper', 6 July 1971.

attack and the US refused to publicly acknowledge Portugal's role, but it was clear that the operation had in fact been authorized from the highest levels of the Portuguese government.[127] French and American officials worried the attack would have a negative impact on Western interests in Guinea, as Touré's dependence on the Soviet Union only deepened in its wake.[128] Guinea had been almost exclusively armed with Soviet equipment prior to the attack, but this was further strengthened by the growing number of Soviet military assistants.[129] Nonetheless, French and American reports emphasized that Guinea's heavy armaments and number of troops did not translate into capacity, which was limited by a lack of technical skill and logistical support, and the diversion of soldiers to non-military tasks.[130]

The attack in Conakry marked the start of a particularly dark period in Guinean history. In 1971, convinced the attackers had benefitted from inside cooperation,[131] Touré ordered the arrest of sixty Guineans who were accused of involvement in the attack. They were subsequently condemned to death or forced labour.[132] Among those who received capital punishment were twelve soldiers, who offered public confessions suggesting that their participation in the Portuguese-led attack was related to what they viewed as the negative attitude of the Guinean government towards soldiers.[133] Though

---

127 Ray C. Cline, Director of the Bureau of Intelligence and Research, US Department of State, to Secretary of State, 'Guinea Touré's opponents strike by sea', 24 November 1970, FNGUIN 1970–1973, Box 891, CGRDS, NARA; US Department of State, 'Memorandum of conversation: Antonio Cabruta Matias, Counselor, Embassy of Portugal; George Trail, Jerrold North, Guinea-Sierra Leone Defense Pact; and Portuguese views', 27 April 1971, DEFGUIN 1970–1973, Box 1740, CGRDS, NARA.

128 General Secretariat for National Defence, Intelligence Exploitation Centre, 'Pénétration Soviétique en Guinée', 1 March 1968.

129 Sherer, 'Prospects of Sékou Touré's regime', 11 October 1971; US Department of State, 'Memorandum of conversation: Antonio Cabruta Matias, Counselor, Embassy of Portugal; Trail and North, Guinea-Sierra Leone Defense Pact; and Portuguese views', 27 April 1971.

130 General Secretariat for National Defence, Intelligence Exploitation Centre, 'Les forces armées guinéennes', 17 April 1970, GR9Q5122, SHD, 'Pénétration de l'URSS en Guinée', 1 November 1968, GR9Q5122, SHD, and 'Aviation militaire guinéenne', 21 July 1971, GR9Q5122, SHD; US Embassy Conakry to Department of State, 'Bi-weekly', 20 January 1964, POLGUIN 1964–1966, Box 2256, CGRDS, NARA; Graham, 'Guinean military strength: Personnel and weapons', 19 April 1966.

131 Intelligence Exploitation Centre, 'Guinée: Le grand procès populaire de la cinquième colonne', 24 August 1971, GR9Q5122, SHD.

132 Lewin, *Ahmed Sékou Touré (1922–1984)*, vol. 5, Chapter 65.

133 Mamadi Keïta, 'Rapport sur les méfaits de agents de la 5eme colonne', 18 November 1971.

the Guinean investigation of the attack focused on domestic actors, Guineans with foreign connections were accused of involvement as well.[134] France and West Germany were linked to the attack through Foccart's so-called 'fifth column', but somewhat surprisingly, West German Nazi networks were also mentioned in the confessions of participants published in Guinean state newspaper *Horoya*. The scenarios presented in some of these confessions seem almost fantastical, but five French nationals and two West Germans received sentences in connection to the incident.[135]

Guinea subsequently broke off diplomatic relations with West Germany and expelled thirty-seven West German technical assistants.[136] Researchers have questioned what reason West Germany would have had to be involved in the Portuguese operation,[137] and American officials have argued that the 'evidence' against alleged West German participants was fabricated. Though connections between West German officials and FLNG in Dakar were clear,[138] it is worth noting that Guinea had established diplomatic relations with East Germany just two months prior to the attack.[139] What is known is that French intelligence reports indicate that former Guinean ambassador to Bonn and Paris, Nabi Youla, who had defected to France in 1967, had a central role in organizing the Guinean opposition, and met with Portuguese authorities. Youla had apparently advised that the Guinean military could organize a coup against Touré, that Deputy Chief of Staff of the Armed Forces Kaman Diaby would be suitable to lead the effort, and that Chief of Staff Noumandian Keïta was unlikely to oppose it.[140] It is possible that West Germany was involved in the attack, and the location of some West German citizens during the event as well as suicides in the diplomatic corps following

---

[134] US Embassy Conakry to Department of State, 'The November 22 raid: The revolutionary tribunal on the role of the front liberation national of Guinea (FLNG)', 15 February 1971, POLGUIN 1970–1973, Box 2340, CGRDS, NARA.

[135] Lewin, *Ahmed Sékou Touré (1922–1984)*, vol. 5, Chapter 65.

[136] Lewin, 'La Guinée et les deux Allemagnes'.

[137] Ibid.

[138] US Embassy Conakry to Department of State, 'The November 22 raid: The revolutionary tribunal on the role of the front liberation national of Guinea (FLNG)', 15 February 1971.

[139] Winrow, *The foreign policy of the GDR in Africa*; US Embassy Conakry to Department of State, 'Bi-weekly no. 14', 21 September 1970, POLGUIN 1970–1973, Box 2340, CGRDS, NARA.

[140] Ministry of Armed Forces, SDECE, 'Guinée: au sujet de M. Nabi Youla', 23 May 1967, 5AG/1646, FFAN, and 'Projet d'action du front libération national de la Guinée', 23 November 1967, 5AG/1646, FFAN.

the event lend some support to this theory, but the evidence is thin. It is also possible that any German role in the operation was insignificant, but Touré – knowing that relations with West Germany would be severed in any case – implicated the West Germans in order to divert attention from the Guinean role in the attack.[141] Touré had previously regularly exploited external threats to foster national unity.[142]

The Portuguese attack pushed Guinea further towards communist states. Aid from China and Arab countries increased,[143] while the West tried to protect its economic interests.[144] For the US, this meant safeguarding almost US$ 200 million in private American investment in the Guinean mining industry.[145] When the US ambassador met with Touré soon after the attack, Touré claimed he had known the timing of the attack beforehand, and that both French and Soviet actors wanted him out of the way to gain better access to bauxite – to which he said Americans had privileged access.[146] US officials acknowledged that there were now even fewer alternatives to Touré than before, as most 'moderates' had been eliminated.[147] Any concern Touré felt about Soviet domination did not stop him from becoming ever more reliant on Soviet military assistance after 1970. Soviet military aid to Guinea was well suited to both Soviet and Guinean objectives, as it helped assure Guinea's survival without requiring the Soviet Union 'to commit

141 Lewin, 'La Guinée et les deux Allemagnes'; Sherer, 'Prospects of Sékou Touré's regime', 11 October 1971; McIlvaine, US Embassy Conakry, to State Department, 'The plotters are sentenced', 19 May 1969, CGRDS 1967–1969, POLGUIN, Box 2165, NARA; Hughes, Director of the Bureau of Intelligence and Research, US Department of State, to Secretary of State, 'Guinea CIA syndrome', 17 January 1969, CGRDS 1967–1969, POLGUIN, Box 2165, NARA.
142 The High Commissioner representing the President of the French Community in Dakar to President of the Community, General Secretariat, 25 May 1960.
143 Sherer, 'Prospects of Sékou Touré's regime', 11 October 1971.
144 Intelligence Exploitation Centre, 'Evolution de la situation en Guinée et développement diplomatique', 24 January 1971, GR9Q5122, SHD.
145 Roy Haverkamp, US Embassy Conakry, to Department of State, 'Guinea: Guidelines for Policy', 3 February 1970, POLGUIN 1970–1973, Box 2341, CGRDS, NARA; US Embassy Conakry to Department of State, 'Policy Planning Paper', 6 July 1971; John P. Walsh, Acting Executive Secretary, 'Memorandum for Mr. Henry Kissinger: Letter from President of Guinea and suggested reply', 20 May 1969, POLGUIN 1967–1969, Box 2164, CGRDS, NARA.
146 Sherer, US Embassy Conakry, to Department of State, 'Conversation with President Touré', 19 December 1970, POLGUIN 1970–1973, Box 2340, CGRDS, NARA.
147 Sherer, 'Prospects of Sékou Touré's regime', 11 October 1971; Haverkamp, 'Guinea: Guidelines for Policy', 3 February 1970.

... to new economic assistance projects'.[148] In Mali and in Guinea, Soviet economic assistance had been a failure, but by focusing on military assistance instead, the Soviet Union could still assert its political influence. This is how the Soviets came to control the military sphere in Guinea while Western countries dominated the economic sphere.

Mali's relation with the two blocs

Despite its socialist orientation, the government of Mali was less radical, less internationalist, and less pan-Africanist than that of Guinea, which allowed for smoother relations with France and the US. Between 1960 and 1968, the administration of Malian president Modibo Keïta skilfully managed American, French, Chinese, Israeli, and Soviet offers of assistance and thereby maximized its receipt of foreign aid. However, these foreign resources were not used efficiently, and as the Malian economy shrank, popular dissatisfaction grew. By the time Malian soldiers carried out a coup in 1968, there was little resistance from the population, and foreign powers readily transferred their assistance to the military government.

Unlike Guinea, Mali and the other former colonies in francophone West Africa had voted to join the French Community in 1958, attaining their independence two years later, when they signed cooperation agreements with France. Mali did, however, distance itself from France soon after independence. In January 1961, for example, Mali demanded the withdrawal of French forces and the return of Malian soldiers serving in the French military.[149] Aware that the French position in Mali was weakening, US officials opted to provide training to parachutists in the Malian armed forces, as well as vehicles and uniforms.[150] Nevertheless, the socialist orientation of Mali's government made them hesitant to grant further security assistance to the country, and opinions differed inside the Kennedy administration as to whether US assistance to either Guinea or Mali would mitigate the communist influence. The American ambassador in Abidjan signalled that more US assistance to Mali would anger Western-oriented African countries and send the message 'that flirtations with the communist bloc pay off'.[151]

---

148 Ibid.
149 General Secretary for African and Malagasy Affairs, 'Instruction pour la Chargé d'affaires au Mali', 9 February 1961, 5AGF/580, FFAN.
150 General Secretariat for National Defence, Intelligence Exploitation Centre, 'L'armée malienne' 23 October 1962, GR9Q5128, SHD.
151 US Embassy Abidjan, 31 March 1961, MAL60–63, 770e, Box 1952, CGRDS, NARA.

US Secretary of State Dean Rusk, fearful of entering into an arms race with the Soviet Union, was likewise opposed to granting military assistance to Mali, arguing that it would be expensive for the US and could create 'artificial arms establishments on the Latin American model'.[152] President Kennedy's Assistant Secretary of State for African Affairs, Mennen Williams, did support the decision to grant assistance to Mali, not least because President Keïta was already under the impression that the US ambassador had promised military assistance. It was on this basis that he had agreed to send the Malian minister of defence to the US.

Williams contended that Mali had only reached out to communist countries because it had not received aid from the West. He believed the US could leverage engineering equipment to convince the Malian government to renounce Soviet assistance, and only then deliver arms. Williams also seemed convinced by the insistence of Mali that an urgent decision needed to be made, arguing that:

> The Mali question requires an immediate decision; it is one of those problems where a failure to take a decision constitutes a decision by default. If we delay even a few more days in confirming the invitation to the Mali Secretary of State for Defense, it will be as though we had decided to give no assistance.[153]

He also pointed out that Mali had recently received US$ 44 million of economic credit from the Soviet Union and said the US should seek to influence the military, which was 'western-oriented, unlike the government'.[154] In hindsight, it is clear that Williams grossly overestimated the potential impact of US military aid, as well as the sincerity of Malian officials. Mali had also requested arms from Israel for Malian militias, which had already received small arms from Czechoslovakia in October 1960.[155] American officials assumed that Mali had done so because it wanted to avoid an exclusive dependence on the communist bloc.[156] However, in October 1961, Israel alerted the US that it had provided 4,000 personal weapons

152 Rusk to Chester Bowles, US Department of State, 4 April 1961, MAL61–63, 770e, Box 1952, CGRDS, NARA.
153 Williams to Undersecretary of State, US Department of State, 6 April 1961, MAL61–63, 770e, Box 1952, CGRDS, NARA.
154 Williams to Undersecretary of State, US Department of State, 4 April 1961, MAL61–63, 770e, Box 1952, CGRDS, NARA.
155 Directorate of African and Malagasy Affairs, 'fournitures d'armes à Mali', 13 October 1961, INVA299, CADC.
156 Williams to Undersecretary of State, 4 April 1961.

to Mali in February 1961 but had no news about their location or what kind of militia forces Mali planned to create. Israeli officials said they had no desire to assist Mali further; they were already frustrated by the fact that Mali had more than once reopened talks on additional military aid, only to withdraw when Czechoslovakia provided the equipment they needed.[157] The French saw the Israeli experience as reason to engage more with the Americans, as 'Israel offers arms with US support'.[158] Even if it was US policy to encourage assistance from Western countries to African militaries, the Americans were keen not to be identified with Israeli projects.[159]

Mali received such quantities of military equipment from the Soviet Union that Western offers looked insignificant in comparison. It acquired one hundred and four vehicles, sixteen cannons, one hundred armoured cars, and twenty-five trucks in July 1961 alone. A French military attaché noted to US officials that the Soviets had to be operating the equipment and were likely training Malian soldiers to use them, 'as there is not a single qualified artilleryman in the Malian armed forces'.[160] In December of that year, when Mali announced it was not interested in any further training from the US, the US Embassy in Bamako concluded that the Malian government had 'decided to rely exclusively on the bloc for its foreign military training requirements'.[161] American officials reported the presence of fifteen Soviet trainers at the main military base in Kati and characterized this as proof of Mali's alignment with the Soviet Union.[162]

In early 1962, when Mali received further weapons deliveries from both the Soviet Union and Czechoslovakia, French intelligence services noted that the weapons amassed in Mali were four times the needs of its troops,

---

[157] US Embassy Tel Aviv, 'Military aid to Mali', 30 August 1961, MAL61–63, 770e, Box 1952, CGRDS, NARA; General Secretariat for National Defence, Intelligence Exploitation Centre, 'L'armée malienne', 23 October 1962.

[158] Directorate of African and Malagasy Affairs, 'Fournitures d'armes à Mali', 13 October 1961.

[159] Williams, US Department of State, to Governor Harrison, 'Scheduling of US-Israeli talks on Africa', 31 July 1964, DEF-AFR 64–66, Box 1614, CGRDS, NARA.

[160] US Embassy Bamako, 'Summary list of soviet bloc military equipment now in Mali', 17 July 1961, MAL61–63, 770e, Box 1951, CGRDS, NARA.

[161] US Embassy Bamako, 'Malian military personnel selected for training in the Soviet Union', 12 December 1961, MAL61–63, 770e, Box 1951, CGRDS, NARA.

[162] US Embassy Bamako, 'Activities of soviet military personnel in Mali', 17 July 1961, MAL61–63, 770e, Box 1951, CGRDS, NARA, and 'Internal Security Assessment of Mali,' 1 June 1962, MAL61–63, 770e, Box 1951, CGRDS, NARA.

who lacked the technical skills to operate the equipment.[163] The number of Soviet trainers in Mali thus increased over the next few years, rising to forty by 1962 and almost 60 by 1967.[164] As it seemed Mali had been lost to the communist bloc, US officials found it easier to decide against providing police assistance in 1962, 'as it would most likely be used against anticommunist elements in Mali'.[165] The US Embassy portrayed American and Malian objectives as incompatible.

In 1963, the US Department of Defense stipulated that military assistance programmes should focus on internal security and should target three key US objectives: to eliminate 'Sino-Soviet influence', foster 'an anticommunist western orientated military community', and 'contribute to stable and viable friendly governments'.[166] The US thus sought to maximize contact between American trainers and Malian soldiers, but the Malians preferred 'maximum material with a minimum working contact' in order to reduce US influence and intelligence gathering on their military.[167] US officials were convinced that assistance from a less threatening capitalist country could help maintain some sort of contact with Malian security forces, so they encouraged the British to provide Mali with police assistance.[168] This began in May 1962,[169] but it was short-lived and Mali eventually received police training from Czechoslovakia instead.[170]

163 General Secretariat for National Defence, Intelligence Exploitation Centre, 'L'armée malienne', 23 October 1962; Advisor to the Squadron Battalion Commander, 'Rapport fin de mission, aôut 1962–juillet 1965', 29 June 1965, GR14S268, SHD; US Embassy Bamako, 'Security forces of the government of Mali', 24 May 1962, MAL61–63, 770e, Box 1951, CGRDS, NARA.

164 French officials reported similar numbers: ten Bulgarians and thirty Soviets. See General Secretariat for National Defence, Intelligence Exploitation Centre, 'L'armée malienne', 23 October 1962, and 'L'armée malienne et l'aide militaire française', 28 April 1972, 5AGF/582, FFAN.

165 US Embassy Bamako, 'Internal Security Survey', 28 May 1962, MAL61–63, 770e, Box 1951, CGRDS, NARA.

166 Assistant US Secretary of Defense to Deputy Undersecretary of Defense, 19 February 1963, POL-AFR63, Box 3809, CGRDS, NARA.

167 US Embassy Bamako, 'Police assistance programs', 17 September 1962, MAL61–63, 770e, Box 1951, CGRDS, NARA and 'Internal Security Assessment of Mali', 1 June 1962.

168 US Embassy Bamako, 'Internal Security Survey', 28 May 1962.

169 US Embassy Bamako, 'Internal Security Assessment of Mali', 1 June 1962.

170 US Embassy Bamako, 'Discontent Among the Provincial Gendarmerie', 8 February 1966, POL 1964–1966, Box 2463, CGRDS, NARA.

One year into the programme, the British had announced that it would no longer train Malian officers because of a lack of French-speaking personnel.[171] This need for French-speaking Africa specialists also hindered the US in its military cooperation with Mali. According to the US Ministry of Defense, the problem extended from the fact that aid had been granted to countries that had refused to accept US military missions on their territory or US trainers for their armed forces. In 1963, the Ministry had identified lessons learned to avoid repeating failures of the past, and determined it was particularly important to respond to requests and implement decisions promptly. Furthermore, receiving states needed to have the technical skills to use US equipment, or accept appropriate training and an in-country US military mission. The Ministry advised that any programmes that did not should be terminated.[172] Nevertheless, in 1964, the US began training a Malian engineering company to build runways in Bamako and Tessalit. Shortly thereafter, a Malian soldier was convicted for selling confidential information to the Americans – who had acted carelessly and unwisely, according to the French ambassador, and for information he considered insignificant.[173]

There were notable ways in which the actions of the US and Soviet Union complemented each other in Mali in the 1960s. For instance, the Soviets provided enormous amounts of light and heavy weapons, planes, and vehicles to the country, but Mali lacked the necessary infrastructure to use them.[174] With so many Soviet cars and only a few roads,[175] Mali's use of Soviet planes and vehicles was dependent on US help to build roads and runways. From 1965 onwards, China became increasingly active in Mali, and trade between the two countries grew when China granted a FM 30 billion loan to Mali and reportedly provided the Malian military with enough personal weapons to re-equip its entire force. Chinese military

---

171 US Embassy Bamako, 'Police Assistance Programs', 4 September 1963, Box 3981, NARA.

172 Assistant US Secretary of Defense to Deputy Undersecretary of Defense, 19 February 1963.

173 Ambassador Pelen, 'Condamnation à la peine de mort d'un ancien sous-officier malien accusé d'espionnage au profit des Etats-Unis', 30 June 1966, 62POL–15, CADN.

174 Colonel Charles to Alain Richard, 7 April 1972, 5AGF/2708, FFAN; US Embassy Bamako, 'Discontent Among the Provincial Gendarmerie', 8 February 1966.

175 Pelen, 'Quelques réflexions sur l'armée malienne', 2 December 1966, GR6Q44, SHD.

advisors started working on Malian bases in Kati, Gao, Kidal, and Tessalit, and were particularly active in training militias.[176]

The rising presence of both the Soviets and Chinese was a cause of friction inside the Malian armed forces and it also sparked criticism from the wider population.[177] Despite this, just a few months prior to the November 1968 military coup, the Malian government signed a military assistance agreement with the Soviet Union. The promise of new Soviet equipment would reduce the Chinese influence, as would sending additional Soviet officers and technicians to Mali. While Malian officers did welcome the new equipment, they did not welcome the presence of additional Soviet officers.[178] Indeed, by 1962, the French ambassador had reported that Malian soldiers were hostile towards their Soviet instructors, who they said did not understand the Malian mentality.[179]

In 1967, French officials notified Paris that Malian officers had expressed interest in receiving training from the French.[180] The Ministry of Foreign Affairs explained that such requests would be considered favourably but providing military equipment would be difficult.[181] Yet, after the 1968 coup, France did grant military assistance to Mali, providing military material worth FF 2–2.5 million and training twenty to twenty-five Malian soldiers each year over the course of the next decade.[182] The US also offered assistance to parachutists when the Soviets refused to do so, as the military government

176 US Embassy Bamako, 'French military counselor reviews military situation in Mali', 8 December 1965, DEF 1964–1966, Box 1679, NARA, and 'Discontent Among the Provincial Gendarmerie', 8 February 1966; Pelen, 'Quelques réflexions sur l'armée malienne', 2 December 1966; General Secretary for African and Malagasy Affairs, 'Aides extérieures accordées au Mali', 28 April 1972, 5AGF/582, SHD.

177 US Embassy Bamako, 'French military counselor reviews military situation in Mali', 8 December 1965.

178 Intelligence Exploitation Centre, 'Pénétration de l'URSS au Mali', 14 August 1968, GR9Q5128, SHD, and 'Pénétration de la PRC au Mali', 1 November 1968, GR9Q5128, SHD.

179 Ambassador Wibeaux, Ambassador of France in Mali, to the General Secretary for African and Malagasy Affairs, 28 April 1962, 5AGF/583, FFAN.

180 Lieutenant-Colonel Lebe, Military Advisor, 'Rapport fin de mission October 1965–November 1967', 27 October 1967, GR14S268, SHD; Ambassador Pelen, 'Quelques réflétions sur l'armée malienne', 2 December 1966.

181 Directorate of African and Malagasy Affairs, 'Assistance technique militaire au mali,' 15 December 1966, INVA180, CADC.

182 Secretary of State for Foreign Affairs, 'Forces armées Maliennes et notre Assistance militaire au Mali', 11 October 1971, INVA320, CADC; French Embassy Bamako, 'Coopération militaire franco-malienne', 10 November 1978, 62PO1-72, CADN.

in Mali sought to avoid receiving more Chinese assistance,[183] which was generating conflict among Malian officers.[184] Largely as a result of the coup, military equipment and expertise from a variety of countries augmented the training needs of the Malian armed forces, the air force in particular.[185]

Most Malian soldiers were trained in either the USSR or Mali, which allowed the Soviet Union to maintain its influence after 1968.[186] Although the coup against a socialist president did little to dampen the desire of the Soviets or Chinese to provide military assistance to the country, there were some simmering disagreements between the Malian and Soviet governments. In March 1971, for example, the Soviet military mission led by General Sokolof left Bamako on bad terms and without responding as to whether Moscow would furnish the equipment Mali had requested. Soviet officials complained that the Malians were not maintaining their equipment,[187] and as relations grew more tense, the Soviet military mission was reduced to six instructors.[188] At this point, there were some sixty Chinese assistants in the country.[189]

The strength of the Malian army worried neighbouring states, especially after a brief conflict over the Agacher strip between Mali and Upper Volta in 1974. Although Soviet military assistance became less visible, especially during the 1980s, a French military attaché noted that Mali still needed foreign assistants to maintain its equipment and keep its forces operational.[190] Western powers did remain economically important to Mali, but, in 1979,

183 US Embassy Bamako, 'Malian developments', 8 November 1968, POLMALI 67–69, Box 2331, CGRDS, NARA.
184 Ambassador Dallier, French Embassy Bamako, 'Arrestation de deux membres du CMLN', 5 April 1971, 61PO160, CADN; Maurice Courage, Chargé d'affaires, French Embassy Bamako, 'Procès des capitaine Yoro Diakite et Malik Diallo,' 2 August 1972, 61PO160, CADN; Col Charles to Richard, 7 April 1972.
185 General Secretary for African and Malagasy Affairs, 'Audience du lieutenant Moussa Traore', 3 November 1970, 5AGF/2708, FFAN; Secretary of State for Foreign Affairs, 'Forces armées Maliennes et notre assistance militaire au Mali', 11 October 1971.
186 Lieutenant-Colonel Chenevoy, Military Advisor, 'Rapport fin de mission 25 October 1973–31 August 1976', GR14S268, SHD; French Embassy Bamako, 'Coopération militaire franco-malienne', 10 November 1978.
187 Colonel Charles to Richard, 7 April 1972.
188 General Secretary for African and Malagasy Affairs, 'L'armée malienne et l'aide militaire française', 8 April 1972, 5AGF/582, FFAN.
189 Secretary of State for Foreign Affairs, 'Forces armées maliennes et notre assistance militaire au Mali', 11 October 1971.
190 Lieutenant-Colonel Chenevoy, 'Rapport fin de mission 25 octobre 1973–31 aôut 1976'.

the French Chargé d'affaires concluded that the 'Soviets control the army, and therefore the country' and that 'by taking charge of the army, the Soviets have made a political investment which they intend not to lose.'[191]

It would have been difficult for the Malian government to reduce the presence and influence of the Soviets, who they needed to maintain military equipment and furnish spare parts. Furthermore, Mali owed over FM 100 billion (one and half times the Malian budget at the time) to the Soviet Union. In comparison, the significant economic assistance provided by Western countries bought them little political influence in Mali.[192] France and the US had essentially 'lost' Guinea and Mali to the Soviet bloc, despite keeping all other francophone West African countries within France's sphere of influence. The 'loss' of these countries, Guinea in particular, heightened the fears of French intelligence actors about the Soviets' increasing penetration into Africa, and the growing economic influence of the US in France's richest former colonies. As Robert explained:

> The Americans did not intend to allow themselves to be out-maneu-
> vered by the Soviets, who saw certain African states as fertile ground
> for the expansion of communism. As long as France was able to
> protect its area of influence from Soviet penetration, the Americans
> were not too eager to intervene. On the other hand, as soon as the
> American perceived a weakness on our part, our declined presence
> or our influence in a given country, they mustered the financial and
> human resources that would allow them to step up their game and
> occupy the place before the Soviets. Sometimes the Americans did not
> even wait, so great was their eagerness to see the natural resources of
> some countries turn into dollars bills.[193]

This explains the hostile attitude of French officials towards American activities in francophone West Africa, where France felt it needed to protect its economic interests and sought to help former colonies from having to take part in violent Cold War struggles between the two global super-powers. From the American perspective, especially during the Kennedy administration, diversifying their sources of economic and military aid was thought to give African governments more credibility. However, French officials were firm in their position that all other actors should be kept out of the region's sphere of defence. This required significant resources, both

---

191 French Embassy Bamako, 'La présence militaire soviétique au Mali', 17 January 1979, 62PO1-72, CADC.
192 Ibid.
193 Robert, *'Ministre' de l'Afrique*, p. 112.

Table 1. Major weapons transfers 1959/60–1974 and French troops in francophone West Africa, 1962–1972.

	Guinea	Mali	Senegal	Côte d'Ivoire	Niger	Mauritania	Upper Volta	Togo	Dahomey
vehicles	48	49	80	40	17	60	44	41	28
artillery	34	30	6	4				4	4
planes	35	30	20	17	18	15	8	8	9
helicopters	8	1	6	6				2	
French troops									
1962			5,575	1,270	1,400	2,850			820
1964			4,520	1,280	1,400	1,530			235
1966			2,239	313	214				
1972			2,200	313	214				

Source: SIPRI arms transfers database, https://www.sipri.org/databases/armstransfers, accessed 27.12.2021; INVA, CADC.

military and economic, and France sought to match Soviet arms transfers to Guinea and Mali by allocating weapons to Senegal and Côte d'Ivoire (see Table 1). The Senegalese and Ivorian governments thus became key French allies against Soviet penetration in Africa. Of course, being a key ally gave the Senegalese and Ivorian presidents considerable power, both to negotiate the amount of French military assistance they received and to act against French interests and advice.

Life Insurance: French Relations with the Presidents of Côte d'Ivoire and Senegal

One important feature of decolonization in former French West Africa was that it took place in cooperation rather than confrontation with France. The wars in Indochina and Algeria had convinced French policymakers that power should be transferred to Africans who had been loyal to France and would enable the French to maintain influence in the region.[194] Thus, throughout the 1960s, France dedicated significant resources to this end, [195] justifying support for one-party systems and authoritarian regimes as necessary and unavoidable due to the threats newly independent countries were facing not to mention the weakness of their state institutions.

For French officials, the two most important means of safeguarding French interests in Africa were military cooperation and close interpersonal relationships with African decision-makers.[196] African elites saw this cooperation with the former colonial power as essential because France was providing vital material resources in the midst of difficult political and economic conditions.[197] The relations of Ivorian President Félix Houphouët-Boigny with French officials is an obvious example of how parties mutually benefitted.[198] The Senegalese president, Léopold Senghor, was another key ally for France. Of the nine francophone West African countries, Senegal and Côte d'Ivoire were the most economically important to France and hosted the largest French populations (see Figure 5).

---

194 Chafer, *The End of Empire in French West Africa*, pp. 185–9, 215–16, 226, and 232; Bat, *Le syndrome Foccart*, p. 81; Foccart, *Foccart Parle*, p. 217.

195 Bat, *Le syndrome Foccart*, pp. 81, 137–42, and 158.

196 Ibid., pp. 137–42, 150–58, 216, and 248–54; Chafer, *The End of Empire in French West Africa*, p. 233.

197 Chafer, *The End of Empire in French West Africa*, pp. 88 and 234.

198 Cooper, 'Possibility and Constraint', p. 176.

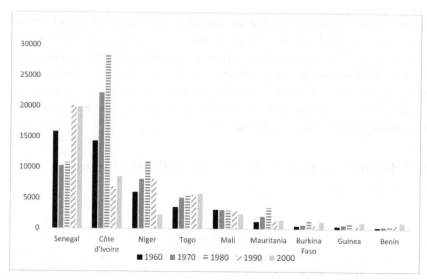

Figure 5. French populations in francophone West Africa (Source: World Bank migration databank, https://databank.worldbank.org/home.aspx, accessed 3.1.2019).

Senegal had significant strategic value to France, while Côte d'Ivoire was economically important. France nevertheless signed military assistance and cooperation agreements with both, and clearly relied on them to counter potential threats from communist countries.[199] The impact of economic and military assistance from France on the social, economic, and political development of its former colonies has been a source of intense debate. Some have argued that the role of France was widely beneficial,[200] and others that French activities in Africa only benefitted the elite and led to increased corruption.[201] The focus here is on the defence and foreign policy decision-making of African governments, not on corruption, but the World Bank's Good Governance Index (GGI) for 1996–2019 (see Figure 6) indicate that many of the main recipients of French military and economic assistance experienced high levels of corruption. However, the fact that Upper Volta

---

[199] Ministry of Cooperation, 'Domaine de l'assistance militaire', 18 September 1974, INVA318, CADC.
[200] Marine Lefèvre, *Le soutien américain à la Francophonie: Enjeux africains, 1960–1970* (Paris: Presses de la Fondation Nationale des Sciences Politiques, 2010).
[201] François-Xavier Verschave, *La Françafrique: le plus long scandale de la République* (Paris: Stock, 1998).

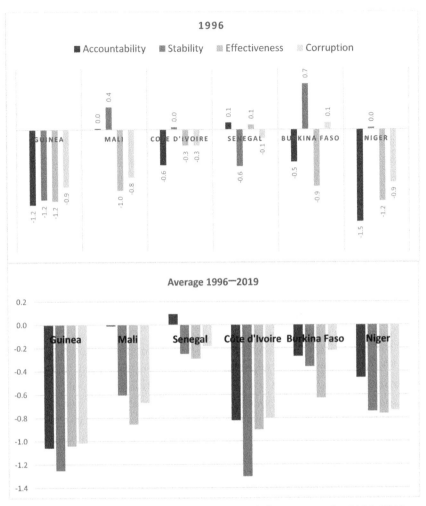

Figure 6. Good Governance Index for 1996 and the averages for 1996–2019; scale 2.5 to -2.5; world average 0 (Source: info.worldbank.org/governance/wgi/, accessed 12.2.2021).

(Burkina Faso) and Senegal remain exceptions to this trend suggests that the policies and decisions of African governments are indeed a decisive factor in how foreign assistance impacts a society.[202]

202 This has also been suggested by Hodzi in relation to Chinese assistance. See Hodzi, 'China and Africa'.

Comparing the defence policies of Senegal to those of Côte d'Ivoire is thus instructive. The Ivorian president chose to weaken the army and rely on French protection, whereas the Senegalese president built national military capacities. Understanding the differences between their policies adds nuance to the view that France was an all-powerful puppeteer who controlled the politics of African states through its military presence.[203] Sometimes the opposite was true, and figures like Houphouët-Boigny were thought by some to have too much influence on French policies. Still, the fact that Côte d'Ivoire voted with France and the US in the United Nations General Assembly with some frequency, unlike most francophone West African countries did not follow the French lead (see Figure 2), may be explained by the Ivorian president's own ideological views or the country's economic position. However, as Houphouët-Boigny was so close to members of the French political and economic elite, it is hard to untangle his views from theirs, and there was clearly a convergence among them. In 1970, for example, as the Ivorian president undertook a controversial and failed effort to encourage African countries to establish relations with the apartheid regime in Pretoria,[204] the French significantly increased trade with South Africa.[205]

In 1967, a French ambassador referred to Houphouët-Boigny specifically when he complained to American colleagues that French policy in Africa was unsustainable, as it was based on relations with political elites who could not remain in power forever, but whose departure would lead to chaos because they had built political systems so dependent on themselves that their countries lacked viable parliamentary institutions. The ambassador criticized Paris for its continued support of Houphouët-Boigny and warned that anything could happen when the Ivorian president eventually left power.[206] This prediction was accurate; after the death of Houphouët-Boigny, Côte d'Ivoire experienced years of instability, including a military coup and a civil war.

Previous studies have suggested that French influence in Côte d'Ivoire was most pervasive in the economic sphere. Supposedly, French exports to Africa helped non-competitive industries in France and French economic

203 Luckham, 'French Militarism in Africa'; Martin, 'Continuity and Change in Franco-African Relations'.
204 Ivorian diplomatic archives, South Africa box.
205 Data from the International Monetary Fund (IMF).
206 US Embassy Ouagadougou, 19 December 1967, AFR 66–69, Box 1776, CGRDS, NARA.

aid in Africa was ineffective, mainly benefitting French companies.[207] However, the average share of French exports to sub-Saharan Africa in the 1960s and 1970s was close to 7%, which was less than that of its European neighbours. Britain's exports to sub-Saharan Africa during this period were more voluminous, much of which went to South Africa. Senegal and Côte d'Ivoire were the most important sub-Saharan destinations for French exports, and both countries exported a large part of their own agricultural produce to France.[208] These two countries received the most economic assistance from France, which suggests that French economic interests played a role in aid allocations (see Figures 3 and 4).

The continuity of French aid or export patterns in certain industries can partly be attributed to the fact that language, infrastructure, and a long-term physical presence becomes more important when sophisticated equipment is transferred to new environments and new users. The challenges faced by the Germans, Soviets, and Americans in providing military assistance in Africa demonstrate as much. Until the 1970s, France's objective was to guard its exclusive role in the sphere of defence in its former colonies. It was concerned about US involvement, which was considered particularly dangerous as it was believed it would invite competition from the communist bloc. French officials also worried about the technological superiority of the US and thus saw military cooperation as vital to maintaining French influence in Africa,[209] especially in order to guard Senegal and Côte d'Ivoire against foreign interference. Moreover, the military assistance agreements they had signed with France also limited the freedom of these countries to obtain military equipment from elsewhere.

In 1970, the Senegalese president asked to renegotiate the terms of the agreement to allow his forces to procure equipment from other countries. France responded by increasing French military assistance. Two years earlier, American and Germans officials, aware of these constraints and the sensitivities of French officials, concluded that they should cast their activities in Africa as those of 'junior partners'. This would allow them to avoid offending the French, and to better coordinate their assistance with French officials, as

207 Jean-Pierre Dozon, 'L'état français contemporain et son double, l'état franco-africain', *Les Cahiers du Centre de Recherches Historiques* 30 (2002) [DOI: https://doi.org/10.4000/ccrh.432]; Martin, 'The Historical, Economic, and Political Bases of France's African Policy', *The Journal of Modern African Studies* 23, no. 2 (1985), pp. 189–208.
208 Data from the IMF.
209 General Secretary for African and Malagasy Affairs, 'Coopération militaire avec les états de l'Afrique noire francophone', 30 June 1970, 5AGF/2707, FFAN.

they recognized that African governments had used past offers of assistance as a lever to acquire more French assistance.[210] President Houphouët-Boigny, for example, skilfully exploited French fears of US commercial and techno- logical superiority to increase the amount of aid.

The particularity of French-Ivorian relations is reflected in the amount of time Côte d'Ivoire received over half its economic assistance from France. In the 1960s, an average of 62% of both Ivorian and Senegalese aid came from France. By the 1980s, Senegal had reduced the amount to 30%, but Côte d'Ivoire was still receiving 58% of its assistance from France (see Table 2 and Figures 4 and 7). This is not to say that French economic assistance was unimportant to Senegal, as its economic growth was slow and based largely on the export of peanuts to France. In the 1960s, France was the source of over half of Senegal's imports and served as the destination for 77% of Senegal's exports.

In Côte d'Ivoire, cocoa and coffee production had boomed, attracting buyers in Europe and the US, and as a result just 39% of Ivorian exports went to France in the 1960s.[211] However, French investments and knowhow were important factors for growth in Côte d'Ivoire, and Houphouët-Boigny welcomed French expertise and its contribution to the development of the Ivorian economy. In the two decades from 1960 to 1980, the number of French migrants in Côte d'Ivoire doubled from 14,000 to 28,000 (see Figure 5). As their numbers increased, dissatisfaction rose among Ivorians, who complained that the French were stealing their jobs and the country's wealth. By 1990, the economic downturn and the political instability that followed had convinced over 20,000 French citizens to leave.

Senegalese president Senghor had taken a different approach, aware that the visibility of French migrants or soldiers might displease the Senegalese population. During his time in office, the number of French expatriates in Senegal was reduced from 16,000 to 10,000 (see Figure 5). The number of French citizens in Africa gave France a reason to maintain military bases in certain countries, and they were located to allow French forces to intervene to protect French citizens, or to provide security for African presidents favoured by France. Both the Senegalese and Ivorian presidents benefitted from this protection – with around 2,200 soldiers in Senegal and some 300 in Côte d'Ivoire (see Table 1) – but such was not the case for all African presidents.

---

[210] 'US/FRG talks on Africa', 13 February 1968, AFR 67–69, Box 1775, CGRDS, NARA.
[211] Data from the IMF.

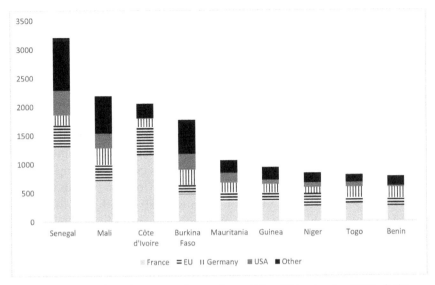

Figure 7. Economic assistance to francophone West Africa in the 1980s (US$ million) (Source: World Bank DataBank, https://databank.worldbank.org/home. aspx, accessed 21.5.2022).

Table 2. Official development assistance from France.

	Benin	Burkina Faso	Côte d'Ivoire	Guinea	Mali	Mauritania	Niger	Senegal	Togo
1960	56%	57%	62%	–14%	37%	48%	64%	62%	24%
1970	27%	33%	49%	–9%	24%	11%	29%	39%	21%
1980	21%	21%	58%	18%	22%	17%	21%	30%	25%
1990	18%	22%	45%	21%	19%	23%	28%	36%	31%
2000	15%	15%	43%	17%	15%	11%	18%	26%	34%
2010	7%	7%	18%	12%	7%	9%	7%	19%	13%

Source: World Bank DataBank, https://databank.worldbank.org/home.aspx, accessed 30.12.2021.

Senghor and Houphouët-Boigny shared the view that French military bases on their territory were important for the stability of their countries, objecting on multiple occasions to French troop reductions. In fact, without Houphouët-Boigny's insistence, the French base in Abidjan would have been closed. Even if a French military presence did provide the two countries with stability, it was a cause for popular dissatisfaction and the main threat facing both these presidents was internal rather than external. In light of this, Senghor suggested that the French base in Dakar be moved to Thies, thereby freeing up valuable buildings in Dakar for Senegalese officers.

Houphouët-Boigny had signed a special agreement allowing him to request French assistance to maintain order.[212] During two periods of instability – in 1962 and 1963, and from 1968 to 1970 – both of which were related to domestic dissatisfaction with government policies, the Ivorian president relied on French troops because he distrusted his Ivorian forces. This highlights a key difference to the approaches taken by Houphouët-Boigny and Senghor. The latter listened to the calls of Senegalese officers to Africanize important posts, whereas Houphouët-Boigny wanted more technical assistants from France. Houphouët-Boigny was also willing to weaken his army to ensure regime security, a decision that had long-term consequences.

France as the guarantor of stability in Côte d'Ivoire

In August 1961, President Houphouët-Boigny spoke before the Ivorian parliament, acknowledging that, 'as we needed security for the construction of our country, it seemed opportune, even necessary, to secure the support of a great friendly nation in order to discourage any attempt at aggression against us.'[213] This view dovetailed with the perspective French officials, who faced some criticism for cooperating with dictators but argued that 'African countries needed political stability to set up their institutions, their administrations, and consequently, they needed … men capable of establishing and maintaining stability.' The head of French intelligence services in West Africa believed these should be 'strong men, able to command respect and to control ancestral ethnic rivalries, to maintain a minimum of

---

212 Convention spéciale sur les conditions de participation éventuelle des forces armées françaises au maintien de l'ordre public en Côte d'Ivoire (Special agreement on the conditions for the possible participation of French armed forces in maintaining public order in Côte d'Ivoire), February 1962, GR11S153, SHD.
213 President Houphouët-Boigny, Message to Parliament, 3 August 1961, 324QONT/9, CADC.

order in countries which had just attained sovereignty and were subject to considerable internal and external pressure.'[214]

Hence, in April 1961, two months before the Ivorian national armed forces were created, Côte d'Ivoire signed a military assistance agreement with France that enabled the French to send technical assistance personnel to train the Ivorian military and provide military equipment for free or on very favourable terms. A military cooperation agreement allowed French forces to participate in maintaining order in Côte d'Ivoire at the request of the Ivorian president.[215] France secured an exclusivity clause in the agreement to ensure it had the first option to supply any military equipment to Ivorian forces.[216]

In his August 1961 speech to Parliament, Houphouët-Boigny described the continuing French role in Ivorian defence affairs as disinterested. Côte d'Ivoire needed security to build its institutions and was lucky that it happened to have the help of its great friend France. The French similarly downplayed their involvement with leaders like Houphouët-Boigny, but did sometimes defend it, like Robert did in his memoirs. He insisted that young African nations needed 'strong' and 'determined' men in power, so that others would respect their authority and they would be able to maintain order.

He was undoubtedly describing men like Houphouët-Boigny, but the description also fits Guinean president Sékou Touré. In many ways, their positions and rationales behind decision-making were in opposition, but both were charismatic authoritarian figures who distrusted their own national armies. As a result, their defence policies were similarly oriented towards preventing soldiers from organizing coups. They also shared strategies of extraversion, with external resources and actors playing key roles in both countries' defence strategies.

Côte d'Ivoire faced few external dangers, but its stability was threatened by internal opposition.[217] Radical anti-colonialist, nationalist, and socialist ideals had become popular among students and labour unions, which

---

214 Robert, *'Ministre' de l'Afrique*, p. 119.
215 Convention spéciale sur les conditions de participation éventuelle des forces armées françaises au maintien de l'ordre public en Côte d'Ivoire, February 1962.
216 'L'accord d'assistance militaire technique entre la République française et la République de Côte d'Ivoire (Technical military assistance agreement between the French Republic and the Republic of Côte d'Ivoire), 24 April 1961, GR11S84, SHD.
217 This position was also presented by President Houphouët-Boigny to the French Ambassador. See Telegram, French Embassy Abidjan, to Directorate of African and Malagasy Affairs, Paris, 27 February 1964, 324QONT/9, CADC and Directorate

opposed Houphouët–Boigny's close alliance with France, as well as his capitalist policies.[218] The Ivorian president worried that his soldiers would be as equally susceptible to foreign influences as student protesters,[219] and his fears of being deposed by the military were only amplified by the January 1963 coup in Togo.[220] In fact, the coup in Togo marked a change in the attitude of many African presidents towards their national armies, and soldiers were increasingly perceived as a main threat to power.

The Togolese regime may not have been as pro-French, but the military coup and sorry end of President Olympio in Togo did worry the Ivorian leader. The French, on the other hand, who did not contribute directly to the demise of Olympio, were not displeased by the event.[221] Seemingly unaware of this, Houphouët–Boigny demanded that France intervene militarily in Togo to punish those soldiers responsible for Olympio's death. He believed it would be dangerous to accept the coup as a fait accompli and allow their crimes to go unpunished, because 'committing a crime must not be rewarded'. He argued that the coup could impact development in all African countries, and set a bad example for 'still young states where the respective leaders do not all have a solid position among the masses of their countries'.[222] Although the Ivorian president's fear was that the events in Togo may be contagious if Togolese soldiers were permitted to remain in power after killing Olympio,[223] de Gaulle declined these calls to intervene

---

of African and Malagasy Affairs, 'Problèmes militaires franco-ivoiriens', 3 June 1961, 5AGF/1787, FFAN.

218 *Crise politique en Côte d'Ivoire*, 1PO/1/14, CADN; Directorate of African and Malagasy Affairs, 'République de Côte d'Ivoire', 3 July 1963, 324QONT/9, CADC.

219 Houphouët-Boigny, quoted in telegram, French Embassy Abidjan to Directorate of African and Malagasy Affairs, 27 February 1964, 324QONT/9, CADC.

220 Telegram, Raphaël-Leygues to Directorate of African and Malagasy Affairs, Paris, 13 December 1963, 324QONT/10, CADC; Telegram, French Embassy Abidjan to Directorate of African and Malagasy Affairs, 27 February 1964, 324QONT/9, CADC; Raphaël-Leygues to Ministry of Foreign Affairs, 'Politique militaire en zones d'outre-mer no. 4' 26 December 1963, 5AGF/2661, FFAN.

221 Robert, *'Ministre' de l'Afrique*, pp. 74–5. According to Robert, '… *nous n'avons rien fait pour calmer le mécontentement des militaires nordistes, car l'impopularité du régime grandissait et nous espérions de laisser faire.*' ('… we did nothing to calm the discontent of northern soldiers, as the unpopularity of the regime was growing and we hoped to let it go.')

222 Letter from Houphouët-Boigny to de Gaulle, 2 March 1963, 5AGF/535, FFAN. Houphouët-Boigny expressed similar positions in discussions with French Ambassador Raphaël-Leygues.

223 General Secretariat for African and Malagasy Affairs, 'Projet d'instruction pour Raphaël-Leygues', 5 March 1963, 5AGF/535, FFAN.

in Togo, instead assuring Houphouët-Boigny that France would not fail to provide assistance to Côte d'Ivoire if necessary.[224]

Two alleged coup plots against the Ivorian president were made public in Côte d'Ivoire in 1963. In January, communists were accused of having plotted to assassinate Houphouët-Boigny. This led to a number of political figures being imprisoned and later condemned to death or a lifetime of forced labour.[225] French Ambassador Léon Brasseur expressed scepticism about the charges in a report to Paris, hinting that the president and his allies had plotted to silence the opposition. Brasseur further suggested that the ensuing arrests had been a means by which individuals from the president's own ethnic group, the Baoulé, could occupy all the central positions in the state administration. The ambassador noted that communists were not even active in the country.[226] French officials in Paris took the communist threat more seriously than Brasseur, but acknowledged that ambitious members of the president's entourage may have used coup allegations for their personal benefit. Their conclusion was that the liberal character of the Ivorian regime was in danger, and France should therefore assist in reinforcing Ivorian institutions.[227] Soon afterwards, Brasseur was replaced by Jacques Raphaël-Leygues, who was less critical of the authoritarian tendencies of the Ivorian regime and less sceptical of the Ivorian president's concerns about security.

The second coup plot in Côte d'Ivoire was announced in August 1963. It implicated the armed forces and had long-term effects on the development of the military. Houphouët-Boigny had been out of the country for over four months when allies warned him that his opponents were planning to stage a coup upon his return. French officials questioned the existence of the plot and assumed that individuals in the president's inner circle were exaggerating the threats against him in order to cast suspicion on his rivals, once again for personal profit. Even so, the Ivorian ministers of interior and defence, both of whom were suspected of being involved, were called

---

224 Letter from General de Gaulle to Houphouët-Boigny, 5 March 1963, 5AGF/535, FFAN.

225 The verdict was delivered on 10 April 1973. Eighty people were accused; seven were condemned to death. See French Embassy Abidjan, 'Situation Politique du 5 avril au 12 avril 1963', 1PO/1/10, CADN.

226 Ambassador Léon Brasseur to Directorate of African and Malagasy Affairs, 'Crise politique en Côte d'Ivoire', 23 January 1963, 1PO/1/14, CADN.

227 Directorate of African and Malagasy Affairs, 'Note: Situation politique en Côte d'Ivoire', 13 January 1963, 1PO/1/14, CADN.

to Paris and suspended from their duties, and some members of the armed forces were arrested.[228]

Whilst in France, Houphouët-Boigny met more than once with the French ambassador and with de Gaulle, who personally pledged that France would intervene if his opponents staged a coup when he returned to Abidjan.[229] In July, Houphouët-Boigny requested an increase in French troop numbers in Côte d'Ivoire in order to discourage potential mutinies.[230] Despite admitting he had a right to request French military assistance, French officials thought it would be politically unwise if it was granted. Foccart's office noted that 'recourse by an independent state to the French armed forces for an internal police operation should only be carried out as a last resort, when the government has used all the normal means in its possession.'[231] Houphouët-Boigny insisted that, by the summer, the situation had grown more dire than it was in January, and he claimed the purpose of the August plot was to separate Côte d'Ivoire from France.[232] Ambassador Raphaël-Leygues suspected the plot may have been exaggerated, but concluded nevertheless that 'the physical and political survival of President Houphouët-Boigny seems ... very important for Africa; if he would disappear, his country, which is now a stable state, could congolise [sic], the Sanwi region would separate itself on one side [and] the Bété region on the other.'

Nonetheless, Raphaël-Leygues emphasized that France should not allow itself to be compromised and said it was preferable if the Ivorian president did not completely forsake his own security forces.[233] Despite this advice, Houphouët-Boigny decided to disarm the national military. On 14 August

[228] Ambassador of France in Abidjan, 'Situation politique du 4 au 17 septembre 1963', 17 September 1963, 324QONT/3, CADC; Telegram, Abidjan to Paris, 14 August 1963, 324QONT/10, CADC; Directorate of African and Malagasy Affairs, 'Situation politique en Côte d'Ivoire', 29 August 1963, 324QONT/10, CADC, and 'République de Côte d'Ivoire', 3 July 1963.

[229] Plantey, General Secretariat for African and Malagasy Affairs, 'Note à l'attention de monsieur le président de la république', 7 August 1963, 5AGF/535, FFAN; Raphaël-Leygues, 'Note: compte-rendu l'entretien avec Houphouët-Boigny', 5 August 1963, 5AGF/535, FFAN.

[230] Directorate of African and Malagasy Affairs, 'République de Côte d'Ivoire', 3 July 1963.

[231] Plantey, 'Note à l'attention de monsieur le président de la république', 7 August 1963.

[232] Raphaël-Leygues, 'Note: compte-rendu l'entretien avec Houphouët-Boigny', 5 August 1963.

[233] Ibid.

1963, while he was still out of the country, he asked the French to assist in inspecting the ammunition and arms of the Ivorian army and gendarmerie.[234] Using technical failures and the visit of the French inspector as the rationale, Houphouët-Boigny instructed Ivorian forces to hand over their weapons. These armaments would be kept by French forces until Houphouët-Boigny returned.[235]

The Ivorian president had also requested that French forces participate in maintaining public order, but the French were not eager to respond to an Ivorian popular uprising. French diplomats and military delegates found the situation in Côte d'Ivoire untenable: having disarmed the military, Houphouët-Boigny was left with no means to respond to potential resistance. The only forces capable of maintaining order in the country were the French, but their numbers were insufficient to do so, much less to re-establish it. French authorities thus urged Houphouët-Boigny to immediately return seized armaments to any Ivorian units he considered loyal.[236]

Events in Congo at the time largely informed the decision-making of Houphouët-Boigny. Despite a similar military assistance agreement, France had not sent troops to support the President of Congo, Foulbert Youlou,[237] and he was deposed in a popular uprising. After returning to Côte d'Ivoire in late August 1963, the Ivorian president decided to establish party militias that would form a counterforce to the military.[238] French officials opposed the idea, as they thought French allies might perceived it as a step towards fascism.[239] They also feared that party militias would have a negative effect

---

234 French Embassy Abidjan, 'Situation politique 17 aôut 1963', 25 August 1963, 1PO/1/14, CADN; Directorate of African and Malagasy Affairs, 'Situation politique en Côte d'Ivoire', 29 August 1963, 324QONT/10, CADC.

235 Raphaël-Leygues, 'Retour de Houphouët-Boigny à Côte d'Ivoire', 28 August 1963, 1PO/1/14, CADN; Telegram, Abidjan to Directorate of African and Malagasy Affairs, Paris, 14 August 63, 324QONT/10, CADC.

236 Raphaël-Leygues, 'Retour de Houphouët-Boigny à Côte d'Ivoire', 28 August 1963.

237 Robert, *'Ministre' de l'Afrique*, pp. 216–22.

238 Raphaël-Leygues, 'Situation politique 26 octobre au 8 novembre 1963,' 9 November 1963, 324QONT/3, CADC; Directorate of African and Malagasy Affairs, 'Situation politique en Côte d'Ivoire', 29 August 1963; Raphaël-Leygues, 'Situation politique 13 au 20 décembre 1963', 24 December 1963, 324QONT/3, CADC, and 'Retour de Houphouët-Boigny à Côte d'Ivoire', 28 August 1963; French Embassy Abidjan, 'Actualités politiques', 10 September 1963, 1PO/1/14, CADN, and 'Extrait du bulletin de renseignements hebdomadaires, 19–25 aôut 1963', 25 August 1963, 1PO/1/14, CADN.

239 French Embassy Abidjan, 'Situation politique', 3 September 1963, 1PO/1/14, CADN; Telegram, Abidjan to Paris, 31 August 1963, 324QONT/10, CADC.

on the morale and efficiency of the Ivorian armed forces, which had been trained and equipped by France,[240] even though they described these forces as lethargic, mediocre, and inefficient.[241]

The introduction of militias was not the first change to the Ivorian military structure that France opposed. They had also objected to the Ivorian adaptation of an Israeli agricultural programme where soldiers trained the youth in agricultural techniques as part of their obligatory national service.[242] The idea that the armed forces could also directly contribute to the economy appealed to Ivorian decision-makers.[243] Hence, in May 1962, they signed an agreement with Israel to bring the system to Côte d'Ivoire. French officials felt the system's structures and techniques were 'completely foreign to Africa', and were concerned that Ivorian officials were more interested in developing civic service than creating an effective army.[244] As a result, France demanded that the Ivorians separate the civic service system from the armed forces, so that it would no longer fall within the remit of the defence minister. They got their wish in August 1963.[245] In 1964, the French softened slightly and the Ministry of Cooperation communicated that civic service programmes were acceptable as long as they did not lead to the neglect of military training or the maintenance of defence capacities.[246]

240 French Embassy Abidjan 'Actualités politiques', 10 September 1963; Telegram, Abidjan to Paris, 31 August 1963, 324QONT/10, CADC.
241 Brasseur to Minister of Cooperation, 'Organisation de l'armée ivoirienne et l'assistance militaire technique', 8 February 1963, 5AGF/2661, FFAN; Military advisor, French Embassy Abidjan, 'Rapport annuel pour 1965' 7 December 1965, GR14S251, SHD; Intelligence Exploitation Centre, Section B, 'Les problèmes de défense en Côte d'Ivoire' 23 January 1968, GR9Q5113, SHD; Telegram, Raphaël-Leygues to Directorate of African and Malagasy Affairs, 13 December 1963.
242 Abel Jacob, 'Israel's Military Aid to Africa, 1960–66', *Journal of Modern African Studies* 9, no. 2 (1971), pp. 165–87; Zach Levey, 'Israel's Strategy in Africa, 1961–67', *International Journal of Middle East Studies* 36, no. 1 (2004), pp. 71–87.
243 Chargé d'affaires, French Embassy Abidjan, to Ministry of Foreign Affairs, 'Situation politique du 21 au 17 juillet 1962', 28 July 1962, 324QONT/2, CADC.
244 Ambassador of France in Côte d'Ivoire to Minister of Foreign Affairs, 'Situation politique du 30 juin au 6 juillet 1962', 7 July 1962, 324QONT/2, CADC; Brasseur to Minister of Cooperation, 'Organisation de l'armée ivoirienne et l'assistance militaire technique', 8 February 1963. In general, French officials were worried about the increasing influence of Israel on Ivorian decision-makers. See Telegram, Abidjan to Paris, 12 September 1963, 324QONT/10, CADC.
245 Telegram, Abidjan to Paris, 31 August 1963, 324QONT/10, CADC.
246 Ministry of Cooperation, 'Directive concernant l'orientation et l'évolution des armées nationales africaines et malgache', 27 August 1964, INVA318, CADC.

Perhaps the French antagonism towards a civic service system was rooted in genuine concern about the efficiency of Ivorian forces, but given the willingness of French forces to help in disarming their Ivorian counterparts, it was most likely motivated by a desire to reduce Israel's influence.[247] In this case, France's opposition demonstrated its readiness to exert its own influence to persuade the Ivorians to maintain inherited military structures inherited in order to preserve their exclusive relationship with Côte d'Ivoire.[248] Later, when it was reported that Israel had been training Ivorian intelligence officers, the French again strongly disapproved.[249]

Limiting the role of other foreign actors in Côte d'Ivoire was not only important to France's defence policy, but also to its commerce.[250] This drove the French response to US activities in Côte d'Ivoire,[251] and allowed Houphouët-Boigny to use their fears of increasing American influence to obtain more aid. For example, when he requested French equipment for the navy and air force in 1962, French officials were hesitant to comply for fear that other former colonies would demand the same.[252] However, they were even more worried that the US would provide the equipment, as well as American technical assistants who would work alongside the Ivorian military.[253] Côte d'Ivoire ultimately received the equipment from France.[254] Even US assistance to the Ivorian police raised concerns among

247 Ambassador of France in Côte d'Ivoire to Minister of Foreign Affairs, 'Situation politique du 30 juin au 6 juillet 1962' 7 July 1962.
248 The French believed their exclusive relationship should at least be assured in training troops and providing military equipment. See Directorate of African and Malagasy Affairs, 'Problèmes militaires franco-ivoiriens', 3 June 1961.
249 Diefenbacher, Ministry of Interior, Director of International Police Technical Cooperation Services, 'Note concernant les activités d'Israël en matière de police en Côte d'Ivoire', 13 October 1970, 5AGF/1797, FFAN.
250 Raphaël-Leygues, French Embassy Abidjan, to Ministry of Foreign Affairs, 'L'action des Etats-Unis en Côte d'Ivoire dans le domaine économique et les positions françaises', 24 March 1972, 5AG/5F/1810, FFAN.
251 Raphaël-Leygues to Ministry of Foreign Affairs, 'Note de l'influence américaine en Côte d'Ivoire', 12 May 1965, 324QONT/12, CADC; Directorate of African and Malagasy Affairs, 'Note: Situation en Côte d'Ivoire', 7 June 1968, 324QONT/ 9, CADC.
252 Côte d'Ivoire, Constitutions de la marine (1961–1965) et forces aériennes (1962), GR11S382, SHD; Joint Staff to the Minister of Armed Forces, 'Demande de cession de deux hélicoptères de type Alouette II par le gouvernement de la Côte d'Ivoire', 7 March 1962, GR11S382, SHD.
253 'Renforcement de moyens aériens de l'armée de l'air de la république de Côte d'Ivoire', 21 February 1962, GR11S382, SHD.
254 Raphaël-Leygues to Minister of Cooperation, 'Personnel de l'armée de l'air pour deux hélicoptères Alouette III', 8 October 1964, 5AGF/2661, FFAN, and

French officials, in part because American equipment was newer and better quality.[255] Still, when the Americans ended their assistance to Ivorian police in 1962, it was supposedly because French assistance was so 'excessive' that it was no longer needed.[256]

The reports of multiple French officials suggest that Côte d'Ivoire refused US offers of military assistance.[257] American diplomatic reports state the opposite, with Ivorian politicians having contacted the US Embassy about the possibility of negotiating assistance. Either way, US officials were clear that they had 'neither the desire nor capacity to displace the French' in Côte d'Ivoire, especially given the volume of French aid in the country, which was seen to dominate 'almost all sectors of Ivorian life'.[258] In the opinion of one Ivorian soldier interviewed for this study, it was the exclusivity of this assistance that provided the best available basis for development of the Ivorian military.[259]

American diplomatic papers indicate that the US was in fact less interested in providing assistance to Côte d'Ivoire than to Upper Volta. American officials saw no immediate danger of Soviet influence in Côte d'Ivoire, and Upper Volta was notable for both its geographic and political positioning. Still, the US felt the Ivorian dependency on France should be reduced, in part through aid from other countries, particularly Israel. Their

---

'Hélicoptères Alouette II pour la Côte d'Ivoire', 8 March 1963, 5AGF/2661, FFAN; General Secretariat for African and Malagasy Affairs, 'Note à l'attention de monsieur le président de la république au sujet du prêt d'un patrouilleur côtier rapide, à la marine ivoirienne', 25 March 1963, 5AGF2661, FFAN; C. Piernet, Minister of Cooperation, to the Ambassador of France in Côte d'Ivoire, 'Création d'une forces lagunaire', 23 January 1963, 5AGF/2661, FFAN.

255 Ambassador of France in Côte d'Ivoire to Ministry of Foreign Affairs, 'Situation politique du 22 au 28 septembre, 29 September 1962, 324QONT/2, CADC.

256 Alfred Wellborn, Deputy Chief of Mission US Embassy Abidjan, 'Public safety review', 30 October 1965, CGRDS 1964–1966, DEFIVCAST, Box 1663, NARA.

257 Raphaël-Leygues to Minister of Cooperation, 'Personnel de l'armée de l'air pour deux hélicoptères Alouette III', 8 October 1964, and 'Hélicoptères Alouette II pour la Côte d'Ivoire', 8 March 1963; General Secretariat for African and Malagasy Affairs, 'Note à l'attention de monsieur le président de la république au sujet du prêt d'un patrouilleur côtier rapide, à la marine ivoirienne' 25 March 1963; Piernet, Minister of Cooperation, to the Ambassador of France in Côte d'Ivoire, 'Création d'une force lagunaire', 23 January 1963.

258 James Wine, US Embassy Abidjan, 'Ambassador's political–economic assessment', 12 February 1964, CGRDS 1964–1966, POLIVCAST, Box 2370, NARA.

259 General Ouassenan Kone, Commander of the Ivorian Gendarmerie from 1964 to 1974, interview by author, 26 November 2015, Abidjan; Colonel André Gouri, interview by author, 23 November 2015, Abidjan.

concern was that French military assistance was 'patently self-serving' and aimed at 'consciously limit[ing] the capability of the Ivorian forces, both to compel dependence on France as well as to discourage the growth and efficiency of local forces', and that this could eventually provoke a violent response by local actors.[260]

The focus of the US in Côte d'Ivoire was on increasing American investment in the country, but as US Ambassador James Wine noted, this was 'in some ways most sensitive as it impinges upon the French commercial and industrial hegemony'.[261] France was indeed prone to paranoia about US involvement. For example, American diplomatic papers show that Côte d'Ivoire made requests to the US for equipment for the Ivorian police and gendarmerie in 1964 and 1965, after France informed Houphouët-Boigny that it would be closing its military base in the country.[262] When the US offered to send a team of military cartographers to assist the Ivorian army in 1965, France saw this as a means of infiltration.[263]

To some degree, the French could sympathize with America's aspirations in Africa. Having failed to push progressive countries such as Guinea and Mali back towards neutralism, support for Côte d'Ivoire was considered less risky.[264] Houphouët-Boigny's regime presented itself as willing to cooperate with anyone, as long as relations were profitable.[265] This quid pro quo was the basis of Ivorian relations with Israel, whose assistance Côte d'Ivoire enjoyed until 1973, when the Ivorian government decided its relations with oil-producing countries were more important. To the annoyance of Israel, the Ivorians severed relations publicly, but privately expressed a desire to continue to profit

---

260 Wine, 'Ambassador's political-economic assessment', 12 February 1964.

261 Ibid.

262 Lloyd M. Rives, Chargé d'affaires, to Colonel William O. Gall, Assistant for West and Central Africa, 'Ivory Coast Request for Military Assistance', 29 April 1964, DEFIVCAST 1964–1966, Box 1663, CGRDS, NARA; Alfred Wellborn, 'Public safety review', 30 October 1965.

263 Raphaël-Leygues 'Compte-rendu de l'audience du général de Gaulle', 25 June 1965, 5AGF/535, FFAN.

264 Directorate of African and Malagasy Affairs, 'Note: Etats-Unis et de la Côte d'Ivoire', 1 April 1965; Raphaël-Leygues, 'Note de l'influence américaine en Côte d'Ivoire' 12 May 1965.

265 In 1970, the Ivorian Minister of Foreign Affairs announced that, in relation to Ivorian neutrality in the Cold War: '… *les contingences de notre développement économique détermineront le choix de nos amis*' ('… the contingencies of our economic development will determine the choice of our friends'). See A. Usher, Minister of Foreign Affairs, statement at conference, Technical School Abidjan, April 1970, Discours de Félix Houphouët-Boigny 1961–1965, CADC.

from cooperation.[266] Houphouët-Boigny, again motivated by the prospect of profit, also proposed negotiations with white South Africa, an initiative that was dismissed by other African presidents.[267] The Ivorian president did not see relations with communist countries as profitable, and it was not until January 1967 that Côte d'Ivoire established diplomatic ties with the Soviet Union. These relations were quickly severed in 1969, when Côte d'Ivoire accused the Soviets of inciting and radicalizing Ivorian students.[268]

In the end, Côte d'Ivoire always remained firmly allied with France, and the French influence on Ivorian defence was always significant. Houphouët-Boigny was convinced that just the presence of French soldiers dissuaded military coups, an opinion shared by the US.[269] In 1965, when de Gaulle and French officers wanted to close the French military base in Port-Bouët, Houphouët-Boigny initially agreed, but when military coups struck multiple neighbouring countries in 1966 – Upper Volta, Togo, Ghana, and Dahomey – he demanded the French maintain troops in the country. His own minister of defence worried that reversing this withdrawal would negatively impact the morale of Ivorian soldiers.[270] French officials also hesitated, as operating

266 Levey, 'Israel's Exit from Africa, 1973: The Road to Diplomatic Isolation', *British Journal of Middle Eastern Studies* 35, no. 2 (2008), pp. 205–26; François Giraudon, Chargé d'affaires of France in Côte d'Ivoire, to Minister of Foreign Affairs Michel Jobert, 'Rupture des relations diplomatiques entre la Côte d'Ivoire et Israël', 26 November 1973, 5AGF/1812, FFAN.
267 'Relations entre Côte d'Ivoire et Afrique de Sud,' Archives Diplomatiques de Côte d'Ivoire.
268 Hubert Debois, Chargé d'affaires French Embassy Abidjan, to Ministry of Foreign Affairs, 'Établissement de relations diplomatiques entre la Côte d'Ivoire et l'URSS', 25 January 1967, 324QONT/12, CADC; Raphaël-Leygues to Ministry of Foreign Affairs, 'Après la rupture des relations diplomatiques entre la Côte d'Ivoire et l'URSS', 6 June 1969, 324QONT/12, CADC.
269 US Embassy Abidjan, 'Assessment of Internal Situation in Ivory Coast', 22 January 1966, POLIVCAST 1964–1966, Box 2370, CGRDS, NARA and 'Assessment of Military Coup Possibilities', 9 April 1964, DEFIVCAST 1964–1966, Box 1663, CGRDS, NARA.
270 Maurice Perrier, General Secretariat for the Community, 'Audience du Président Houphouët-Boigny' 25 June 1965, 5AGF/535, FFAN; Raphaël-Leygues, 'Compte-rendu du visite à Couve de Murville 2 juillet 1965 en Abidjan', 5AGF/535, FFAN; Ministry of Foreign Affairs to the Minister of Armed Forces, 'Maintien d'un escadron a Port-Bouët', 10 February 1966, 5AGF/1806, FFAN; Perrier, Technical Advisor, Intelligence Exploitation Centre, Section B, 'Attitude du ministre ivoirien des forces armées', 1 March 1966, 5AGF/1806, FFAN; Perrier, General Secretariat for the Community, 'Maintien des garnisons françaises de Port-Bouët et Nianmey', 29 October 1966, 5AGF/1806, FFAN.

the base, which was less strategically vital from a military perspective than bases in Senegal, Madagascar, and Djibouti, cost the French a significant FF 2 million per year.[271] However, a compromise was struck, and France agreed to leave approximately 300 French soldiers in Port-Bouët.[272]

There were benefits for the French to remaining, however, as the base was an important intelligence-gathering point, and from there it was possible to listen to both Guinean and Ghanaian radio transmissions. Moreover, the French were still concerned that if they withdrew they would soon be replaced by the Americans.[273] Indeed, by the early 1970s, France increasingly believed the US was also trying to displace the French in other African countries with the greatest economic potential, including Zaire, Nigeria, Gabon, and Cameroon. According to the US Embassy in Abidjan, 'American officials … [were] more likely to be amused by such allegations than to take them seriously', as they knew 'how little we would care to assume the French burden in Africa.'[274]

American officials admitted that the US and France were competitors in global markets, and they criticized 'trade restrictions inherent in France's special relationship with the associated African states.' The embassy

271 Premier ministre de la France, 'Note d'orientation pour les généraux délègues à la défense dans les zones d'outre-mer no 1, 2 et 3 "Bases stratégiques en Afrique"', 24 November 1961, GR9Q118, SHD; Presidency of the Republic, Naval Vice-Admiral of the Special Staff, 'Les forces française en Côte d'Ivoire', 17 December 1966, 5AGF/535, FFAN; General Secretariat for the Community, 'Audience du Président Houphouët-Boigny–De Gaulle', 19 February 1969, 5AGF/535, FFAN; Raphaël-Leygues, 'Compte-rendu de l'audience du général de Gaulle', 25 June 1965; Telegram to Directorate of African and Malagasy Affairs, 25 September 1965, 5AGF/1793, FFAN; Ministry of Foreign Affairs to the Minister of Armed Forces, 'Maintien d'un escadron à Port-Bouët', 10 February 1966; Perrier, General Secretariat for the Community, 'Maintien des garnisons françaises de Port-Bouët et Nianmey', 29 October 1966.

272 General Secretariat for African and Malagasy Affairs, 'Note à l'attention de monsieur le président de la république: Le président Houphouët-Boigny et les gouvernements militaires de la Haute-Volta, du Togo et du Dahomey', 26 April 1967, 5AGF/1806, FFAN; Chief of Staff, Secretariat for African and Malagasy Affairs, 'Forces françaises en Côte d'Ivoire', 15 June 1967, 5AGF/1800, FFAN; General Secretariat for African and Malagasy Affairs, 'Réunion outre-mer à l'état major des armées du 20 octobre', 20 October, 1966, AG5/5F/1806, FFAN; General Secretariat for the Community, 'Audience du Président Houphouët-Boigny', 15 July 1969, 5AGF/535, FFAN; General Secretariat for African and Malagasy Affairs, 'Note coopération militaire franco-ivoirienne', 12 June 1970, 5AGF/1806, FFAN.

273 Raphaël-Leygues, 'Compte-rendu de l'audience du général de Gaulle' 25 June 1965.

274 US Embassy Abidjan, 'US policy aims in Africa', 27 October 1972, AFR-US 1970–1973, Box 2035, CGRDS, NARA.

complained that while the US tried to 'emphasize the hard, economic truths of supply and demand in discussion of coffee, cocoa and commodity problems with the producing states, France somehow manages to pose as the champion of third-world interest', but it did concede that, 'what we see as the natural and desirable development of cooperation between contiguous anglophone and francophone states may indeed represent a threat to French pre-eminence in the latter.'[275] The friction between French and American interests was economic, not political, and the US concluded that it should aim to avoid French 'sensitivities ... especially in the manner in which we do things. Where conflict is unavoidable, we should be doubly careful that our policies stand on their merits, particularly in African eyes.'[276]

The French were particularly keen to limit the US military presence in Africa and maintain their own monopoly on assisting and training African soldiers, in part because of the importance of technical assistants in gathering intelligence. Early on, Robert had observed that the Soviets understood the best way to penetrate countries of West Africa was, namely, through technical assistance. As French military equipment was regularly accompanied by technical assistance personnel, they were key to understanding and influencing events on the ground.[277] These assistants worked alongside the local armed force and were in a good position to evaluate military capacities and the morale of soldiers. French military personnel were thus encouraged to gather information,[278] and military technical assistants were seen as a way of assuring continuous intelligence-gathering for France when the number of French troops was reduced in 1965. They were instructed not to engage in any actions that may arouse suspicion, and to report all information the military attaché, especially regarding the morale of troops.[279]

275 Ibid.

276 Ibid.

277 Robert, *'Ministre' de l'Afrique*, pp. 115 and 120.

278 Premier ministre de la France, Letter No. 20842/GEMOA/ON, 'Les instructions du premier ministre concernant le réorganisation du renseignement outre-mer', July 1959, GR9Q118, SHD; Lieutenant-General Brebisson, Supreme Commander of Overseas Zone No. 1, to the Army Chief of the General Staff, 'Recherche de renseignement d'ordre militaire au Mali, en Guinée et au Ghana', 29 August 1961, GR9Q118, SHD; Lieutenant-General René Cogny, Commander of French Forces in Central Africa, to Prime Minister, General Staff, 'Recherche du renseignement intérieur en Afrique centrale', 2 April 1962, GR9Q118, SHD.

279 'Note pour le secrétaire d'état, instruction aux conseillers militaires sur le rôle des cadres de l'assistance militaires technique dans le domaine du renseignement', 1 July 1965, INVA19, CADC.

For Houphouët-Boigny, French technical assistance was another way to assure control of the armed forces. As a 1964 US report noted, French assistants ensured that soldiers executed the orders of the Ivorian government.[280] While technical assistance by France was also significant in other states, in 1966, only Madagascar received more than Côte d'Ivoire.[281] That year, 25% of the officers in the Ivorian army were French, as were 85% of its naval officers and 90% of its officers in the air force. In fact, the Ivorian air force had only one Ivorian pilot, although it had many French-made planes and helicopters.[282] By the early 1970s, the number of French officers in the army had been cut to 15%, but French troops still accounted for 44% of Ivorian naval officers and 24% of Ivorian air force officers.

Until 1970, the Ivorian navy and air force had been commanded by French technical assistants, who also taught in Ivorian military schools.[283] The role of these assistants had slightly diminished by 1972, after which they served only in technical and administrative roles, particularly in the Ministry of Defence and the Military Cabinet.[284] Houphouët-Boigny had never made the Ivorization of state institutions a priority, even if French reports occasionally noted the dissatisfaction that maintaining a French military base and keeping French officers in command positions had generated among Ivorian soldiers.[285] The Ivorian president continued to be suspicious of the

---

280 Leslie Rood, US Embassy Abidjan, 'Ivorian internal security forces', 19 February 1964, POLIVCAST 1964–1966, Box 2371, CGRDS, NARA; US Embassy Abidjan, 'Assessment of military coup possibilities', 9 April 1964.
281 French Embassy Abidjan, 'Évolution des effectifs et aspects qualitatifs de la coopération technique en Côte d'Ivoire et coût de l'assistance technique', 9 November 1966, 324QONT/12, CADC.
282 General Secretariat for National Defence, Intelligence Exploitation Centre, 'Bulletin quotidien des renseignements', 4 April 1967, 5AGF/1800, FFAN.
283 General R. Couetdic, Ministry of Cooperation, to General Secretariat for African and Malagasy Affairs, 'Note sur les forces armées ivoiriennes et sur notre assistance technique en Côte d'Ivoire', 17 March 1970, 5AGF/2717. The command of the navy and gendarmerie were given to Ivorian officers in 1971. See Couetdic, Ministry of Cooperation, to Secretariat for Foreign Affairs, 'Note sur les forces armées ivoiriennes et sur notre assistance technique en Côte d'Ivoire', 9 December 1971, 5AGF/2717, FFAN.
284 Raphaël-Leygues, 'La Côte d'Ivoire et l'Armée', 30 August 1974, 1 PO/1/16, CADN.
285 General Secretariat for African and Malagasy Affairs, 'L'armée ivoirienne et l'aide militaires française', 2 July 1973, 5AGF/1813, FFAN; Françoise Giraudon, French Embassy Abidjan, 'L'ivoirisation des cadres', 11 September 1973, 5AGF/1813, FFAN; French Embassy Abidjan, 'Malaise au sein de l'armée ivoirienne', 6 July 1965, 5AGF1793, FFAN; Telegram, Abidjan to Ragunet, Paris, 6 July 1965, 5AGF/1793, FFAN; Minister

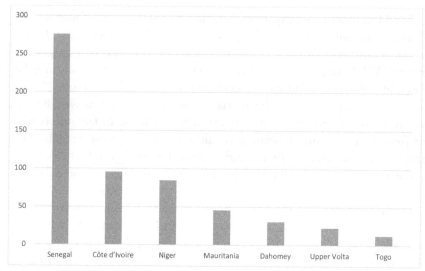

Figure 8. French military assistance, 1960–1968 (FF million) (Sources: CADC: INVA/320).

military, and another alleged coup plot within the armed forces in 1973 convinced him that the organization and mission of the military did not correspond to the needs of society.[286]

Houphouët-Boigny had always envisaged the Ivorian armed forces as an army for peace, which would make their military capacities irrelevant to their purpose. However, the reliance on France and the prevalence of French migrants in the Ivorian economy continued to deepen inequality and discontent in the country throughout the 1980s and 1990s, and, combined with the weaknesses of the national military, left the country ill-prepared to face the rebellion from the North in 2002. President Senghor left behind a different legacy by having placed a high priority on creating a strong professional army. Though Senegalese officers used their influence to reduce the French military presence in their country, Senegal still received more military assistance than Côte d'Ivoire (see Figure 8), in part because its strategic location. The country being the westernmost point in Africa saw

of Armed Forces, SDECE, 'Côte d'Ivoire: les progrès de opposition', 14 May 1973, 5AGF/1812, FFAN.
286 Raphaël-Leygues, French Embassy Abidjan, to Minister of Foreign Affairs, Michel Jobert, 'Complot des jeunes officiers contre le regime ivoirien', 13 September 1973, AG/5F/1812, FFAN; Houphouët-Boigny quoted in Raphaël-Leygues, 'La Côte d'Ivoire et l'Armée', 30 August 1974.

France being willing to provide important military and economic resources, which gave Senghor a unique leverage.

The strategic importance of Senegal

In Senegal, as in Côte d'Ivoire, France's objective was to maintain its exclusivity in relation to military assistance. In 1961, when the Senegalese government requested engineering equipment for the army from the US after the French refused to provide it, American officials asked France whether it objected and the French responded that the US could deliver the equipment on two conditions: any training would be provided by France and the Senegalese government needed to have the necessary budgetary resources to use the equipment.[287] Assistant US Secretary of State Williams condemned the French stance, which denied American access to the Senegalese military and forced the 'western-oriented Senegalese government to have to choose between exclusive dependence upon France or recourse to the Soviet bloc'. Williams advised that the US should still try to establish a 'modest' military presence in Senegal and develop contacts in the Senegalese military due to Dakar's strategic location.[288]

The importance of Dakar made the US more eager to get involved in Senegal than in Côte d'Ivoire. However, when the Kennedy administration ordered US embassies in Africa to undertake needs assessments in 1962, diplomatic officials in Dakar recommended against providing internal security assistance to Senegal.[289] France was likely to oppose it, they noted, and Senegal would refuse. American officials knew that Senegal was planning to build an army of close to 7,000, and that the French considered this excessive. For tactical reasons, the US Embassy in Dakar recommended that the US should wait until Senegalese officials made requests.[290] Several years later, their conclusion was unchanged: Senegal did not need US assistance and, even if it did, France would pressure the Senegalese into rejecting it.[291]

---

287 US Embassy Dakar, 'French Views on Military Aid to Senegal', 12 December 1961, SENEGAL 60–63, 770t, Box 1989, CGRDS, NARA.
288 Williams, US Department of State, to Mr Chenery, 'Furnishing military assistance to Senegal', 12 December 1961, SENEGAL 60–63, 770t, Box 1989, CGRDS, NARA.
289 US Embassy Dakar, 'Senegal Internal Security', 6 June 1962, SENEGAL 60–63, 770t, Box 1989, CGRDS, NARA.
290 Ibid.
291 US Embassy Dakar, 'Public Safety Review', 29 June 1965, 770t, Box 1989, CGRDS, NARA.

Senegal's approach to French assistance differed to that of Côte d'Ivoire. Senghor wanted a strong, independent army and emphasized training over technical assistance. By 1963, most of the French technical assistants in Senegal had been withdrawn from command positions in the army and gendarmerie. Those that remained led the administrative, and logistic services of the army, but Senegalese forces were capable of maintaining internal order without French involvement. In the navy and air force, however, French assistants continued to hold the most important positions, and Senegalese authorities continued to rely mostly on France for training its armed forces. Senegal had over 200 soldiers in French military schools in 1963;[292] and 250 Senegalese officers and 850 non-commissioned officers had been trained in France by 1969.[293]

The ongoing presence of French technical assistants was a source of dissatisfaction for some Senegalese soldiers. In 1965, an article appeared in a Senegalese newspaper, criticizing the command of the Senegalese armed forces and contending that French assistants acted as 'gods and fathers, not because they teach Senegalese how to be soldiers but because they maintain the key positions, putting aside competent Senegalese.' The author – who a French military attaché identified as Amadou Kone, a former air force sergeant – claimed that French assistants had misused their power in deciding promotions, and found amusement in 'making and unmaking the careers of Senegalese soldiers'.[294] Other members of the Senegalese armed forces also complained about the corruption of French technical assistants.[295] In 1968, when the logistics services of the military were still led by French assistants, Senegalese soldiers sought to gain control.[296]

At the same time, French observers signalled grave problems with corruption among Senegalese gendarmes and police, which was on a scale that could undermine public trust in the security sector. President Senghor felt these problems may have been caused by too hasty a process

---

[292] Ambassador Paye, French Embassy Dakar, 4 November 1963, INVA180, CADC.
[293] General Secretary for African and Malagasy Affairs, 'Audience de monsieur Leopold Senghor', 16 December 1969, 5AGF/609, FFAN.
[294] Military advisor, French Embassy Dakar, 'Article sur l'aide technique militaire française au Sénégal', 24 August 1965, 184PO1–1043, CADN; French Embassy Dakar, 'Opinions sénégalaises sur l'assistance technique française', 17 July 1968, 184PO1–104, CADN.
[295] French Embassy Dakar, 'Opinions sénégalaises sur l'assistance technique française', 17 July 1968, 184PO1–1043, CADN.
[296] General Secretary for African and Malagasy Affairs, Special Staff, 'Visite du président Senghor', 30 July 1968, 5AGF/609, FFAN.

of Africanization.[297] Moreover, it was not only military personnel who were dissatisfied by the continuing significant role of the French in Senegal. The number of French citizens in the country may have fallen from 16,000 to 10,000 between 1960 and 1970, but it was argued that too many French expatriate workers still held jobs that Senegalese workers could do.[298] A lack of career opportunities and Senegal's alignment with France took Senegalese students and workers to the streets in 1968, which was a year of global political turmoil. President Senghor responded by using the armed forces against protestors and requested assistance from the French, which they promised.[299]

For Senegalese officers, the role they played in suppressing the protests helped them understand the extent of their own political bargaining power as military actors. Senghor's reliance on security forces had given more power to Army Chief of Staff Alfred Diallo, for example. When a Senegalese officer subsequently accused Diallo of corruption, the accuser found himself charged with plotting a coup. Even if there was no real plot to speak of, the US Embassy estimated that 'the French would never intervene', as that could entail conflict with Senegalese soldiers. The Americans described the Senegalese officer corps as '90% pro-French, as many of them have French wives, almost all are trained by the French and served in the French army' and hypothesized that, 'if junior officers turn[ed] against Diallo, France could do nothing.'[300]

The French were aware of the increasing power of the Senegalese military and when President Senghor requested, at the end of 1969, that the 1962 military assistance agreement signed between Senegal and France be modified, Foccart's office suspected he had been 'pushed in that direction by the Army Chief of Staff, who had been approached by the US offering planes to the air force'.[301] France did not object to modifying the agreement, but according to the SIPRI Arms Transfers Database, Senegal continued

297 General Secretary for African and Malagasy Affairs, Special Staff, 'Visite du président Senghor', 30 July 1968.
298 French Embassy Dakar, 'Situation au Sénégal', 13 May 1969, 184PO1–517, CADN.
299 Blum, 'Sénégal 1968: révolte étudiante et grève générale', *Revue d'histoire moderne et contemporaine* 59-2, no. 2 (2012), p. 144.
300 US Embassy Dakar, '*Le monde* correspondent Pierre Biarnes' views on alleged military plot', 29 January 1969, POLa9 67–69, Box 2477, CGRDS, NARA.
301 General Secretary for African and Malagasy Affairs, 'Audience de monsieur Léopold Senghor', 16 December 1969, 5AGF/609, FFAN; General Secretary for African and Malagasy Affairs, 'Accords de défense franco-sénégalais', 27 November 1969, GR6Q44, SHD.

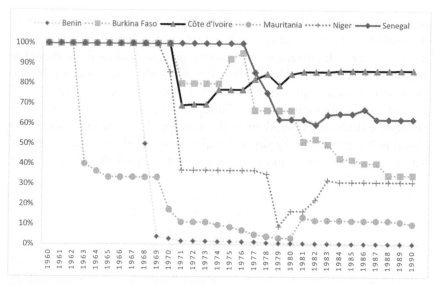

Figure 9. Major weapons transfers from France (Source: SIPRI arms transfers database, https://www.sipri.org/databases/armstransfers, accessed 27.12.2021).

to import only French equipment in the years that followed (see Figure 9). Between 1960 and 1968, Senegal had already received more French military assistance (FF 280 million) than any other country in franco-phone West Africa (see Figure 8). In 1971, when the anti-colonial conflict against Portugal in Guinea-Bissau risked spreading to Senegal, Senegalese officials requested additional aid – seeking equipment for border defence and French technical assistance for the intelligence services. The French Foreign Ministry responded positively[302] but first reminded Senghor that France has already agreed to renew Senegalese military equipment, which would cost 36 million FF in the next five years.[303]

Increased military assistance from France to Senegal in 1970 and 1971 was coupled with decreased economic assistance, which dropped from nearly US$ 29 million in 1969 to about US$ 13 million in 1971. However, it would return to previous levels by 1974.[304] This temporary reduction in economic assistance may have reflected the simple calculation by France that it was

[302] SAM 'Audience du président Léopold Senghor' 10 septembre 1971, 5AGF/610, FFAN.
[303] SAM 'Entretien avec Léopold Senghor' 6 février 1971, 15 février 1971, 5AGF/610, FFAN.
[304] Data on net foreign economic assistance from the World Bank DataBank.

important to reallocate resources to the military in order to strengthen its loyalty to Senghor and raise satisfaction among soldiers regarding their service conditions. Or, it may have been linked to difficulties in bilateral relations between the countries, which were complicated by the wish of Senegalese officials to obtain military equipment from third countries, as well as the issues of the French military base and the housing assigned to French technical assistants.

Although President Senghor supported the French military presence,[305] the visibility of the French base in Dakar did cause him political problems. He had asked on multiple occasions that the French troops be moved to Thies, thereby vacating French installations in Dakar for Senegalese officers. He also argued that this would look better to those arriving in Dakar to attend international conferences.[306] Senegalese Chief of Staff Diallo raised this issue again in 1971. In his opinion, the quarters assigned to French soldiers exceeded their needs. The officers' villas, for example, were in a prestigious neighbourhood surrounding the headquarters of the Senegalese armed forces, and Diallo requested that some should be given to Senegalese officers. He justified this by noting that the Senegalese military lacked housing, forcing officers to rent from the private sector, at a cost of CFA 70 million a year. The French ambassador refused to entertain Diallo's demand, explaining that French forces also lacked housing in Senegal.[307]

Later that year, Senghor, Diallo, and the Senegalese minister of interior, Abdou Diouf, again expressed their desire to take possession of the villas, they were again rebuffed. By then, Foccart's office noted, the dispute had grown beyond the mere question of housing, as the new urban plan for Dakar included the intention to build highways that would traverse the French villas.[308] The housing issue demonstrated that Diallo and Senegalese military officers could influence Senegalese politics, which could incentivize Senghor to renegotiate with French officials. When Diallo retired in 1972, his successor, General Fall, was no more welcoming of the French military

---

305 General Secretary for African and Malagasy Affairs, 'Entretien avec le président Léopold Senghor, 6 February 1971', 15 February 1971.
306 French Embassy Dakar, 'Demande sénégalaise', 18 September 1964, 184PO/1/325, CADN.
307 Ambassador of France in Dakar, 'Demande d'aide exceptionnelle au profit des forces armées sénégalaises', 9 April 1971, 184PO1–1043, CADN.
308 General Secretary for African and Malagasy Affairs, 'Lettre au président Senghor', 27 July 1971, 5AGF/610, FFAN.

presence, and this most likely reflected the broad opinion of the soldiers he commanded.

What emerges from this history of French military assistance to Côte d'Ivoire and Senegal is not a story of neo-colonial domination, but one of a series of negotiations in which the Senegalese and Ivorian presidents played key roles. The major difference between these countries was that Senegalese officers had more influence on these negotiations than their Ivorian counterparts. However, France would not have allowed Senghor or Houphouët-Boigny to be ousted by a military coup, reflecting its special relationship with both presidents. By contrast, the presidents of Upper Volta, Niger, Mauritania, Togo, and Dahomey all lost power as a result of a coups and had no preventative protection from France. These five countries were also poorer than Senegal and Côte d'Ivoire and received less French military and economic assistance. As a result, they had to face the challenge of building their national armies with very limited resources.

Surviving on Leftovers: Building National Militaries with Limited Resources

In Niger, Upper Volta, Mauritania, Togo, and Dahomey, national armies had to be built from far fewer resources than those enjoyed by the governments in Mali, Guinea, Senegal, or Côte d'Ivoire. Maintaining a national army is equally expensive, and the cost of salaries and military equipment can account for a large part of national budgets. Every country in the region thus sought to reduce their costs by requesting foreign military aid. With the exception of Guinea and Mali, all francophone countries automatically looked to France for assistance, and all signed military assistance agreements with France in 1961.[309] These agreements promised French equipment and training, but clearly stipulated that partner countries could not receive military equipment from elsewhere without French authorization. This assured a French monopoly on this assistance in francophone West Africa. However, French resources were limited, and those countries that were strategically and economically less vital to France received less military assistance (see Figures 8 and 10). Thus, where French trade, investment, and expatriate populations were limited, so was the amount of military aid.

309 Directorate of African and Malagasy Affairs, 'Conventions sur la participation des forces armées françaises au maintien de l'ordre', 13 August 1963, INVA 17, CADC.

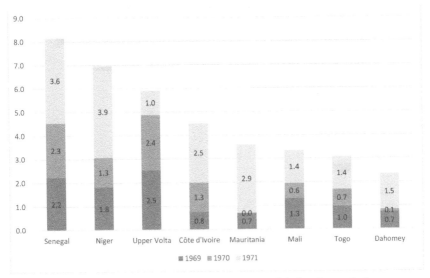

Figure 10. French military assistance (equipment only) for the period 1969–1971 (FF million) (Source: SHD; CADC).

The amounts of military and economic assistance France allocated also depended on factors such as the local needs and capacity of each government, as well as the potential risk of corruption and mismanagement. There was a clear quid pro quo in some cases. In Upper Volta, for example, the government's refusal to host a French military base saw France reduce its military assistance, so that by 1974, the Voltaic military was the least equipped of all those in francophone West Africa (see Figure 11). The situation was mirrored in Togo and Dahomey, and soldiers in all three countries took on political roles, with Togo experiencing its first military coup in 1963, Dahomey in 1964, and Upper Volta in 1966.

Upper Volta also had to confront the challenge of integrating the largest number of colonial soldiers released from the French army, which furthered the ability of military actors to influence the political sphere. Togo and Dahomey, by contrast, had contributed few soldiers to French forces under colonial rule (see Table 3). The Voltaic, Togolese, and Dahomeyan governments also received minimal economic assistance, and thus had badly equipped militaries built with limited resources. This explains why Niger and Mauritania experienced their first coups as well, although their larger geographical size and the presence of a French military base only saw coups taking place in 1974 and 1978, respectively.

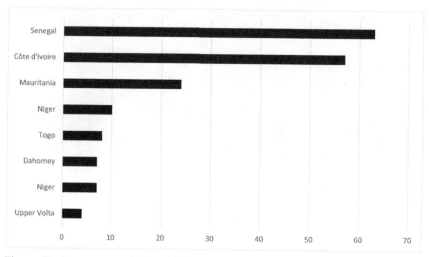

Figure 11. Arms accumulation, 1960–1974 (Source: SIPRI arms transfers database, https://www.sipri.org/databases/armstransfers, accessed 2.5.2022).

Table 3. Soldiers in colonial and postcolonial francophone West Africa.

	African soldiers before and after independence in 1961			Soldiers in 1954		
	French army	Officers	National army	European	African	Total
Guinea	12,600	(21)	3,500	11%	89%	1,890
Upper Volta	11,360	(19)	800	16%	84%	2,530
Mali	7,610	(30)	4,000	20%	80%	3,500
Côte d'Ivoire	5,710	(10)	3,400	13%	87%	3,100
Senegal	4,700	(26)	3,000	47%	53%	6,780
Dahomey	3,000	(4)	600	12%	88%	1,350★
Niger	2,970	(2)	800	10%	90%	3,280
Mauritania	1,440	(0)	1,300	32%	68%	4,280
Togo	870	(1)	200	12%	88%	1,350★

Source: SHD: GR5H27, GR5H28, GR5H40.
★ Total for Dahomey and Togo is combined.

Clearly, France could not freely impose its will on its former colonies, as seen in the refusal of the Voltaic, Guinean, and Malian governments to allow French military bases on their territories. Although the French signed defence agreements with Togo, Dahomey, Mauritania, and Niger promising mutual aid,[310] and initially had military bases in Dahomey, Mauritania, and Niger, by 1966 only the base in Niger was still operational (see Table 1). There, French troops remained on the insistence of President Diori, who signed a special agreement allowing him to request French assistance to maintain order. However, neither the French base nor this special agreement protected Diori in 1974 when Nigerien soldiers carried out a coup, despite the presence of 200 French troops in the country. The military government that took over subsequently asked the France to withdraw.

The different decisions francophone West African governments made reflect the agency of African actors, which was sometimes exerted under considerable pressure, as was seen when officials in Upper Volta refused to host a French military base. This decision came at the price of reduced French military assistance, which was especially limited prior to 1962, when the first Voltaic Defence Minister – who had frustrated French officials during negotiations on defence cooperation – was replaced. During its first eight years of independence, Upper Volta had already received significantly less French military assistance than Niger, Mauritania, and Dahomey. Only Togo received less than Upper Volta (see Figure 8). However, French military assistance increased in the late 1960s. Between 1969 and 1971, for example, the military government of Upper Volta obtained French military equipment worth FF 5.9 million, putting it close behind Niger (FF 7 million) and Senegal (FF 8.9 million).

Even so, there were a number of constraints on African agency, as French military assistance agreements limited the freedom of cooperating countries. First, France insisted that recipient countries spend a maximum of 10% of their budget on the military, or in exceptional situations, such as being faced with an external threat, 15% for a short period of time.[311] These budgetary limitations partially explain why France objected to offers of US

---

310 Camille Evrard, 'Retour sur la construction des relations militaires franco-africaines', *Relations internationals* 165, no. 1 (2016), pp. 23–42.
311 Ministry of Cooperation, 'Directive concernant l'orientation et l'évolution des armées nationales africaines et malgache', 27 August 1964. NB: Such a limit could have been beneficial to populations in newly independent states, if it had resulted in spending being directed towards education and health at higher rates.

and West German equipment being accepted by former colonies – France did not want to pay the additional costs of operating and maintaining this equipment.[312]

Second, France criticized any large-scale use of the military against civilian populations. French officials emphasized that armies receiving French assistance should be used to maintain interior order *only* in exceptional situations, when security forces (Republican Guards, the police, and the gendarmerie) had already been deployed.[313] French policies towards coups were, however, more ambiguous. While soldiers who assumed power in regional coups were all former members of the French military and were viewed as favourable to France, military rulers were also influenced by fellow soldiers who advocated strength and independence. Nonetheless, like the West Germans and Americans, French diplomats thought that in the absence of democratic systems that offered checks and balances to governmental power, military coups were often the only way to unseat corrupt, authoritarian rulers.[314]

Third, French policy until 1970 was one of exclusivity, aimed at preventing other actors from entering its defence sphere in former colonies, supposedly to ensure that they did not become Cold War battlegrounds. African governments, however, tested the limits of French policy by accepting non-military material for armed and security forces from elsewhere. In the 1970s, the French Ministry of Cooperation finally suggested that French policy on military assistance change in order to make aid more selective. This was partly due to the recognition that the military assistance provided by the UK, US, and the Soviet Union was targeted at countries they deemed most strategically and economically important, with the Americans seen to have a commercial motivation and the Soviets focused on intelligence-gathering and influencing the air forces.[315] In other words, all military aid was part of the global struggle for influence.

In 1970, when the French concluded that every major foreign power was interested in providing military aid to West Africa due to the actual and potential power of armies in the region, the key recommendation of the Ministry of Cooperation was that France should no longer offer assistance

---

312 Ministry of Cooperation, 'Domaine de l'assistance militaire', 18 September 1974.
313 Ministry of Cooperation, 'Directive concernant l'orientation et l'évolution des armées nationales africaines et malgache', 27 August 1964.
314 'US/FRG talks on Africa', 13 February 1968.
315 Colonel Charles, General Secretariat for African and Malagasy Affairs, 'Coopération et aides militaires étrangères en Afrique noire', 27 June 1970, 5AGF/2707, FFAN.

to countries with whom it had poor diplomatic relations. The ministry also noted that a choice should be made between giving rich countries additional equipment in order to get them to buy more, or favouring poorer countries that could not afford to buy equipment themselves. The French feared that their previous approach of 'giving little to all, in the end, made everyone unhappy'.[316]

When French policy changed, the US, West Germany, and others were finally free to provide military equipment to francophone West African countries. Niger received one plane from the US in 1969, and five from West Germany in 1970. Togo obtained military material from West Germany, Canada, and the UK throughout the 1970s, and also from Libya, which also supplied Upper Volta with equipment. Western powers as well as the Soviet Union also provided Dahomey (Benin) and Mauritania with military equipment. The decisions made by military governments in the region to accept weapons from states on opposing sides of the Cold War underline their agency vis-à-vis France, but may also reflect the soldiers' disappointment in terms of what French officials could offer, militarily and ideologically. A new generation of officers had come to power that had not served in the French military. They thus supported the rise of revolutionary ideology within the armed forces, which motivated military governments to distance themselves from France, as was the case of Upper Volta in the 1980s.

Comparing the decision-making of the Voltaic and Nigerien governments to that of leaders in Guinea, Mali, Côte d'Ivoire, and Senegal facilitates an analysis of African agency, in that Upper Volta and Niger largely took an opposite approach. Such a comparison is possible, in part, because these states all share certain characteristics, which cannot be said of Mauritania, Togo, or Dahomey. They are the outliers: Togo and Dahomey are geographically so small that it required fewer resources to build their national military capacities. Togo, as a former German colony, was politically and economically least connected to France, and Mauritania is culturally and politically closer to North Africa than to West Africa.

While Mauritania cannot be easily analysed in a comparative context alongside other francophone West African countries, it does highlight the shift in African foreign policy that emerged as a result of the 1973 oil crisis.[317] The sudden wealth of oil-producing countries increased the influence of

316 Ibid.
317 Evrard, 'Quelle transmission du "pouvoir militaire" en Afrique? L'indépendance mauritanienne vue par l'armée française', *Afrique contemporaine* 235, no. 3 (2010), pp. 27–42.

Saudi Arabia, Kuwait, Libya, Algeria, and the United Arab Emirates in the majority of Muslim West Africa, to the extent that these countries seemed to provide an alternative to France. That year, the Six Day War also led every government in francophone West Africa to break diplomatic ties with Israel, as relations with oil-producing countries were deemed more important once these countries began providing aid and loans across the region. This was a huge disappointment to Israel, which had spent significant resources cultivating relations with African political and military elites.[318] However, Niger and Mauritania were soon similarly disappointed by their cooperation with the *Organization of the Petroleum Exporting Countries* (OPEC) countries, and both turned again to France – Niger, when it needed help finding buyers for its uranium, and Mauritania when it needed French assistance confronting the conflict in Western Sahara in 1976. In fact, all the franco-phone West African countries that experienced a conflict sought protection or equipment from foreign partners. This was true for Niger's operation against the Sawaba rebellion in 1964 and Upper Volta's border war against Mali in 1974, as well as Mauritania's conflict in the Western Sahara, and in every instance, the need of these countries for military equipment and assistance brought them back to France.

No base for France in Upper Volta

In his memoir, the first Chief of Staff and second president of Upper Volta, Sangoulé Lamizana, said of France's departure from the country in 1962 that:

> In Ouagadougou, the transfer of various materials, in accordance with the agreements, was carried out very strictly. By a very fine needle. 'You do not give gifts to people who kick you out' was whispered here and there by some French officers .... In Bobo-Dioulasso, the situation was worse. The disastrous departure of the French troops deprived us of many things. Instead of leaving the equipment that they could not take with them, the French preferred to destroy it ... the electric wires were sabotaged or simply torn off. It was the price to pay for our refusal to grant military bases to France.[319]

---

318 Levey, 'Israel's Exit from Africa, 1973: The Road to Diplomatic Isolation' and 'Israel's strategy in Africa, 1961–67'.

319 Sangoulé Lamizana, *Sur la Brèche trente années durant: Mémoires*, vol. 2 (Paris: Jaguar, 1999), p. 32.

Six months prior the establishment of Upper Volta's national armed forces in November 1961, the country's leadership had signed a military assistance agreement with France, but, to the disappointment of the French, the Voltaic government demanded the withdrawal of French troops by January 1962.[320] Despite acknowledging that this request was a reflection of nationalist popular opinion in Upper Volta, French officials were irritated by the approach of the Voltaic minister of defence, Bamina Nébié, during negotiations.[321] According to US officials, conflict between Nébié and the French military attaché was partly due to Nébié's desire to create a Voltaic force of 10,000 soldiers, which the French considered excessive.[322]

Although the transfer of French military bases in Ouagadougou and Bobo-Dioulasso (the two largest cities in Upper Volta) was presented to the world as having taken place on the most amicable terms, a US military envoy soon heard complaints about how the French had behaved as they withdrew.[323] The Voltaic experience of an abrupt and bitter French departure is similar to that of Mali and Guinea, except that Upper Volta had a military assistance agreement with France that promised the equipment it needed to establish a national army. The refusal of Voltaic leadership to host a French military base, however, was met by an unwillingness on the part of France to offer any substantial aid. In public, Upper Volta's first president, Maurice Yaméogo, praised French assistance, in the hope that he could secure more, especially after it became obvious that no other country was going to provide significant aid.[324]

Why Yaméogo refused the request for a French base is not completely clear. He appeared to be as much a Francophile as Côte d'Ivoire's Houphouët-Boigny or Niger's Diori.[325] The key difference may have been the number

320 Ibid., pp. 24–5.

321 Ibid., pp. 24–6 and 32; Ambassador of France to the President of Upper Volta, 27 December 1961, 6V13, Centre National des Archives du Burkina Faso (ANB); Estes, US Embassy Ouagadougou, to Department of State, 'Defense Ministry Change', 24 May 1962, 770k 1960–1963, Box 1983, CGRDS, NARA, and 15 May 1962, 770k 1960–1963, Box 1983, CGRDS, NARA.

322 Antony Dalsimer, US Embassy Ouagadougou, to Department of State, 'Upper Volta Gains an Army', 20 October 1961, 770k 1960–1963, Box 1983, CGRDS, NARA.

323 Estes, US Embassy Ouagadougou, to Department of State, 'Report of Voltaic-French III: Feeling at Bobo-Dioulasso military camp', 15 June 1962, 770k 1960–1963, Box 1983, CGRDS, NARA.

324 Levasseur, 'Synthèse No XLIII/65', 3 November 1965, 313QONT/7, CADC.

325 Jean-Marc Palm, *Rassemblement Démocratique Africain (RDA) en Haute-Volta (1947–1980)* (Burkina Faso: DIST/CNRST, 2011), pp. 190 and 208.

and sentiment of soldiers in Upper Volta. In 1960, there were some 11,000 Voltaic troops serving in the French army, along with an estimated 100,000 retired soldiers living in Upper Volta,[326] and these soldiers were lobbying for the establishment of a strong, independent national armed force. As Voltaic soldiers interviewed for this study noted, allowing a French military base in Upper Volta at the time was inconceivable, as it would have undermined the country's independence.[327] This was also expressed by Yaméogo during a visit to Israel in July 1962,[328] and US officials observed that he and other Voltaic politicians were 'anxious to tell their more neutralist neighbors that they have no foreign forces on their soil.'[329]

In the end, rejecting the French base had negative consequences for the Voltaic armed forces. One Voltaic officer suggested in an interview that Yaméogo should have resisted popular opinion and accepted the base to ensure sufficient equipment for the military.[330] Instead, with French-Voltaic relations weakened, politicians in Upper Volta turned to the US for military assistance. While then Chief of Staff Lamizana claimed in his memoir that Voltaic requests were turned down by the Americans,[331] US archives indicate that the Americans provided seventy tonnes of military equipment to the Voltaic armed forces in April 1962.[332] US interest in Upper Volta had to do with its strategic location, bordering six other African countries, as well as its close relations with progressive countries Guinea, Mali, and Ghana.[333]

---

[326] 'Rapport de fin de commandement du général de CA Gardet, commandant supérieur des forces armées de la ZOM 1 du mai 1958 au 15 fevrier 1960', GR 5H28, SHD. Also see weekly reports of the French Embassy Ouagadougou, February through May 1961, in File 313QONT/3, CADC.

[327] Capitaine Didier Felicieu Compaore, Colonel Major Aly Paré, and Adjutant-Chef Major Macaire Yaméogo, interview by author, 15 January 2016, Ouagadougou.

[328] 'Conférence de presse du 12 juillet 1962 à Jérusalem – déclaration de monsieur le président Maurice Yaméogo, Président de la république de Haute-Volta', 6V8, ANB.

[329] John A. Bovey, US Embassy Paris, to Donald Dumont, Acting Director, Office of West African and Malagasy Affairs, 16 May 1962, 770k 1960–1963, Box 1983, CGRDS, NARA.

[330] Colonel Barthélémy Kombasre, interview by author, 18 January 2016, Ouagadougou.

[331] Lamizana, *Sur la Brèche*, p. 33.

[332] US Embassy Ouagadougou, 'Airlift of Military Equipment to Upper Volta', 26 May 1962, 770k 1960–1963, Box 1983, CGRDS, NARA.

[333] US Department of State, 'Memorandum of conversation: Guy de Commines, Counselor French Embassy; Donald Dumont, AFW; Martin Herz, AF; Robert Foulon B/FAC', 17 May 1961, 770k 1960–1963, Box 1983, CGRDS, NARA; US Embassy Ouagadougou to Department of State, 'US Overseas Internal Defense Policy in Upper Volta', 23 November 1962, 770k 1960–1963, Box 1983, CGRDS, NARA.

Documents from the US Department of State also indicate that American officials thought Voltaic requests should be fulfilled, or else there would be 'an even great danger that Upper Volta might accept assistance from undesirable quarters'. Furthermore, they believed US assistance would bring credibility to Voltaic independence by diversifying the sources of assistance to Upper Volta.[334]

The French view was contrary to that of the Americans. They feared US assistance would draw reactionary aid from communist countries and made it clear that American assistance to Upper Volta was unwelcome.[335] As early as 1961, the US Embassy in Ouagadougou was aware of French sensibilities on the subject and warned that it was 'undesirable' to US objectives if it at all appeared as though the US 'wished to replace French officers with Americans, even as technical advisers'. It advised that American assistance could 'be confined to vehicles, perhaps special communication equipment, construction of buildings and other items which the French are less inclined or less able to provide', and 'should require a minimum of US military personnel for training and supervision for minimum length of time.'[336]

American diplomatic reports throughout the early 1960s continued to emphasize that the US had no wish to 'supplant French [assistance], only complement' it in Upper Volta.[337] The Americans would offer only limited

---

334 US Department of State, 'Memorandum of conversation: Guy de Commines, Counselor French Embassy; Donald Dumont, AFW; Martin Herz, AF; Robert Foulon B/FAC', 17 May 1961.

335 US Embassy Ouagadougou to Department of State, 'Memorandum of conversation: Henry Bernard, French Chargé d'affaires, and Anthony Dalsimer, Third Secretary', 12 May 1962, 770k 1960–1963, Box 1983, CGRDS, NARA; Major Frank, US Embassy Ouagadougou, to Deputy Chief of Staff for Operations and Plans, 'Military mission to Upper Volta', 12 June 1962, 770k 1960–1963, Box 1983, CGRDS, NARA; US Department of State, 'Memorandum of conversation: Guy de Commines, Counselor French Embassy; Donald Dumont, AFW; Martin Herz, AF; Robert Foulon B/FAC', 17 May 1961.

336 US Embassy Ouagadougou to Department of State, 'Interview with Maurice Yaméogo: Review of Upper Volta affairs', 28 August 1961, 770k 1960–1963, Box 1983, CGRDS, NARA.

337 Ibid. Also see Estes, US Embassy Ouagadougou, to Department of State: 'Improving Police Forces Capabilities', 23 May 1962, 770k 1960–1963, Box 1983, CGRDS, NARA; 'Internal Security Assessment', 30 May 1962, 770k 1960–1963, Box 1983, CGRDS, NARA; and 'Upper Volta: Problems and Prospects During 1963', 10 January 1963, 770k 1960–1963, Box 1983, CGRDS, NARA.

aid and would not take on the responsibility of supporting the entire Voltaic military establishment, which they saw as 'something the French were more willing to do'.[338] Despite these assurances, French officials remained suspicious of US activities.[339] They did their best to convince the Americans that French assistance was underutilized, claiming, for example, that places allocated to Voltaic soldiers in trainings went unfilled, and arguing that there was thus no need for US training.[340]

Voltaic complaints to US officials about the lack of training opportunities in French military schools gave the opposite impression.[341] Nevertheless, the French objective to guard its exclusive role in the West African military sphere led the US to tailor its assistance to the Voltaic police, providing communication equipment, vehicles, and training.[342] Much of this assistance could not be used due to insufficient budget resources, however, and the

338 Major Frank, 'Military mission to Upper Volta', 12 June 1962. Also see US Embassy Ouagadougou to Department of State, 'Interview with Maurice Yaméogo: Review of Upper Volta affairs', 28 August 1961; Estes, 'Internal Security Assessment', 30 May 1962; US Embassy Ouagadougou, 'Vulnerabilities of the Government of Upper Volta', 18 March 1964, POLUVOLTA 1964–1966, Box 2907, CGRDS, NARA.

339 US Embassy Ouagadougou, 'Memorandum of conversation: participants Henri Bernard, French Chargé d'affaires; Major Demondiere, French military attaché, and Major Frank, MTT Upper Volta', 18 May 1962, 770k 1960–1963, Box 1983, CGRDS, NARA, and 'Memorandum of conversation: Henry Bernard, French Chargé d'affaires, and Anthony Dalsimer, Third Secretary', 12 May 1962; Frank, 'Military mission to Upper Volta', 12 June 1962; Bovey, First Secretary, US Embassy Paris, to Cunnigham, Economic Affairs, Office of African and Malagasy Affairs, 25 June 1962, 770k 1960–1963, Box 1983, CGRDS, NARA.

340 US Embassy Ouagadougou, 'Memorandum of conversation: Herni Bernard, French Chargé d'affaires; Major Demondiere, French military attaché; and Major Frank, MTT Upper Volta,' 18 May 1962; Frank, 'Military mission to Upper Volta', 12 June 1962; Bovey, US Embassy Paris, to Cunnigham, Office of African and Malagasy Affairs, 25 June 1962.

341 US Embassy Ouagadougou to Department of State, 'Memorandum of conversation: Major Henry Frank, MTT Upper Volta, and Major Demondiere, French military attaché Ouagadougou', 3 May 1962, 770k 1960–1963, Box 1983, CGRDS, NARA; Estes, US Embassy Ouagadougou, to Department of State, 'French Military Attaché – Views on United States Military Assistance', 9 May 1962, 770k 1960–1963, Box 1983, CGRDS, NARA; US Embassy Ouagadougou to Department of State, 'Memorandum of conversation: Henry Bernard, French Chargé d'affaires, and Anthony Dalsimer, Third Secretary,' 12 May 1962; Frank, 'Military mission to Upper Volta', 12 June 1962.

342 French Embassy Ouagadougou, 'Proposition d'aide américaine et israélienne à la Haute-Volta en matière de police', 5 June 1962, 499PO/1/386, ANB; Estes, 'Improving Police Forces' Capabilities', 23 May 1962, and 'Internal Security Assessment', 30 May 1962; Frank, 'Military mission to Upper Volta', 12 June 1962.

Americans concluded that it would be better to coordinate their assistance with France.[343] US Ambassador Thomas Estes believed the Voltaic police and military would 'be inclined to ask for everything and then hope the resources will be made available in the forthcoming budget' and recommended the Americans 'ensure that requests for equipment are coordinated' with the Voltaic government's planning minister, but that the US should first 'double-check with the French'.[344]

French authorities insisted the US provide no equipment that would engender extra costs, including 'more vehicles, more radios, more heavy equipment that would require more fuel and more trained personnel and maintenance.'[345] The US refused any further military assistance to Upper Volta thereafter, 'pending assurance that budgetary resources ... be made available for operation and proper maintenance of what had already been provided.'[346] American officials felt that they could still assist the Voltaic gendarmerie, but assistance to the army would be beneficial only with 'evidence of the ability of the government to support its growth'.[347] US reports also alluded to the fact that President Yaméogo had delayed increasing the manpower of the national army for political reasons, even when the French were willing to equip a second battalion.[348]

The government of Upper Volta also solicited assistance from the Israelis,[349] sending a delegation to Israel in April 1962 to discuss its needs.[350] Voltaic

343 Estes, 'Improving Police Forces' Capabilities', 23 May 1962, and 'Internal Security Assessment', 30 May 1962; Estes, US Embassy in Ouagadougou, to Deputy Chief of Staff for Operations and Plans, 'Future of US military assistance in Upper Volta', 12 June 1962, 770k 1960–1963, Box 1983, CGRDS, NARA.

344 Estes, 'Internal Security Assessment', 30 May 1962.

345 Estes, 'Improving Police Forces Capabilities', 23 May 1962. Also see Estes, 'Internal Security Assessment', 30 May 1962, and 'Future of US military assistance in Upper Volta', 12 June 1962.

346 Estes, 'Improving Police Forces Capabilities', 23 May 1962.

347 Estes, 'Future of US military assistance in Upper Volta', 12 June 1962.

348 Bovey, US Embassy Paris, to Donald Dumont, Office of West African and Malagasy Affairs, 16 May 1962; US Embassy Ouagadougou to Department of State, 'Memorandum of conversation: Major Henry Frank, MTT Upper Volta, and Major Demondiere, French military attaché Ouagadougou.' 3 May 1962; US Embassy Ouagadougou, 'Memorandum of conversation: Herni Bernard, French Chargé d'affaires; Major Demondiere, French military attaché; and Major Frank, MTT Upper Volta,' 18 May 1962; Bovey, US Embassy Paris, to Cunnigham, Office of African and Malagasy Affairs, 25 June 1962.

349 French Embassy Ouagadougou, 'Proposition d'aide américaine et israélienne à la Haute-Volta en matière de police', 5 June 1962.

350 Lamizana, *Sur la Brèche*, p. 33.

Defence Minister Nébié was particularly interested in the Israeli model of civic service.[351] However, soon after the delegation returned, Nébié was replaced by Michel Tougouma, who had been the minister of youth and sports. US reports noted that Tougouma and Nébié had clashed over Israeli assistance in the days preceding this ministerial change, and neither Israeli nor American assistance was thereafter solicited by Upper Volta.[352] The French, who were pleased about the ousting of Nébié,[353] seemed to have been aware of it beforehand.[354] In fact, American officials assessed that Tougouma's appointment was a condition of the Voltaic government receiving more French aid.[355] After Tougouma was in place, the French were indeed more willing to provide assistance.

The problems in Franco-Voltaic relations had left Voltaic forces lacking even the most basic equipment. Unlike Nébié, who had had grandiose plans, Tougouma's goals for the military were more moderate.[356] Nevertheless,

351 Estes, US Embassy Ouagadougou, to Department of State, 'Minister of Defense Nebie Comments on Israeli Visit', 9 May 1962, 770k 1960–1963, Box 1983, CGRDS, NARA; US Embassy Ouagadougou to Department of State, 'Memorandum of conversation: Major Henry Frank, MTT Upper Volta, and Major Demondiere, French military attaché Ouagadougou,' 3 May 1962.

352 US Embassy Ouagadougou, 'Memorandum of conversation: Defense Minister Bamina Nebie, Chief of Staff Lamizana Sangoulé, Bureau Chief Sidiki Keita, Ambassador Thomas Estes, Major H. Frank', 9 May 1962, 770k 1960–1963, Box 1983, CGRDS, NARA; Bovey, US Embassy Paris, to Cunnigham, Office of African and Malagasy Affairs, 25 June 1962; US Embassy Ouagadougou, 'Memorandum of conversation: Herni Bernard, French Chargé d'affaires; Major Demondiere, French military attaché; and Major Frank, MTT Upper Volta,' 18 May 1962; Estes, 'Upper Volta: Problems and Prospects During 1963', 10 January 1963.

353 Lamizana, *Sur la Brèche*, pp. 34–5; Estes, US Embassy Ouagadougou, to Department of State, 15 May 1962.

354 US Embassy Ouagadougou, 'Memorandum of conversation: Major Henry Frank, MTT Upper Volta, and Major Demondiere, French military attaché Ouagadougou,' 3 May 1962.

355 Estes, US Embassy Ouagadougou, to Department of State, 15 May 1962.

356 US Embassy Ouagadougou, 'Memorandum of conversation: Defense Minister Bamina Nebie, Chief of Staff Lamizana Sangoulé, Bureau Chief Sidiki Keita, Ambassador Thomas Estes, Major H. Frank, 9 May 1962; Estes, 'Defense Ministry Change', 24 May 1962; US Embassy Ouagadougou, 'Memorandum of conversation: Defense Minister Michel Tougouma, Ambassador Thomas Estes, Major H. Frank, 28 May 1962, 770k 1960–1963, Box 1983, CGRDS, NARA, and 'Memorandum of conversation: Herni Bernard, French Chargé d'affaires; Major Demondiere, French military attaché; and Major Frank, MTT Upper Volta,' 18 May 1962; Estes, US Embassy Ouagadougou, to State Department, 'MAP planning', 5 June 1962, 770k 1960–1963, Box 1983, CGRDS, NARA.

French officials were frustrated by what they saw as extravagant requests. In 1964, for example, Foccart's office noted that Yaméogo had insisted on submitting a plan for the development of the Voltaic military that exceeded the country's entire budget. The French ambassador refused to send the plan on to de Gaulle, asking Yaméogo to revise it. Initially, Yaméogo was willing to amend the plan, but pressure from Voltaic soldiers led him to change his mind.[357]

This kind of mismanagement of the economy by the Voltaic president spurred France to reduce its budgetary aid to Upper Volta, from CFA 573 million in 1964 to CFA 500 million in 1965. Voltaic budget deficits were large and state debt had mounted, and by 1964, the deficit was over CFA 600 million, of which CFA 400 million was completely unexplained.[358] The year before, the French ambassador had already noted that Voltaic state finances were the most poorly managed in all of francophone Africa,[359] and French officials grew ever more sceptical of Yaméogo's abilities to manage the Voltaic economy.[360]

When the government of Upper Volta asked the US to restart its assistance to the Voltaic police, which had ended in 1962, it was again Yaméogo who was identified as a liability when Estes recommended against providing this assistance, specifically citing the Voltaic president's authoritarian tendencies and the risk that the US would 'inherit the same sort of irrational suspicion and criticism' faced by the French, who he said were 'now in trouble in Upper Volta … [where] Yaméogo blamed French technical assistants of subversive activities in the military'. On top of this, US officials remained keenly aware that 'the French may … react unfavorably to an attempt to exert US influence in what they feel to be an area of paramount French interest.'[361] Moreover, American officials thought the Voltaic police had more serious problems than a lack of equipment, including poor organization,

---

357 Perrier, General Secretariat for the Community, 'Principales questions militaire concernant la Haute-Volta', 7 December 1964, 5AGF/1847, FFAN.
358 Ibid.
359 Levasseur, Ambassador of France in Upper Volta, 'Forces d'opposition et force de l'opposition en Haute-Volta', 10 July 1963, 313QONT/11, CADC.
360 Palm, *Rassemblement Démocratique Africain*, pp. 204–6 and 208–11. Also see documents in File 499po/1/1, CADN; File 313QONT/7, CADC; File AG/5F/1848, FFAN; and File POLUVOLTA 1964–1966, Box 2909, CGRDS, NARA.
361 Estes, US Embassy Ouagadougou, Department of State, 'Special program for Foreign Government Civilian officials', 23 February 1965, POLUVOLTA 1964–1966, Box 2909, CGRDS, NARA.

parallel and ill-defined tasks, and ranks who were appointed based on 'personal consideration rather than merit'.[362]

Yaméogo's decision to centralize power to himself, in addition to his extravagant lifestyle, also generated tension with his domestic associates and opponents. The final blow to his regime was the announcement of austerity measures at the end of 1965, to which labour unions responded by organizing protests. The armed forces assumed power on 3 January 1966.[363] Although these events apparently came as a surprise to the French,[364] they were not altogether unhappy about this change in leadership.[365] The French ambassador told his American colleagues that military rule was actually likely to improve Voltaic governance, and deserved US support.[366] The position of the US Embassy in Ouagadougou was similar, as officials felt the change 'improve[d] advancement of US objectives' in Upper Volta, where Yaméogo's rule had become increasingly authoritarian and corrupt.[367]

Within several months of the coup in Upper Volta, militaries had assumed power in six other African countries: Algeria, Congo, Dahomey, the Central African Republic, Nigeria, and Ghana. The US perspective was that military rule benefitted Africa and advanced American interests, of which a coup was a clear example. Coups were thought to improve governance, as soldiers were said to have a 'lower tolerance of corruption; a greater emphasis on competence, especially in the field of governmental activities; and a stronger emphasis on national integrity.' As far as the Americans were concerned, African coups aligned with US goals by refocusing African militaries on internal economic and political development rather than on advancing

---

362 Estes, 'Improving Police Forces Capabilities', 23 May 1962, and 'Special program for Foreign Government Civilian officials', 23 February 1964, POLUVOLTA 1964–1966, Box 2909, CGRDS, NARA.

363 Lamizana, *Sur la Brèche*, pp. 55–6.

364 Levasseur, 'Crise politique en Haute-Volta', 4 January 1966, 313QONT/10, CADC; Military Advisor, French Embassy Ouagadougou, 'Rapport mensuel mois de décembre, 6 January 1966, GR14S261, SHD; Roberts, US Embassy Ouagadougou, 'Upper Volta coup and US–French relations', 18 January 1966, POLUVOLTA 1964–1966, Box 2909, CGRDS, NARA, and 'Upper Volta coup', 26 February 1966, POLUVOLTA 1964–1966, Box 2909, CGRDS, NARA.

365 Levasseur, 'Situation en Haute-Volta', 5 February 1965, 313QONT/10, CADC.

366 US Embassy Ouagadougou, 19 December 1967, AFR 66–69, Box 1776, CGRDS, NARA.

367 US Embassy Ouagadougou, 'Annual Policy Assessment for Upper Volta', 26 March 1966, POLUVOLTA 1964–1966, Box 2907, CGRDS, NARA. Also see Roberts, 'Upper Volta coup', 26 February 1966, and 'Ouagadougou Rigged Election', 3 February 1966, POLUVOLTA 1964–1966, Box 2908, CGRDS, NARA.

neutralist foreign policies. Additionally, the view of soldiers as 'less emotional' led US officials to expect 'more practical cooperation with the former metropoles' in countries under military rule. These officials proposed that the US should 'hit hard to seize the present opportunities' by directing loans and investment to countries that had recently experienced military coups, including Upper Volta.[368]

The Americans also understood that military coups had the potential to create openings for Soviet influence in Africa. In the absence of any leading communist parties, Soviet subversion efforts in Africa had become increasingly difficult, but a coup presented a possible shortcut. The Soviets, aware of this, implemented a strategy of establishing personal contacts with African military elites. A 1969 US intelligence report noted that the Soviet Union was clearly trying to match the influence of former colonial powers on these military actors; it warned that Moscow had reduced its economic aid to African states in favour of military aid, which the Soviets viewed as the most effective and inexpensive way to wield influence in Africa. While world powers had cooperated to some extent to avoid weapons build-ups in Africa in the 1960s, by the end of the decade the CIA concluded that the Soviets had 'exploited Western reluctance to meet some of the more extravagant African arms requests'.[369]

After the military coup in Upper Volta, Soviet officials showed a growing interest in developing relations with the country, and in June 1968, former defence minister Nébié was appointed ambassador to Moscow. The move annoyed the French.[370] However, a more serious challenge lay in Soviet offers of military equipment. When information on a Soviet proposal for aid was leaked to the French in 1969, the French ambassador threatened President Lamizana with serious repercussions if the Soviet offer was accepted. The Voltaic government refused Soviet assistance, and French officials presumed it was because their previous assistance had convinced young Voltaic officers

368 Deputy Assistant Secretary of State for African Affairs Fredericks to Secretary of State Rusk, 'Memorandum: Opportunities in the New African Situation,' 5 March 1966, Document 207, FR-US 1964–1968, vol. XXIV, Africa, CGRDS, NARA.

369 Intelligence Memorandum, No. 1393/67, 'Some aspects of subversion in Africa', 19 October 1967, Document 230, FR-US 1964–1968, vol. XXIV, Africa, CGRDS, NARA.

370 Telegram, Raul Délaye, French Embassy Ouagadougou, to the Directorate for African and Malagasy Affairs, 3 November 1968, 5AGF/1854, FFAN; Elliot Skinner, US Embassy Ouagadougou, to State Department, 'Proposed Voltaic Ambassador to URRS', 24 May 1968, POLUVOLTA 1967–1969, Box 2696, CGRDS, NARA.

that it was not worth risking future aid from France.[371] Upper Volta did eventually receive military assistance from the Soviet Union, but only after a 1983 coup by revolutionary soldiers. The Voltaic military had in fact acquired already aid from Soviet allies; soldiers interviewed for this research referenced assistance received from Libya.[372] Indeed, Upper Volta received Libyan aid in 1974,[373] one year after it severed diplomatic relations with Israel and formed closer ties with oil-producing states.[374]

The French had started renewing Voltaic equipment in 1968, providing material worth more than FF 7 million over three years.[375] French officials hoped this assistance would convince Voltaic soldiers to abandon governing and return to their military duties. Towards the end of the 1970s, the military government came under even more pressure to transfer power to civilians. This coincided with French assessments that the once highly competent and well-trained Voltaic military had become increasingly ineffectual and politicized.[376] Lamizana escaped French criticism,[377] but US diplomats reported that he was not particularly eager to transfer power to civilians.[378]

[371] Telegram, Délaye, French Embassy Ouagadougou, to the Directorate for African and Malagasy Affairs, 'Communique via le département à Minarmées: Le projet de livraison des matériels soviétiques a l'armée nationale', 7 February 1969, 5AGF/1855, FFAN; Military advisor, French Embassy Ouagadougou, 'Bulletin de renseignements d'un projet d'accord de livraison de matériel militaires soviétiques à la Haute-Volta', 11 February 1969, 5AGF/1855, FFAN; General Secretariat for African and Malagasy Affairs, 'Audience du général Lamizana', 26 August 1969, 5AGF/2719, FFAN; Ministry of Planning and Public Works, 'Compte-rendu de la réunion tenue le 8 janvier 1968 à 8 heures à la direction des travaux publics en vue de faire le point des projets susceptibles d'être présentes à l'aide soviétique', 2V18, ANB.
[372] Interviews by author, January 2016, Ouagadougou.
[373] Ministry of Cooperation, 'Domaine de l'assistance militaire', 18 September 1974, INVA318, CADC.
[374] See documents in File 5AGF/1858, FFAN; and Files GR14S262, GR9Q5122, and GR14S263, SHD.
[375] See documents in Files 5AGF/1847 and 5AGF/2719, FFAN.
[376] Military advisor, French Embassy Ouagadougou, 'Rapport de fin de mission du Colonel Laroussinie, Conseiller militaire auprès de l'Ambassade de France en Haute-Volta', 6 April 1965, GR14S263, SHD.
[377] Colonel Jean Parisot, Military attaché, French Embassy Ouagadougou, 'Rapport de fin de mission', 25 June 1975, GR9Q5122, SHD.
[378] US Embassy Ouagadougou, 'The biographic Handbook Program', 30 July 1971, POLUVOLTA 1970–1973, Box 2766, CGRDS, NARA; Ray C. Cline, Director of the Bureau of Intelligence and Research, US Department of State, to Secretary of State, 'Upper Volta: First Step on the Road Back to Civilian Government', 26 November 1969, POLUVOLTA 1967–1969, Box 2696, CGRDS, NARA.

Nevertheless, elections were held in December 1970, and a new government consisting of both soldiers and civilians was formed in February 1971.[379] The military returned to power in 1974, however, after prolonged economic and political crisis.[380] That year also marked the start of conflict between Upper Volta and Mali. The course of that conflict and the performance of Voltaic troops made clear to the French all that was wrong with the Voltaic army: soldiers were poorly trained and demoralized, equipment was old and out of order, and logistical arrangements were non-functional. [381]

The conflict also revealed the benefits of Soviet assistance. At the outset, the Malian armed forces were much better equipped, having Soviet planes and armaments.[382] Upper Volta had to rely instead on limited equipment provided for free by France.[383] Despite a population suffering from severe famine,[384] the Voltaic military government decided they would need to spend more budgetary funding to obtain military equipment, and made a sizeable acquisition of new material from the French.[385] The Voltaic military budget for soldier salaries alone already accounted for a large part of the overall state budget, and military spending was disproportionate to spending on health or education, which French officials had disparaged.[386] Although

379 Telegram, Délaye, French Embassy Ouagadougou, to Paris, 'Elections en Haute-Volta', 22 December 1970, 5AGF/1856, FFAN; General Secretariat for African and Malagasy Affairs, 'Haute-Volta', 23 February 1971, 5AGF/2719, FFAN; Azais, Military Advisor, French Embassy Ouagadougou, 'Rapport de fin de mission', 30 June 1972.

380 General Secretariat for National Defence, Intelligence Exploitation Centre, 'Eléments destines à l'élaboration d'une directive pour le conseiller militaire à Ouagadougou', 8 June 1972, GR9Q5122, SHD; Parisot, 'Rapport de fin de mission', 25 June 1975.

381 National Defence General Staff, Intelligence Division, 'Le différend frontalier Malo-Voltaïque', 27 November 1974, GR9Q5122, SHD; Parisot, 'Rapport de fin de mission', 25 June 1975; Battalion Commander Debacker, 'Fiche d'analyse du rapport annuel de l'Ambassade de la France en Haute-Volta', June 1974, GR14S263, SHD; National Defence General Staff, Intelligence Division, 'Le différend frontalier Malo-Voltaïque', 27 November 1974; Azais, 'Rapport de fin de mission', 30 June 1972; Parisot, 'Rapport de fin de mission', 25 June 1975.

382 National Defence General Staff, Intelligence Division, 'Le différend frontalier Malo-Voltaïque', 27 November 1974; Military attaché, French Embassy Ouagadougou, 'Rapport de fin de mission du Colonel Jean Parisot', 25 June 1975.

383 Ministry of Cooperation, 'Domaine de l'assistance militaire', 18 September 1974.

384 Parisot, 'Rapport de fin de mission', 25 June 1975.

385 Ibid.

386 Ministry of Cooperation, Defence Cabinet, 'Directive concernant l'orientation et l'évolution des armées nationales africaines et malgache', 27 August 1964, 324QONT/23, CADC.

the choice of Voltaic officials to spend more on the military may not have been the wisest, it was certainly autonomous.

After the conflict with Mali erupted, French military assistants in Upper Volta were suspended from their duties, antagonizing and perplexing the French, who saw this as precisely the moment when their assistance could have been of great use.[387] Interviews with former Voltaic soldiers indicate that the conflict clearly revealed their dissatisfaction with the military aid provided by France, from which Mali was perceived to have benefitted much more than Upper Volta.[388] At the time, French reports noted increasing anti-French sentiment among the Voltaic population, especially the youth.[389] French officials realized that their influence on the country's armed forces was waning. Older officers, who had been trained by the French and had served in the French military, still expressed a closeness and loyalty to France, but few younger officers shared these sentiments.[390] Nevertheless, it took another ten years for the revolutionary potential of the Voltaic armed forces to materialize.[391] The military coup in Niger in 1974 had similar roots, with a younger generation of Nigerien officers calling for a more independent defence policy, an end to government corruption and more resources for the army.

French know-how and Nigerian defence

Hamani Diori, the first president of Niger, had a keen interest in international politics, not unlike Upper Volta's Maurice Yaméogo. But while Yaméogo rejected a French base in his country, Diori's foreign policy approach took the opposite track. He embraced the French military presence

387 Parisot, 'Rapport de fin de mission', 25 June 1975.

388 Capitaine Compaore, Colonel Major Paré, and Adjutant-chef Major Yaméogo, interviews by author, 15 January 2016, Ouagadougou; Colonel Barthélémy Kombasre, interview by author, 18 January 2016, Ouagadougou; Lieutenant Gariko Yaya and Commandant Paul Tonde, interview by author, 22 January 2016, Ouagadougou.

389 French Embassy Ouagadougou, 'Situation politique', 21 April 1972, 5AGF/1857, FFAN; Diefenbacher, Director of International Police Technical Cooperation Services, to Foccart, 'Note sur situation en Haute-Volta', 18 May 1972, 5AGF/1857, FFAN; Delayé to Minister of Foreign Affairs Maurice Schuman, 'La Haute-Volta et la révision des accords de coopération', 12 August 1972, 5AGF/1857, FFAN; Diefenbacher, Ministry of Interior, Director of International Police Technical Cooperation Services, to Foccart, 'Note sur la politique étrangère voltaïque', 18 May 1973, 5AGF/1858, FFAN.

390 Parisot, Military attaché, French Embassy Ouagadougou, 'Rapport annuel', 15 June 1973, GR9Q5122, SHD.

391 Pierre Englebert, *Burkina Faso: Unsteady Statehood in West Africa* (Boulder, CO: Westview, 1996) and *La Révolution Burkinabe* (Paris: Harmattan, 1986), pp. 201–7.

in Niger, insisting on multiple occasions that France maintain a base there, In 1962, when the French announced that they would be reducing their troop numbers from 1,400 to 200, Diori objected, citing the accumulation of heavy weapons in neighbouring Mali.[392] Then, as the French government was closing multiple military bases across Africa in 1964, an armed rebellion against the government in Niger by the exiled opposition Sawaba movement convinced France to maintain a base in Niamey, with around 200 soldiers.[393] The French ambassador further reported that Diori was likely to object to removing French troops from Agadez, however, as he was having problems with the Tuareg population. The ambassador recommended that France maintain the base in Agadez to secure uranium exploration.[394]

By 1965, the Nigerien government had succeeded in suppressing the Sawaba rebellion, and French troops could be reduced. Diori accepted the French departure from Kaouar and from Agadez, but demanded more French technical assistance to complement new equipment the Nigerien military had recently obtained.[395] France planned to withdraw all of its troops from Niger in July 1966, as it had done in Côte d'Ivoire, but the date was first postponed to March 1967 and then cancelled in 1969.[396] This decision was driven by multiple military coups in neighbouring countries as well as French strategic interests in uranium mining. Indeed, in 1967, Diori requested that French troops be reinstalled in Agadez in order to provide security for a uranium mine near Arlit.[397]

Diori's insistence that Niger host a French military base was not unheard of, as both the Ivorian and Mauritanian presidents had made similar demands.[398] Notably, what these three states had in common was a

392 Foreign Affairs Advisor, 'Compression militaires françaises', 9 October 1962, 478PO1–1, CADN.

393 Fouchet, 'Note en vue de l'audience de Diori Hamani', 5AGF/598, FFAN.

394 'Conférence des ambassadeurs dans les états francophones d'Afrique noire', 12 June 1964, INVA317, CADC; French Embassy Niamey, 'Dépenses de fonctionnement des forces armées nigériennes: Note pour secrétaire d'état', 9 September 1964, 5AGF/2694, FFAN.

395 General Secretary for African and Malagasy Affairs, 'Audience du président Diori Hamani', 2 February 1965, 5AGF/598, FFAN.

396 Air Force General Fourquet, Chief of Staff of the Armed Forces, to Minister of Armed Forces, 'Implantation à Niamey', 22 April 1969, 5AGF/2694, FFAN.

397 General Secretary for African and Malagasy Affairs, 'Audience du président Diori Hamani', 10 November 1967, 5AGF/598, FFAN.

398 Directorate for African and Malagasy Affairs, 'La réunion d'experts tenue à Nouakchott 8 July 1964 remaniement du diapositive militaire françaises en république de Mauritanie', INVA318, CADC.

small number of returning colonial soldiers (see Table 3). Having few or no experienced officers, they needed foreign technical assistance to build their national militaries. This also meant that these governments faced less domestic pressure to build a strong, independent armed force. Despite this, Diori expressed concerns as early as 1962 about the prospect of exerting control over 1,000 Nigerien soldiers returning from the French military.[399] His fears were only heightened by the military coup in Togo in 1963 and a mutiny of soldiers in Niger in 1964, and they were made worse by the fact that the French had refused to intervene. After French forces were put in a difficult position during the August 1963 military coup in Congo, French officials had communicated to African governments that French troops could not be used to support their unpopular decisions or to take sides in disputes between the local government and the army. Further, French forces would in no case substitute for local forces and would only open fire according to the rules of the French military.[400] Ultimately, the French government maintained discretionary power over whether and how to intervene.

One important lesson learnt from Congo was that French technical assistants should not be responsible for maintaining order and should thus be withdrawn from command positions as soon as possible.[401] In Niger, French Ambassador Paul Fouchet expedited transfer of the command of the gendarmerie to a Nigerien officer, but noted that it would take until 1968 before the air force could be led by a Nigerien, as there were no qualified personnel.[402] It was clear to both French and US officials that this lack of experienced officers meant the Nigerien forces would continue require external technical assistance for an extended period of time. American observers attributed this situation to France's failure to educate colonial soldiers and criticized a French postcolonial policy they said was motivated by 'dreams of international prestige, of high commercial profit (largely at the expense of the French taxpayer and not somewhat of the common market) or of keeping alight the flame of French cultural influence.'[403]

---

399 Foreign Affairs Advisor, 'Compression militaires françaises' 9 October 1962.
400 Diplomacy Paris to French Embassies Abidjan, Fort-Lamy, Bangui, Dakar, Yaoundé, 'Communique Brazzaville', 23 August 1963, 184PO/1/325, CADC.
401 Ibid.
402 Fouchet, Ambassador to Niger, 'Question sur l'évolution de l'assistance technique militaire au Niger', 30 January 1964, INVA180, CADC.
403 US Embassy Niamey, 'The French presence in Niger', 23 April 1966, POL 1964–1966, Box 2514, CGRDS, NARA.

Training a new generation of officers increased the political ambitions of the military in Niger, and in 1969, the French Chief of Staff of Armed Forces grew doubtful as to whether Diori could trust his own forces. He recommended that the number of French troops be increased,[404] and the French ambassador agreed.[405] French officials were also concerned about rising mismanagement, tax evasion, and budget deficits in Niger, as direct budgetary allocations from France represented 36% of the Nigerien budget, which did not take into account French military assistance.[406] Niger only became strategically important to France once uranium production began near Arlit, where a reserve of 20,000 tons of uranium was first found in 1965. A company of both French and Nigerien ownership was established in 1967, and in 1971, the Nigerien state received over CFA 4 billion from sales of uranium (to France). These returns represented between 17% and 33% of the state budget, and the Nigerien government planned to use uranium profits to diversify the country's economy, which had previously been based on peanuts and pastoralism. The French, for whom the 750 tonnes of uranium produced by Niger in 1971 satisfied about half the country's consumption, expected Nigerien production to double by 1974, if transport, technical, and political challenges were solved.[407]

Other countries also grew interested in providing military assistance to Niger after uranium production began. The Nigerien government, bound by its agreement with France, had to refuse a West German proposal in 1966. In the 1960s, the Nigerien military wanted more equipment for its air force, France denied their request because of the extra costs a new plane would incur in technical assistance, maintenance, and training.[408] When Diori communicated to the French that he wished to renegotiate the military cooperation agreement, France agreed to provide four airplanes, and another in 1974. Still, Niger did obtain one aircraft from the US and

404 Air Force General Fourquet, 'Implantation à Niamey', 22 April 1969.

405 French Embassy Niamey to Ministry of Foreign Affairs, 'Problèmes de sécurité', 29 April 1969, 5AGF/2694, FFAN.

406 General Secretary for African and Malagasy Affairs, 'Audience du President Diori Hamani', 18 October 1969, 5AGF/598, FFAN.

407 Intelligence Exploitation Centre, 'L'exploitation du gisement d'uranium d'Arlit', 3 February 1970, GR 9Q5131, SHD; French Embassy Niamey, 'Dépenses de fonctionnement des forces armées nigériennes: Note pour secrétaire d'état', 9 September 1964.

408 Secretary of State for Foreign Affairs in charge of Cooperation, 'Note sur les forces armées nigérienne et l'assistance militaire technique au Niger', 13 November 1968, 5AGF/2694, FFAN.

five from West Germany in 1969 and 1970. The Germans also provided ten technical assistants, along with vehicles and construction materials.[409]

Most of the military equipment in Niger still came from France, and most of its soldiers were trained in France.[410] Nigerien soldiers interviewed for this study said that relations with French technical assistants had nevertheless been strained, as some still held on to a colonialist mentality. They had more positive memories of German military assistants, whom they considered more direct and effective than the French. One gendarme noted that Germany was also quick to react if anything was needed.[411] These soldiers regretted that cooperation with West Germany had ended when its assistants were withdrawn from Niger due to media reports about the brutal treatment of Tuaregs by Nigerien armed forces.[412] The traditional pastoralist livelihoods of Tuaregs had been disturbed by uranium mining activities, for which they had not been recompensed.[413] In fact, uranium production contributed little to the economic development of Niger in general, and the popular perception in the country is that France profited from Nigerien riches while the population was left with nothing. In 1996, the first World Bank Good Governance Index rated Niger as the most corrupt country in francophone West Africa after Guinea (see Figure 6), and in both countries, mineral rents benefitted the local political and military elite.

The value of uranium rose after the 1973 oil crisis, and Diori sought to renegotiate the selling price to France. French officials knew Diori was pragmatic enough to recognize that Niger could not harvest its uranium on its own, as the process requires considerable investment and technical knowhow, which France could provide.[414] Though negotiations stalled, an agreement was supposedly reached just before Chief of Staff of the Nigerien Armed Forces Seyni Kountché carried out a successful coup in April 1974.[415] The Nigerien military justified the coup as a remedy to the corruption of the government and its inability to provide relief to Nigeriens suffering the effects of severe drought and famine (see Chapters 3 and 5). There were

---

[409] Ministry of Cooperation, 'Domaine de l'assistance militaire', 18 September 1974.
[410] Ibid.
[411] Interview by author, June 2019, Niamey.
[412] Ibid.
[413] Anna Bednik, 'Bataille pour l'uranium au Niger', *Le Monde diplomatique*, June 2008, p. 16.
[414] General Secretariat for National Defence, Intelligence Division, to General Secretary of National Defence, 26 May 1974, GR9Q5131, SHD.
[415] Richard Higgott and Finn Fuglestad, 'The 1974 Coup d'État in Niger: Towards an Explanation', *Journal of Modern African Studies* 13, no. 3 (1975), pp. 383–98.

other motivating factors, including the ongoing presence of the French military, their opposition to a defence agreement with Libya, and soldiers wanting a share of the country's uranium profits.

Some thought France was behind the coup, as French troops had not intervened to keep Diori in power. France gained little in its aftermath as the military government requested the evacuation of French troops and uranium negotiations re-started.[416] Eventually, President Kountché reached a deal that allowed Niger to sell its share of the uranium to whoever it wished. While France continued to purchase the bulk of the production, and at a higher price, Niger is thought to have sold some to Libya, Pakistan, and Iraq as well. In the 1980s, however, when Niger faced difficulties in finding reliable customers, France reassumed its role in marketing and selling Niger's share.[417]

After the 1974 military coup, French military assistance to Niger was reduced, but its economic assistance continued. When Libya came to be seen as a threat to Niger in the 1980s, the US increased both its military and economic assistance.[418] This was maintained for over three decades, but Nigerien soldiers, students, and academics had a negative opinion of American and French military bases in the country and of the increased foreign military presence after the 2011 crisis in Libya. A common view was that foreign soldiers had not been deployed in the country to provide security for Nigeriens but to protect foreign economic interests and keep corrupt politicians in power.[419] This widespread perception is important in itself, whether true or not.

Conclusion

As this chapter illustrates, foreign actors did influence the building of national militaries in francophone West Africa by putting pressure on newly independent governments and providing resources that created opportunities for African presidents and elites. Nevertheless, external actors could not dictate defence policy in these countries, as seen in the very different decisions made by West African presidents in the postcolonial period. Guinean and Malian leaders refused to allow French military bases in their countries and opted for military assistance from communist states, while

---

416 Ministry of Cooperation, 'Domaine de l'assistance militaire', 18 September 1974.
417 Gabrielle Hecht, *Being Nuclear*, pp. 100–3.
418 Interview by author, June 2019, Niamey.
419 Ibid.

they received most of their economic aid from the capitalist West. The Cold War climate allowed Guinean president Sékou Touré to shift alliances from 'East' to 'West' depending on what each side had to offer at the time. Malian socialist president Modibo Keïta used a similar strategy. Though Upper Volta remained in the French sphere of influence, its government also refused to host a French military base, despite considerable pressure from France. By contrast, the first Ivorian, Nigerien, Senegalese, and Mauritanian presidents all insisted that French troops stay in their countries. In 1963, Ivorian president Houphouët-Boigny actually chose to disarm the Ivorian armed forces and establish party militias, despite France's objections. Nigerien president Diori purposefully weakened the national armed forces in Niger as well, relying on the French military presence for security. Léopold Senghor took an altogether different approach by welcoming French assistance and building Senegal's military capacities.

The varied strategies these leaders employed make it clear that France did not play a definitive role in their decision-making. However, these governments undeniably faced outside pressure regarding policy choices, and not only from France. Hence, French officials viewed it as their responsibility to 'protect' former French colonies from becoming pawns in Cold War struggles, even though this 'protection' came with the price of exclusive military cooperation with France. The French pressured the Ivorian president to reduce the role that Israel played in the defence of Côte d'Ivoire, for example, and to limit the role of militias.

In addition to presenting pressures and constraints, the Cold War environment and the ambitions of the former colonial power presented opportunities for both African presidents and soldiers. Even if the decisions of the Ivorian and Guinean presidents could not have been more opposite in many regards, their choices were motivated by a similar desire to mobilize as many resources as possible from the external environment. In Guinea, Touré exploited Cold War rivalries to receive aid from both sides, while in Côte d'Ivoire, Houphouët-Boigny used French fears of increasing American and Israeli influence to obtain more aid from France. The French military presence also allowed presidents such as Houphouët-Boigny to weaken their national armed forces if they considered national soldiers a threat to their regime. From the perspective of African presidents, one of the advantages of foreign technical assistance was that foreign experts were unlikely to plan a coup.

Military cooperation agreements with France may have limited the choice of francophone West African governments as to the equipment they received but it did grant them more aid than any other Western power alone could have provided. Free military equipment from France also made it possible for recipient governments to boost soldiers' morale by improving their service conditions and salaries. In countries with high numbers of returning colonial soldiers, this was particularly important, as officers released from the French army tended to pressure civilian governments to invest in their national militaries. This was a key factor in making decisions about defence in Senegal, Upper Volta, Guinea, and Mali. For instance, the Guinean and Malian governments seem to have calculated correctly that Senegal and Côte d'Ivoire would receive the most French assistance, and that France would be unable to provide sufficient resources with what was leftover in its budget to satisfy the needs of the high number of colonial soldiers returning to Guinea and Mali. As a result, they looked to the communist bloc for military aid.

It is important to note, however, that francophone West African governments had objectives that went beyond maximizing external assistance. For example, Touré sought to preserve his image as a pan-Africanist leader, which would have suffered had he been totally dependent on the Soviets. In Upper Volta, the rejection of a French military base was motivated by the nationalism of Voltaic politicians and their domestic constituency. The case of Upper Volta also demonstrated that strategies of extraversion were not available to all presidents nor did they provide the same benefits. Upper Volta lacked the strategic and economic importance that attracted significant foreign military assistance to its neighbours. This notwithstanding, the willingness of Western countries to provide military assistance diminished as corruption, mismanagement, the excessive use of force against civilians, and decreasing legitimacy plagued African governments across the region, although these concerns had less impact on the allocation of Soviet assistance.

3

Sovereignty: Strategies to Control Populations and Territories

Countries created as the result of decolonization clearly deviate from the notion that statehood is a matter of effectiveness, as their statehood has never depended on internal capacities but rather on the external recognition of their sovereignty.[1] International laws and foreign relations practices are based on traditional conceptions of states as organizations with the capacity to govern and control a specific territory and the population therein.[2] However, the capacity to govern and control a territory and population, and to implement and enforce decisions, depends largely on their administrative and coercive structures. At independence, many African governments inherited the administrative structures of its former colonial occupier, which tended to be minimal by design, being based on the premise that colonies should be fiscally self-sufficient.[3] This left these governments with weak capacities to manage and control their territories.[4] Hence, significant efforts were made, both national and international, to build administrative and coercive capacities in newly independent states.

This chapter analyses the decision-making of francophone West African governments as they developed state capacities to control their populations

---

[1] James Crawford, *The Creation of States in International Law* (Oxford: Clarendon Press, 2006), pp. 57–8, 60, 107–8, and 150; Robert H. Jackson, *Quasi-States: Sovereignty, International Relations, and the Third World* (Cambridge University Press, 1990).

[2] Montevideo Convention on Rights and Duties of States, Seventh International Conference of American States, 26 December 1933; Stephen D. Krasner, *Sovereignty: Organized Hypocrisy* (Princeton University Press, 1999), p. 229; Crawford, *The Creation of States*, p. 97.

[3] Young, *The African Colonial State in Comparative Perspective*, p. 97; Ewout Frankema and Marlous van Waijenburg, 'Metropolitan Blueprints of Colonial Taxation? Lessons from Fiscal Capacity Building in British and French Africa, c.1880–1940', *Journal of African History* 55, no. 3 (2014), pp. 317–400; Cooper, *Colonialism in Question*, p. 157; Chabal and Daloz, *Africa Works*, p. 12.

[4] Cooper, *Colonialism in Question*, p. 157; Chabal and Daloz, *Africa Works*, p. 12.

and territories and examines how the availability of human and material resources influenced their national military and administrative capacities. As colonial structures had created a basis for postcolonial state institutions, their impact on national armed forces was significant. In francophone West Africa, colonial legacies determined who became the first members of new national armies, where military installations were located, and how forces were armed.

One question that is central to this chapter is: When does it make sense for a government to use its economic and military resources to extend the presence of the state to areas that have no financial or political value? Tilly proposed that this makes sense when a government faces an external threat. He has linked the process of state formation in Europe to war-making, as administrative structures were needed to gather the resources that would increase the coercive capacities of the state.[5] Africa, however, did not undergo a similar process by which war-making augmented state administrative capacities. The administrations of newly independent African states were financed mostly through trade tariffs, as well as foreign assistance and credit.

The ability of these governments to access resources depended on their control over the capital city and any other main areas of economic activity, such as ports and cash crop-producing areas.[6] As a result, the foreign economic assistance that flowed into Africa after independence reduced the incentives for African presidents to extend their administrative reach of their states to include economically unimportant regions. State administrations were thus located in the few largest cities of a country and the political reliance of African governments on urban constituents meant they often neglected rural populations.[7] Significant resources are required to provide services and infrastructure to rural areas, and these governments often chose to focus their spending on capital cities in order to consolidate their main base of support.

The neglect of rural areas was especially evident in the postcolonial development of roads and railways. During colonial times, these areas had been neglected because infrastructure was designed to export raw materials to

---

5   Tilly, *Coercion, Capital and European States*, pp. 14–15 and 195–6.

6   Cooper, 'Possibility and Constraint', pp. 186–7 and *Africa Since 1940*, pp. 156–90; Clapham, *Africa and the International System*; Herbst, *States and Power in Africa*.

7   Cooper, 'Possibility and Constraint', pp.186–7 and *Africa Since 1940*, pp. 156–90; Bayart, *The State in Africa*, pp. 63–5; Robert Bates, *Essays on the Political Economy of Rural Africa* (Cambridge University Press, 1983), pp. 108–33.

ports, rather than to link cities.[8] However, as political scientist Jeffrey Herbst has noted, this lack of transport infrastructure served a potential political purpose for post-independence governments in Africa, as it decreased the likelihood that their opposition in the hinterlands could reach the capital. Neglect was only a viable option because political elites and their most important supporters faced no immediate external threats, which could have forced these governments to extend their control to areas further from the capital. In the absence of such threats, security provision was limited and did not reach economically unproductive or remote areas within their borders.[9]

This chapter seeks to explain the decisions of francophone West African governments regarding control over their territories by considering the resources, both external and internal, they had at their disposal. Historian Leigh Gardner has suggested that understanding the purpose for which a state exists requires examining its budget, as revenue (aid, debt, and taxes) and spending (on education, health, and the military) reflect the nature of a state.[10] The analysis will focus on the ways states acquired and allocated resources, and what this can tell us about postcolonial state-building and the role of the armed forces in this process. For example, this chapter considers whether the sources of a government's income influenced the strategies it used to develop state capacities. However, in postcolonial countries, state budgets often failed to fully reflect a government's economic or coercive resources, as so much was provided by foreign powers.

The main argument of this chapter is that government strategies to control populations, territories, and their armed forces hinged on the resources at their disposal. The wealthiest governments in francophone West Africa, which also received the greatest amount of economic assistance, chose to consolidate their power by providing opportunities, benefits, or services to their populations, either on an individual or collective basis. We will call this process cooptation and will refer to these governments as *coopting states*. This was a different strategy to the one applied by governments that received the greatest amount of military and security assistance yet remained poor. They used coercion, and the influence of ideology, to maintain power. These we will call *coercive states*. There were also governments with very few economic

---

8   Herbst, *States and Power in Africa*, pp. 36, 55–6, 72, and 93; Nugent, *Smugglers, Secessionists and Loyal Citizens on the Ghana-Togo Frontier* (Oxford: James Currey, 2002), pp. 77–113.

9   Herbst, *States and Power in Africa*, pp. 85, 170–3, 225, and 253–8.

10   Leigh Gardner, *Taxing Colonial Africa: The Political Economy of British Imperialism* (Oxford University Press, 2012).

or military resources. They often centralized power and resources to their capital city and they will be referred to as *centralized states*.

It must be noted that resources alone did not predetermine national decision-making, as internal and external threats, as well as the personal opinions of presidents, were also important factors. Nonetheless, based on similarities and differences in the strategies and resources of francophone West African governments, Côte d'Ivoire and Senegal can be examined as coopting states; Guinea and Mali as coercive states, and Niger and Upper Volta as centralized states. Côte d'Ivoire and Senegal each had a high gross domestic product (GDP) per capita and could thus use their local resources to coopt large parts of their populations. Both also had relatively good access to foreign credit and economic aid and were reasonably effective at taxing officially recorded economic activity. They relied primarily on the distribution of economic benefits to control their populations and militaries, although the Ivorian strategy was aimed more at coopting individuals whereas the approach of Senegal was more collective.

Notably, in both of these coopting states, military and security spending did not account for a particularly large share of the budget, partly due to French military assistance.[11] However, unlike Côte d'Ivoire, Senegal faced more internal pressure to build its national military capacities. At independence, a high number of Senegalese officers and non-commissioned officers were serving in the French military, and they lobbied for building a strong armed force in newly independent Senegal. The Ivorian regime was not under this pressure, as it reintegrated fewer colonial officers, the loyalty of whom it was able to ensure by providing them with promotions and administrative positions.

The coercive states of Guinea and Mali both had low GDPs, and their socialist economic policies offered limited resources with which to provide economic benefits to their populations. However, the military assistance these governments received from communist countries meant they had considerable coercive resources at their disposal, allowing them to control the population and the military. While the population density and agricultural potential of these two states differed, their socialist governments sought to extend party control to the countryside. They succeeded in taxing their populations and allocated a large part of their state budgets to their security and armed forces. Controlling these forces required ideological training, but the Guinean government did not shy away from using violence as well. The

---

11 Journaux officiels, Ivorian and Senegalese national archives.

first Malian government mostly avoided this, but it might have regretted it later, when Malian soldiers carried out a coup in 1968.

Niger and Upper Volta – countries we are calling centralized states – not only had low GDPs, but also had limited access to foreign aid and credit. This made it extremely difficult for them to extend control over their populations, territories, and militaries. The governments of both states chose to focus their resources on their largest city, as weak agricultural potential and low population density made it unprofitable to widen state control beyond this. These centralized states thus had minimal capacities to tax their populations, and because they obtained the bulk of their resources from their capitals and spent the most there as well, their governments became increasingly irrelevant to many of their citizens.

Coopting States: Côte d'Ivoire and Senegal

Compared to other francophone West African countries, Côte d'Ivoire and Senegal were able to draw from greater state resources in order to provide better benefits and services to their populations. Both governments also used a similar strategy of cooptation to control military actors, although they applied this in different ways to very different militaries. In both the civilian and military spheres, this cooptation was facilitated by the ability of their administrations to generate state resources through taxation, and to access foreign aid and credit.

The economics of coopting states

Their relative success in taxing economic activity set Côte d'Ivoire and Senegal apart from the rest of francophone West Africa. Both governments also accessed to foreign economic assistance and credit, although Senegal was generally more dependent on this aid than Côte d'Ivoire. In 1964, the amount of foreign assistance each country received as a percentage of their state budget peaked, accounting for almost one-third of the Ivorian budget and over three-quarters of the Senegalese budget.[12]

The most marked difference between the economies of Côte d'Ivoire and Senegal was the phenomenal rate of Ivorian growth until 1978 (see Figure 12). However, Ivorian state spending rose even faster, which made its economy vulnerable when the global price of cocoa, the country's main

[12] Ibid; data on foreign assistance and government expenditures from the World Bank DataBank. Available at http://databank.worldbank.org/data/home.aspx.

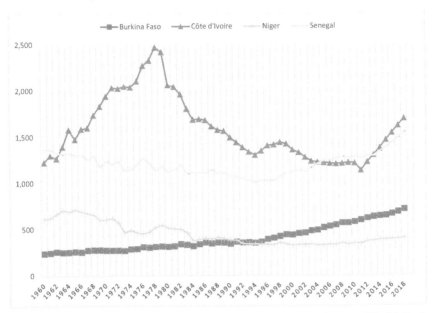

Figure 12. GDP PPP per capita constant, 1959–2017 (US$) (Source: World Bank DataBank, https://databank.worldbank.org/home.aspx, accessed 28.2.2020).

export, fell in the 1980s. Another difference between these countries had to do with their tax bases. In Côte d'Ivoire, taxes on trade generated a slightly larger share of state revenue (on average 53% from 1960 to 1974) than in Senegal (46%), and taxes on salaries and profits generated slightly less (17%) compared to Senegal (20%).[13] In recent years, the Ivorian government has continued to draw a significant part of its state budget from foreign trade. While cash crop agriculture directed to external markets is easier to tax, this relies on global prices and the willingness of rural populations to grow cacao and coffee. Côte d'Ivoire may thus be considered more of a gatekeeping country than Senegal, as the Ivorian government could extract greater resources from the flow of agricultural produce out of the country.

In both of these states, the successful taxation of economic activity has been facilitated by higher levels of urbanization. Between 1960 and 1974, the Ivorian urban population grew from 18% to 31% and the Senegalese from 23% to 33%. Today, about half the population in both countries lives in urban areas.[14] Côte d'Ivoire and Senegal can also be labelled as coopting

13 Journaux officiels, Ivorian and Senegalese national archives.
14 Data on urbanization from the World Bank DataBank.

states because this level of urbanization enabled their governments to tax and spend more than other francophone West African countries.

In the decades after independence, government spending was also reflected in the health of the Ivorian and Senegalese populations, for they had the highest life expectancy and lowest child mortality rates in the region. The percentage of health spending from GDP increased over time in both countries (see Figure 13) and, with the exception of Mauritania, was always higher than that of other francophone West African states. By contrast, the military spending of Côte d'Ivoire and Senegal – around 10% of the state budget in each – was lower, and from 1960 to 1974, both spent slightly more of their budget on education (14–16%) than the rest of francophone West Africa.

Côte d'Ivoire and Senegal also spent 8–9% of their budgets on health in the fifteen years after independence, although spending on health has reduced to 4% in Côte d'Ivoire and 7% in Senegal since 2000. Allocations to education continues to account for over 20% of their state budgets (and over 4% of GDP).[15] Even though the low literacy rates in both countries do not necessarily reflect this level of education spending, the continued capacity of these countries to provide services to their populations can be seen in the fact that, in 2017, Ivorians and Senegalese had the best access to clean water (81% and 73% of their populations, respectively), electricity (66% and 62%), and the internet (46% and 44%) in the region.[16] There is nevertheless a significant disparity between the access of urban and rural populations to electricity and water.[17]

The strategies of Côte d'Ivoire and Senegal cannot be explained by economic factors alone, as the availability of foreign assistance, the existence of external threats, and the attitude of their presidents also played key roles. While, these two coopting states adopted similar strategies to control their populations through the provision of services, opportunities, and benefits, their approaches to building their national militaries and security forces differed. For example, the Ivorian government was much less interested in increasing its national military capacities than Senegal, where a relative lack of private sector opportunities for returning colonial soldiers resulted in increased pressure to build a strong Senegalese armed force.

---

15 Journaux officiels, Ivorian and Senegalese national archives.
16 Data on access to water, internet, and electricity from the World Bank DataBank.
17 Ibid.

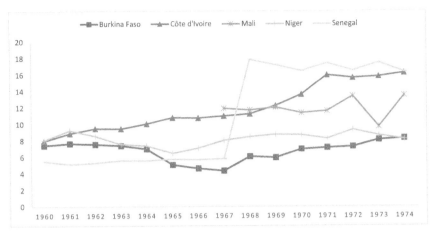

Figure 13. Government spending as a percentage of GDP, 1960–1974 (Source: World Bank DataBank, https://databank.worldbank.org/home.aspx, accessed 28.2.2020).

Individual and collective cooptation of military actors in Côte d'Ivoire and Senegal

In 1961, President Houphouët-Boigny told lawmakers in Côte d'Ivoire that 'everyone knows the dominant element of the politics of our country is peace, peace within, peace without. Above all, we want peace among all Africans.' He pledged that if peace in Africa was realized, Ivorians would 'be the first to give up maintaining a ruinous army, in order to devote almost all of our modest budget to the economic and social development of the country.' However, he did note that 'in the event that we are victims of an aggression, we have concluded a defence agreement with France which allows the latter to lend us its support.'[18]

In this regard, two factors made Côte d'Ivoire reliant. First, as few experienced soldiers had transferred into the national military at independence, the Ivorian forces needed extensive French assistance over a prolonged period.[19] Second, Houphouët-Boigny had a negative view of the military negatively (which he made no secret about), as he had prioritized economic

---

18 President Houphouët-Boigny, Message to Parliament, 3 August 1961, 324QONT/9, CADC.
19 Brebisson, 'Rapport de fin de commandement du général commandement (16 fevrier 1960–30 juin 1962)', 30 June 1962, GR5H28, SHD.

development, to which he felt the armed forces contributed little.[20] His strategy, and these priorities, brought initial success as Ivorian cash crop production grew between 1960 and 1974, partly due to foreign investment.[21] Africans from neighbouring countries began immigrating to Côte d'Ivoire in search of a better life, and the population thus increased by 58% over the first ten years of Ivorian independence.

Being the wealthiest West African country, Côte d'Ivoire was in the best position to develop a national military. Even the 10% of the Ivorian state budget directed to the military amounted to more, in monetary terms, than allocations to militaries across the region.[22] Ivorian defence decisions were, however, shaped by a lack of external threats and paranoia about internal threats.[23] Military coups in neighbouring countries made Houphouët-Boigny wary of Ivorian officers and reluctant to develop Ivorian military capacity. The coup in Togo in 1963 thus spurred the Ivorian president to temporarily disarm his forces, create a party militia system as a counterforce, and increasingly rely on the French for defence.[24]

Houphouët-Boigny presented his desire to limit the role of the national military as a cost-cutting measure, but this was hardly his main motivation. He envisioned that the Ivorian military could engage in the country's economic development through a civic service model in which soldiers

20 Raphaël-Leygues to Ministry of Foreign Affairs, 'Situation intérieure', 17 December 1968, 1PO/1/1, CADN; Colonel Mathieu, Military Advisor, French Embassy Abidjan, 'Rapport de fin de mission', 16 December 1968, GR14S254, SHD.

21 Data on Ivorian GDP and GDP growth, 1960–1974, from the World Bank DataBank.

22 Data on military spending in local currency from the World Bank DataBank.

23 Telegram, French Embassy Abidjan to Directorate of African and Malagasy Affairs, 27 February 1964; French Embassy Abidjan, 'Problèmes militaires', 15 November 1961, 1PO/1/1, CADN; Raphaël-Leygues to Ministry of Foreign Affairs, 'Situation intérieure', 17 December 1968.

24 Raphaël-Leygues to Ministry of Foreign Affairs, 'Politique militaire en zone d'outre-mer no.4', 26 December 1963; Delegation for the Defence of Overseas Zone 4, 'Note à l'attention de M. Ambassadeur de la France', 13 December 1963, 5AGF/2661, FFAN; Presidency of the Republic, 'Réunion outre-mer a l'état-major des armées du 20 octobre, 20 October 1966, 5AGF/1806, FFAN; Ministry of Foreign Affairs to Minister of Armed Forces, 'Maintien d'un escadron à Port Bouet', 10 February 1966, 5AGF/1806, FFAN; Perrier, Technical Advisor, Intelligence Exploitation Centre, Section B, 'Attitude du ministre ivoirien des forces armées', 1 March 1966; Directorate of African and Malagasy Affairs, 'République de Côte d'Ivoire', 3 July 1963, 324QONT/9, CADC; Telegram, French Embassy Abidjan to Directorate of African and Malagasy Affairs, 27 February 1964; Brasseur to Directorate of African and Malagasy Affairs, 'Crise politique en Côte d'Ivoire', 23 January 1963; Mathieu, 'Rapport de fin de mission', 16 December 1968.

would train Ivorian youth in agricultural techniques. This came to fruition in the early 1960s,[25] but was met by the disapproval of French officials, who said the programme diverted resources from 'integral tasks' of the armed forces. These officials argued that non-military tasks were likely to reduce Ivorian capacities, which were considered weak from the outset.[26] Frustrated that the significant material and personnel assistance provided by France had not led to the development of a better Ivorian military, which they felt was undermined by the decisions of political leaders, French officials had low expectations of Ivorian forces. Throughout the early 1960s, they noted that the Ivorians were unable to respond to external attacks and could only carry out police operations if the opposing side was neither well-organized nor well-armed.[27]

Conversely, the Senegalese military was described as the best force in francophone Africa.[28] Senegal had the longest colonial history and the most sizeable French presence, as Dakar had been the administrative capital of French West Africa (FWA). Hence, during the colonial period, more soldiers – and more French soldiers – were located in Senegal than anywhere else in Africa. In fact, in 1954, there were 24 soldiers for every 10,000 people in Senegal. This rate dropped in newly independent Senegal but increased to 20 soldiers per 10,000 people by 1974.

25 Jacob, 'Israel's Military Aid to Africa, 1960–66', pp. 165–187; Levey, 'Israel's Strategy in Africa, 1961–67', pp. 71–87; Chargé d'affaires, French Embassy Abidjan, to Ministry of Foreign Affairs, 'Situation politique du 21 au 17 juillet 1962', 28 July 1962; French Embassy Abidjan, 'Problèmes militaires', 15 November 1961.

26 Ambassador of France in Côte d'Ivoire to Minister of Foreign Affairs, 'Situation politique du 30 juin au 6 juillet 1962', 7 July 1962, 324QONT/2, CADC; Telegram, Abidjan to Paris, 12 July 1963, 324QONT/10, CADC; French Embassy Abidjan, 'Problèmes militaires' 15 November 1961; Directorate of African and Malagasy Affairs, 'Etudes de comportement des armées nationales en 1963', 1PO/1/16, CADN; French Embassy Abidjan, 'Rapport concernant Monsieur Banny Jean, Ministre de la Défense de Côte d'Ivoire', 15 November 1961, 1PO/1/1, CADN.

27 Brasseur to Minister of Cooperation, 'Organisation de l'armée ivoirienne et l'assistance militaire technique', 8 February 1963, 5AGF/2661, FFAN; Military Advisor, French Embassy Abidjan, 'Rapport annuel pour 1965', 7 December 1965; Colonel Courtiade, Military Advisor, 'Rapport de fin de mission', 5 July 1971 GR14S254, SHD; Telegram, Raphaël-Leygues to Directorate of African and Malagasy Affairs, 13 December 1963; Directorate of African and Malagasy Affairs, 'Etudes de comportement des armées nationales en 1963'; French Embassy Abidjan, 'Problèmes militaires', 15 November 1961.

28 General Secretary for African and Malagasy Affairs, 'Audience de monsieur Leopold Senghor' 16 December 1969.

The high number of soldiers in Senegal led to the Senegalese population actively participating in the development of the military. Moreover, it meant that Senegalese authorities were in a good position to control the territory and the population. The situation was different in Côte d'Ivoire, where the number of soldiers as a percentage of the population was nearly half that of Senegal (see Figure 14).

In 1961, when the development of the Ivorian armed forces began, the first soldiers were split among the three garrisons left empty after the withdrawal of French troops in Abidjan, Bouaké, and Man. By the end of that year, the force consisted of some 1,000 colonial soldiers, along with 2,500 new recruits.[29] The country was divided into three military regions, headquartered in Abidjan, Bouaké, and Daloa.[30] Troops were also stationed in Man, Séguéla, and Odienné, and were concentrated in the western part of the country, near the Guinean border.[31] Four legions of gendarmes were based in Abidjan, Bouaké, Daloa, and Korhogo, and mobile companies of the gendarmerie were posted in Odienné, Man, Séguéla, Dimbokro, Bingerville, and Aboisso.[32] During most of the 1960s, the Ivorian armed forces numbered just over 5,200, including the gendarmerie. By 1974, force manpower in Côte d'Ivoire had risen to 6,600, more than twice the number in Upper Volta,[33] but less than the nearly 7,000 soldiers and 2,000 gendarmes that comprised the Senegalese forces (see Table 4).

The number of gendarmes and police in Côte d'Ivoire was much higher than in other francophone West African countries due to the Ivorian government's focus on internal security.[34] Prior to independence in May 1960, the Ivorian gendarmerie had numbered only 610, but it grew after

---

29   Brebisson, Supreme Commander of Overseas Zone No. 1, to Land Forces Chief of Staff, 'Rapport annuel 1961', GR5H27, SHD; Duvauchelle, Chargè d'Affaires of France, to Minister of Cooperation, 'Note du Commandant Fusier concernant l'organisation et les effectifs de l'armée de terre ivoirienne', 2 June 1962, 1PO/1/16, CADN.

30   Raphaël-Leygues, 'La Côte d'Ivoire et l'Armée', 30 August 1974.

31   Colonel François, Military Advisor, French Embassy Abidjan, 'Rapport de fin de mission', 5 September 1966, GR14S254, SHD; Military Advisor, French Embassy Abidjan, 'Rapport mensuel mars 1966', 6 April 1966, GR14S251, SHD.

32   General Secretariat for National Defence, 'Evolution récente et problèmes de la Côte d'Ivoire', 22 June 1970, 5AGF/2717, FFAN; Colonel François, 'Rapport de fin de mission', 5 September 1966.

33   Military advisor, French Embassy Ougadougou, 'Rapport annuel du juin 1973–15 juin 1974', 15 June 1974, GR14S263, SHD.

34   Colonel Revol, Ministry of Foreign Affairs, 'Visite de Monsieur Houphouët-Boigny et problèmes Ivoiriennes en matière de sécurité et défense', 16 May 1960, 324QONT/8, CADC.

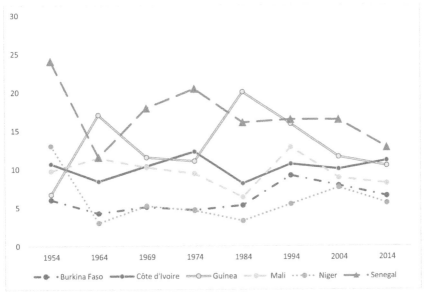

Figure 14. Soldiers per 10,000 people in francophone West Africa, 1954–2014 (Sources: 1954–1984: AAOF, SHD, ADN, CADC; from 1984: World Bank DataBank, https://databank.worldbank.org/home.aspx, accessed 28.2.2020; Population statistics: Affaires militaires, Rapports de recrutement: 4D1, 4D2, 4D3, 4D8, 4D9, 4D11, 4D12, 4D15, 4D16, 49D, Archives d'Afrique Occidentale Française, Dakar, Sénégal (AAOF). The Frankema-Jerven African Population Database 1850–1960, version 1.0; published in Frankema, E. and M. Jerven (2014), 'Writing History Backwards and Sideways: Towards a Consensus on African Population, 1850–present', *Economic History Review* 67, S1, pp. 907–31, available at: https://www.aehnetwork.org/data-research/.).

independence, doubling to 1,214 by 1964, and doubling again to 2,446 by 1974 – almost four times the number of gendarmes in Upper Volta.[35] In Côte d'Ivoire, these forces represented 16% of the security apparatus, reflecting Houphouët-Boigny's calculations that the internal opposition posed the most immediate threat and that France would protect the country against external enemies. Accordingly, the Ivorian gendarmerie took the key role in responding to internal disturbances, including ethnically motivated protests in the Gagnoa and Aboisso regions and student protests in Abidjan (see Chapter 5).

35 Military advisor, French Embassy Ougadougou, 'Rapport annuel du juin 1973–15 juin 1974', 15 June 1974.

Table 4. Manpower in the security and armed forces in francophone West Africa, 1961–1975.

	1961	1962	1963	1964	1965	1966	1967	1968	1969	1970	1971	1972	1973	1974	1975
Benin															
army			856	1,298	1,456	1,521	1,813	912	1,126	1,196	1,450	1,150	1,141	1,150	
air force			12	16	40			34	32	34	45	32	36	40	
navy				89											
police				565					600	667			613		
Upper Volta															
army	770	800	960	1,199	1,503	1,578	1,931	2,062	2,062	2,100	2,237	2,056	2,019	2,084	
air force					1	12	33	33	33		49	52	76	82	
gendarmerie	364	479	554	667	661	759	714	712	722	700	690	743	662	620	661
republican guard			992		1072						1822	1841			
police					236										
Côte d'Ivoire															
army	3,600	3,400	3,500	3,500	2,696	3,294	3,260	3,207	3,171	3,321	3,331	3,007	3,409	3,498	
air force					57	153	112	153	146	157	155	166	169	200	
navy	74			85	128	127	128	125	140	134	133	184	195	192	200
gendarmerie	1,400	1,450	1,318	1,418	1,239	1,697	1,754	1,758	1,766	2,169	2,100	2,361	2,566	2,750	2,746
milice			3500			999	875	879			906	890	909	1000	
police								1803							

	1961	1962	1963	1964	1965	1966	1967	1968	1969	1970	1971	1972	1973	1974	1975
Niger															
army	651	788	823	860	1,865	2,283		1,900	1,779	1,800		1,988	1,891	1,721	1729
air force	40	40	14	27	27	47		70	65				77	60	77
gendarmerie	191	242	274	250	301	401	436	450	450	450	473	512	527	550	527
republican guard			950	1,000	1,000	1,000		1,100				1,200			1,260
presidential guard					100	100		150							
police						800		800							
milice				50		1500									
Senegal															
army	3,000		4,230	2,502	5,147	4,739	5,159	5,200	5,690	5,720	5,865	5,784		6,328	7,000
air force			70	168	168	149	168	180	159	160				145	500
navy			11	109	109	116	160	170	141	160				242	320
gendarmerie		1,070	1,115	1,356	866	1,193	1,312	1,400	1,427	1,420	1,407	1,504		1,792	2,000
republican guard		1545		1536	1536			1200							
police		1070		2023	2023			2600							

Table 4 *continued*

	1961	1962	1963	1964	1965	1966	1967	1968	1969	1970	1971	1972	1973	1974	1975
Togo															
army			1,400	560		846	846		944	2100		2500	2500	2,300	
air force						24	14		11	20				30	
gendarmerie			550	231	958	583	570	570	588	600		700	700	710	
republican guard		730							350	300					
police		260							350	360				664	
Mauritania															
army	1,051	1,051	1,118			1,255	1,287		1,329	1,330		1,200		1,300	
air force	14	14	60		13	17	26		24	25		25	100	100	
navy	35	35				31	26		56	60		100	100		
gendarmerie	251	241	553		296	307	321		314	300		450		450	
republican guard			300			843	889					930		950	
police						145	177					200			
Mali															
army	1,658	2,500	3,800		3,000	3,250	3,310	3,200	3,200	3,200	3,000	4,000	4,500	4,500	7,500
air force								102	60	80	80	100	103	103	
gendarmerie		650	650		1,400	1,420	1,420	1,400	1,400	1,400	1,420	2,000	1,500	1,500	

	1961	1962	1963	1964	1965	1966	1967	1968	1969	1970	1971	1972	1973	1974	1975
republican guard		1,900	1,900		1,935	1,942	1,942	2,500	2,000	2,000	1,000	1,000	2,000	2,000	
police		3,150	500	600	493	882	914	1,000	700	700	2000	1000	1000	1000	
milice		3,000	3,500	4,000		4,000		5,000							
Guinea															
army	3,500	3,500								4,500	4,600				
air force									100						
gendarmerie	500	3,000	900							2,500					
milice								5,000		8,000					34,000

Sources: ADN, CADC, SHD.

French estimates of the capacities of the Ivorian gendarmerie were frequently more positive than those of the Ivorian army.[36] The French likewise described the Senegalese gendarmerie as the best trained and most disciplined of Senegal's security institutions.[37] Until the mid–1960s, the resources allocated to the military and gendarmerie in the two countries were similar, but as Senegalese numbers remained steady, the Ivorians reduced the relative share of defence spending allocated to the army and redirected some to party militias (see Table 5). One might assume that because these militias were established to provide a counterforce to the military and deter potential military coups, they would be better armed and better paid than the rest of the Ivorian armed forces, but the personnel costs per militia member were actually lower than those for gendarmes or soldiers.[38] Although French reports in 1963 mention that the equipment for Ivorian militias was initially taken from the army,[39] there is no indication that this practice continued.

Despite their opposition to the establishment of party militias, French officials were not of the opinion that the militias had the same divisive and corrosive effect on the armed forces in Côte d'Ivoire as they had in Guinea. This may be because the tasks of Ivorian militias diverged from those of the military, as they were restricted to providing security for the political elite. Furthermore, after their initial establishment, their size was reduced from 3,500 to less than 1,000 individuals (see Table 4), and they were enjoined to the Presidential Guard, which only operated in Abidjan and Yamoussoukro.[40]

36 French Embassy Abidjan, 'Problèmes militaires' 15 November 1961.
37 General Secretary for African and Malagasy Affairs, 'Les forces armées togolaises', 1 September 1967, 5AGF/619, FFAN.
38 Military advisor, French Embassy Abidjan, 'Rapport mensuel mars 1966' 6 April 1966; Colonel Mathieu, 'Rapport de fin de mission', 16 December 1968; Military advisor, 'Rapport annuel 1969', 22 December 1969, GR14S252, SHD; Military advisor, French Embassy Abidjan, 'Rapport mensuel mois de fevrier 1971', 6 March 1971, GR14S252, SHD; Colonel Aron, Military advisor, 'Rapport fin de mission', 25 June 1974, GR14S254, SHD.
39 Raphaël-Leygues, 'Retour du Président Houphouët-Boigny en Côte d'Ivoire', 28 August 1963, 1PO/1/14, CADN; French Embassy Abidjan, 'Extrait du bulletin de renseignements hebdomadaires 19–25 August 1963', 1PO/1/14, CADN; Directorate of African and Malagasy Affairs, 'Situation politique en Côte d'Ivoire', 29 August 1963.
40 French Embassy Abidjan, 'Extrait du bulletin de renseignements hebdomadaires 19–25 August 1963'; Directorate of African and Malagasy Affairs, 'Situation politique en Côte d'Ivoire' 29 August 1963; Mathieu, 'Rapport de fin de mission', 16 December

Military spending in Côte d'Ivoire and Senegal differed from that of governments in the rest of the francophone West Africa, in that both countries spent more on equipment and less on salaries. The share allocated to personnel costs in the Ivorian and Senegalese gendarmerie was greater than in their armies, as the average salaries and benefits for gendarmes were higher because most of them held permanent positions and made frequent circuits around the country. The equipment used by gendarmerie was also less expensive than that used by military forces.[41] In Côte d'Ivoire, however, the average spending on personnel costs was higher in both army and gendarmerie budgets. In Senegal, these rates were lower (see Table 6), which allowed the government to spend a higher percentage of its budget on equipment and meant that Senegalese forces were likely to be better equipped than their Ivorian colleagues.

Spending on military equipment alone does not tell the full story of how well these troops were equipped, as France provided most of it free of charge. The Ivorian armed forces received an initial transfer of equipment from France in April 1962 (mainly weapons, munitions, vehicles, and transmission and construction equipment).[42] Despite further requests for equipment needed by the Ivorian navy and air force, the latter of which was comprised entirely of French pilots until 1969,[43] France at first declined.[44] After the end of the war in Algeria, and France reduced its presence in Africa in 1964

1968; Colonel Courtiade, 'Rapport de fin de mission' 5 July 1971; Colonel Aron, 'Rapport de fin de mission', 25 June 1974.

41   Mathieu, Military advisor, French Embassy Abidjan, 'Rapport mensuel de janvier 1968', February 1968, GR14S252, SHD; Military advisor, 'Rapport annuel 1969', 22 December 1969; Military advisor, 'Rapport annuel année 1970', 26 January 1971, GR14S252, SHD; Courtiade, 'Rapport de fin de mission', 5 July 1971; Aron, 'Rapport fin de Mission', 25 June 1974; Miliary advisor, French Embassy Abidjan, 'Rapport mensuel mois de fevrier 1971', 6 March 1971; French Embassy Abidjan, 'Rapport annuel mois de janvier 1972', 7 February 1972, GR14S253, SHD.

42   Ministry of Armed Forces, 'Mission d'inspection en ZOM no 4 1962', GR9H470, SHD.

43   Letter to Félix Houphouët-Boigny from Foccart, 4 July 1969, 5AGF/2717, FFAN; Letter from Foccart to Félix Houphouët-Boigny, 27 August 1969, 5AGF/2717, FFAN; Raphaël-Leygues to Minister of Cooperation, 'Personnel de l'armée de l'air pour deux hélicoptères Alouette III', 8 October 1964; Raphaël-Leygues to Minister of Cooperation, 'Moyens aériens de la Côte d'Ivoire', 30 June 1964, 5AGF/2661, FFAN; Military advisor, French Embassy Abidjan, 'Rapport mensuel mois de décembre 1965', 5 January 1966, GR14S251, SHD; Colonel Wursten, Military advisor, French Embassy Abidjan, 'Rapport de fin de mission', 9 June 1965, GR14S254, SHD.

44   See documents in File 5AGF/2661, FFAN and File GR11S382, SHD.

Table 5. Allocation of military spending: the army and gendarmerie, 1962–1974.

	1962	1963	1964	1965	1966	1967	1968	1969	1970	1971	1972	1973	1974
Côte d'Ivoire													
army	69%		0%	62%	63%		33%	31%	33%	32%	34%	33%	32%
gendarmerie	31%		0%	28%	27%		25%	26%	27%	27%	28%	30%	30%
militia			6%	8%	7%	6%	6%	6%	7%	6%	7%	6%	6%
Burkina Faso													
army	54%	55%	56%	47%		53%	65%			67%	68%	68%	67%
gendarmerie	37%	35%	37%	34%		34%	35%		33%	33%	32%	32%	33%
Benin													
army			48%	52%		47%	41%						
gendarmerie			52%	48%									
Mali													
army				73%	73%		50%	48%	78%		62%	78%	77%
gendarmerie				23%	23%		15%	16%	22%		18%	22%	23%
Senegal													
army		67%	69%	64%	64%			69%	69%	62%	61%	61%	63%
gendarmerie		27%	25%	25%	24%			21%	21%	28%	29%	29%	27%
Niger													
army					40%	61%	63%	63%			59%	56%	57%
gendarmerie					16%	26%	26%	26%			26%	27%	29%

Table 5 *continued*

	1962	1963	1964	1965	1966	1967	1968	1969	1970	1971	1972	1973	1974
Mauritania													
army	47%	72%	75%	78%	76%	76%	66%	72%	72%	71%	70%	69%	69%
gendarmerie	53%	28%	25%	22%	24%	23%	32%	26%	26%	27%	29%	30%	29%

Sources: ADN, CADC, SHD.

Table 6. Personnel cost in armed and security forces.

	1961	1962	1963	1964	1965	1966	1967	1968	1969	1970	1971	1972	1973	1974	**Average**
Army															
Benin						85%				68%	74%		82%	80%		78%
Côte d'Ivoire									78%	79%	69%	71%	68%			73%
Mali						77%	74%	65%	75%	76%	65%	68%	66%	64%	65%	70%
Mauritania			39%	46%	63%	64%	63%	65%	95%	66%	68%	69%	65%	61%	52%	63%
Niger							49%	47%	48%	49%			53%	58%	59%	52%
Senegal		51%	53%	54%	53%	62%	61%			53%	53%	59%	58%	55%	56%	56%
Upper Volta			64%	83%	76%	91%			87%			88%	88%	89%	83%	83%

Table 6 *continued*

	1961	1962	1963	1964	1965	1966	1967	1968	1969	1970	1971	1972	1973	1974	Average
Gendarmerie															
Benin					87%				84%	86%		83%	83%		85%
Côte d'Ivoire								92%	92%	90%	92%	86%			90%
Mali								87%	85%	82%	83%	79%	82%	84%	83%
Mauritania		79%	78%	79%	79%	77%	80%	80%	79%	79%	78%	79%	74%	72%	78%
Niger				77%	76%	72%	73%	72%	76%			80%	79%	74%	75%
Senegal			79%	77%	76%	77%					73%	73%	74%	71%	75%
Upper Volta		82%	87%	94%	95%			92%			92%	92%	93%	94%	91%
Republican guard															
Mali		92%	92%	93%	90%	89%	89%				93%	93%	93%	93%	93%
Mauritania								90%	89%	90%	90%	91%	86%	80%	89%
Niger						89%	88%	88%	88%	90%		88%	88%	89%	89%
Police															
Mali police								84%	84%	87%	87%	87%	87%	87%	87%
Mauritania police		71%	59%	69%	68%	79%	81%	82%	84%	83%	88%	85%	82%	77%	77%
Niger police						89%	87%	87%	87%			85%	83%	86%	86%
Military															
Guinea	80%						85%	86%	89%						85%

Sources: ADN, CADC, SHD.

and in 1965, equipment was transferred to the Ivorian navy and air force. By 1965, the air force had two C47 planes and four Alouette helicopters at its disposal, and by 1971, it had acquired 6 Cessnas and a fifth Alouette.[45] According to French reports, Côte d'Ivoire received FF 107 million of military aid between 1960 and 1970, of which 25% was in the form of military equipment. Only Madagascar and Senegal received more military aid from France.[46] Nevertheless, in 1970, the Ivorian president complained to Jacques Foccart that Côte d'Ivoire was not receiving the same amount of military assistance as other former French colonies.[47]

As Côte d'Ivoire's economic growth meant that it was able to buy French equipment, rather than receive it as part of its free military assistance package, Ivorian officials chose to receive the bulk of French aid in the form of technical assistance. The number of French assistants in the country was justified by the need to develop Ivorian capacities, but as this French assistance was not directed wholly towards building those capacities, but actually substituted for them in some cases, it did have unavoidably negative effects. Compared to other former French colonies, there were a considerable number of French technical assistants in Côte d'Ivoire, both military and civil; in 1966 only Madagascar received more technical assistance.[48] When the Ivorian president requested more assistants in 1965, the French were hesitant to respond positively, as there were already 1,550 in the country.[49]

French assistants were especially plentiful in the command of the Ivorian armed forces and made up a large proportion of officers. Even when important positions were transferred to Ivorians, French officers often remained as advisors.[50] For Houphouët-Boigny, the Ivorization of the state administration in general, and the armed forces in particular, was never a priority. When the army was first established in 1961, the number of French officers (fifty) was more than twice the number of Ivorian officers

---

45 Couetdic, 'Note sur les forces armées ivoiriennes et sur notre assistance technique en Côte d'ivoire', 17 March 1970, and 'Note sur les forces armées ivoiriennes et sur notre assistance technique en Côte d'Ivoire', 9 December 1971.

46 General Secretariat for African and Malagasy Affairs, 'Note à l'attention de monsieur le secrétaire général: aide militaire à la Côte d'Ivoire', June 1970, 5AGF/2717, FFAN.

47 Foccart, 'Note à l'attention du Colonel Maldan', 12 June 1970, 5AGF/2717, FFAN.

48 French Embassy Abidjan, 'Evolution des effectifs et aspects qualitatifs de la coopération technique en Côte d'Ivoire et coût de l'assistance technique', 9 November 1966.

49 'Président Houphouët-Boigny audience par général de Gaulle samedi 26 juin 1965,' 5AGF1783, FFAN.

50 Ambassador of France in Côte d'Ivoire to Ministry of Foreign Affairs, 'Situation politique du 30 juin au 6 juillet 1962', 7 July 1962, 324QONT/I2, CADC.

(eighteen).[51] In the ensuing years, the number of French military assistants in Côte d'Ivoire multiplied, more than doubling between 1962 and 1963, for example (see Table 7). By 1965, their number had dropped slightly, but there were still 131 French technical assistants in the army, seventy-eight in the gendarmerie, thirty-two in the air forces, and thirteen in the navy. In 1968 – when 16% of the officers in the Ivorian gendarmerie and 25% of those in the army were French – a French military attaché emphasized that these assistants remained crucial, as they had 'prevented the Ivorian army from sinking into disorganisation, chaos and mismanagement.'[52]

In Senegal, the number of French technical assistants fell much faster than in Côte d'Ivoire. As Ivorians were requesting additional assistants, their number in Senegal was cut in half from 1963 to 1964. Ten years later, in 1974, only thirty-nine French assistants remained in Senegal, less than one-third the number in Côte d'Ivoire. That year, only 3% of the officers in the Senegalese army were French, compared to 32% of the officers in the Ivorian army.[53] These numbers clearly reflect the choice of the Ivorian president to rely heavily on a French military presence. However, the significant role of the French and a resulting lack of career opportunities for Ivorian soldiers fostered dissatisfaction among Ivorian troops.

The Senegalese government's decision to Africanize its military made for easier relations between French assistants and Senegalese soldiers. Indeed, members of the Senegalese military who were interviewed for this study mostly had positive experiences working with French technical assistants. They noted that it had been essential for these assistants to learn a few words of Wolof, with one officer sharing the example of a French assistant who had learned to say 'I want it done this way' in the local language. These soldiers also viewed the sporting activities that brought the French and Senegalese together as a way of maintaining friendly relations.[54]

In Côte d'Ivoire, Houphouët-Boigny was unwilling to decrease the number of French assistants, but sought ways to provide advancement opportunities for Ivorian soldiers. As a consequence, the proportion of officers to soldiers in the Ivorian forces was higher than in other francophone West African countries (though only slightly higher than in Senegal). This changed after an attempted military coup in 1973, when the pace of

51 Brebisson, 'Rapport annuel 1961'.
52 Mathieu, 'Rapport de fin de mission', 16 December 1968. Also see Military advisor, French Embassy Abidjan, 'Rapport annuel pour 1965', 7 December 1965.
53 Ministry of Cooperation, 'Domaine de l'assistance militaire', 18 September 1974.
54 Interviews by author, July 2019, Dakar.

Table 7. French technical assistants in the military in francophone West Africa, 1961–1975.

	1961	1962	1963	1964	1965	1966	1967	1968	1969	1970	1971	1972	1973	1974	1975
military															
Benin			42	47	48	52	34		51	35	34	33	33	24	21
Upper Volta	111	88		69	52	47	36	32	40	33	31	32	29	27	13
Côte d'Ivoire	149	141	304	303	254	181	162	138	114	107	116	111	94	140	108
Niger	381		90	144	127	118		95	33	91	78	79	73	70	66
Senegal			230	112	136	128	131	94	102	77	53	51	44	39	39
Mauritania	206	209			152	141	104		57	82	67	61	7		
Togo			25	35	31	33	40	29	25	22	29	26	29	30	41
army															
Benin				16	16	21			17	12	13	13	14	11	6
Upper Volta	49	57		45	35	34	28	25	22		19	19	17	15	8
Côte d'Ivoire	149		135	176	131	102	94	68	54	49	53	54	41	100	31
Niger	104	104	95	71	70	64					43	43	39	34	31
Senegal			230		85	76	70		48						
Mauritania	206	209			110	94	72			44	30	29	3		
Togo				17	11	13	15			25	9	9	10	10	16
gendarmerie															
Benin			26	21	11	11			7	7	10	7	7	5	6
Upper Volta	62	31	11	17	9	3					1	1	1	2	0

Table 7 *continued*

	1961	1962	1963	1964	1965	1966	1967	1968	1969	1970	1971	1972	1973	1974	1975
Côte d'Ivoire	141		119	85	78	38	28	28	23	22	27	25	25	15	25
Niger		61	55	32	37	34		26			18	17	17	18	17
Senegal			68	59	17	13	13		13		10	10	11	15	15
Mauritania	65	65			23	27	15				12	11	3		
Togo			25	17	54	12	12		8		10	9	7	8	7
air force															
Benin				10	14	15		13	13		10	10	9	5	7
Upper Volta				7	8	10	8	7	8	9	9	10	10	10	11
Côte d'Ivoire			26	27	32	29	29	32	28	27	27	25	23	22	21
Niger	8		9	11	13	14	14				10	10	7	10	10
Senegal			21	16	16	15	15	14			9	9	7	4	3
Mauritania			60		11	9	6			9	7	6	0		
Togo				3	3	3	3			5	6	5	8	9	14
navy															
Côte d'Ivoire			24	15	13	12	11	10	9	9	9	7	5	3	
Mauritania				0	0	6	9		13	13	12	10	0		
Senegal		18	18	5	9	8	5	4	2	2	2	2	2	4	4

Sources: SHD, ADN, CADC.

Ivorization in the military slowed and twenty-two of the most capable Ivorian officers were given roles in civil administration.[55] Nevertheless, some French technical assistants in important positions were replaced by Ivorians, and Chief of Staff Thomas d'Aquin Ouattara was replaced by General Coulibaly, whom the French considered more capable and more popular with the troops. The fact that Houphouët-Boigny had kept d'Aquin as chief of staff until 1974, despite his unpopularity and perceived incompetence, demonstrated the Ivorian president's desire to ensure his armed forces were kept weak.[56]

French officials noted that after Coulibaly returned from training in France, he no longer automatically acquiesced to d'Aquin.[57] This reflected the challenges that arose in the Ivorian military as a result of the different experiences of younger and older officers. Younger officers had been rigorously trained in France, but older officers who transferred into the Ivorian forces from the French military had received promotions fairly soon after independence without extensive training or command experience. French reports complained that older Ivorian officers often concentrated more on profiting from their positions instead of carrying out their duties, and claimed that various forms of fraud went unpunished. Moreover, younger officers were believed to admire soldiers in neighbouring countries who had successfully seized power rather than their own older colleagues.[58]

Disparities in the training, experiences, and perspectives of these younger and older generations of officers generated mutually animosities in every former French colony. Interviews with younger Nigerien and Senegalese soldiers revealed that the older officers they served with were often poorly educated and many were practically illiterate. Younger officers were now being trained at the same military schools – whether in France or in Africa – as the military presidents in nearby countries.[59] French officials were aware

55 Ministry of Cooperation, 'Domaine de l'assistance militaire', 18 September 1974.
56 Raphaël-Leygues, 'La Côte d'Ivoire et l'Armée', 30 August 1974.
57 Hynin, Military attaché, French Embassy Abidjan, 'Rapport mensuel mois de juillet à aôut 1974', 14 September 1974, GR 14S254, SHD; Raphaël-Leygues, French Embassy Abidjan, to Minister of Foreign Affairs Jean Sauvagnargues, 'Synthèse politique du 1 juin au 31 juillet 1974', 19 August 1974, 1PO/1/5, CADN.
58 Raphaël-Leygues to Ministry of Foreign Affairs, 'Situation intérieure', 17 December 1968; Mathieu, 'Rapport de fin de mission', 16 December 1968; Courtiade, 'Rapport de fin de mission', 5 July 1971; Telegram, Raphaël-Leygues to Directorate of African and Malagasy Affairs, 10 January 1966, GR6Q42, SHD; SDECE, 'Malaise dans l'armée ivoirienne', 3 August 1970, 5AGF/2717, FFAN.
59 Interviews by author, 2019, Dakar and Niamey.

of the problems related to these differences in training, and the generational conflicts that had emerged as a result. It was suggested as early as 1964 that most African soldiers be trained in Africa, either locally or in joint African military schools as the French considered training in France unsuited to African needs, arguing that the high number of foreign students lowered the level of instruction in French military academies. At the time, there were 1,500 foreign students in French military schools and, according to French authorities, many were unable to keep up with the courses offered.[60]

In April 1964, a French committee recommended that African soldiers be trained in France only in exceptional cases, putting forth reasons both psychological and technical. The committee concluded that the training soldiers received in France did not correspond to work conditions on the ground in Africa, or to the equipment and resources of African national armies. Furthermore, they said young soldiers who spent many years in French military schools often had difficulties readapting when they returned to their country of origin, and that many had a tendency to take on political roles or even believed they were 'called upon' to do so.[61] Nevertheless, most Ivorian and Senegalese officers continued to be trained in France. In fact, after 1964, Senegal sought to send as many soldiers to train in France as possible. Both Senegalese and French decision-makers defended this by arguing that it was better for all officers to receive similar training. In fact, sending African soldiers to France for training was also seen as a way to ensure that those soldiers developed links with the French military elite.

The French debate about training African officers in France was revisited in 1969, with nearly identical framing. Of the more than 3,300 foreign trainees in France in 1968, 28% of them were from Africa, a rate that jumped to 35% (of 2,600 trainees) in 1969. French officials were unhappy that the number of foreign soldiers in French academies surpassed the overall limit set at 15%. They advised that local military attachés should be given more control over which soldiers were selected for training in France, and that France should seek to train African soldiers locally by developing military academies in Africa. This would assure that their training was better adapted

---

60 Directorate of African and Malagasy Affairs, 'Conférence prononcé par Messner à la réunion tenue au comité central français pour outre-mer 10 April 1963', 14 April 1963, INVA17, CADC.
61 Directorate of African and Malagasy Affairs, 'Réunion de défense du 12 avril 1964: situation des armées nationales africaines et malgache', 20 April 1964, INVA317, CADC.

to the real needs of the national armies in which they served.[62] Soldiers who needed technical training could still be trained in France,

A French foreign ministry report of 1970 questioned whether military training for African soldiers in France could even be considered as military aid, as it had not resulted in any real improvements to African armed forces. It echoed earlier sentiment that some military academies in France were simply not adapted to African needs and that, as far as possible, African soldiers should be trained in African military academies, which had been established by then in Madagascar, Côte d'Ivoire, Cameroon, and Chad.[63] French authorities claimed the insistence on French training had come from African governments, who wanted their officers to have the same education and qualifications as the French officers with whom they collaborated, and who they would ultimately replace.[64] Four years later, the French Ministry of Cooperation noted that while local training had its advantages, it was not always practical for each state to have its own military academy. In some fields, the ministry contended, foreign training was an absolute necessity, as local training was thought to have led to failures in many countries. The argument was again made that training African soldiers in France helped build camaraderie between French and African military elites.[65]

The Soviet Union similarly understood that training African soldiers was the best way to influence African military elites, as they had done in Guinea and Mali. From the 1960s through 1990, the Soviets increasingly focused on providing military aid because its economic assistance had been largely ineffective. Indeed, what most clearly separates Guinea and Mali from coopting states like Côte d'Ivoire and Senegal is the economic opportunities available to citizens. Economic failures in Guinea and Mali bred popular dissatisfaction, to which their socialist governments responded by deploying armed and security forces. However, many of these soldiers objected to using violence against civilians, breeding dissatisfaction in the military. The Guinean government arrested soldiers who expressed discontent, while the Malian government increasingly used party militias to dispose of any

---

62 Secretariat for the Training of African Soldiers in France, 29 January 1970, 5AGF/2707, FFAN; General Staff, 'Stagiaires étrangères dans les écoles et formations françaises', 3 December 1969, 5AGF/2707, FFAN.

63 Military advisor, 25 September 1970, INVA320, CADC.

64 'Note à l'attention de monsieur général d'armée gazelles', 16 October 1970, INVA 320, CADC.

65 Ministry of Cooperation, 'Domaine de l'assistance militaire' 18 September 1974.

opposition. This use of violence to control society and the military characterizes these coercive states is described in the next section.

Unlike coercive states, Côte d'Ivoire and Senegal were able to provide
sufficient economic opportunities and benefits to a large enough number of
citizens that their governments did not feel the need to constantly deploy
the military to silence popular protests. These coopting governments used
their economic resources to extend the reach and service provision of the
state to civilians, and also had sufficient economic and military resources to
keep their soldiers content. Nonetheless, by comparing these two coopting
states, it is easy to see that economic resources did not always translate into
superior military capacities if leaders considered their armies as potential
threats to their security, as in the case of Côte d'Ivoire.

Coercive States: Guinea and Mali

Guinea and Mali were the only francophone West African countries to
receive most of their military assistance from communist states. However,
their socialist economic policies, together with aid from the communist bloc,
did not succeed in creating growth, which meant these countries had more
coercive capacity to control their populations than economic resources to
co-opt them. Hence, both governments ruled mostly through intimidation,
violence, and ideological influence.

The economics of coercive states

An analysis of Guinean and Malian development strategies is made difficult
by the lack of historical data. This is true in relation to both militaries,
and accurate information on economic development in Guinea before the
mid-1980s is also hard to find, as the Guinean government was secretive
about state finances. Reliable information on the Guinean GDP is only
available after 1984, and it suggests the country was much poorer at that time
than Senegal, Côte d'Ivoire, and Mauritania. Until the 1990s, Mali's GDP
was among the lowest of francophone West African countries (see Figure
15). One can thus conclude that both countries were consistently poor.
Throughout the 1960s and 1970s, they also had the lowest life expectancy
and highest child mortality rates in FWA.[66]

Conversely, Guinea and Mali maintained relatively large military and
security agencies. In Mali, force numbers increased from 10,000 in 1962

---

[66] Data on life expectancy and child mortality from the World Bank data bank.

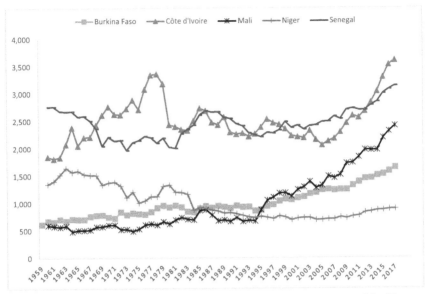

Figure 15. GDP PPP per capita, 1959–2017 (US$) (Source: Pennworld tables, https://www.rug.nl/ggdc/productivity/pwt/, accessed 28.2.2019).

to 13,000 just before the military coup in 1968, while in Guinea, they rose from 6,500 in 1962 to almost 15,000 prior to the Portuguese-led attack in 1970. This growth in the size of both country's security forces was largely the result of an increase in the number of party militias, which soon surpassed the size of the Guinean and Malian armies (see Table 4). The size of the Guinean military hovered around 5,000 until 1974, while Malian forces ranged between 7,000 and 8,000 troops throughout the late 1960s and into the 1970s. However, the size of Mali's territory and population were much greater, and the government spent more on its military as a function of GDP than other francophone West Africa countries between 1960 and 1980. Though comparative data on Guinea is unavailable, accessible information suggests that the Guinean government spent an average of 8% of its budget on the military, about half that of Mali (15%). Still, given the large size of other security agencies in these countries, overall spending to 'maintain order' must have been much higher.

The Guinean and Malian governments each allocated 8–9% of their budgets to healthcare, not unlike other francophone West African states. However, incomplete and unreliable data indicates that Guinea spent as much as 20% of its budget on education, compared to only 11% in Mali. In terms of spending on education, Guinea ranked the highest in francophone

West Africa, and Mali the lowest.[67] Nonetheless, Guinean literacy rates are meagre. While the adult literacy rate in Guinea is consistently higher than that of Mali, rates in both countries are lower than those in Senegal and Côte d'Ivoire.[68]

Access to water and electricity in Guinea and Mali were also inferior to those in the coopting states of Senegal and Côte d'Ivoire, though it was similar to access in the centralized states of Niger and Upper Volta. The Guinean and Malian governments could have taken better advantage of urbanization to facilitate service provision, as the urban population in Guinea doubled between 1960 and 1974, and growing from 10% to 16% in Mali.[69] Not only did they fail to sufficiently provide services to urban populations, they also neglected the service provision of rural populations. In 2000, less than 1% of Guineans or Malians living in rural areas had access to electricity.[70]

The agricultural potential and population density of Mali and Guinea were, however, strikingly different. Guinea had a higher agricultural potential and more than three times the population density of Mali. In these two regards, Guinea resembles Côte d'Ivoire, and Mali its Sahelian neighbours Niger and Burkina Faso (Upper Volta). During the period examined herein, Mali differed from these Sahelian states in that its socialist government did seek to extend coercive control to the countryside. It also taxed officially recorded economic activities at a greater rate than Niger or Upper Volta, but less than Côte d'Ivoire and Senegal, receiving 20 to 25% of its revenues from taxation, primarily of salaries.[71] The Malian government had little incentive to extend its service provision to those parts of its territory that were sparsely populated and where little taxable economic activity took place.

In Guinea, data on state revenue and spending is only available after 1985. It shows that the soldiers who assumed power after President Touré's death in 1984 barely taxed officially recorded economic activity and spent close to 20% of the budget on the military. The military government surely benefitted from the country's bauxite mining industry in ways not recorded in official state revenue, but that was enough to maintain the large

67 See documents on Mali and Guinea in Record Group 59 (CGRDS), NARA.
68 Data literacy rates from the World Bank DataBank.
69 Data on urbanization and population density from the World Bank DataBank.
70 Data on electricity access from the World Bank DataBank.
71 Journal officiel, Mali.

security and military force characteristic of a coercive state.[72] However, the opportunity to generate significant state income from mining activities (in addition to foreign investments, credit, and aid), combined with the difficulty of building and maintaining infrastructure in a tropical climate and the increasing unreliability of its security sector, reduced the incentives for the Guinean government to extend its coercive control to any areas that were not needed in order for the government to access key resources.

The ability to access credit and assistance from Western countries also became increasingly important for both the Guinean and Malian governments. Their state-led economies had failed, as had Soviet economic assistance – which the American ambassador in Guinea argued had been ineffective because it was allocated to '"grandiose" and "inefficient" projects, originally requested and insisted upon by Guinea itself, often despite repeated bloc warnings that something smaller and less showy would do the job better.'[73] By 1960, the black market was flourishing in Guinea and most of the products available came from communist countries. Imports from elsewhere were difficult to obtain. State structures created to deal with import-export trade were soon dismantled and private companies reassumed this task.[74]

Western states were a key source of investment in the Guinean mining industry, and soon after independence, the government had assured investors it would not nationalize mining companies. Important inflows to the Guinean economy were connected to bauxite mining specifically, and large projects were funded by both the US and the Soviet Union.[75] The most valuable company was FRIA, the ownership of which was 48.5% American, 26.5% French, 10% British, 10% Swiss, and 5% West German.[76] In 1963, FRIA produced US$ 29 million worth of aluminium, representing 60% of Guinea's annual exports.[77]

In conversations with their American, French, and West German counterparts, Guinean officials discussed the disappointment and failures of Soviet assistance to Guinea. While Western observers connected these failures not

72 Data from the World Bank DataBank.
73 Cassidy, 'Sino-Soviet Bloc Political-Economic Relationships with Guinea', 18 July 1963.
74 Ibid.
75 See documents in Files 5AGF/1637, 5AGF/1638 and 5AGF/558, FFAN; File 51QONT/34, CADC, and Files 770b 1960–1963, Box 1944, and POLGUIN 1963, Box 2257, CGRDS, NARA.
76 Francis Hure, 'Situation économique de la Guinée', 31 March 1959.
77 Donald Herdeck, US Embassy Conakry, 'Politico-economic assessment of Guinea for 1963', 16 May 1963, POLGUIN 1963, Box 2257, CGRDS, NARA.

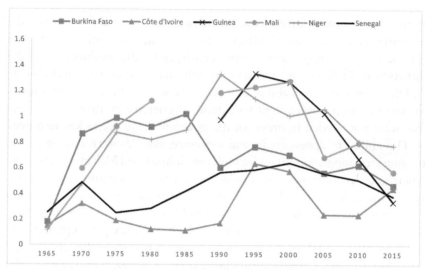

Figure 16. Foreign aid as a percentage of state spending in francophone West Africa, five-year average for the period 1965–2015 (Source: World Bank DataBank, https://databank.worldbank.org/home.aspx, accessed 28.2.2020).

only to socialism but also to the inefficiency of the Guinean administration,[78] a French report referred to the comment of a Guinean official that the 'myth of altruistic aid' from socialist countries had been exposed, 'and now Guinea was bound by agreements they could not get out of'.[79] According to the French, Guinea had therefore relied on the US for economic survival from 1964 onwards.[80] The importance of US aid to the Guinean government challenges the belief that Touré was ultimately dependent on and allied with the communist bloc. By the late 1960s, private American investment in Guinea measured close to US$ 200 million and it was clear that Touré's regime was economically reliant on the US.[81]

[78] Jean-Louis Pons, Ambassador of France in Guinea, to Ministry of Foreign Affairs, 'La crise des rapports Russo-Guinéens', 15 January 1962, 51QO/59, CADC; Jean-Pierre Hadengue, 'Aides extérieures reçues par Guinée: Comte-rendu de l'attaché militaire à Bonn sur l'attitude de Fodéba Keita, ministre guinéen de la défense, lors de son récent voyage officiel en Allemagne fédérale', 19 September 1962, 5AGF/1640, FFAN.
[79] Jean Mialet, 'Note à l'attention de Monsieur le président de la république, president de la communauté: Situation de la Guinée', 23 March 1962.
[80] French Embassy in the US to the Directorate for Africa-Levant, 'Relations entre les états-unis et la Guinée', 17 November 1971.
[81] See documents in Files USGUIN 1964–1966, Boxes 2258 and 2256; POLGUIN 1967–1969, Boxes 2164 and 2165; and POLGUIN 1970–1973, Box 2341, CGRDS, NARA.

The role of foreign credit and assistance was also significant in Mali, which was the most indebted of the nine francophone West African countries until Mauritania surpassed it in 1976. Hence, throughout the 1970s and 1980s, the Guinean and Malian governments increasingly depended on Western economic assistance. Over time, their populations were also increasingly reliant on Western aid, which amounted to an average of 1.2 times the state budgets of these countries from 1985 to 2000 (see Figure 16). This is not surprising given the character of these coercive states, which taxed economic activities, maintained a large security apparatus – spending much of their state budget on security forces and the military – but provided few economic opportunities and services to their populations.

The socialist development of Guinea and Mali and the capacity of their armed forces

In newly independent Guinea and Mali, the size of their national armed forces had quickly exceeded the number of soldiers stationed in each colony during the colonial period, with Guinea more than doubling the number of soldiers for every 10,000 people in the country from 1954 to 1964 (rising from 7 to 17). One reason for these governments to establish large forces was to integrate the high numbers of returning colonial soldiers, and in Guinea, the government was also concerned about both internal and external threats. The Guinean government had in fact been subject to French hostility since independence, after it refused to joined the French Community.[82] Moreover, some former colonial soldiers had participated in operations against Touré, who also faced internal opposition related to the country's poor economic conditions.[83] In Mali, where the government did not face similar external threats, the number of soldiers per 10,000 people increased only slightly after independence. Yet, like Guinea, the failures of Mali's socialist economic policies led to public dissatisfaction, and both governments turned to their security and armed forces to silence domestic opposition.

82 National Defence General Staff, Intelligence Division, 'Le problème Guinéen', 17 April 1959, GR9Q5122, SHD; Charles de Gaulle, 'Note', 2 April 1962, 5AGF/558, FFAN; De Gaulle, 'Note pour monsieur Foccart', 31 March 1962, 5AGF/558, FFAN.
83 General Secretary for African and Malagasy Affairs, 'Situation de l'armée nationale de Guinée', 11 September 1962; Diefenbacher, Ministry of Interior Director of International Police Technical Cooperation Services, to Foccart, 'Note concernant les activités au Sénégal opposants au régime de Sékou Touré', 22 July 1970; SDECE, 'Note d'information autour des événements de Conakry du 22 novembre 1970', 15 February 1971, 51QONT/33, CADC; Africa Branch, 'Note pour le cabinet du ministre: activités de certaines milieux Guinéens en France', 28 August, 1970, 51QONT/29, CADC.

Table 8. Territory, borders, population density and soldiers per km².

| Country | Land area km² | Borders km | Neighbours | km² per soldiers | | Population | | People per km² |
				1964	1974	1960	1974	1974
Benin	112,760	1,989	4			2,431,617	3,187,413	28
Burkina Faso	273,600	3,193	6	127	97	4,829,289	6,040,045	22
Côte d'Ivoire	318,000	3,110	5	92	42	3,503,559	6,121,295	19
Guinea	245,720	3,399	6	38	51	3,494,164	4,424,030	18
Mali	1,220,190	7,243	7	157	207	5,263,727	6,368,346	5
Mauritania	1,030,700	5,074	4			850,377	1,291,857	1
Niger	1,266,700	5,697	7	1,114	543	3,388,774	5,040,795	4
Senegal	192,530	2,640	5	48	20	3,206,757	4,797,188	25
Togo	54,390	1,647	3			1,580,508	2,356,620	43

Source: World Bank DataBank, accessed 28.2.2020.

Using force against civilians did create unease among national troops, and the Guinean and Malian governments responded to this in different ways. While the Malians sought to mitigate discontent by assuring the material wellbeing of soldiers, the Guineans relied on ideological indoctrination, arrests, and executions. The violent means by which the Touré regime confronted its opposition had ripple effects across Guinean society. Its population growth and life-expectancy were both low, and in some years, population growth was negative. From 1960 to 1974, life expectancy in Guinea grew by only three years, making it the lowest in all of francophone West Africa.[84]

Furthermore, during Touré's time in office (1958–1984), two million Guineans reportedly left the country, most without official authorization, indicating the limited capacities of the government to control the movement of people and goods across state borders.[85] French reports also described a thriving black market and increases in smuggling activity soon after independence. This emerged in response to the establishment of a state monopoly on imports, and again after Guinea adopted its own currency in 1960. The truth is, Guinean borders were hard to control, or 'practically impossible' if one believes the French evaluations of 1959.[86]

The borders of Mali were not very easy to control either. In total, they stretch over 7,000km, more the twice of the length of the Guinean border, encompassing a territory five times the size of Guinea (see Table 8). This meant there was one soldier or gendarme per 200km2, whereas in Guinea there was one per 50km2. These numbers suggest that the coercive reach of the Guinean state was more extensive than that of Mali. In the early 1960s, the Malian army had extended its reach to the more sparsely populated

---

84 Data from the World Bank DataBank
85 The Regional Delegate in West Africa, Dakar, 'Situation des Guinées (Conakry) qui vivent en dehors de leur pays', 21 June 1977, UNHCR Fonds 11, Records of the Central Registry, Series 2, Classified Subject Files 1971–1984, 100.GEN.GUI Refugees from Guinea – General 1967/1984, 11.02.BOX.0023; The Regional Delegate in West Africa, Dakar, 'La sitation des Guinées vivant à l'etranger', 26 November 1976, UNHCR Fonds 11, Records of the Central Registry, Series 2, Classified Subject Files 1971–1984, 100. GEN.GUI Refugees from Guinea – General 1967/1984, 11.02.BOX.0023; Message from the Regional Branch Office for West Africa to the High Commissioner, 2 June 1971, UNHCR Fonds 11, Records of the Central Registry, Series 2, Classified Subject Files 1971–1984, 100.ICO.GUI Refugees from Guinea in Ivory Coast [Volume 1 – 1.ICO.GUI]1966/1971, 11.02.BOX.0095.
86 National Defence General Staff, Intelligence Division, 'Le problème guinéen' 17 April 1959.

areas in the north, in a response to Tuareg rebellions in 1963 and 1964, and French and American observers noted that this fight against the Tuareg had allowed the military to demonstrate its effectiveness and usefulness to the Malian government.[87] Other than these operations, soldiers in Mali were generally quite centralized and remained on their bases, with other organizations playing the primary role in controlling the population.

Various Malian security agencies, police, and republican guard units all had a role in maintaining internal order. In 1963, some 1,200 gendarmes were responsible for border security, 1,500 republican guards secured the capital, and 1,500 police officers were tasked with monitoring crime and engaging in counterintelligence.[88] Governments in both Mali and Guinea also developed party militias to counter the force of their national militaries. In Guinea, intelligence services trained by Czechoslovakian experts would also become increasingly important. Their role was to gather information on foreign nationals and on Guinean political elites. French officials noted that even if Guinean police lacked vehicles and transmission equipment, the assistance they received from Czechoslovakia had enabled them to function relatively effectively.[89]

Assessing the strategies and capacities of the Guinean and Malian militaries is made rather difficult by the scarcity of information available on their development. What is known is that the first 2,500 soldiers in the Guinean armed forces were selected from the 11,000 colonial soldiers who chose to leave the French military, including 16 officers. Choosing personnel for the military was not an easy task, and French reports suggest that the loyalty of returning soldiers to the Guinean regime was not guaranteed.[90] However,

---

87 US Embassy Bamako, 'French military counselor reviews military situation in Mali 8 décembre 1965', DEF 1964–1966, Box 1679, NARA; Secretary of State for Foreign Affairs, 'Forces armées maliennes et notre assistance militaire au Mali', 11 October 1971.
88 US Embassy Conakry to Department of State, 'Capacities of Guinea Police Forces Adequate to Present Needs: no US aid recommended', 29 May 1963, 770b 1960–1963, Box 1944, CGRDS, NARA; Attwood, 'Factors which may produce subversion, violent disturbance and lead to disorder', 14 June 1962.
89 See documents in Files 51QO/34 and 51QO/32, CADC; Files 5AGF/1644, 5AGF/555, 5AGF/1639, and 5AGF/1637, FFAN; and File 770b 1960–1963, Box 1944, CGRDS, NARA.
90 National Defence General Staff, Intelligence Division, 'Fiche sur le potentiel militaire de la Guinée', 17 April 1959, GR9Q5122, SHD; SDECE, 'Moyens consacrés à la défense de l'état Guinée', 5 January 1959, 51QO/32, CADC. Attwood, US Embassy Conakry, to Department of State, 'Police assistance program', 21 August 1962, 770b 1960–1963, Box 1944, CGRDS, NARA; General C. A. Gardet, 'Rapport de fin de commandement', 15 February 1960, GR5H28, SHD.

by 1961, force numbers in the Guinean military had increased to 3,500, and an additional 1,300 Guineans were selected to join the gendarmerie and Republican Guard. By 1965, the Guinean military consisted of 4,200 soldiers,[91] more than twice the size of the force in Upper Volta. Until the 1970s, the Malian army consisted of around 3,000 soldiers, despite its considerably larger territory (see Table 4).

Communist countries transferred a significant amount of military equipment to the Guinean and Malian governments, the value of which, according to SIPRI, was much higher than French aid to other francophone West African countries (see Figure 1). Western officials were convinced that the volume of equipment flowing into Guinea and Mali from the communist bloc exceeded the military needs of each country, amounting to more than their armed forces could even use. The Americans and French also questioned whether these transfers of military equipment were helping to build Guinean and Malian military capacities, suggesting for example that a shipment of arms from Czechoslovakia and the Soviet Union to Guinea was used 'to flatter the government's taste for the spectacular presentation of power' rather than increase actual military capabilities.[92] Western reports also referred to the dissatisfaction of soldiers in Guinea and Mali with Soviet assistance, as Soviet equipment often became quickly unusable as a result of inadequate maintenance and adverse climatic conditions.[93] In addition, those soldiers who had transferred from the French military into the Guinean and Malian national forces often only had experience with French light weapons and thus lacked the technical aptitude to maintain more sophisticated Soviet military equipment, which made these forces reliant on Soviet technical assistance.[94]

In Guinea, the first technical assistants from Czechoslovakia arrived in 1959, together with a significant shipment of arms.[95] Most of the French

91 Presidency of the Republic, Special Staff, 'Forces armées de la république de Guinée', 12 March 1965, 5AG/1646, FFAN.

92 General Secretary for African and Malagasy Affairs, 'Situation de l'armée nationale de Guinée', 11 September 1962.

93 General Secretariat for National Defence, Intelligence Exploitation Centre, 'Les Forces Armées Guinéennes', 17 April 1970; Attwood, 'Factors which may produce subversion, violent disturbance and lead to disorder' 14 June 1962; Pierre Graham, 'Guinean military strength: Personnel and weapons', 19 April 1966.

94 See documents in Files 51QO/3 and 51QO/34, CADC; File GR9Q5122, SHD; and Files 5AGF/1639 and 5AGF/555, FFAN.

95 The shipment consisted of 8,000 rifles, 3,000 automatic pistols, twenty machine guns, six canons, six anti-tank canons, and armoured vehicles and grenades.

technicians in the country had departed straight after independence, leaving a considerable gap in knowledge, but they were quickly replaced by counterparts from communist countries.[96] According to the French, there were over 500 technicians from the 'east' assisting the Guinean administration in 1960. These included 240 from China, working in agriculture; forty-five from the USSR, assisting with railroad construction; eighty-five from Czechoslovakia, working in the armed forces; as well as sixty technicians from Yugoslavia and forty from East Germany.[97] American reports noted that this increased to close to 1,000 technicians from the communist bloc in 1963, including forty-seven Soviet military advisors and ninety-five Czechoslovakian military and security experts.[98] Mali received its first Soviet trainers two years after Guinea, in 1961. French intelligence reports indicate that there were forty Soviet technical assistants in Mali by 1962, and sixty by 1967.[99] On top of this, many Guinean and Malian soldiers were trained in communist countries.[100]

Nonetheless, Guineans officials complained that Soviet aid did not correspond with their needs. For example, Fodéba Keïta, the minister of defence and security, informed West German officials that the training offered to Guinean soldiers was more effective at ideologically indoctrinating them than it was at increasing their technical capacities.[101] Despite this, military coups elsewhere in Africa made the socialist governments of Guinea and Mali wary about increasing the size or capacities of their national armed

---

96   French Intelligence Service, 'Situation en Guinée', 18 January 1959; National Defence General Staff, Intelligence Division, 'La pénétration communiste en république de Guinée', 12 April 1960.

97   Presidency of the Community, 'Note à l'attention de monsieur le secrétaire général – experts étrangères en Guinée', 22 December 1960; National Defence General Staff, Intelligence Division, 'La pénétration communiste en république de Guinée', 12 April 1960.

98   Cassidy, 'Sino-Soviet Bloc Political-Economic Relationships with Guinea', 18 July 1963.

99   General Secretariat for National Defence, Intelligence Exploitation Centre, 'L'armée malienne' 23 October 1962; General Secretary for African and Malagasy Affairs, 'L'armée malienne et l'aide militaire française' 28 April 1972.

100 French Intelligence Service, 'Situation en Guinée' 18 January 1959; National Defence General Staff, Intelligence Division, 'Fiche sur la Guinée', 7 April 1959; Commander of the Armed Forces in the AOF-Togo Defence Zone, 'Guinée forces armes et de sécurité 1961'.

101 Hadengue 'Aides extérieures reçues par Guinée: Compte-rendu de l'attaché militaire à Bonn sur l'attitude de Fodéba Keita, ministre guinéen de la défense lors de son récent voyage officiel en Allemagne fédérale', 19 September 1962.

forces, and both countries relied to some degree on ideological training to secure their soldiers' loyalty.

Soldiers were also asked to participate in the agricultural and industrial development of Guinea and Mali, a by-product of which was decreased military capacity.[102] Initially, these economic tasks were meant to strengthen the state, but later they were used as a means of reducing the capacities of their forces and thus the likelihood of a military coup.[103] Following the coup in neighbouring Ghana in 1965, the ability of soldiers in Guinea to access munitions was limited.[104] Where the Guinean government resorted to the use of force against soldiers it deemed disloyal, the government on Mali relied on strategies of cooptation in its military, and until the 1990s, a significant portion of its resources were allocated to the armed forces (see Figure 17). Only the Voltaic government spent a higher share of its budget on the military, but this was only true until the 1968 military coup in Mali.

In both Guinea and Mali, most military spending was earmarked for personnel costs rather than equipment. While the Malian government allocated 70% of its military spending to these costs, the rate appears to have been even higher in Guinea, although the available data is incomplete. Guinea did indeed spent a considerable portion of its state budget on countering security threats from the time of its independence, allocating nearly 20% of the 1959 budget to this purpose, nearly all of which went on personnel costs.[105] The importance of ensuring that security forces were satisfied was reflected in the fact that their salaries were paid on time and were maintained at consistent levels from the colonial into the postcolonial

102 General Secretary for African and Malagasy Affairs, 'Situation de l'armée nationale de Guinée', 11 September 1962.

103 General Secretariat for National Defence, Intelligence Exploitation Centre, 'Les Forces Armées Guinéennes', 17 April 1970; US Embassy Conakry to Department of State, 'Information needed for assessment of new civic action program proposals for African countries', 19 June 1964.

104 Graham to Rusk, 'Guinean military preparedness', 18 March 1966; McIlvaine, US Embassy Conakry, to Rusk, 13 December 1966, DEFGUIN 1964–1966, Box 1649, CGRDS, NARA; Hughes, 'Guinea: Touré Demilitarizes the Military', 16 January 1969.

105 Directorate of African and Malagasy Affairs, 'République de Guinée: Moyens consacrés à la défense de l'état', 8 January 1959, 51QO/34, CADC; Directorate of African and Malagasy Affairs, 'Note sur le budget 1959 de la Guinée', 30 April 1959, 51QO/11, CADC; SDECE 'Moyens consacrés à la défense de l'état Guinée', 5 January 1959; Ambassador Francis Hure to the Ministry of Foreign Affairs, 'Dépenses nationale 1959', 23 March 1959, 51QO/32, CADC.

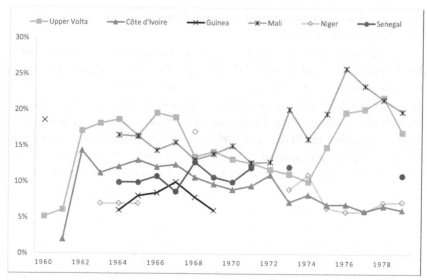

Figure 17. Military spending as a percentage of the state budget, 1960–1974
(Source: World Bank DataBank, https://databank.worldbank.org/home.aspx,
accessed 28.2.2020; Journaux Officiels Senegal, Mauritanie, Niger).

period, unlike the salaries of other state employees.[106] It was because they
expected foreign countries to provide them with military equipment for
free that the Guinean and Malian governments were able to spend so much
of their defence budgets on personnel costs.

In the 1960s, the Guinean government started to reduce its spending
on the army due to the threat soldiers were presumed to pose and reallo-
cating these resources to other security agencies.[107] Similarly, the Malian
government reduced the army's share of the military budget prior to the
1968 military coup and began to emphasize the development of militias
and police, increasing the number of party militia members from 5,000 to
7,000. The Malian militias were assigned unpopular political policing tasks
that army soldiers did not want to carry out and, when the militias were

106 Ministry of Foreign Affairs, Directorate for Africa-Levant, 'Guinée', 2 July 1960;
Ministry of Foreign Affairs, 'Situation intérieure', 28 May 1960, 5AGF/1637, FFAN;
SDECE, 'Guinée: Le complot contre le régime', 9 May 1960; General Secretary for
African and Malagasy Affairs, 'Situation de l'armée nationale de Guinée', 11 September
1962.
107 Ibid.

dissolved after the coup, the share of the state budget allocated to the army was raised by the military government.

The impact of the military coup on the wellbeing of soldiers in Mali, and on military effectiveness, was not altogether positive. In its wake, the use of violence to control the armed forces increased as the new military president sought to secure his control. After four years of military rule, a French report noted that although the Malian army looked modern, its actual capacities were limited by a lack of exercises and training.[108] With the most experienced officers involved in governing the country, the administration and organization of the armed forces had been neglected. A French military attaché attributed the superiority of Malian forces in the 1974 border conflict with Upper Volta to Soviet military assistance rather than domestic military capacity.[109]

Distrust of the military made it more difficult for the Guinean and Malian governments to prepare for and respond to external threats. The Guinean president, even more than Malian leaders, solved this dilemma by relying on party militias to consolidate his power. Youth militias established at independence were trained by Czechoslovakian assistants.[110] In 1967, in response to military coups in neighbouring countries, these militias were armed and trained by Cuba. By 1968, there were 5,000 militia members in Guinea, slightly more than the number of soldiers in the country, and by 1970, the militias had grown to 8,000 members, almost twice the number of Guinean soldiers. The tasks of militias overlapped with those of the army and gendarmerie, and included controlling the population, the borders, and the country's most important towns.[111]

---

108 General Secretary for African and Malagasy Affairs, 'l'armée malienne et l'aide militaires française', 28 April 1972.

109 Lieutenant-Colonel Chenevoy, Military advisor, 'Rapport fin de mission 25 October 1973–31 August 1976'.

110 General Secretary for African and Malagasy Affairs, 'Situation de l'armée nationale de Guinée', 11 September 1962.

111 Lewin, *Ahmed Sékou Touré (1922–1984)*, vol. 5, pp. 251–70; General Secretariat for National Defence, Intelligence Exploitation Centre, 'Les Forces Armées Guinéennes', 17 April 1970; General Secretariat for National Defence, Intelligence Exploitation Centre, 'Organisation de la Milice Populaire et du Service Civique en République de Guinée', 13 May 1968, GR9Q5122, SHD; General Secretariat for National Defence, Intelligence Division, 'La Guinée du Président Sékou Touré: Annexe G – Les forces armées Guinéennes et l'assistance militaire soviétique, chinoise et cubaine', 3 June 1977; Ministry of Armed Forces, SDECE, 'Guinée-Cuba: stage de formation de la milice à cuba', 5 January 1968.

Militias were also used to respond to external threats, such as in November 1970, when Portuguese-led forces attacked Conakry over Guinean support of the anti-colonial movement in Guinea-Bissau. The main purpose of the attack was to free Portuguese prisoners held in Conakry, and although it was led by Portuguese officers, the force included exiled Guinean opposition forces based in France, Côte d'Ivoire, and Senegal – which accounted for about half the 300 assailants.[112] It is difficult to assess the effectiveness of the Guinean security response to the attack, because the attackers may have also intended to overthrow the Guinean president and kill Amílcar Cabral, the leader of the anti-colonial movement in Guinea-Bissau. If the objective was only to free the prisoners, the attack was successful, apart from the considerable diplomatic problems it caused Portugal. Had the objective also been to depose Touré and assassinate Cabral, the attack was largely a failure, and badly planned, as Cabral was not even in Guinea at the time.

The opinion of foreign observers was that had the assailants intended to oust Touré and expected to receive support from the Guinean population, it did not materialize. According to the French, the assailants' most significant failure was not to capture the main radio station, which allowed the Guinean government to call for assistance.[113] American officials reported that Guinean President Sékou Touré was subsequently suspicious of complicity within the armed forces due to the 'lethargic response' of soldiers.[114] In

112 Directorate for Africa-Levant, Sub-Directorate for Africa, 'Note pour le ministre: Guinée', 5 February 1971, 51QO/33, CADC; State Minister for National Defence, SDECE, 'Note d'information autour des événements de Conakry du 22 novembre 1970', 15 February 1971; Intelligence Exploitation Centre, 'Les événements de Guinée et leur développements diplomatiques', 1 April 1971, GR9Q5122, SHD; SDECE, 'Activités de l'opposition guinéenne', 8 December 1972, 51QO/33, CADC.
113 SDECE, 'Note d'information autour des événements de Conakry du 22 novembre 1970', 15 February 1971; SDECE, 'Activités de l'opposition guinéenne', 8 December 1972; Directorate for Africa-Levant, Sub-Directorate for Africa, 'Note pour le ministres', 28 November 1970, 51QO/29, CADC; General Secretariat for National Defence, 'Évolution de la situation en Guinée et développement diplomatique', 3 February 1971, 51QO/33, CADC; Intelligence Exploitation Centre, 'Les événements de Guinée et leur développements diplomatiques', 1 April 1971; US Embassy Conakry to Department of State, 'Policy Planning Paper', 6 July 1971; US Department of State 'Memorandum of Conversation: Guinea Industry visitors', 2 December 1970, FNGUIN 1970–1973, Box 891, CGRDS, NARA.
114 US Embassy Conakry to Department of State, 'Policy Planning Paper', 6 July 1971. Also see US Embassy Conakry to Department of State, 'Fifth column in Guinea', 20 July 1970.

this way, the attack in November 1970 destroyed a considerable amount of military human capital and reinforced Guinea's dependence on Soviet military assistance. The rise in internal repression saw nearly one hundred Guineans executed for their alleged cooperation with the assailants.[115]

The attack was also particularly harmful to Western interests in Guinea.[116] As Soviet ships were patrolling the Guinean coast, the US reduced its aid.[117] No economic assistance came from the Soviets to compensate, not that this had ever been very successful. In fact, increased military assistance from the Soviets, as well as China, better suited the plans of the Guinean and Soviet governments.[118]

In April 1970, a few months prior to the attack, French military intelligence had produced a comprehensive report on Guinean military capacities that described the Guinean armed forces as the most powerful in francophone Africa in terms of troop numbers and equipment. Guinea was the only state in the region to possess large numbers of armoured vehicles, artillery, and fighter aircraft. Even so, French observers reported that a lack of maintenance and technical knowledge had reduced the operational value of this equipment, and that most was no longer functional.[119] The reports suggested that the capacities of Guinean soldiers were further limited by the failure of the military to engage in exercises and training because most soldiers were involved with agricultural and road-building tasks.[120] It was the Guinean air force that was most significantly impacted by this lack of technical skill and knowledge, which made it largely dependent on Soviet and Czechoslovakian technical assistants. This was the case even in 1970,

115 Directorate for Africa-Levant, Sub-Directorate for Africa, 'Assertions guinéennes sur une nouvelle agression: entretiens franco-allemands du 25 juin 1971', 23 June 1971, 51QO/34, CADC; General Secretariat for National Defence, 'Évolution de la situation en Guinée et développement diplomatique', 3 February 1971.

116 Directorate for Africa-Levant, Sub-Directorate for Africa, 'Assertion guinéennes sur une nouvelle agression: entretiens franco-allemands du 25 juin 1971', 23 June 1971.

117 French Embassy in the US to the Directorate for Africa-Levant, 'Relations entre les États-Unis et la Guinée', 17 November 1971; General Secretariat for National Defence, 'Afrique noire: ingérences étrangères en Guinée', 11 February 1972, 51QO/34, CADC.

118 US Department of State, 'Memorandum of conversation: Antonio Cabruta Matias, Counselor, Embassy of Portugal; George Trail, Jerrold North, Guinea Sierra Leone Defense Pact; and Portuguese views', 27 April 1971.

119 General Secretariat for National Defence, Intelligence Exploitation Centre, 'Les Forces Armées Guinéennes', 17 April 1970, and 'Aviation militaire guinéenne', 21 July 1971.

120 General Secretariat for National Defence, Intelligence Exploitation Centre, 'Les forces armées guinéennes', 17 April 1970.

when the air force consisted of some fifteen officers and one hundred airmen.[121] After the attack, the air force received two new MIG-17s from the Soviets, and in the five years that followed, Soviet military assistance to Guinea amounted to an estimated US\$ 40 million. There were reportedly 110 Soviet assistants working within the Guinean military during this period, mostly in the air force. Around one hundred Guinean airmen departed yearly to the Soviet Union for training as well.

From 1971 to 1975, approximately 300 sailors were said to have been trained in China. At the same time, the Chinese doubled the number of technical assistants they deployed to Guinea. Additionally, Cuba became more involved in training the Guinean military, there being around 310 Cuban advisors working in the country.[122] Even so, French reports suggest that purges in the Guinean military – including the armed forces chief of staff and commandant of the gendarmerie, both of whom were executed – undermined any improvements in capacity otherwise enabled by the equipment and assistance provided by foreign partners.[123] In the short term at least, the Portuguese attack had increased Guinean reliance on foreign military aid, rather than improving the capacities of the state to control its population and territory.[124]

By contrast, Mali's conflict with Upper Volta in 1974 demonstrated the superior military capacities of the Malian armed forces, and the military government's relatively better use of Soviet military assistance. The conflict did not have the same negative consequence for Malian forces as the Portuguese-led attack had had for Guinea. However, there is no indication that it led to an increase in state administrative capacities. What Guinea and Mali had in common was the fact that their government's state-led economic policies, along with Soviet military assistance, resulted in military capacities that were superior to those needed to provide economic opportunities or services to their populations. In centralized states like Niger and Upper Volta, the reverberations of external military and economic assistance were fewer, because this assistance was much less significant. The refusal of the Voltaic government to host a French military base meant that Upper

---

121 Ibid.

122 See documents in File GR9Q5122, SHD, and File 51QO/34, FFAN.

123 Intelligence Exploitation Centre, 'Guinée: Le grand procès populaire de la cinquième colonne', 24 August 1971.

124 Terence Todman, US Embassy Conakry, 'Report on fifteen-day inspection tour of border military installations by Guinea's chiefs of staff (army and airforce)', 1 November 1973, DEFGUIN 1970–1973, Box 1740, CGRDS, NARA.

Volta received minimal French military assistance, and the Nigerien civilian government had little interest in increasing national military capacities. With limited resources, these governments focused on both economic and military development in their capital cities.

Centralized States: Niger and Upper Volta

The resource restraints faced by Niger and Upper Volta, and the narrow reach of their state administrations, set them apart from coercive states. The Nigerien and Voltaic armed and security forces were small and ill-equipped, and the capacities of both governments to tax their populations were weak. They also had limited access to foreign credit, which made them reliant on foreign aid. As these centralized states focused their limited economic and military resources on their capitals, they had a minimal impact on the lives of most of their populations.

The economics of centralized states

From 1960 to 1974, Niger and Upper Volta taxed the officially recorded economic activities relatively little.[125] By 1974, the governments were collecting the lowest amounts of taxes in all of francophone West Africa. The agricultural potential of these countries was weak, and productivity was low, which meant there was very little that could be taxed. Niger and Upper Volta were also the least urbanized states in the region,[126] which made it more cumbersome and expensive to recover taxes and provide services to the majority of their populations. Niger was also sparsely populated, which further magnified these challenges.

However, sudden changes to the state finances of these countries in the 1970s and 1980s suggest that limited tax collection was not only a question of capacity but also one of willingness. In Niger, state spending as a function of GDP nearly doubled between 1974 and 1977, and throughout the 1980s, the revolutionary military government in Burkina Faso (previously Upper Volta) likewise raised spending, more than doubling it between 1980 and 1991. In both countries, the bulk of the taxes collected were from salaried workers, as these governments could not capture as much in tariffs as other

125 Data on percentage of government spending from the GDP World Bank DataBank.
126 Data on urbanization from the World Bank DataBank

francophone West African countries due to the limited volume of their international trade.[127]

The military coups in Niger and Upper Volta served to slightly modify the economic situation in each country, but in different ways. Following the 1966 military coup in Upper Volta, the state began generating more revenue from trade than it had before, whereas the military government that ruled Niger after 1974 collected more in taxes from personal and corporate income than the civilian government that preceded it.[128] Even so, their weak economic potential meant that both countries continued to have limited access to foreign credit and remained largely dependent on French financial assistance. Upper Volta managed nonetheless to be the least indebted francophone West African country. Niger, on the other hand, started accumulating considerable debt after the 1974 military coup and the 1973 oil crisis, essentially erasing any temporary benefit gained by the government through its ability to better access foreign credit in the earlier 1970s when uranium production began. In the decade from 1980 to 1990, Niger's already large debt ballooned to over 75% of its gross national income (GNI) (see Figure 18). Notably, Niger was still much less indebted than Mauritania, which relied on foreign credit to fund almost all of its budget after the oil crisis.

Upper Volta was more reliant on foreign aid than foreign credit. In 1967, the Voltaic government received foreign assistance equal to its state budget, and during the 1974 famine, foreign assistance accounted for more than 1.5 times the national budget in both Upper Volta and Niger. Niger's dependence on foreign aid surpassed that of Upper Volta in the 1980s, despite Nigerien mineral resources and the country's access to foreign credit.[129] The reliance on foreign aid had important political implications for both countries, especially in combination with their limited state capacities. As a result, these governments and their citizens were more dependent on foreign benefactors than they were on each other.

Service provision in centralized states like Niger and Upper Volta was poor. During the 1960s and 1970s, health spending represented just under 10% of their state budgets, not unlike other francophone West African countries. Spending on education was just over 10%, which was slightly

---

[127] Budgets 1960–1980, Burkinabe and Nigerien National Archives.
[128] Ibid.
[129] Journaux Officiels, Nigerian and Burkinabe National Archives. Data on official foreign assistance, official government spending, and national debt from the World Bank DataBank.

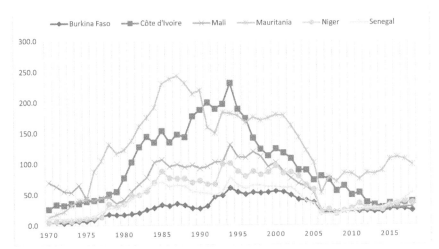

Figure 18. Government debt as a percentage of GNI (Source: World Bank databank, https://databank.worldbank.org/home.aspx, accessed 28.2.2020).

lower than other states in the region.[130] However, because the GDPs and GDP spending of the Nigerien and Voltaic governments were low (see Figure 13), the resources available to provide services were minimal. Nigerien health indicators reflect the limited ability of the Nigerien government to meaningfully improve the living conditions of its population. Even after 1967, child mortality in Niger increased, and the country long had the lowest adult literacy rate in all of francophone West Africa. Upper Volta had the second lowest adult literacy rate, and slightly better indicators overall, but it still trailed behind the coopting states of Côte d'Ivoire and Senegal. In both Niger and Upper Volta, infrastructure development was similarly inadequate. By 2000, only 7–8% of their populations had access to electricity. When it came to potable water, around half the population of Burkina Faso had access to it, compared to about one-third of the population of Niger.[131]

The limited material resources of both of these countries were reflected in their military capacities, although Niger and Upper Volta differed in how much they spent on their national armed forces. The Voltaic government sometimes allocated as much as 19% of the state budget to the military, a proportion that would only drop to less than 10% after the mid-1990s. In Niger, military spending was consistently lower before 1974, constituting

130 Journaux Officiels, Nigerian and Burkinabe National Archives.
131 Data on access to water, electricity, and internet from the World Bank DataBank.

less than 10% of the state budget, except in 1966 (see Figure 17). This difference may be partly explained by the larger number of colonial soldiers who returned to Upper Volta (see Table 3).

Limited resources and weak military capacities in Niger and Upper Volta

Colonial soldiers who returned to Upper Volta were respected by Voltaic society, and the need to offer them positions in a credible national armed force made the creation of a strong military a priority for the Voltaic government.[132] The development of the national military in Upper Volta was thus facilitated by the inclusion of experienced soldiers.[133] This did generate financial problems, as integrating these soldiers into the Voltaic forces was expensive. In Niger, which had only a quarter of the number of returning colonial soldiers to reabsorb, the government faced less pressure to create a strong national army. Unlike the armed forces of Upper Volta, the Nigerien military was hampered by the low educational levels and skills of soldiers, which imposed limits on its development. In 1960, only two Nigerien officers were serving in the French army compared to nineteen Voltaic officers (see Table 3). French officials therefore anticipated that the Nigeriens would require French military technical assistance for an extended period.

In addition to the issue of returning soldiers, their limited resources and the size of their territories made it even more challenging for the Nigerien and Voltaic governments to control the populations and territory within their borders. French reports often referred to the limited financial means of Niger and Upper Volta being the main obstacle to developing their military capacities. Although Niger's GDP was more than twice that of Upper Volta until the 1970s (see Figures 14 and 15), its territory is far larger – about five times the size of Upper Volta – and has the longest borders in all of francophone West Africa. Niger also shares borders with seven countries, which made the task of controlling its territory even more difficult. Despite the size of Nigerien territory, the country's armed forces were small. In 1964,

---

132 Ministry of the Armed Forces, Overseas Office, 'Notice sur Haute-Volta', 8 July 1960, GR5H150, SHD; French Embassy Ouagadougou, 'Compte-rendu hebdomadaire', 4 August 1961, 313QONT/3, CADC; Special Envoy of France and the Community to Upper Volta, 'Etat d'esprit des anciens combattants en Haute-Volta', 19 April 1961, 313QONT/20, CADC.
133 Brebisson, 'Rapport annuel 1961'.

for example, there was only one Nigerien soldier per 1,114km2, compared to one soldier per 127km2 in Upper Volta (see Table 8).

As the number of troops in both Niger and Upper Volta had been relatively small during the colonial period, increasing the size of their postcolonial forces created extra costs associated with enlarging military bases and establishing new ones. In 1954, Niger had just over 3,300 soldiers and gendarmes, and Upper Volta around 2,500.[134] It was not until 1965 that the Voltaic military surpassed this number, whereas the size of the Nigerien national military peaked at 2,500 in 1972 and had dropped below 2,400 by 1975 (see Table 4).

The Voltaic army was established in November 1961, more than a year after formal independence, and consisted of 770 Voltaic soldiers – including twenty-four officers – who had transferred from the French forces.[135] They were only able to move into their barracks on the 1 January 1962, however, as they had to wait for the French to fully leave their military bases. Although the number of Voltaic soldiers increased at a slower pace than in other francophone West African countries, there was a significant growth in the size of the Voltaic force between 1963 and 1965, when in rose from roughly 1,200 to more than 2,500. The number of soldiers rose significantly in this time, from 960 to some 1,500, and the size of the gendarmerie increased from about 550 to 660. The Voltaic air force finally added its first Voltaic member in 1965 and its first Voltaic officer in 1966. By 1968, however, Upper Volta had only increased the size of its military by several hundred troops, and until 1974, it stood at around 2,100 army and air force soldiers and 700 gendarmes (see Table 4).

Voltaic forces were centred in the country's two largest cities, Ouagadougou and Bobo-Dioulasso, where French military bases had previously been located. There were also companies of gendarmes in Koudougou and Fada

---

134 Major-General Nyo, Commander of the Armed Forces, AOF–Togo Defence Zone, to the Secretary of State for War, 'Situation d'effectifs à la date du 1 janvier 1954, Commandement supérieur des forces armées de la zone état-major, 1er bureau', 21 January 1954, GR5H40, SHD.

135 Brebisson, 'Rapport annuel 1961'; Military advisor, French Embassy Ouagadougou, 'Rapport de fin de mission du Colonel Laroussinie', 6 April 1965; French Embassy Ouagadougou, 'Compte-rendu hebdomadaire no. 98', 18 August 1961, 313QONT/3, CADC; French Ambassador in Upper Volta to the Secretary of State for Foreign Affairs, 'Transfert d'officiers voltaïques à l'armée nationale de la république de Haute-Volta', 20 October 1961, 313QONT/4, CADC.

N'Gourma.[136] In Niger, military and security forces were spread more widely because the government had been faced with responding to attacks from a rebel movement that mainly operated from neighbouring countries. Niger's physical size and the length of its borders provided an inherent challenge to the Nigerien military.[137] Nevertheless, Nigerien soldiers interviewed for this research said that difficult missions in the northern part of the country were not a cause for dissatisfaction, but simply part of the job.[138] Some soldiers from Upper Volta, on the other hand, had referred to missions in the northern regions of their country as a form of punishment, and had refused to go. Conditions in these remote locations were difficult, and a lack of infrastructure and service provision in these regions reflected the absence of the state, but the reluctance of soldiers to relocate to areas such as these was one of the reasons it was so hard for both countries to organize the provision of services beyond urban zones. Hence, in Niger and in Upper Volta, the state apparatus and political power were both concentrated in their capitals. The inhabitants of each were highly influential, while the remainder of their populations often had little ability to impact political decision-making.[139]

This centralization of power left their presidents in fragile positions, as demonstrated in 1966 when Voltaic President Maurice Yaméogo was ousted in a military coup, and in 1974 when Nigerien President Hamani Diori was deposed in the same manner. While Yaméogo had succeeded in eliminating organized Voltaic opposition at independence, his development of a single-party state was poor, as politicians had few contacts in rural areas and positions in ministries depended on personal relationships with the president.[140] The French reported that populations in the western part of Upper Volta, particularly in Bobo-Dioulasso, were also dissatisfied

---

136 Military Advisor, French Embassy Ouagadougou, 'Rapport annuel 1971', 31 January 1972, GR14S262, SHD; National Defence General Staff, Intelligence Division, 'Le différend frontalier Malo-Voltaïque', 27 November 1974.
137 Colonel Mahamane Koraou, Nigerien Chief of Staff 1994–1995, interview by author, 20 May 2019.
138 Sabo Yahouza, Captain of the Gendarmerie, interview by author, 22 May 2015.
139 Jean Le Cannellier, French Ambassador in Upper Volta, 'Rapport Fin de Mission (24 June 1977–31 August 1981)', 499po/1/15, CADN.
140 Levasseur, 'Forces d'opposition et force de l'opposition en Haute-Volta', 10 July 1963; Levasseur, French Ambassador in Upper Volta, to Minister of Foreign Affairs Couve de Murville, 'Rapport fin de mission 16 June 1963–18 December 1967', 18 December 1967, 313QONT/13, CADC, and 'La Haute-Volta en 1964', 6 January 1965, 313QONT/10, CADC.

by the fact that the Voltaic government directed benefits to members of the president's ethnic group, the Mossi. The rural population remained largely indifferent to the prerogatives of the government as it had no means to influence it.[141] By the mid-1960s, labour unions represented the only organized opposition in Upper Volta beyond the military, and their political importance far exceeded their numerical strength. In fact, in 1966, when unions played a key role in overthrowing Yaméogo, the country had only had a few thousand salaried workers .[142]

In Niger, President Diori also exhibited a tendency to engage in ethnic favouritism, which contributed to the centralization of his regime. He too was said to favour his own ethnic group, the Djerma, and narrowly distribute the benefits of political power among his close entourage in the capital, Niamey. Exiled Nigerien opposition managed to organize an armed insurrection from neighbouring countries and their movement found support within labour unions, among peasants, and with members of the majority ethnic group, the Hausa. However, their movement had been brutally dismantled by 1965, and power remained centralized to Diori and to the capital.

In both Niger and Upper Volta, this centralization and the weak capacities of the state were linked to the lack of incentives for leaders to extend control beyond their capital and main trade routes. States that obtain the bulk of their resources by taxing trade, or through aid, have little need for administrative or coercive structures to collect taxes from the majority of the population. The Nigerien and Voltaic governments attained most of their revenues from interntional trade and aid, which influenced to whom they were accountable, as politicians tend to listen to those who have contributed sizably to their state or personal budgets.

In Upper Volta, the state relied on foreign aid as well as taxes collected from salaried workers in main cities, which helps explain the political power of labour unions. One French report quoted a Voltaic informant who said that Voltaic labour unions often represented the country's well-educated minority, who failed to take into account the economic realities

---

141 See documents in Files 313QONT/11 and 313QONT/4, FFAN; and File 313QONT/9, CADC.
142 Levasseur, 'Rapport fin de mission 16 juin 1963–18 décembre 1967', 18 December 1967, 'Crise politique en Haute-Volta', 4 January 1966, and 'La Haute-Volta en 1964', 6 January 1965; Levasseur to Minister of Foreign Affairs Couve de Murville, 'La Haute-Volta en 1965', 22 March 1966, 313QONT/9, CADC.

of the state.[143] The same complaint was made about colonial soldiers who had transferred into Voltaic forces from the French army and who had put pressure on politicians to create a strong national military despite the country's limited resources. The large number of colonial soldiers in Upper Volta drove the government's decision to create an army of career soldiers, even though conscripts would have reduced personnel costs.[144] Integrating these colonial soldiers meant the Voltaic military featured high numbers of officers, and therefore high salary costs. Between 1960 and 1974, an average of 83% of the Voltaic military budget was allocated to salaries (see Table 6).

The Nigerien government allocated only an average of 52% of its military budget to salaries (see Table 6). This was a direct result of the smaller number of returning colonial soldiers the armed forces had to absorb. In 1965, officers in the Nigerien forces equalled 1.7% of the total number of troops, which was about half that of the Voltaic forces. After the 1974 military coup, the number of officers in the Nigerien military increased dramatically for two years in a row, first rising to approximately the same rate as Upper Volta (near 4%) before jumping to 5.4% in 1975.[145] This was because the Nigerien military government that assumed control in 1974 promoted a large number of officers after taking power. Interviews with Nigerien soldiers suggest that significantly more resources were directed to both the army and gendarmerie after the coup, largely in the form of more trainings and equipment. Nigerien soldiers further noted that more army contracts went to Nigerien companies. Previously, French equipment meant French training and French business opportunities.[146]

Despite this greater flow of resources to the Nigerien armed forces, military spending in the country did not increase significantly after the coup, as the government secured foreign assistance from West Germany and the US.[147] Even so, Niger received far more military assistance from France than Upper Volta, its fellow centralized state. In fact, the amount of French

---

[143] The report read: '*Depuis l'indépendance, les syndicats … se conduisent comme ils avaient encore en face de la richesse de la puissance coloniale; ils ne tiennent pas compte de la pauvreté du pays*' ('Since independence, the unions … behave as though they still have the wealth of the colonial power before them; they do not take into account the poverty of the country'). See Military attaché, French Embassy Ouagadougou, 'Rapport mensuel mois de septembre 1971', 30 September 1971, GR 14S262, SHD; Delaye, French Ambassador in Upper Volta, 'Synthèse no XX69', 30 September 1969, 313QONT/9 CADC.
[144] See documents in Files 313QONT/3, 313QONT/20, and 313QONT/4, CADC.
[145] SHD.
[146] Interview by author, May 2019, Niamey.
[147] Ibid.

assistance to the militaries of these countries was a key difference between them, as the decision of the Voltaic government to refuse a French military base resulted in it automatically receiving considerably less (see Figure 8). A direct result was that the Voltaic armed forces was still lacked even the most basic equipment in 1964,[148] and only 67% of its 1,500 soldiers had firearms.[149]

Of all nine francophone West African countries, the value of arms transfers to Upper Volta was the lowest. Togo, Dahomey, and Niger also received relatively little in arms transfers, and in all these countries, military coups and military rule became frequent. The inverse was true in countries where the value of arms transfers was high, such as Guinea, Côte d'Ivoire, and Senegal, where no coups occurred between 1960 and 1974 (see Figure 1). While a lack of material resources may have motivated the military overthrow of civilian governments, and French reports often referenced the dissatisfaction of young officers in Upper Volta with the material conditions of the army,[150] the soldiers who assumed power in Dahomey, Togo, Niger, and Upper Volta did not make significant weapon purchases. Niger did receive more weapons transfers from France and Germany after the 1974 military coup, however, and similar increases in arms transfers were observed after other coups in francophone West Africa. For example, transfers from the Soviet Union to Mali increased after the 1968 coup, and the Soviets did the same after coups in Mauritania in 1978 and Guinea in 1984.[151]

---

148 French Embassy Ouagadougou: 'Compte-rendu hebdomadaire', 4 February 1961, 313QONT/4, CADC; 'Compte-rendu hebdomadaire', 28 April 1961, 313QONT/4, CADC; 'Compte-rendu hebdomadaire', 4 August 1961; 'Compte-rendu hebdomadaire' 19 May 1961, 313QONT/3, CADC; 'Compte-rendu hebdomadaire', 7 October 1961, 313QONT/3, CADC; 'Compte-rendu hebdomadaire', 10 November 1961, 313QONT/3, CADC; 'Compte-rendu hebdomadaire', 26 May 1962, 313QONT/4, CADC. Directorate of African and Malagasy Affairs, 'Questions militaires en Haute-Volta', 2 November 1961, 313QONT/20, CADC; SDECE, 'Synthèse de renseigne-ments: January 1962' 17 February 1962, GR5H170, SHD; Lamizana, *Sur la Brèche*, pp. 24–6, and 32; Ambassador of France to the President of Upper Volta, 27 December 1961.

149 Lamizana, 'Rapport annuel du 1er janvier 1964 au 31 December 1964 sur le moral et le fonctionnement de forces armées voltaïques', 4V37, ANB.

150 Parisot, 'Rapport annuel', 15 June 1973; Military attaché, French Embassy Ouagadougou, 'Rapport mensuel mois de septembre 1971', 30 September 1971; Delaye, French Ambassador in Upper Volta, to Minister of Foreign Affairs Schumann, 'Synthèse no XXVI69', 23 December 1969, 313QONT/8, CADC; Intelligence Exploitation Centre, 'Éléments destines à l'élaboration d'une directive pour le conseiller militaire à Ouagadougou', 17 October 1969, GR9Q5122, SHD.

151 SIPRI Arms Transfers Database.

Francophone West African countries started accummulating more weapons after the mid-1970s, when many postcolonial governments in francophone Africa began obtaining military equipment from sources other than France.[152] The French policy on military aid in Africa in the 1960s differed to that of the UK, which allowed its former colonies to attain military equipment from other providers. Throughout the 1960s, the strategy of the French had been to keep any other actors out of its sphere in Africa, on the premise that this protected newly independent states from undue foreign intervention. France also had the objective of limiting the weapons arsenals of its former colonies, and it often dissuaded postcolonial governments from buying new equipment by reminding them of the extra financial costs and human resources involved in its operation and maintenance. The French policy was also to provide only a few spare parts, to control how it equipment was used and to reduce the eagerness of countries to request more. France believed this would force African militaries to recognize the costs of operating and maintaining the equipment they received, and that otherwise, their 'appetite would be insatiable.[153] However, in 1970, when the French Ministry of Cooperation underlined the need for France to help its former colonies renew much of the material that had been transferred to their militaries in the early 1960s, it determined that maintaining rather than replacing the old equipment would be more expensive.[154]

The Voltaic government, which spent the bulk of its military budget on soldiers' salaries, lacked the resources to maintain or use its military equipment. The government chose not to institute obligatory military service due to financial restraints, because even if the French provided equipment for free, the costs of maintenance would be too high.[155] The governments of Togo and Dahomey also had problems maintaining their military equipment. In 1973, a French military attaché in Dahomey reported that the army was not maintaining its equipment because it was so old that commanders thought that replacing it would be more practical. He characterized Dahomean soldiers as more interested in politics than in building military capacity, and said French technical assistants were the only ones

---

152 Ibid.
153 Ministry of Cooperation, 'Domaine de l'assistance militaire' 18 September 1974.
154 General Secretary for African and Malagasy Affairs, 'Coopération militaire avec les états de l'Afrique noire francophone', 30 June 1970; Military advisor, 25 September 1970.
155 See documents in Files 313QONT/3, 313QONT/20, and 313QONT/4, CADC.

carrying out their duties with professional integrity.[156] Even if this is not wholly accurate, it reflects the challenges of making military cooperation effective, enabling technical assistants to transmit their skills to local soldiers.

In Niger, where the role of French technical assistants was significant until the military coup in 1974, some soldiers who were interviewed for this research criticized French military assistance and noted that prior to 1974 most of the equipment used by the armed forces was old and of poor quality. These soldiers shared the opinion that Niger's civilian president, Hamani Diori, had been disinterested in developing the army.[157] However, in the late 1960s, the Nigerien government under Diori had launched an effort to attract recruits with technical skills to the army and the gendarmerie. One interviewee was studying in a technical school in 1968 when he was recruited by the government to train in the military. According to him, he was one of a group of thirty-six students, twenty-one of whom completed a nine-month training in a military school in Niamey. Only two of his trainers were Nigerien, the rest were French.[158]

Leaders in Upper Volta had made the Africanization of the Voltaic military more of a political priority than Diori.[159] In 1961, the Voltaic military had about half the number of French assistants that were in the Nigerien military. This trend continued, more or less, and by 1973, 7% of Voltaic officers were French, compared to 18% in Niger. The difference was even more marked in the gendarmerie. After 1965, there were never more than three French assistants in the Voltaic gendarmerie at any one time, while in Niger, their numbers fell from thirty-seven in 1965 to eighteen in 1974. After 1969, the number of French assistants in the Voltaic armed forces overall remained close to thirty, two to three times less than in Niger and four times less than in Côte d'Ivoire (see Table 7).

In every francophone country, it took longer to build technical capacities for an air force than for other military branches. Hence, French technical assistants continued to play important roles in francophone West African air forces well into the 1970s. In Upper Volta, the air force had exclusively French officers in 1965; but by 1973, 50% of officers and 75% of non-commissioned officers in the air force were Voltaic. The number of French technical assistants serving in the Nigerien air force was slightly

---

156 Lieutenant-Colonel Kern, Military Advisor, French Embassy Cotonou, 'Rapport fin de mission', 30 May 1973, GR9Q5107, SHD.
157 Interview by author, May 2019, Niamey.
158 Ibid.
159 French Embassy Ouagadougou, 'Compte-rendu hebdomadaire', 10 November 1961.

higher at the time, but in the 1970s and 1980s, West Germany and the US started to provide Niger with equipment and training.[160]

Nigerien soldiers and gendarmes had positive memories of German cooperation, but their opinions of French technical assistance were mixed. Some soldiers felt French assistants had little to no confidence in Nigerien abilities, which created distrust on both sides.[161] Indeed, the early development of armed forces in both Niger and Upper Volta was challenged by the fact that neither country attracted the most motivated or talented French soldiers. A French report from 1964, for example, described problems recruiting qualified assistants for Upper Volta.[162] A recent study on military cooperation in Mali concludes that challenges related to lack of trust on both sides, and to Malian soldiers feeling underestimated, continue to limit the effectiveness of military aid.[163]

Of course, some French technical assistants in Niger did succeed in building good relationships with Nigerien soldiers. One soldier who was interviewed described his experience of serving under three different French assistants, the first two of whom were not focused on building Nigerian capacities. 'When they arrive, they know nothing', he commented of assistants such as these, 'they need us, use us, and then, they share nothing and leave.'[164] This same soldier did say that the last French assistant he worked with, who was appointed as his head of service in 1976, had 'invited us to work together with him', noting that 'he bought material we needed and sent a lot of people to training in France and in Niamey.'[165] Even if the experiences of Nigerien soldiers and gendarmes with French technical assistants were mixed, their experiences of training in France or by French officers in Niamey were mostly positive. In their evaluations of their French trainers, these Nigerien soldiers gave good reviews and said they were accustomed to working with Africans.[166]

One Nigerien soldier, who received training at an officer school in Madagascar from 1968 to 1971, said that the class of students one year behind him had included soldiers who would subsequently become heads

160 Interview by author, May 2019, Niamey.
161 Ibid.
162 Levasseur to Minister of Foreign Affairs Couve de Murville, 'La Haute-Volta en 1964', 6 January 1965.
163 Denis Tull, 'Rebuilding Mali's army: the dissonant relationship between Mali and its international partners', *International Affairs* 95, no. 2 (2019), pp. 405–22.
164 Interview by author, May 2019, Niamey.
165 Ibid.
166 Ibid.

of state, such as Thomas Sankara and Siad Barre. He described the school in positive terms and said his trainers were all French, apart from a few Malagasy. The school in Madagascar was later closed, but similar schools existed in Morocco and Cameroon.[167] Upper Volta also established a military academy in Ouagadougou to train future Voltaic military elite. The school was run by a French officer until 1973, when the job was finally transferred to a Voltaic officer,[168] but most Voltaic and Nigerien officers would be trained in France until 1974.[169]

French officials also had a largely positive view of the military potential of Voltaic forces but saw a lack of resources as the main obstacle to their development.[170] Military rule in the country had at first done little to change the situation, as austerity measures had been implemented. During five years of military rule from 1966 to 1971, state spending grew less than 1% per year, but the economy grew an average of 3%.[171] However, Voltaic military spending always accounted for more than 10% of the state budget. This was more than the limit stipulated by France in a 1964 directive from the Ministry of Cooperation to any states receiving its assistance.[172]

French reports thus spoke disapprovingly of the large percentage of the Voltaic budget spent on the military. In 1970, the French Embassy noted, for example, that Upper Volta had spent CFA 1056 million on soldier salaries but only CFA 130 million on medical equipment, concluding that 'even if Upper Volta wants to be independent in its defence, its healthcare is based on external assistance.'[173] Nevertheless, the country's low GDP and low spending from GDP meant that Upper Volta's spending on the military could not provide the armed forces with significant resources. In 1965, when

---

167 Ibid.

168 Ministry of Cooperation, 'Domaine de l'assistance militaire', 18 September 1974.

169 Military advisor, French Embassy Ouagadougou, 'Rapport annuel 1971', 31 January 1972.

170 See documents in Files GR9Q5122, GR14S262, and GR11S85, SHD; and File 313QONT/3, CADC.

171 Azais, 'Rapport de fin de mission', 30 June 1972; Military advisor, French Embassy Ouagadougou, 'Rapport mensuel fevrier 1971', 27 February 1971, GR14S262, SHD.

172 French Embassy Niamey, 'Dépenses de fonctionnement des forces armées nigériennes: Note pour secrétaire d'état', 9 September 1964, 5AGF/2694, FFAN; Ministry of Cooperation, 'Directive concernant l'orientation et l'évolution des armées nationales africaines et malgache', 27 August 1964, INVA318, CADC.

173 French Embassy Ouagadougou to Directorate of African and Malagasy Affairs, Paris, 'Finances publiques Haute-Volta', 31 August 1970, 499PO/1/1, CADN.

Upper Volta spent CFA 953 million on its military, Côte d'Ivoire (which was of comparable size) could spend three times as much.

While there was no meaningful difference between military spending in Upper Volta during the period of military rule from 1966 to 1970 and the years of transitional rule from 1971 to 1974, spending was at its highest in 1969 and 1971 – just before and after the transition. Evidently, military leaders sought to guarantee resources for the armed forces before trans-ferring partial political power to civilians. One aspect that did change across these years was the distribution of the military budget. In 1970, a year prior to elections, the Voltaic army and air force received 82% of the military budget, which the transitional government reduced to 67% by 1974. This was still more than President Yaméogo had allocated to the army during his rule from 1960 to 1965, when around 54% of military spending went to the army and 36% to the gendarmerie.[174]

In newly independent Niger, the civilian government had also allocated less of the military budget to the army, which received 40% in 1965 with Diori in power, and 57% in 1974 after the military coup. Fearful of the coup that would eventually come, Diori had looked to create a strong counter-force to the Nigerien military, and the country's Republican Guard was thus the second largest security force after the army. Niger also had party militias, membership of which numbered around 1,500. Notably, under Diori, the Nigerien gendarmerie does not seem to have held a privileged position vis-à-vis other security forces, despite playing an important role in responding to the Sawaba rebellion in early 1960s. In fact, according to interviewees, the equipment of the Nigerien gendarmerie was in poor condition prior to the military coup. This changed after 1974, when it was able to access more resources, including spare parts and engineering equipment.[175]

Unlike their counterpart in Niger, the Voltaic military government reduced both the manpower and resources of the Voltaic gendarmerie. According to the French, most of the equipment provided by France went

---

174 Cde Lieutenant Zingue Wété, Lieutenant-Colonel Bbaye Fayma, 'La gendar-merie nationale du Burkina Faso', 10 March 1992, 7V429, ANB; French Embassy Ouagadougou, 'Compte-rendu hebdomadaire', 12 May 1962, 313QONT/4, CADC; Levasseur, 'Forces d'opposition et force de l'opposition en Haute-Volta', 10 July 1965, 313QONT/11, CADC; French Embassy Ouagadougou to the Directorate for African and Malagasy Affairs, 'Les forces politiques', 31 December 1964, 499PO/1/1, CADN.
175 Interview by author, May 2019, Niamey.

to the Voltaic army, leaving the gendarmerie with only a modest inventory.[176] Moreover, because so much military spending went to personnel costs, the gendarmerie could not afford to purchase equipment, and relied on aid. The salaries of Voltaic soldiers and gendarmes were comparable to those in Côte d'Ivoire, despite the lower cost of living. Nonetheless, Voltaic officers often complained that their service to the nation was inadequately compensated, especially during the period of military rule from 1966 to 1970.[177]

As raising military salaries in these years was not an option due to austerity measures, promotions were used to increase the pay of individual soldiers. These promotions were only given to the older generation of Voltaic officers close to President Lamizana, however, which led to criticism.[178] Upper Volta's younger generation of officers was better educated, and arguably more qualified for promotion in many cases, but they were more critical of the military government. The promotions also began to stir discontent among the public, who saw this as a clear circumvention of austerity policies with which the civilian administration had complied. As public criticism of the military leadership grew louder, political parties were allowed to organize beginning in November 1969. Labour unions in Upper Volta accused soldiers of corruption and inaction, and the army was increasingly seen by the public to safeguard the personal and institutional interests of soldiers rather than to move the country forward.[179]

Whilst salaries, benefits, and promotions ensured the loyalty of Voltaic soldiers to Lamizana, the privileged position of the military during the years of its rule actually reduced the country's overall military capacity. Supervision suffered, as the most experienced officers were engaged in governance and no longer assured that their orders were followed. As a result,

176 Azais, 'Rapport de fin de mission', 30 June 1972.

177 Battalion Commander Vadogo Ouédraogo, Chief of Staff of the Armed Forces, 'Rapport annuel du 1 janvier 1966 au 31 décembre 1967 sur le moral et le fonctionnement et les activités des forces armées nationales', 21 March 1968, 4V37, ANB.

178 Levasseur, French Ambassador in Upper Volta, to Minister of Foreign Affairs Maurice Couve de Murville, 'Synthèse XVI/67', 28 April 1967, 313QONT/22, CADC; Delaye, French Ambassador in Upper Volta to Minister of Foreign Affairs Maurice Couve de Murville, 'Synthèse IV68', 23 February 1968, 313QONT/8, CADC.

179 Géraud de la Batut, Chargé d'affaires, to Minister of Foreign Affairs Maurice Schumann, 'Synthèse XVII69', 19 August 1969, 313QONT/9 CADC; Delaye, 'Synthèse no XX69', 30 September 1969; Delaye, French Ambassador in Upper Volta, to Minister of Foreign Affairs Schumann, 'Synthèse no XXIV69' 26 November 1969, 313QONT/8 CADC; Military advisor, French Embassy Ouagadougou, 'Rapport mensuel mois de mars 1970', 31 March 1970, GR14S262, SHD.

the forces lacked training and discipline, and military equipment was insufficiently maintained. French military attachés reported that older officers were overwhelmed by their administrative duties and talented younger officers were discouraged by the absenteeism of their superiors.[180]

In Togo and Dahomey, military rule also led to declining discipline within the forces and reduced national military capacities. When soldiers took the role of deciding policy, diverging views were debated within the armed forces, creating permanent conflicts – often between older and younger generations of officers.[181] In Niger, generational conflicts were less severe, perhaps because of the small number of colonial soldiers who had transferred into the national forces from the French military. A Nigerien soldier noted in an interview that the key difference between these generations in Niger had to do with the technical capacities of younger officers, but he noted that the experiences of older soldiers were appreciated.[182]

In Upper Volta, where a huge number of colonial soldiers had transferred into Voltaic forces, political matters increasingly caused disagreement within the military. This was especially true of the transfer to civilian rule in 1971, when many soldiers disputed the ambitious and expensive plans to augment force numbers and army resources. French reports noted that a number of soldiers opposed the transfer of power to civilians, and that some even wanted a government consisting solely of military ministers.[183] One French military attaché complained that Voltaic soldiers had begun to show more interest in politics than in their own profession, noting that the country had once been well-known for the quality of its soldiers.[184] Absenteeism, poor supervision, and indiscipline had become endemic among Voltaic forces during military rule, and this continued after 1971 under the transitional government.[185] Protests in April 1973, for example, were met by

---

[180] General Secretary for African and Malagasy Affairs, 'Les forces armées togolaises', 1 September 1967 and 'Audience de monsieur Hubert Maga, président du conseil et du gouvernement dahoméen', 30 August 1971, 5AGF/547, FFAN; General Couëdic, 'Les forces togolaises et notre assistance militaire au Togo', 27 February 1970, 5AGF/2721, FFAN; Lieutenant-Colonel Kern, 'Rapport fin de mission', 30 May 1973.

[181] Ibid.

[182] Interview by author, May 2019, Niamey.

[183] Military advisor, French Embassy Ouagadougou: 'Rapport mensuel mois de janvier', 31 January 1970, GR14S262, SHD; 'Rapport mensuel mois d'avril', 30 April 1970, GR14S262, SHD and 'Rapport mensuel mois de mars 1970', 31 March 1970.

[184] Parisot, 'Rapport annuel', 15 June 1973.

[185] See documents in Files GR14S262 and GR9Q5122, SHD.

a violent response that was seen to reflect the lack of discipline, training, and preparation of forces in Upper Volta.[186]

The transition to civilian rule brought financial challenges. Reintegrating military ministers into the armed forces proved expensive, as their salaries had to be drawn from the military budget. Moreover, cooperation between military and civilian ministers was difficult from the start, and the popularity of the government had plunged by 1973. That year, a French military attaché described the ills of the Voltaic political system:

> the persistence of tribalism, search for personal gain and lack of dynamism of state agents, as well as unimaginative and bloated state administration, constrains or even paralyzes the efforts to improve the education and the standard of living of the population and the country's infrastructure.[187]

In 1975, he characterized the military and civilian elites in Upper Volta in similar terms, accusing them of 'egoism, ambitions and absence of commitment to the common good'.[188]

In 1973 and 1974, Upper Volta had received emergency assistance to help those among its population who had been severely affected by drought and famine, but this food aid did not provide for any long-term improvements or development. The apathy of the Voltaic government towards this humanitarian disaster led to domestic and international criticism, and it was assumed that the apathy of the Voltaic political elite was due to the fact that it had not affected the Mossi, their ethnic group.[189] The Nigerien and Malian governments were accused of exhibiting similar disinterest in responding to famine, as well as the misuse of famine relief. Again, ethnic differences between the victims and the government elite, along with the poor transport infrastructure of Niger and Mali, limited the effectiveness of their responses.

In Niger, the poor management of this crisis by the civilian government' was one of the main drivers of the military coup in 1974. When the military also returned to power in Upper Volta in 1974, with Lamizana

---

[186] Military advisor, French Embassy Ouagadougou, 'Rapport mensuel mois de mai', 2 May 1973, GR14S262, SHD.

[187] Parisot, 'Rapport annuel', 15 June 1973.

[188] Parisot, 'Rapport de fin de mission', 25 June 1975.

[189] Military advisor, French Embassy Ouagadougou: 'Rapport mensuel mois de January', 31 January 1973, GR14S262, SHD; 'Rapport mensuel mois de mars 1973', 29 March 1973, GR14S262, SHD and 'Rapport mensuel', 1 June 1973, GR14S262, SHD; Parisot, 'Rapport de fin de mission', 25 June 1975.

as prime minister, few French observers were surprised.[190] Soon after, a border conflict ignited between Upper Volta and Mali in December 1974. There were minimal casualties and the conflict lasted only several days, but the financial costs were high. In Upper Volta, the conflict also marked a permanent increase in the number of soldiers deployed along the northern border. The drought in this region had aggravated a land dispute over the Agacher Strip by amplifying the importance of water resources in the area for pastoralists in both countries. Yet, French reports also connected the conflict to Malian domestic politics.[191] It was said to have demonstrated how years of military rule had weakened the Voltaic army, as its commanders lacked control and its operations were hampered by logistical problems and inadequate training. The war also revealed how much better prepared Malian forces were as the result of having acquired Soviet equipment.[192]

While Tilly's theory of warfare and state-building proposes that states must expand their administrative reach to collect more taxes in order to finance war, this is unlikely to occur where military capacities are increased through foreign assistance, such as in Mali, which received significant amounts of equipment and technical assistance from the Soviets. Upper Volta received much less foreign military aid, however, and after the 1974 conflict with Mali, it increased its taxation of official economic activities. The conflict also convinced the Voltaic military government to invest in military equipment. In this way, according to a French report, 'the conflict

190 General Secretariat for National Defence, Intelligence Exploitation Centre, 'Eléments destines à l'élaboration d'une directive pour le conseiller militaire à Ouagadougou', 8 June 1972; Military advisor, French Embassy Ouagadougou, 'Rapport mensuel', 1 June 1973, 'Rapport mensuel', 30 November 1973, GR14S262, SHD, and 'Rapport mensuel mois de mars 1973', 29 March 1973; Parisot, 'Rapport de fin de mission', 25 June 1975; Jean Mathivet, Chargé d'affaires, to the Ministry of Foreign Affairs, 'Synthèse no XIV/67', 14 April 1967, 313QONT/22, CADC.
191 Parisot, 'Rapport de fin de mission', 25 June 1975; Colonel Barthélémy Kombasre, interview by author, 18 January 2016, Ouagadougou; Lieutenant Gariko Yaya, interview by author, 22 January 2016, Ouagadougou; Commandant Paul Tonde, interview by author, 22 January 2016, Ouagadougou; Pierre Claver Hien, 'Les frontières du Burkina Faso: genèse, typologie et conflits (1885–1985)' in *Burkina Faso cent ans d'histoire 1985–1995*, edited by Yenouyabe Georges Madiega and Oumarou Na (Paris: Kartala, 2003), pp. 695–720; Pierre Englebert, *La révolution Burkinabe* (Paris: Harmattan, 1986), pp. 193–7.
192 Parisot, 'Rapport de fin de mission', 25 June 1975; Military Centre for Overseas Information and Documentation Upper Volta, 'Synthèse 1975', 25 June 1975; National Defence General Staff, Intelligence Division, 'Le différend frontalier Malo-Voltaique', 27 November 1974.

with Mali [was] particularly beneficial for the Voltaic armed forces'.[193] Upper
Volta had previously relied exclusively on equipment provided free of charge
by the French, but after the conflict, the Voltaic military purchased CFA
160 million worth of equipment, also from France.[194]

A French military advisor doubted that this new equipment would
bring any long-term benefit, however, calling these years 'a particularly
black period' for Voltaic forces and writing that 'the behaviour of senior
officers and staff during recent operations has been appalling.' He criticized
operations at all levels, noting that the Voltaic response to the conflict with
Mali had been:

> … completely improvised, the mobilization of reservists was only
> belatedly accompanied by the necessary logistical arrangements. Very
> large quantities of weapons, ammunition, vehicles, and materials have
> been bought and transported at great expense. But it all risks turning
> into an incredible waste if the army command, taking advantage of the
> government's momentary generosity … does not have a plan to ensure
> the adequate maintenance of the equipment it has received. There
> is a fantastic waste of time and energy in this country. Professional
> conscience is rare … [and] rare are those who are truly penetrated by
> the sense of the common good and driven by the desire to pull their
> compatriots out of underdevelopment.[195]

Even if equipment purchases did not guarantee any enduring benefit, the
conflict and its side-effects had long ranging repercussions for Voltaic state
finances. In the five years following the conflict, Voltaic spending increased
and state revenues doubled, despite the fact that the economy was growing
no faster. Military spending soon accounted for more than 20% of the state
budget, whereas the share allocated to health and education was slightly
reduced.[196] Improvements in the performance of Voltaic troops during a
second conflict with Mali in December 1985 suggest that this investment
did increase Voltaic military capacities.[197]

193 Parisot, 'Rapport de fin dé mission', 25 June 1975.
194 Ministry of Cooperation, 'Domaine de l'assistance militaire' 18 September 1974.
195 Ibid.
196 Republic of Upper Volta, Ministry of Finance, National Budget 1977, 35V128, ANB;
Republic of Upper Volta, Ministry of Finance, National Budget 1979, 35V129, ANB.
197 Hien, 'Les frontières du Burkina Faso' ; Englebert, *La révolution Burkinabe,* pp. 193–7
; Paul Blanc, French Embassy Ouagadougou, 'Fin de Mission (28 March 1973–30 May
1977)', 499PO/1/15, CADN.

The experience of these two centralized states illustrates how challenging and expensive it can be to build military and state capacities, especially in areas far from the capital with little economic potential. It helps make clear how a reliance on foreign economic assistance can contribute not only to the centralization of political power, but also of services and economic opportunities. In both of these countries, the concentration of political power and economic resources into the hands of a few led to discontent with their governments and eventual military coups. However, in each case, military rule did not increase military or administrative capacities. While more of the state budget went to the armed forces under these regimes, the bulk was spent on soldier salaries and benefits, and the control of military governments remained focused on their capitals.

Conclusion

As this chapter illustrates, the decisions made by African governments in building their national military capacities can be explained as a function of economic and military resources. However, the personal views of leaders, colonial structures, and external and internal threats also played a role. Differences in the views of presidents are most clearly exemplified by a comparison of Ivorian President Houphouët-Boigny and Senegalese President Senghor. Houphouët-Boigny made no secret of his negative opinion of soldiers and chose to rely on French protection, while Senghor looked more positively upon the armed forces and sought to build national military capacities. Both Côte d'Ivoire and Senegal generated significant economic resources, which allowed their governments to extend the reach the state and provide economic opportunities and services to a large part of their populations. This is what characterizes them as coopting states.

Guinea and Mali – the two francophone West African countries labelled as coercive states – received significant security and military assistance from the Soviet Union, but neither was able to provide economic opportunities to their populations as a result of their socialist policies. The poor economic conditions faced by the majority of Guineans and Malians led to dissatisfaction with their governments, to which both responded with force. Each of these states maintained a large security apparatus and spent a considerable part of the state budget on security forces and the military. Their civilian governments also relied on ideology to control the population and the army, particularly by targeting youth.

In both Guinea and Mali, the one party-state sought to extend control to rural areas through party structures and party militias. Investing in the latter was considered a necessity in the light of military coups in neighbouring countries and the dissatisfaction of Guinean and Malian troops with being ordered to use force against civilians. These governments grew increasingly dependent on Soviet military assistance, as suspicions of coup plots led to the arrests and executions of Guinean and Malian soldiers, which reduced their national military capacities. In this way, coercive strategies was applied by these countries even to control of the armed forces.

The militaries of Niger and Upper Volta, which this chapter discusses as centralized states, were undermined instead by infighting and politicization. Neither Niger nor Upper Volta had sufficient economic and military resources, which led their governments to focus both political and military power on their capitals and provide very few services and economic opportunities for the rest of the population. This centralization of power and resources reduced the popular support for presidents and left governments in these countries vulnerable to coups. Military coups did not lead to greater military capacities in either country, as most of their respective military budgets were spent on assuring soldiers' material wellbeing. This meant that political and military power, as well as economic opportunities and services, remained centralized.

Military rule failed to improve military capacities because the most experienced officers took on administrative tasks, leaving only a few capable soldiers to supervise the discipline, training, and logistics of the armed forces. This absence of supervision, along with a politicized and contentious internal environment, reduced the likelihood of military orders being followed or that abuses of power or misuse of public funds were punished. This reduced both the effectiveness and cohesion of the national forces in Niger and Upper Volta. The military governments in both countries also tended to rule in isolation.

The efficiency of party organizations had a considerable effect on whether and to what extent this was possible. For example, in Upper Volta, Maurice Yaméogo's Voltaic Democratic Union (UDV) had weak ties to the population, especially in the countryside. In other francophone West African countries, coopting and coercive states had parties that built much more extensive and effective party structures, such as the Democratic Party of Guinea (PDG) and the Democratic Party of Côte d'Ivoire (PDCI). This enabled the Guinean and Ivorian governments to communicate their message and impose their will much further outside their capitals.

Both internal and external threats also influenced how state coercive institutions were developed. In Guinea, the creation of party militias was vindicated in the Portuguese-led attack in November 1970, when these militias played a major role in fighting off the assailants. However, despite the imperative to build coercive capacities due to the immediacy of external threats, Guinea could not find a way to control the movement of people and goods across its borders. Although the first president of Upper Volta allocated significant state resources to the armed forces in response to the high number of returning colonial soldiers, the absence of external threats and the location of former French military bases led the Voltaic armed forces to concentrate troops in the two largest cities. It deployed few soldiers to the borders or the northern part of the country. In Côte d'Ivoire, an absence of external threats and the primacy of internal threats saw the Ivorian president focus largely on developing the gendarmerie.

In some cases, the threats perceived by francophone West African governments actually convinced them to intentionally weaken national military capacities. After the 1963 military coup in Togo and the proliferation of coups across Africa that followed, soldiers in Guinea, Mali, Niger, and Côte d'Ivoire were given alternative tasks, often in agriculture. Their ability to access weapons and ammunition was also sometimes restricted, and networks of informers were created. Anyone seen as a threat was arrested or sent abroad, and new institutions with parallel tasks were created to form a counterforce to the military.

The distrust displayed by some governments towards their national armed forces also made it more difficult to respond to external threats. The Guinean government became more reliant on Soviet assistance after the November 1970 attack, for example, defying Tilly's theory on war-making and state-building, as the external threat Guinea confronted did not increase state capacities. Instead, many well-educated Guineans were executed or imprisoned, which only deepened Guinean dependence on foreign technical expertise. The 1974 conflict between Upper Volta and Mali similarly failed to have any considerable impact on Voltaic state capacities. The government invested more of its resources in developing national military capacities, and although Voltaic tax revenues increased, 20% of the state budget was directed to the military, most of which was spent on soldier salaries rather than on equipment. The conflict did briefly increase nationalist sentiment among the Voltaic population, but this did not lead to negotiations between the regime and the population on the role of state institutions. As Voltaic state capacities to improve the living conditions of the population were limited, so too was the relevance of the government to the majority of its citizens.

In both Guinea and Upper Volta, external conflicts did not lead to state-building, at least not in a way that amplified the voices of citizens and centred on their needs, because the availability of foreign economic and military assistance reduced incentives for these governments to provide economic opportunities or services to their populations. Indeed, the development of state coercive capacities in francophone West Africa was contingent on how much and what kind of external military assistance could be accessed, and when. The Ivorian, Senegalese, Voltaic, and Nigerien armed forces largely depended on the availability of French assistance to build capacity, for instance. France was able to increase its transfers of military equipment to francophone states after the war in Algeria ended in 1962, by which time its overall presence in Africa had been dramatically reduced. Similarly, the French decision to repatriate all its African soldiers by 1964 enabled the force size of national militaries in francophone West Africa to be augmented fairly quickly. France was also more willing to provide equipment after 1964, especially to African air forces, where it took longer to build technical capacities, which meant that the role of French assistants continued to be important. Other branches of the military were commanded by local officers. From 1969 onwards, France largely concentrated on assisting national air forces.

From 1969 onwards many countries in francophone West Africa acquired planes and helicopters from other Western states as well. In the 1970s, West Germany and The Netherlands were permitted to provide equipment to the Nigerien and Senegalese armed forces, and by the 1980s, many countries that were formerly reliant on French assistance, such as Mauritania and Benin (previously Dahomey), turned to the Soviets for military assistance. Guinea and Mali, which opted for Soviet assistance immediately after independence, tied the building of the bulk of their national military capacities to aid from the Soviet Union, even though both countries received significant economic assistance from Western powers. This made Guinea and Mali economically reliant on Western countries but militarily reliant on the Soviets. Nevertheless, as insufficient maintenance of Soviet equipment reportedly rendered it quickly unusable, it did not increase the military capacities of these two countries as much as the extent of their weapons arsenal would suggest. As in all francophone West African countries, the limited training provided to colonial soldiers increased the dependency of these militaries on the technical assistance of foreign actors. The impact of colonial structures on national armed forces, and the various approaches African governments used to deal with difficult colonial legacies is discussed in the next chapter.

4

Legitimacy and Colonial Legacies:
The Use of Force and Institutions of Coercion

At independence, francophone West African governments faced the difficult challenge of building national armed and security forces from the personnel, equipment, and infrastructure previously intended to keep the French empire secure. These governments needed sufficient human and material resources to build a military, and to assure the reintegration of those colonial soldiers who could not be included in national armed forces. They also needed to build the legitimacy of coercive institutions and the use of force. As violence had been used as a means of repression during colonialism, African populations looked upon any continuity in colonial structures or in the elevated role of foreign resources in national security with much cynicism. This made it more challenging to develop national security and armed forces so that they would be seen as legitimate by the population.

This chapter shines a light on the strategies used by governments in francophone West Africa to address difficult legacies of colonialism, particularly as it relates to legitimizing the use of force and institutions of coercion. The decisions of these governments diverged when it came to the role of the former colonial power, which had implications for the legitimacy of their national militaries. Where France played a continuing important role in national security, it was more difficult to mark a clear break from colonial structures and practices. Hence, in countries like Guinea, Mali and Upper Volta – which refused to host French military bases – the government could more easily legitimize their national armed forces through nationalist discourse. However, the fact that the Malian and Guinean governments did not depend on France to equip and train their national militaries did not mean they avoided a reliance on foreign aid.

Notably, Guinea, Mali, and Upper Volta were also the three countries with the highest numbers of returning colonial soldiers (see Table 3), which suggests that these soldiers may have played a part in pushing their governments to build strong and independent militaries. The return of colonial soldiers posed various challenges for every francophone country in West

Africa. They were so numerous that it was impossible for all of them to be incorporated into the new national armed forces. Those who could not be reintegrated possessed few professional skills that could be employed outside of the military. Worse, France had largely relied on African soldiers throughout the colonial period, as the number of French soldiers in West Africa was small (see Table 3). The role colonial soldiers had played in defending the French empire and ensuring local order made governments in newly independent African states wary about their loyalty, as they had not participated in national struggles. They were also inadequately trained and had little experience in using any military equipment other than light weapons. The French had also recruited most of these soldiers from the rural youth, who were uneducated and underprivileged, quite unlike the political elite. Hence, this all increased the challenge of building a national military out of colonial soldiers in francophone West Africa.

In some cases – such as in Mali, Senegal, or Upper Volta – soldiers' poor level education and their ethnic background seems to have facilitated better relations with the regime, as suggested by the relatively positive attitudes of these governments towards colonial soldiers. However, the 1963 military coup in Togo shifted the perspective of many African governments towards their national militaries, with soldiers being increasingly seen as a threat. Even so, despite concerns about their loyalty, all leaders in newly independent francophone built their national armies using colonial soldiers. The gendarmes and police officers in these states were also former colonial soldiers. This continuity of personnel from the colonial period was an obstacle to legitimizing the institutions of coercion in these states.

Colonial security systems and infrastructure also posed a challenge to postcolonial African governments. The recruitment, training, equipment, and logistics of the French military in Africa had not been designed for the purposes of independent states; yet making changes to colonial structures required human and material resources these nascent states lacked. This forced francophone West African governments to seek foreign aid – from equipment to technical skills and training – in order to develop national military capacities, and many received this assistance from France. This additional hangover from the colonial period, whether in the form of technical assistance or military bases, created further problems in legitimizing institutions of coercion and the use of force. The challenge was clearly greatest for governments that remained aligned with France, as they could not so easily mark the point at which a rupture from the colonial past had occurred.

It was somewhat unavoidable, though, that postcolonial state institutions in all of francophone West Africa would be shaped by colonial social structures, and this was particularly true for the national armed forces. In the region that became French West Africa (FWA) in 1895, colonial conquest had been driven by military interests rather than economic or political objectives, which made military structures important to the administration of newly acquired territories and led to the absorption of conquered African forces into the French military.[1] In this way, African soldiers became vital to the expansion and maintenance of the French empire.[2] Their inclusion within the 'forces of order' did not mean, however, that Africans had any influence over how coercion was used. In fact, studies of colonial policing emphasize that its purpose was not to provide security to the African population, but to keep order and guarantee African labour for European enterprise.[3]

Nevertheless, the structures, practices, and objectives of postcolonial national military and security forces across francophone West Africa were based on their French equivalents. However, practices related to the use of force in the colonies had long differed from those applied by France in the metropole.[4] The *indigénat* system had authorized colonial administrations to punish colonial subjects without a court order, leading to the despotic and arbitrary use of force. Postcolonial governments, hence, faced the challenge of legitimizing the state monopoly on the use of force. States usually have good reason to establish practices, using the tools at their disposal, that legitimize the use of force, at least in order to reduce the extent to which force is actually needed. In other words, if the use of coercion is widely accepted, a state is less likely to encounter active or passive resistance to its power or demands. The acceptance of a state's use of force ultimately depends on how coercion is exercised.

This is not to say that no other means exist by which a state can legitimize violence. Coercion can be legitimized by qualifying its use – claiming it is only used with restraint, in exceptional circumstances, and according

---

1   Michael Crowder, *West Africa under Colonial Rule* (London: Hutchinson, 1982), pp. 69–78.

2   Myron Echenberg, *Les Tirailleurs sénégalais en Afrique occidentale française, 1857–1960* (Paris: Karthala, 2009), pp. 25, 58–9, and 291, and 'Paying the Blood Tax: Military Conscription in French West Africa, 1914–1929', *Canadian Journal of African Studies* 9, no. 2 (1975), pp. 172–3, and 176.

3   Jean-Pierre Bat and Nicolas Courting, *Maintenir l'ordre colonial: Afrique et Madagascar xixe–xxe siecles* (Presses universitaires de Rennes, 2012); Martin Thomas, *Violence and Colonial Order: Police, Workers and Protest in the European Colonial Empires, 1918–1940* (Cambridge University Press, 2012).

4   Ibid.

to some mutually agreed principles, such as national or local laws. A state may also work to convince internal or external audiences that force must be used to advance shared collective or individual interests, for example, to combat a domestic or international threat. Defining such shared interests would of course require some degree of consultation between a state and its population, but any such practice was largely absent in the colonial period and therefore did not develop in most postcolonial states. Indeed, as this chapter and the next will show, francophone West African governments preferred top-down approaches to legitimizing their use of force or institutions of coercion to strengthening systems of political participation. Commonly, this entailed public presidential discourse about the necessity to assure national unity or fight foreign plots of subversion.

In addition to rules and practices, the structure of colonial coercitive institutions represented another difficult legacy of colonialism, and newly independent African countries faced the challenge of legitimizing and reorganizing the means of coercion itself. This meant reimagining the people, infrastructure, and equipment that had exercised colonial coercion, even as every postcolonial francophone West African state built its national armed forces from personnel, bases, and equipment transferred from the French military. This chapter will show that despite these continuities, francophone West African governments took different approaches to legitimizing and reorganizing their forces. Guinean President Sékou Touré took the most radical approach, requesting the immediate departure of French troops upon Guinean independence in 1958. He turned to the communist bloc for aid, and until the 1990s, Guinean forces were equipped and trained almost entirely by communist countries.

Mali also received significant assistance from the communist bloc. Together with Upper Volta, both Mali and Guinea had been the most important source of recruits to the French military, and therefore had high numbers of returning colonial soldiers. The pressure to equip a large army may have contributed to the decision of the Guinean and Malian governments to turn to communist states for military aid. While the Voltaic government did not make this same choice, it did refuse to host a French military base and asked that French troops be withdrawn. Hence, the three countries with the highest numbers of former French colonial soldiers all saw the departure of French troops, marking a break from the colonial past.

As this chapter will demonstrate, postcolonial governments in francophone West Africa that retained a French military base on their territory had a harder time navigating colonial legacies. The approaches of these countries to colonial soldiers and to building their national armed forces were far from uniform, however. The Ivorian president, who disliked the military and was suspicious of colonial soldiers, established party militias and assigned his troops to non-military agricultural tasks, much like the socialist governments in Guinea and Mali. By contrast, the Senegalese president respected the sophistication and experiences of Senegalese officers and heeded their concerns about the political development of the country.

For context, this chapter analyses the similarities and differences in the approaches of governments in these countries to managing colonial legacies. It will start by describing the colonial security system and the recruitment of African soldiers by France. French recruitment of Africans is discussed in existing literature as it relates to the period leading up to the Second World War, but there are gaps in our understanding of how this process worked in the 1950s as well as the role of African soldiers in the conflicts of Indochina and Algeria. However, the focus here is on the impact of colonial structures in the postcolonial period, and how the recruitment and use of African soldiers by France influenced the building of national militaries in newly independent francophone West Africa. Disparities in French recruitment, for example, meant that the number of returning colonial soldiers in some of these countries was four to ten times higher than the number of soldiers recruited to their national armed forces.

Blood Tax: West African Soldiers in the French Army

In 1933, the head of the French military cabinet dismissed the idea that African recruits to French forces in its colonies should serve 'voluntary commitments, which, by definition, exclude any idea of obligation, and are the expression of an individual will'. Instead, he argued, 'the principle of recruitment in French West Africa is essentially based on the idea of contribution. Military service is a veritable "blood tax" due by all, and regardless of the ability or desire of each to bear arms.'[5] However, commanders on the ground in FWA had already complained that 'newly arrived recruits are completely illiterate … and among the native population the conviction is spread that only the poor and the sons of captives are required to perform military service.' This was a stain on France, claimed one commander in 1928, and for the sake of 'French prestige', it needed to change.[6]

---

5   Chief of the Military Cabinet in Dakar to Directorate of Political and Administrative Affairs, 'Recrutement indigène', 18 December 1933, 4D2, AAOF.
6   Battalion Chief Charbonneau, Commander of the Military Subdivision of French Guinea, to Lieutenant-Governor of French Guinea, 'Au sujet du recrutement', 11 January 1928, 4D8, AAOF.

French debates on the recruitment of African soldiers often involved contestations between different colonial actors on the means and objectives of colonialism. The French civilian administration supported universal conscription as a way of teaching republican values to the colonized. This was the 'blood tax', *l'impôt du sang*, that all subjects were required to pay. The French military complained, however, that universal conscription was damaging its reputation, as its ranks were filled with the most underprivileged youth of FWA. While young people who had received even minimal education were left off recruitment lists, French practices in this regard varied over the colonial period. In the earliest years, for example, recruits had been members of conquered forces or former slaves. [7]

An influential proponent of recruiting African soldiers into the French military was Charles Mangin, a French general who suggested in 1910 that France should recruit an increasing number of African soldiers to match Germany's increasing strength and population growth.[8] Two years later, a law on universal conscription in the colonies imposed a quota of conscripts to each colony.[9] In other words, all of FWA was expected to pay a blood tax by supplying a certain number of recruits to the French military, although Mauritania and Niger were often exempt because their widely dispersed nomadic populations made recruitment cumbersome.[10] Despite the difficulties of recruiting soldiers from some parts of FWA, politicians in Paris were insistent that the burden of military service should be shared equally among all groups and regions, as this would enforce a sense of community belonging among colonial subjects and establish reciprocal responsibilities between the republic and the colonized. Universal conscription was seen as the only way to supply a sufficient number of African soldiers to the French military.[11]

---

7   Echenberg, *Les tirailleurs sénégalais*, pp. 25, 58–9, and 291; Echenberg, *Paying the Blood Tax*, pp. 172–3, and 176.

8   Charles Mangin, *La force noire* (Paris: Harmattan, 2011).

9   Echenberg, *Les tirailleurs sénégalais*, pp. 25, 58–9, and 291; Echenberg, *Paying the Blood Tax,* pp. 172–3, and 176.

10   The French calculated the number of recruits that could be supplied by each colony by deducting the number of men in good physical condition in their twenties from the total population. Based on these calculations, in 1919, the number that could be recruited from the whole of French West Africa was estimated to be 16,500 out of a population of approximately 10,638,000. See Echenberg, *Les tirailleurs sénégalais*, p. 98.

11   Chief of the Military Cabinet in Dakar, 'Recrutement indigène', 18 December 1933.

This view was not shared by all those parties involved. Officials in Paris, colonial administrators, and the French military all disagreed about how many soldiers should be recruited and what the outcome of recruitment would be.[12] From the perspective of the military, conscription had many unwanted consequences, including the fact that it obligated the recruitment of soldiers who were neither adapted nor motivated for armed service. Moreover, as traditional local chiefs had drafted the list of potential conscripts, this had allowed them to use the process as a tool of social control by listing any individuals they did not want in their jurisdiction, or vice versa.[13] In Guinea, for example, chiefs were thought to have systematically excluded some names from recruitment tables, which they concealed by adding the names of individuals who were too young or old or physically unfit for military service.[14]

French officers believed its own civilian administration was complicit in helping educated Africans escape conscription,[15] and it was true that both the civilian administration and the private sector preferred to keep them out of the military. In 1938, a French report noted that the army could only succeed in recruiting educated Africans if the civil administration and private sector restricted their hiring to candidates who had already fulfilled their military duties.[16] Despite this, individuals who could speak French, read and write, or practice a profession were still not presented to recruitment commissions.[17] The sons of chiefs were also absent from among conscripts, and some French officials felt their successful recruitment could improve the image of the French military in the colonies.[18] One French officer even suggested that the colonial administration should make military service a prerequisite for recognition as a chief. He suggested that chiefs who had been in the military would have greater authority over former soldiers

---

12 Echenberg, *Paying the Blood Tax*, pp. 182–3, and 190.

13 Echenberg, *Les Tirailleurs sénégalais*, p. 115.

14 Captain Nya, 'Rapport ... sur une mission de recrutement effectuée en Guinée en January 1927', 21 February 1927, 4D8, AAOF.

15 Battalion Chief Charbonneau to Lieutenant-Governor of French Guinea, 'Au sujet du recrutement', 11 January 1928.

16 Senior Commander of AOF Troops, 'Rapport annuel sur le recrutement indigène année 1938', 22 October 1938, 4D12, AAOF.

17 Nya, 'Rapport ... sur une mission de recrutement effectuée en Guinée en January 1927', 21 February 1927; Battalion Chief Charbonneau to Lieutenant-Governor of French Guinea, 'Au sujet du recrutement', 11 January 1928.

18 Nya, 'Rapport ... sur une mission de recrutement effectuée en Guinée en January 1927', 21 February 1927.

when they returned to their villages, and that the overseas experiences and connections of these former soldiers could make them valuable to France.[19]

However, the reality of universal conscription was that the most disadvantaged in colonial society paid the blood tax, while educated and wealthier Africans did not. As a result, most conscripts did not speak French and only a handful could read and write, which limited the training they could receive. The 'poor quality' of African recruits was then used as a reason to block their gradual absorption into European ranks. To improve the level of aptitude, French military authorities proposed reducing quotas in certain regions and increasing them in regions that had produced the most motivated and physically fit soldiers.[20] Colonial and military officials agreed that the quota for the Fouta-Djallon region in Guinea should be diminished,[21] as members of the Fulani ethnic group were considered physically unfit for military service.[22] Additionally, the number of absent Fulani conscripts was very high.[23] Yet Paris refused to reduce the quota in Fouta-Djallon, as it had already reduced quotas for border areas with the Gold Coast (now Ghana) and Liberia, and it was feared that further compromises would lead to the separation of certain groups from the empire. French officials argued that further reductions would compromise the egalitarian principles of recruitment and would 'reverse the achievements already made in creating a sense of community between "us and them".'[24]

19 Ibid.
20 Governor-General of French West Africa, Military Cabinet, to Lieutenant-colonels of the colonies, 1 October 1930, 4D2, AAOF; Major General Thiry, Senior Commander of the French West Africa Group, to the Governor-General of French West Africa (Military Cabinet), 'Recrutement indigène', 7 December 1933, 4D2, AAOF.
21 Governor-General van Vollenhoven, Military Cabinet, to Mr Maginot, Ministry of Colonies, July 1917, 4D1/81, AAOF; Governor-General of French West Africa, Military Cabinet, to lieutenant-colonels of the colonies, 1 October 1930; Major General Thiry, to the Governor-General of French West Africa (Military Cabinet), 'Recrutement indigène', 7 December 1933.
22 Major General Benoît, Senior Commander of French West Africa Group, 'Rapport … sur les opérations des recrutement indigène en 1929–1930', 21 August 1930, 49D, AAOF; Dr Colonel Colombani, Head of the Health Service of French Guinea, 'Rapport sur le recrutement 1935–1936', 4D11, AAOF, and 'Rapport sur le recrutement 1934–1935', 5 June 1935, 4D11, AAOF.
23 Nya, 'Rapport … sur une mission de recrutement effectuée en Guinée en January 1927', 21 February 1927.
24 Chief of the Military Cabinet in Dakar, 'Recrutement indigène', 18 December 1933.

It must be emphasized that French recruitment was and would never be never egalitarian. The wealthiest, most educated, and most influential Africans were always able to escape conscription. Moreover, the conditions and rights of service available to French and African soldiers were nothing alike. Racial prejudices clearly influenced the treatment of Africans within the French military, leading to preferences for members of certain ethnic groups and their disproportionate promotion to the ranks of non-commissioned officers.[25] In fact, it was only in the mid-1950s that African soldiers had the opportunity to join the officer ranks.

The recruitment of African soldiers by France during the First World War had unmasked the benevolent face of colonialism. The survival of the republic was a priority, and the wellbeing and development of the colonies was secondary. All told, 170,000 African troops, or *tirailleurs sénégalais*, participated in the conflict.[26] Yet, the recruitment practices that had been used by the French concerned both the colonial administrators and the local population. In the years from 1914 to 1916, there were protests against conscription in Haut-Senegal-Niger and in Dahomey. One of the most vocal critics of French recruitment was French colonial administrator and soldier Joost van Vollenhoven – who was appointed Governor-General of FWA in May 1917. He opposed any further recruitment of African soldiers, contending it would result in economic catastrophe in a region already lacking a sufficient agricultural workforce.[27] Van Vollenhoven sought to convince decision-makers in Paris that West Africa was not the reservoir of manpower Mangin had described, saying that:

> We always talk about FWA as a reservoir of black troops. The word was made fashionable by General Mangin. Will it be recalled that the area of FWA not including the Saharan territories is equal to four times that of France and has only twelve million inhabitants! If France, which is not overpopulated, however, had the same population density as FWA, it would have three million inhabitants. Here is the reservoir ....The physiological misery and weak constitution of blacks is so great that the recruiting commissions were only able to take 10-20% of the conscripts already previously selected by the district commanders. The

25   Michel Bodin, *Les Africains dans la guerre d'Indochine, 1947–1954* (Paris: Harmattan, 2000), pp. 150, and 162–4; Echenberg, *Les Tirailleurs sénégalais*, pp. 116–17.

26   Echenberg, *Les Tirailleurs sénégalais*, pp. 59 and 91.

27   Governor-General van Vollenhoven, Military Cabinet, to Mr Maginot, Ministry of Colonies, July 1917.

start of a new recruitment campaign would only offer poor results because the locals are faint.[28]

Van Vollenhoven also criticized the recruitment practices of the French, especially in campaigns undertaken between 1914 and 1917, which a French inspector-general had also found excessive in both their outcomes and methods.[29] French officials did later admit that the practices used by France during the First World War were harmful, but excused them by noting the number of atrocities committed by traditional chiefs.[30]

According to historian Myron Echenberg, van Vollenhoven was correct that French recruitment in Africa during the First World War hampered the development of African societies by leaving an inadequate workforce for the agricultural and industrial sectors.[31] Nonetheless, in 1917, van Vollenhoven was challenged even by leaders in Africa, such as Senegalese politician Blaise Diagne, who welcomed French recruitment. The minister of colonies in Paris found Diagne's position more suitable to his needs and, despite van Vollenhoven's protests, a decision to continue recruitment was made on 17 December 1917. Van Vollenhoven offered his resignation in January 1918, returned to the battlefront, where he died shortly thereafter.

As for Diagne, he succeeded in increasing African recruitment by 52,000 in 1918 and was promoted to serve as a General Commissioner of Recruitment. French officials noted his success and attributed it to the admiration evoked by well-dressed African soldiers among African populations.[32] Indeed, Diagne's recruitment campaign was so effective that he convinced African elites, a group that had largely escaped conscription, to enlist their sons in the French army.[33] In the eyes of decision-makers in Paris, Diagne's success had discredited the colonial administration, as the

28 Ibid.

29 Ibid (quoted in). Inspector-General Picanon had reported in 14 November 1916 that '*les opérations de recrutement qui ont eu lieu de 1914 à 1917 en AOF ont été excessives dans leurs résultats comme dans leurs méthodes*' ('The recruitment operations that took place from 1914 to 1917 in FWA were excessive in their results and methods').

30 Governor-General of French West Africa, Military Cabinet, 'Crise de recrutement en AOF', 30 March 1922, 4D1, AAOF.

31 Echenberg, *Les tirailleurs sénégalais*, p. 82–3 and *Paying the Blood Tax*, pp. 182 and 192.

32 Governor-General of French West Africa, 'Tableau des effectifs recrutes en Afrique occidentale française depuis 1910', 4D1, AAOF; Echenberg, *Les tirailleurs sénégalais*, pp. 88–9.

33 Echenberg, *Les tirailleurs sénégalais*, pp. 82–3, and 88–9; Directorate of Political Affairs, Chief of the Military Cabinet, 'Recrutement indigène 1937', 9 September 1937, 4D12, AAOF; Echenberg, *Paying the Blood Tax*, p. 190.

catastrophic consequences van Vollenhoven and his subordinates had feared did not materialized. Even so, Diagne did not manage to change the fact that French military service remained broadly unpopular in Africa or that many Africans soldiers continued to refuse reenlistment. Notably, these soldiers cited unequal treatment and bad war experiences as reasons for their refusal, rather than the inadequacy of their compensation.[34]

The end of the First World War did not end conscription in FWA. The ongoing threat posed by Germany, the need to maintain a large military, and a lack of workforce in the metropole all contributed to a 1919 law that extended universal conscription into peacetime. French officials calculated that as recruitment had not led to unmanageable violent resistance during wartime, it was even less likely during peacetime. Recruitment by the French was increasingly carried out by using lists compiled by traditional chiefs.[35] Many of those whose names had been included were absent when the mobile recruitment commission arrived, as young men moved either permanently or temporarily outside their village to avoid being forced to sign up. French reports complained that although many of these young men would later return to their villages, the chiefs did not report them to French authorities.[36] In the 1930s, France thus increasingly focused on locating missing youth conscripts in FWA. If found, these '*bons absents*', were directly enlisted. As a result, every year, the French armed forces received African recruits who had absolutely no motivation to serve.[37] Had the process been left to French military leaders, they would have chosen to maintain a small volunteer force, as their British counterparts had done.

Even so, in some regions of FWA, a tradition of military service did develop. This was true of French Sudan (Mali) and Upper Volta, as recruits from these populous and more ethnically homogenous territories often had an easier time integrating into French forces because soldiers could find others who spoke their language. The French also valued the 'warrior qualities' of the Bambara (from Mali) and Mossi (from Upper Volta),

---

34 Governor-General of French West Africa, Military Cabinet, 'Crise de recrutement en AOF', 30 March 1922; Echenberg, *Les tirailleurs sénégalais*, p. 91.
35 Governor-General of French West Africa, Military Cabinet, to lieutenant-colonels of the colonies, 1 October 1930; Governor-General of French West Africa to Minister of Colonies, 'Recrutement indigène en AOF', 9 November 1935, 4D2, AAOF.
36 General Staff, French West Africa Group, 'Rapport sur les opérations de recrutement en 1936', 8 August 1936, 4D11, AAOF.
37 Echenberg, *Les Tirailleurs sénégalais*, p. 138; General Staff, French West Africa Group, 'Rapport annuel sur l'opération de recrutement année 1935', 9 August 1935, 4D11, AAOF.

and members of these ethnic groups were often promoted to serve as non-commissioned officers.[38] In general, populations from savanna regions, such as the Bambara, Bobo, Mossi, or Malinke, were considered by the French to make better soldiers than those from equatorial forest regions.[39]

Some Africans may have submitted to recruitment because it provided one of the few opportunities for work amid the economic crisis of the 1930s, particularly in remote corners of the empire.[40] In any case, Guinea became the most important source of volunteers to the French armed forces.[41] There were also a high number of Voltaic recruits, as Upper Volta was the most populous part of FWA. In contrast, the French typically had only a few conscripts from Mauritania and Niger, if any at all (see Table 9). After the Second World War, France began increasing the number of African volunteers it would accept, but like the First World War before it, the conflict had reduced the willingness of Africans to serve in the French military.[42] Approximately 200,000 *tirailleurs sénégalais* participated in the Second World War, of whom an estimated 17,500 were killed.[43]

In the post-war years, African soldiers were used in unsuccessful efforts to maintain the empire and quell nationalist movements in Indochina, North Africa, and Madagascar.[44] The decision by French officials to use African soldiers in Indochina was a cost-saving measure, and also allowed French

---

38 Echenberg, *Les Tirailleurs sénégalais*, pp. 112–17; Echenberg, *Paying the Blood Tax,* pp. 186–91.

39 Bodin, *Les Africains dans la guerre d'Indochine*, pp. 162–4; Major-General Benoît, 'Rapport … sur les opérations des recrutements indigène en 1929–1930', 21 August 1930.

40 Echenberg, *Les Tirailleurs sénégalais* pp. 58–9, 84–5, 116, and 190; Directorate of Political Affairs, Chief of the Military Cabinet, 'Recrutement indigène 1937', 9 September 1937.

41 Benoît, 'Rapport … sur les opérations des recrutement indigène en 1929–1930', 21 August 1930; General Staff, French West Africa Group, 'Rapport sur le recrutement 1932', 49D, AAOF, and 'Rapport sur les opérations de recrutement indigène en 1939', 14 October 1939, 4D15, AAOF; Report of Lieutenant-General Dubuisson, Senior Troop Commander, 4D15, AAOF; Echenberg, *Les Tirailleurs sénégalais*, p. 194.

42 Ministry of the Overseas, Office of Defence Organization, 3rd Section, to General Commander of the French West Africa Group, 'Recrutement et relève en AOF en 1947', 4D16, AAOF; Governor-General of French West Africa, Military Cabinet, 1st Section, the High-Commissioner of the Republic in French West Africa, Commander of the Legion of Honour, to the governors of the colonies 'Recrutement des africains non originaires de la classe 1948', 18 October 1948, 4D16, AAOF.

43 Echenberg, *Les Tirailleurs sénégalais*.

44 Echenberg, *Paying the Blood Tax*, p. 173.

Table 9. The number of recruits and population sizes in francophone West Africa, 1920–1948.

	1920	1929	1934	1936	1944	1948
Côte d'Ivoire: recruits	1,500	2,000	3,500	2,507	2,000	1,010
% from FWA recruits	12.6	13.3	29.8	32.2	20.0	11.9
% of population FWA	12.4	12.4	32.9	32.9	32.7	12.6
difference	+0.2	+0.9	–3.1	–0.7	–12.7	–0.7
Guinea: recruits	1,776	2,500	2,000	1,289	2,061	1,310
% from FWA recruits	14.9	16.6	17.0	16.5	20.6	15.5
% of population FWA	12.7	12.9	13.0	13.0	13.2	13.2
difference	+2.2	+3.7	+4	+3.5	+7.4	+2.3
Upper Volta: recruits	3,000	3,800	–	–	–	1,560
% from FWA recruits	25.2	25.3	–	–	–	18.5
% of population FWA	20.9	20.5	–	–	–	20.1
difference	+4.3	+4.8	–	–	–	–1.6
French Soudan: recruits	3,001	3,200	3,100	2,124	2,826	2,291
% from FWA recruits	25.2	21.3	26.4	27.3	28.2	27.1
% of population FWA	16.9	16.9	16.8	16.8	16.8	16.8
difference	+8.3	+4.4	+9.6	+10.5	+11.4	+10.3
Senegal: recruits	1,903	1,650	1,870	1,110	1,958	985
% from FWA recruits	16.0	11	15.9	14.3	19.5	11.7
% of population FWA	12.6	12.6	12.7	12.7	12.7	12.8
difference	+3.4	–1.6	+3.2	+1.6	–6.8	–1.1
Dahomey: recruits	600	1,100	860	512	873	730
% from FWA recruits	5.0	7.3	7.3	6.6	8.7	8.6
% of population FWA	9.9	9.9	10.0	10.0	10.0	10.1
difference	–4.9	–2.6	–2.7	–3.4	–1.3	–1.5
Niger: recruits	68	600	380	215	197	416
% from FWA recruits	0.1	4	3.2	2.8	2.0	4.9
% of population FWA	11.2	11.2	11.2	11.2	11.1	11.1
difference	–11.1	–7.2	–8.0	–8.4	–9.1	–6.2

	1920	1929	1934	1936	1944	1948
Mauritania: recruits	50	150	40	30	108	150
% from FWA recruits	0.4	1	0.3	0.3	1.1	1.7
% of population FWA	3.4	3.4	3.4	3.5	3.5	3.5
difference	–3	–2.4	3.1	–3.2	–2.4	–1.8
All recruits FWA	11,898	15,000	11,750	7,787	10,023	8,452
% recruits from overall FWA population	0.009	0.011	0.007	0.005	0.006	0.004

In 1934, 1936 and 1944, Voltaic recruits are reported together with Ivorian numbers. In making this comparison, the populations of Côte d'Ivoire and Upper Volta have been combined. (Sources: Affaires militaires, Rapports de recrutement: 4D1, 4D2, 4D3, 4D8, 4D9, 4D11, 4D12, 4D15, 4D16, 49D, Archives d'Afrique Occidentale Française, Dakar, Sénégal (AAOF). The Frankema-Jerven African Population Database 1850–1960, version 1.0; published in Frankema, E. and M. Jerven (2014), 'Writing History Backwards and Sideways: Towards a Consensus on African Population, 1850–present', *Economic History Review* 67, S1, pp. 907–31, available at: https://www.aehnetwork.org/data-research/.)

soldiers to remain in Europe. Additionally, sending Africans to Indochina was expected to cause less political foment in France than deploying French nationals.[45] This use of colonial soldiers against nationalist movements would have long-term effects on the way former soldiers were perceived by African political elites after independence.

The number of African soldiers in Indochina grew substantially over two years, rising from 2,477 in January 1948 to 12,090 by December 1949. During the same period, the number of French soldiers serving there was reduced by more than 6,000.[46] Nonetheless, French soldiers continued to occupy the most important command positions, while African soldiers were confined to support tasks, kept in low-level positions on the premise that they lacked education. Finally, in the 1950s, when French authorities started to accept the inclusion of African officers, the fact that most recruits came from rural areas where education opportunities were rare, and had weak

---

45 Bodin, *Les Africains dans la guerre d'Indochine,* pp. 13 and 16.
46 Ibid., p.16. Echenberg suggests there were 18,500 *tirailleurs sénégalais* serving in Indochina in 1949, but that number had dropped to 15,000 by 1952. See *Les Tirailleurs sénégalais,* p. 194.

language skills, hampered their training.[47] By 1955, there were 27 African officers in the French military, including 23 from FWA, but there were over 700 French officers in the colonial forces, and it was they who occupied almost every command post.[48]

Previously, the peasant background of soldiers had been valued because the rural youth were believed to be accustomed to hardship and discipline due to their submission to traditional chiefs, and it was expected that their limited education made them less susceptible to nationalist or anti-French propaganda. The French had worried, for example, about the potential influence of Viet Minh propaganda on soldiers in Indochina.[49] Yet it was incorporating Africans into the ranks of officers and non-commissioned officers that was increasingly being considered key to ensuring their loyalty.[50] In fact, this seemed to depend more on their financial remuneration and possibilities for advancement and reenlistment than on ideology.[51] French authorities were convinced nonetheless that soldiers may be swayed by nationalist movements in their home colonies. Thus, as independence movements gained momentum in FWA, French decision-makers prioritized efforts to ensure the loyalty of African soldiers.[52]

In this sense, French military officials felt the end of the conflict in Indochina had negatively impacted the loyalty of African soldiers as well as the security of the colonies. French capabilities to reenlist all returning soldiers had been reduced, and disappointed soldiers were being sent back to home colonies where nationalist movements had already gained momentum. Consequently, the French military considered it a priority to enable reenlistment and provide benefits or employment opportunities for the African soldiers it was repatriating. The most talented individuals, officials suggested, could be employed in the gendarmerie of their home region.[53]

---

[47] Bodin, *Les Africains dans la guerre d'Indochine*, pp. 16 and 211; Echenberg, *Paying the Blood Tax*, p. 175.

[48] See documents from 1955–6 in Files GR5H37, GR5H51, and GR5H37, SHD.

[49] Bodin, *Les Africains dans la guerre d'Indochine*, pp. 27 and 163; Echenberg, *Les Tirailleurs sénégalais*, p. 115.

[50] See documents from 1955–6 in Files GR5H37, GR5H51, and GR5H37, SHD.

[51] Bodin, *Les Africains dans la guerre d'Indochine*, pp. 27, 94, 163, and 215.

[52] General Garbay, Senior Commander, AOF-Togo Defence Zone, 'Plan de renforcement des forces armées de la zone de défense', 8 February 1955, GR5H37, SHD.

[53] General Garbay, Senior Commander, AOF-Togo Defence Zone, to the High-Commissioner of the Republic, Governor-General of French West Africa, 'Effort entrepris concernant la remise en condition des forces terrestres de l'AOF', 23 March 1955, GR5H37, SHD; French Minister of the Overseas to Commanding General of

If soldiers did not join their own militaries, the French hoped they would return to being peasants rather than join the proletariat in the cities, where they would be susceptible to the ideas of nationalist 'agitators'.[54] Indeed, by the mid-1950s, the rise of nationalist movements in Africa had awoken France to the fragility of its colonial security system. Nowhere in FWA were European troop numbers sufficient to respond to potential public disturbances and protests.[55] A 1956 French military report warned that across all the French African colonies, which covered 7,800,000km2 with 23 million inhabitants, there were less than 40,000 'forces of order', most of whom were African.[56] European soldiers represented between 10 and 20% of these troops in most colonies, and slightly more in Senegal and Mauritania (see Table 3).

The French military complained with regularity about its insufficient resources and ever-growing tasks in FWA.[57] France lacked the financial resources to implement all the reinforcements it viewed as necessary.[58] However, by 1959, the number of European soldiers in Africa was increased slightly.[59] New garrisons were also constructed in sensitive locations, such as Conakry, Abidjan, Kaolak, and Cotonou. An emphasis was also placed on reinforcing the gendarmerie because, together with 'garde circles', they

the Armed Forces AOF-Togo Defence Zone, 28 June 1955, GR5H37, SHD; Garbay, 'Plan de renforcement des forces armées de la zone de défense', 8 February 1955.

54 Ibid.

55 The High-Commissioner of the Republic, Governor-General of French West Africa, to the Ministry of the Overseas, 'Politique général concernant les forces armées de l'AOF,' 22 January 1955, GR5H37, SHD; General Larminat, Inspector-General of Overseas Troops, to Chief of Staff of the Armed Forces, 'Plan de renforcement des territoires d'outre–mer en cas de troubles graves', 17 July 1956, GR5H51, SHD.

56 Larminat, 'Plan de renforcement des territoires d'outre–mer en cas de troubles graves', 17 July 1956.

57 See documents from 1955 and 1958 in Files GR5H37 and GR5H28, SHD.

58 Garbay, 'Plan de renforcement des forces armées de la zone de défense', 8 February 1955; French Minister of the Overseas to Commanding General of the Armed Forces AOF-Togo Defence Zone, 28 June 1955; General Garbay, Senior Commander, AOF-Togo Defence Zone, to Minister of the Overseas, 'Étude d'un programme de renforcement des garnisons situées dans certaines zones sensibles', 9 July 1955, GR5H37, SHD; Larminat, 'Projet de rapport du comité technique d'étude pour la défense de l'Afrique', 2 August 1955, GR5H51, SHD.

59 General C. A. Gardet, 'Rapport de fin de commandement', 15 February 1960.

had the most frequent contact with the population and the best knowledge of different regions.[60]

Maintaining order as nationalist movements grew in FWA was considered the primary responsibility of the civilian administration and the forces at its disposal, i.e., the police and gendarmes. They were expected to manifest authority, use force to quell subversive movements, and gather intelligence that could help identify actors with the potential to disturb public order.[61] If these civilian forces were unable to keep the order, help could be requested from the French army. The army thus had a double mission in the colonies: to prepare for potential external conflict and to ensure interior security in peacetime.[62] In 1955, the French commander of troops in FWA under-scored the role of the military in the colonies as being preventive, framing it as a function of 'the social role that the colonial army has traditionally played in our overseas territories.' The objective of France, he said, was 'not only to show strength, but to put the officers and the troops back in contact with the local populations and to maintain or renew the feelings of attachment that the African naturally carries to an army of which he has always constituted an essential element.'[63]

It was also in 1955, however, when French military authorities estimated that the threat of communist subversion in the colonies had elevated the maintenance of interior order to its most important task. Nevertheless, soldiers were told to use force sparingly in order to maintain the respect of

60 Garbay, 'Plan de renforcement des forces armées de la zone de défense', 8 February 1955.
61 Lieutenant-General Borgnis Desbordes, Inspector of Overseas Land Forces, to General Larminat, President of the Technical Study Committee for the Defence of Africa, 'Principes d'emploi des forces armées outre-mer', 5 July 1955, GR5H51, SHD; Larminat, 'Projet de rapport du comité technique d'étude pour la défense de l'Afrique', 2 August 1955.
62 Lieutenant-General Borgnis Desbordes to General Larminat, 'Principes d'emploi des forces armées outre-mer', 5 July 1955; Larminat, 'Projet de rapport du comité technique d'étude pour la défense de l'Afrique', 2 August 1955; French Ministry of National Defence to the Ministry of the Overseas, 'Note sur les principes d'emploi des forces armées dans le territoire de la France d'outre-mer', 7 July 1955, GR5H51, SHD; General Garbay, 'Effort entrepris concernant la remise en condition des forces terrestres de l'AOF', 23 March 1955, and 'Plan de renforcement des forces armées de la zone de défense', 8 February 1955.
63 Garbay, 'Plan de renforcement des forces armées de la zone de défense', 8 February 1955.

the population and ensure their cooperation.[64] French commanders stressed the need to adapt their forces to quick preventive action, as many viewed the failures of the army to do so in North Africa as the main cause of problems in that region. One general noted, for instance, that the lesson learned there was that it is much harder and much more expensive to restore order than to maintain it. He wrote that 'fragility and poor adaptation' had been 'blatantly demonstrated in North Africa' and emphasized that the easiest way to maintain order is to foresee disorder and prevent or eradicate it in its first manifestations, making intelligence-gathering particularly important.[65]

French authorities believed military bases should be situated near important population centres and sensitive zones, to guarantee communication and secure urban centres; and an even greater focus was put on maintaining sufficient mobile forces to provide reinforcement.[66] The precarious political situation also made it even more of a priority to ensure the loyalty of African soldiers,[67] particularly because their deployment to Indochina, Syria, Madagascar, and North Africa was thought to have weakened their loyalty and tarnished the reputation of the French military in the colonies. As the commander of French forces in FWA noted, African soldiers who fought in Indochina, or maintained order in Syria, Madagascar, and North Africa, 'were not indifferent to the circumstances in which [France] had placed them.' He referred to 'the defeat of Indochina in particular' as having 'dealt a definite blow to the prestige and authority of our army'.[68]

The return of 22,000 African soldiers from Indochina from 1954 throughout 1956 therefore posed a challenge to French authorities. These soldiers returned without their European commanders and entered units that were oversized and poorly supervised. A unit that was supposed to number 150 soldiers could comprise 300 to 400 soldiers by 1955, yet still have the

---

64 Lieutenant-General Borgnis Desbordes to General Larminat, 'Principes d'emploi des forces armées outre-mer', 5 July 1955; Larminat, 'Projet de rapport du comité technique d'étude pour la défense de l'Afrique', 2 August 1955.

65 Larminat, 'Projet de rapport du comité technique d'étude pour la défense de l'Afrique', 2 August 1955.

66 Lieutenant-General Borgnis Desbordes to General Larminat, 'Principes d'emploi des forces armées outre-mer', 5 July 1955; Larminat, 'Projet de rapport du comité technique d'étude pour la défense de l'Afrique', 2 August 1955.

67 Garbay, 'Plan de renforcement des forces armées de la zone de défense', 8 February 1955, and 'Effort entrepris concernant la remise en condition des forces terrestres de l'AOF', 23 March 1955.

68 Garbay, 'Effort entrepris concernant la remise en condition des forces terrestres de l'AOF', 23 March 1955.

same number of command officers. In these circumstances, and with some African soldiers seen to be turbulent and undisciplined, their loyalty was increasingly questioned.[69] When African soldiers were no longer willing to inform on their colleagues, French commanders began to take notice of deteriorating relations, which they linked to the constantly changing composition of African units and its effect on cohesion and on the relations of African soldiers with their French superiors.[70]

A number of military officials agreed that these problems extended from the short-sighted recruitment of African soldiers to Indochina. Accepting an unlimited number of African volunteers had been a mistake, they argued, and the recommendation was made to once again cap volunteers at one-third of African forces. They pointed out that these volunteers frequently reenlisted and became career soldiers, increasing their cost without necessarily increasing their effectiveness.[71] Additionally, the characteristics of these volunteers – who often came from specific ethnic groups, meaning they could easily group together against superiors – made it more difficult to ensure their allegiance. In fact, a mixture of soldiers from different groups had traditionally been seen as a guarantee of troop loyalty.[72]

French commanders also felt that the professionalization of the military had weakened links between the French military and African populations. They reported that African soldiers were no longer tied to their communities in a way that facilitated intelligence-gathering, which made the preventive role of the army more difficult. At the same time, too much contact with the civilian population was undesirable as French officers felt that African soldiers who lived outside military bases were at risk of political contamination, especially by nationalist movements.[73]

[69] Ibid.

[70] See documents from 1955 and 1957 in Files GR7T248 and GR5H37, SHD.

[71] Garbay, 'Effort entrepris concernant la remise en condition des forces terrestres de l'AOF', 23 March 1955 and 'Plan de renforcement des forces armées de la zone de défense', 8 February 1955.

[72] Ibid.; French Minister of the Overseas to Commanding General of the Armed Forces AOF-Togo Defence Zone, 28 June 1955; The High-Commissioner of the Republic, Governor-General of French West Africa, to the Minster of the Overseas, 'Politique général concernant les forces armées de l'AOF', 22 January 1955; Lieutenant-General Borgnis Desbordes to General Larminat, 'Principes d'emploi des forces armées outre-mer', 5 July 1955; Larminat, 'Projet de Rapport du Comité Technique d'étude pour la défense de l'Afrique', 2 August 1955.

[73] Garbay, 'Plan de renforcement des forces armées de la zone de défense', 8 February 1955; Lieutenant-General Borgnis Desbordes to General Larminat, 'Principes d'emploi

The conflict in Algeria made the challenges of having to repatriate African soldiers following the end of the war in Indochina a moot point for the French, as 10,000 West Africans were recruited to serve in North Africa, in September 1956.[74] However, French authorities soon came to be view this deployment as problematic as well, and in 1957, the French minister of overseas territories suggested that no new African recruits to North Africa should be accepted.[75] In May 1958, French officials decided that the number of sub-Saharan Africans serving in Algeria should be reduced from 15,300 to 13,000.[76] By the end of that year, Guinean independence spurred more than 11,000 Guinean soldiers to return to their home country, including the 5,000 who had left Algeria. An additional 4,000 African soldiers were recruited to replace them.[77]

Overall, the number of African soldiers serving in the French military started to fall from 1958 onwards.[78] At that time, there were 56,000 African colonial soldiers.[79] This number had been halved to 28,555 by 1959, and by the end of 1962 it stood at just 8,876.[80] In October 1960, French authorities decided to replace all 12,800 sub-Saharan African soldiers in Algeria with

des forces armées outre-mer', 5 July 1955; The High-Commissioner of the Republic, Governor-General of French West Africa, to the Minster of the Overseas, 'Politique général concernant les forces armées de l'AOF', 22 January 1955; Garbay, 'Effort entrepris concernant la remise en condition des forces terrestres de l'AOF', 23 March 1955.

74   General Bourgund, 'Rapport de fin de Commandement', 16 May 1958, GR5H28, SHD.

75   French Minister of the Overseas to Minister of National Defence and Armed Forces, 'Relève des militaires africains en Afrique du nord', 12 March 1957, GR7T248, SHD; Cornut-Gentille, Ministry of the Overseas, to Minister of the Armed Forces, 'Effectifs africains servant en Algérie', 15 October 1958, GR7T248, SHD.

76   See documents in File GR7T248, SHD.

77   Cornut-Gentille to Minister of the Armed Forces, 'Effectifs africains servant en Algérie', 15 October 1958; Gardet, 'Rapport de fin de commandement', 15 February 1960.

78   Colonel Lansoy, Deputy Chief, Military Cabinet, 'Note pour le général d'armée chef d'état-major général des armée: Entretien des effectifs africains en Algérie en 1961', 16 June 1960, GR7T248, SHD.

79   General Mancbou to the Minister of Armed Forces, 'Conséquences de la sécession de la Guinée sur le potentiel des forces terrestres d'outre-mer', 16 October 1958, GR7T248, SHD.

80   Brebisson, 'Rapport annuel 1961', GR5H27, SHD; Brebisson, Delegate for Overseas Defence Zone no. 1, to Army Chief of Staff, 'Rapport annuel 1962', GR5H27, SHD.

French and North African troops,[81] leaving only 2,600 by the end of 1961, all of whom departed in 1962 when Algeria became independent.[82]

French military authorities had feared that the large repatriations of soldiers could cause social and economic problems in newly independent states.[83] Early experiences were, however, considered positive, aside from the repatriation of Guinean soldiers. [84] France thus made the decision to repatriate all remaining African troops, most of whom lacked skills for life outside of the military.[85] This played a role in the decision-making of newly independent governments in francophone West Africa when it came to establishing and building national militaries.

By 1962, every country in francophone West Africa had created a national armed force. This did not mean a complete departure of the French military, as many French soldiers remained on as technical assistants. Given the poor education of most African colonial soldiers and the minimal training they received during their service, foreign assistance was a necessity, especially in logistics and technical matters. This was true despite the fact that the number of West African officers in the French military had grown to sixty-five by 1959.[86] There were also significant regional and ethnic imbalances in promotions. For example, there were numerous Mossi, Bambara, and Malinke officers, but fewer officers hailing from ethnic groups in Côte d'Ivoire.[87] In 1960, this meant there were thirty officers in Mali, twenty-six in Senegal, twenty-one in Guinea, and nineteen in Upper Volta, while there

---

81 General Prieur, Deputy Army Chief of Staff, Ministry of the Armed Forces, to General Commander of Forces in Algeria, 'Militaires africains', 6 December 1960, GR7T248, SHD; Army Staff, 'Retrait d'Algérie de tous les personnels africains', 13 October 1960, GR7T248, SHD; Brebisson, Director of Overseas Troops to the Ministry of Armed Forces, General Staff, 'Note pour le général d'armée chef l'état–major de l'armée: Entretien des effectifs africains en Algérie', 25 April 1960, GR7T248, SHD.

82 Ministry of the Armed Forces, General Staff, to General Commander of Forces in Algeria, 'Transformation des unités mixtes des troupes de marine en Algérie en unités de type normal FSE–FSNA', 16 November 1961, GR7T248, SHD; Lansoy, 'Note pour le général d'armée chef d'état–major général des armée: Entretien des effectifs africains en Algérie en 1961' 16 June 1960.

83 Ministry of the Armed Forces, Military Cabinet, General Staff, to Lieutenant-General Dio, 30 January 1961, GR7T248, SHD.

84 Brebisson, 'Rapport annuel 1962'.

85 Echenberg, *Paying the Blood Tax*, pp. 175 and 190–1.

86 Supreme Command, meeting of senior generals, 20 July1959, GR5H28, SHD; Garbay, 'Plan de renforcement des forces armées de la zone de défense', 8 February 1955.

87 Gardet, 'Rapport de fin de commandement', 15 February 1960.

were just ten in Côte d'Ivoire and few or no officers in Togo, Mauritania, and Niger (see Table 3).

While French authorities would have preferred to organize the security of West Africa around a common defence, the refusal of African governments to do so meant France had to assist each country individually. In turn, French military leaders complained about the fragmentation of the defence system and that their duties had grown but their resources had not. Nevertheless, they saw it as their responsibility to maintain peace and order in West Africa and believed that diminishing French assistance would have been perceived as abandonment, which could have had grave consequences, as African presidents were relying on this aid.[88] French reports also indicate that some colonial soldiers were unenthusiastic about returning to their country of origin after independence, as they considered it a risk to their professional futures and material conditions, even if they saw it as important to participate in state-building tasks in order to avoid becoming outcasts in their communities.[89]

There was a notable difference between the perspectives of younger and older colonial soldiers, and between non-commissioned officers and officers, when it came to the issue of repatriation. Young soldiers and non-commissioned officers were enticed by the prospect of promotion in their national military, while older soldiers and officers worried about how repatriation would impact them financially. If these older soldiers finished fifteen years of service in the French forces, they would gain the right to a French pension, so they were in no hurry to transfer into their national militaries. According to General Brebisson, African colonial soldiers of all ages were also concerned that national armies could become politicized and soldiers would be assigned tasks for which they had not been trained.[90] Soldiers were increasingly being tasked with carrying out public works, for example, in part to justify defence spending. In other words, even if the structures, regulations, and laws of the armed forces in newly independent states were identical to those of France, African governments sought to adapt their national forces to local needs.[91] This generated dissatisfaction

---

88 Brebisson, 'Rapport de fin de commandement du général commandement', 30 June 1962; Deputy Overseas General to the Chief of the General Staff of the Armed Forces, 'Organisation de la défense terrestre', 7 April 1960, GR5H61, SHD.

89 Brebisson, 'Rapport sur le moral 1er semestre', 13 July 1960, GR5H29, SHD.

90 Ibid.

91 Brebisson, 'Rapport de fin de commandement du général commandement', 30 June 1962.

among African colonial soldiers, who Brebisson described in 1960 as fearful 'that their governments will oblige them to do things for which they are neither trained nor made.' He noted that, in Mali, members of the government had complained that African officers, who they accused 'of being too rigid, of not adapting to political realities and of wanting to organize everything according to the perished principles still in effect in the French army', were not obeying their orders.[92]

Brebisson knew that African soldiers were well aware that 'France's time in Africa is over', and argued that the degree to which colonial soldiers were pro-French actors would be determined by their national governments:

> Whatever the deep feelings of African servicemen towards France, one must expect that their attitudes will be that which is dictated to them by their respective governments.... Caught in this political turmoil that overtakes them, they will follow the instructions of African leaders and parties as long as they are given assurances about their material future.[93]

Former colonial soldiers did have an interest in influencing their national governments to adopt pro-French policies, however.[94] Good relations with France were important for their militaries, which depended on French equipment and training. Good relations with France were also important for retired soldiers who received French pensions. Indeed, the downsides of poor relations with France had been exemplified in the problems faced by Guinean soldiers, and had served as a warning to other African governments and soldiers.

From 'Mercenaries' to a People's Armed Force: Military Building in Guinea

Throughout the colonial period, French officials had been aware of the important role colonial soldiers could play in safeguarding the relationship between the colonies and the metropole. Upon independence, however, some African politicians did not hesitate to refer to these colonial soldiers as 'mercenaries'. In the case of Guinean President Sékou Touré, this was not necessarily a term he used because he felt colonial soldiers had joined French forces for financial gain, but because they had served 'a colonial

---

92 Brebisson, 'Rapport sur le moral 1er semestre', 13 July 1960.
93 Ibid.
94 Ibid.

structure where racial segregation, persisting despite constitutions and laws, was applied either in the most brutal way, or with refinements that never ceased to hurt their dignity.'[95] Touré declared:

> ... the officer, the non-commissioned officer, the soldier of the army of the Republic of Guinea is equal to every other officer, non-commissioned officer and soldier of any army in the world. Whether he is a former recruit or a former conscript, he is freed from this state of inferiority which made him, either by constraint or by necessity, a mercenary ... within the French army.[96]

Several years later, Touré was far less content to embrace colonial soldiers. This reflects the difficulties Guinea had experienced in attempting to reintegrate these soldiers, but also the threat former soldiers were seen to pose, and the actions they took against Touré's regime. Touré resented the fact that, having previously occupied their own country, colonial soldiers were now pressuring the Guinean government to provide them jobs in the civilian administration. In 1961, he wrote:

> Now that their country is independent, now that they have found a homeland from which they were dispossessed ... they say, 'If you won't include us in the public administration we will create "havoc"' .... But I ask you, is it thanks to these few disgruntled former soldiers that Guinea became independent? Those who say such things, those who adopt such an attitude, these are the ones we would have found in front of us if we had been forced to take up arms against France. They would never have been on our shores. They would have been on the side of the money, only, because they have no national sense, no patriotic sentiment.[97]

The inconsistency of President Touré's views on colonial soldiers, expressed a few years apart, are emblematic of the conflicting opinions many African politicians held on this issue. On one hand, African political elites wanted soldiers to return, so that they could no longer be used to serve the interests of colonialism or the French. On the other hand, newly independent governments saw former soldiers as a potential threat and wanted France to take

---

95 Sékou Touré, radio speech, to troops, non-commissioned officers, and officers of the Army of the Republic of Guinea, 10 December 1958. Also see Touré, *L'action politique du parti démocratique de Guinée pour l'émancipation africaine* (Conakry: Imprimerie nationale, 1959), p. 152.
96 Ibid.
97 Touré, *Expérience Guinéenne et l'Unité Africaine* (Paris: Présence Africaine, 1961), p. 536.

responsibility for their long-term material comfort. In 1958, when Touré emphasized to Guinean soldiers in the French forces that their service in Guinea would liberate them from an inferior status, he knew these soldiers faced the difficult choice of continuing to serve the French until the end of their contract in order to guarantee their pension, or returning immediately to Guinea to avoid questions about their loyalty. According to French officials, most who chose to return to Guinea before their contracts ended, worried about possible retaliatory actions against them or their families.[98] Touré praised returning Guinean soldiers for having stood up to what he claimed were French lies and intimidation, and said these soldiers had proven their 'courage, sense of sacrifice and love for their country' by doing so.[99]

However, this praise did not bring any material benefits for former soldiers, as Touré felt this was the responsibility of France, not newly independent Guinea. As far as he was concerned, colonial soldiers could either seek employment in the private sector or return to their traditional role as peasants.[100] Jobs in the civilian administration were reserved for party members who had participated in anti-colonial struggles. This lack of opportunities left colonial soldiers disgruntled dissatisfied, particularly those who had forsaken their French pension.[101] In the absence of state action, former soldiers organized protests in Guéckédou and Kankan in 1959, which were quickly silenced by Guinean security forces.[102]

By 1961, when President Touré published his book, *The Guinean Experience and African Unity* [*Expérience Guinéenne et l'Unité Africaine*], his earlier optimism about reintegrating colonial soldiers now 'freed' from French oppression had faded. 'Some former soldiers', he wrote, 'who were used as mercenaries in the French army, believed they could force the government of the Republic of Guinea to give them special conditions.' Not only had the reintegration of these soldiers been difficult from an

---

98 Directorate for African and Malagasy Affairs, 'Option des militaires d'origine Guinéenne', 20 Octobre 1958, 51QO/15, CADC.
99 Touré, radio speech, 10 December 1958.
100 Touré, *Expérience Guinéenne*, p. 537–8.
101 Robert, *Ministre de l'Afrique,* pp. 103–9; Foccart, *Foccart Parle,* p.175.
102 Lewin, *Sékou Touré (1922–1984),* vol. 1, Chapter 29; Camara Kaba, *Dans la Guinée de Sékou Touré: cela a bien eu lieu* (Paris: Harmattan, 1998); SDECE, 'République de Guinée, incidents à Kankan', 20 May 1959, 51QO/32, CADC; Presidency of the Community, General Secretariat, to the Minister of Foreign Affairs, 13 March 1959, 51QO/35, CADC; Office of Overseas Studies, 'Transmission de renseignements: République de Guinée', 13 March 1959, 13 April 1959, and 29 April 1959, 5AGF/555, FFAN; Telegram, General Messmer to Foccart, 27 February 1959, 5AGF/1638, FFAN.

administrative standpoint, but Touré increasingly saw them as a threat to his regime. He questioned the loyalties of colonial soldiers who, while serving the French, 'could have been killed without knowing why.'[103]

Despite this, until the purges of 1969 and 1971, the highest echelons of the Guinean military were occupied by individuals who has served in the French forces, such as Chief of Staff Noumandian Keïta and Deputy Chief of Staff Kaman Diaby. Diaby was executed in 1969 for his alleged connection with a coup plot, along with Guinean minister of defence Fodéba Keïta, while and Noumandian Keïta was executed in 1971 in connection with the November 1970 attack led by Portugal. By this time, Touré's suspicions had grown beyond former soldiers or even Guinean soldiers in the French military. As the mid-1960s arrived, the Guinean president saw nearly all members of the national armed forces as a threat.

To better understand Touré's attitudes and discourse on mercenaries, it is important to consider how the French recruited its soldiers in Guinea by France and how they were used against anti-colonial movements in Indochina and Algeria. Compared to other French colonies, Guinea provided a large number of soldiers to the French military. During the First World War, 27,000 Guinean soldiers were recruited; only Upper Volta and French Sudan provided a greater number.[104] From 1929 to 1949, a further 28,000 Guineans joined the French forces.[105] The number of Guinean recruits increased sharply in the 1950s.[106]

French recruitment in Guinea was highly polarized, regionally and socially, due to French perceptions of the physical and mental abilities of different African 'races', as well as the relative power of local actors vis-à-vis their European counterparts. Racial prejudices and regional imbalances in recruitment were most marked in the case of the Fulani in Fouta-Djallon. From the beginning of universal conscription in 1912 to when volunteers were favoured in the 1950s, the Fulani either escaped recruitment or were considered physically incapable of military service.[107] In contrast, the Malinke were described in colonial reports as the best soldiers, because they were

103 Touré, *Expérience Guinéenne*, p. 536.
104 Governor-General van Vollenhoven, Military Cabinet, to Mr Maginot, Ministry of Colonies, July 1917.
105 Recruitment reports 1929–1949, Files 4D8, 9, 11, 12, 15, and 16, AAOF.
106 Reports on recruitment in Guinea, Côte d'Ivoire, and Upper Volta, 1950–1958, SHD, Pau.
107 Benoît, 'Rapport … sur les opérations des recrutement indigène en 1929–1930', 21 August 1930; General Staff, French West Africa Group, 'Rapport sur les opérations de recrutement en 1936', 8 August 1936.

muscular, hardworking, and easily recruited. The Susu, meanwhile, were characterized as having only modest value.[108]

Earlier studies on colonial Guinea have drawn attention to the dependence of colonial administrators on African actors, who were able to use this to their own benefit.[109] French military recruiters complained, for example, that traditional Guinean chiefs did not respect the egalitarian principles of universal conscription and were easily corrupted. Chiefs were reported to have included or deleted names from recruitment tables in exchange for material compensation. Moreover, almost no sons of chiefs appeared in the tables. Often, men presented to recruitment commissions were either too young or too old for service, as their names had been added to the recruitment tables to replace individuals omitted by the chiefs.[110]

Many men on recruitment lists were also intentionally absent when the commission arrived. In 1929, over 18% of the individuals on Guinean recruitment lists were absent,[111] and in 1937, this rate was 27%,[112] where it hovered for the next decade.[113] Yet, even if almost a quarter of Guinean youth sought to escape conscription, plenty more volunteered for the French military to make up for it. Throughout the 1930s and 1940s, some 80 to 90% of Guinean soldiers were volunteers, far exceeding the average in FWA of 29%.[114] However, most Guinean volunteers were not well educated. Of

---

108 Dr Colonel Colombani, 'Rapport sur le recrutement 1934–1935', 5 June 1935, and 'Rapport sur le recrutement 1935–1936.

109 Emily Osborn, '"Circle of Iron": African colonial employees and the interpretation of colonial rule in French West Africa', *Journal of African History* 44, no. 1 (2003), pp. 29–50.

110 Nya, 'Rapport ... sur une mission de recrutement effectuée en Guinée en January 1927', 21 February 1927.

111 General Staff, French West Africa Group, 'Rapport annuel sur les opérations de recrutement indigène en 1929', 4 August 1929, 4D8, AAOF.

112 General Staff, Senior Commander of AOF Group, 'Rapport annuel sur le recrutement indigène année 1937', 12 September 1937, 4D12, AAOF.

113 Ministry of the Overseas, Office of Defence Organization, 'Note sur les opérations de recrutement concernant la classe 1948 de l'AOF', 23 March 1949, 4D16, AAOF.

114 In 1930, the percentage of Guinean volunteers was 78%, while elsewhere in the colonies the rate was 32%; in 1939, the rate of volunteerism in Guinea was an even higher 88%. General Staff, French West Africa Group, 'Rapport annuel sur les opérations de recrutement indigène en 1929', 4 August 1929; Benoît, 'Rapport ... sur les opérations des recrutement indigène en 1929–1930', 21 August 1930; General Staff, French West Africa Group, 'Rapport sur le recrutement 1932', 49D, AAOF; Colombani, 'Rapport sur le recrutement 1934–1935', 5 June 1935; Lieutenant-General Dubuisson, Commander, French West Africa Group, 'Rapport sur les opérations de recrutement indigène en 1939' 14 October 1939, 4D15, AAOF; Ministry of the Overseas, Office of Defence

the 2,425 men recruited in 1929, only forty-one spoke French and just sixteen were literate.[115] The language skills of Guinean soldiers limited the training the French army could provide them, which made their eventual reintegration more difficult.

In the 1950s, France increased the recruitment of Guinean volunteers to fight in Indochina. Records suggest that from 1950 to 1957, approximately 41,000 Guinean soldiers were recruited into French forces.[116] This was almost four times the number of Ivorian or Voltaic recruits in the same period. The French withdrawal from Indochina saw French military authorities regretting having accepted so many Guinean volunteers, for while they were considered as good soldiers, the French also found them to be easily persuaded to join collective rebellions. This made their large number problematic. Frequent changes in the composition of units were also thought to decrease the loyalty of African soldiers to France, as the relations of soldiers with their French superiors was more distant and less enduring. In 1954, for instance, a battalion of 855 soldiers in Kankan had 4,000 African soldiers pass through it in one year.[117]

The return of so many Guinean soldiers from Indochina worried French military officials who, unable to simply reenlist them, and saw these troops as a potential danger.[118] Nationalist movements were gaining energy in francophone West Africa, and the French were increasingly alarmed about the fragilities of the colonial system.[119] The number of troops in FWA was nowhere near sufficient to ensure security in the case of public disturbances.[120] In 1954, there were less than 1,900 soldiers located in Guinea, of whom only 215 were French (see Table 3). Although the French military

---

Organization, 'Note sur les opérations de recrutement concernant la classe 1948 de l'AOF', 23 March 1949.

115 General Staff, French West Africa Group, 'Rapport annuel sur les opérations de recrutement indigène en 1929', 4 August 1929.

116 Reports on recruitment in Guinea, Côte d'Ivoire, and Upper Volta, 1950–1958.

117 Garbay, 'Plan de renforcement des forces armées de la zone de défense', 8 February 1955; 'Effort entrepris concernant la remise en condition des forces terrestres de l'AOF', 23 March 1955; and 'Rapport de fin de commandement', 15 February 1960.

118 Ibid.

119 Army Staff, Ministry of Land Armies, 'Effectifs de la France d'outre-mer', 27 October 1958, GR7T248, SHD.

120 Head of the Inspection Mission in French West Africa, Inspector-General of the Overseas, to the Minister of the Overseas, 'Organisation de la sécurité intérieure en Guinée Française', 9 July 1956, GR5H170, SHD; Garbay, 'Effort entrepris concernant le remise en condition des forces terrestres de l'AOF', 23 March 1955.

relied on Africans in its ranks to liaise with local communities – as colonial administrators often changed, and their contact with the population was infrequent and insufficient – the popularity of nationalist movements led the French administration to question the allegiance of African soldiers.[121]

A 1956 report of a French inspector general concluded that troop numbers in Guinea should be increased urgently, as the force size there was significantly lower than in French Sudan or Senegal, and was overly concentrated in the cities of Conakry, Kindia, and Kankan.[122] A new garrison had been built in Conakry,[123] and the number of soldiers in Guinea was increased, but there were still only 250 French soldiers in the country by 1956.[124] The number in had doubled by 1958, although African soldiers still represented the majority of 3,000 troops.[125] In October of that year, when Guinea declared independence, President Touré demanded the immediate departure of French parachutists from the capital, and an assessment of remaining French troops within a month. French authorities were unwilling to accept these demands, as French troops were needed to secure the departure of French citizens and equipment. France withdrew these troops two months later, in January 1959.[126]

At independence, the 12,630 Guinean soldiers serving in the French military were given the option to stay on or return to Guinea.[127] Most decided to return home, and the resulting loss of over 11,000 soldiers presented a difficult challenge for the French armed forces. Not only did

---

121 Ibid.

122 Sriber, Head of Mission, Inspector General of the Overseas, 'Rapport les faiblesses du dispositif de sécurité de Guinée', May 1956, GR5H170, SHD.

123 Garbay, 'Plan de renforcement des forces armées de la zone de défense', 8 February 1955, GR5H37, and 'Étude d'un programme de renforcement des garnisons situées dans certaines zones sensibles', 9 July 1955; Governor-General of French West Africa to Minister of the Overseas, 'Plan de réorganisation des forces armées de la zone de défense AOF-Togo', 11 February 1955, GR5H37, SHD.

124 Major General Nyo, 'Situation d'effectifs à la date du 1 janvier 1954', 21 January 1954.

125 Army Staff, Ministry of Land Armies, 'Effectifs de la France d'outre-mer' 27 October 1958.

126 General Garbay, Deputy Overseas Chief of Staff, to the Ministry of Land Armies, Directorate of Overseas Troops, Technical Office, 'Note à l'attention de monsieur le général d'armée: Guinéens en Algérie', 22 October 1958, GR7T248, SHD.

127 Deputy General of the Overseas, Ministry of National Defence and Armed Forces, to Chief of the General Staff of the Armed Forces, 'Note à l'attention du général d'armées chef d'état-major général des armées: évacuation militaire de la Guinée', 23 October 1958, GR7T248, SHD.

this deplete French manpower at the height of the crisis in Algeria, but it was thought that such a massive defection of Guineans could set a negative example for other African soldiers.[128] At the time, Guineans represented 23% of regular soldiers and 30% of non-commissioned officers among the 56,000 African troops in the French military, and there were 7,330 Guinean soldiers serving in FWA (over 75% of whom were volunteers),[129] along with 300 Guinean non-commissioned officers and 4,300 Guinean regular soldiers serving in Algeria.[130] Despite their large number, or because of it, the continued presence of Guinean soldiers in Algeria, after Guinean independence, was viewed by France as a risk to the overall morale of African soldiers.[131]

French reports allude to the surprise, sadness, and disappointment of Guinean soldiers regarding their country's refusal to join the French Community and note that these soldiers worried about their families, their futures, and their pensions.[132] However, French authorities also reported instances of disobedience and collective revolt, with entire units declaring they no longer wished to serve in the French army.[133] For France, the question was how to move nearly 5,000 Guinean soldiers out of Algeria without sending them all directly to Conakry. A transfer to Dakar, where 2,000 Guinean soldiers were already located, was also ruled out. Hence, although there were fears that Guinean soldiers could create problems if they were not liberated from the French military soon after demanding it, the decision was made to delay their repatriation until the end of 1958,

128 Ministry of Land Armies, Directorate of Overseas Troops, Technical Office, 'Situation des militaires originaires de la Guinée en service dans la métropole ou en Afrique du nord', 4 October 1958, GR7T248, SHD; Ministry of the Overseas to Minister of the Armed Forces, 'Effectifs africains servant en Algérie', 16 October 1958, GR7T248, SHD; Gardet, 'Rapport de fin de commandement', 15 February 1960.
129 General Mancbou to the Minister of Armed Forces, 'Conséquences de la sécession de la Guinée sur le potentiel des forces terrestres d'outre-mer', 16 October 1958; Army Staff, Ministry of Land Armies, 'Effectifs Guinéens', 24 October 1958, GR7T248, SHD; Ministry of the Overseas to Minister of the Armed Forces, 'Effectifs africains servant en Algérie', 16 October 1958.
130 Garbay, 'Note à l'attention de monsieur le général d'armée: Guinéens en Algérie', 22 October 1958.
131 Ministry of Land Forces, 'Situation des militaires originaires de la Guinée', 4 October 1958, GR7T248, SHD; Deputy General, Commander of Forces in Algeria, 'Questions posées par les militaires Guinéens' 5 October 1958, GR7T248, SHD.
132 Ibid.
133 Garbay, 'Note à l'attention de monsieur le général d'armée: Guinéens en Algérie', 22 October 1958.

by which time it was hoped relations between France and Guinea would be normalized.[134]

Hence, in 1959, 11,253 soldiers returned to Guinea, of whom 2,500 were selected to establish the Guinean armed forces. Of the twenty-one Guinean officers in the French military, twelve had opted for repatriation. The Guinean government required all of these soldiers to complete additional training in Guinea before joining the national military, however.[135] Soldiers in Guinea were housed in bases left empty by the French in Conakry, Kankan, Kindia, Labe, and Nzerekore, all of which needed to be rebuilt and re-equipped. Fodéba Keïta, Guinea's minister of defence and security from 1960 to 1965, later described the conditions of the Guinean armed and security forces at independence as exceptionally difficult; they had no equipment, no vehicles, no arms, and no uniforms. The French had engaged in a scorched-earth withdrawal, destroying everything from documents to technical security infrastructure. According to Keïta, the Guinean government was left with no choice but to accept assistance from Czechoslovakia and the Soviet Union.[136] A heavy weapons shipment from Czechoslovakia in March 1959 thus helped equip the Guinean military in its early stages. This equipment was accompanied by Czechoslovakian technicians and trainers, as most Guinean soldiers had experienced of only with light personnel weapons.[137]

By April of that year, Guinean forces included sixteen officers, 390 non-commissioned officers, and 2,115 regular soldiers; and by June, the

---

134 General Mancbou to the Minister of Armed Forces, 'Conséquences de la sécession de la Guinée sur le potentiel des forces terrestres d'outre-mer', 16 October 1958; General Gouraud, to military governors general, 'Mesures à prendre à l'égard des militaires originaires de la Guinée', 11 October 1958, GR7T248, SHD; Minister of the Armed Forces to the Minister of the Overseas, 23 September 1958, GR7T248, SHD.

135 Fode Momo Camara, *1 November 1958–1 November 2008: Cinquantenaire de la création l'armée Guinéenne* (unpublished memoir).

136 General Secretary for the Community and African Affairs to General de Gaulle, note dated 4 November 1963. Fodéba Keïta, Minister of Defence, presentation before the Chamber of Deputies, Delegation for the Defence of Overseas Zone 1. See 'Bulletin de renseignements', 8 November 1963, GR5H92, SHD.

137 Brebisson, 'Rapport de fin de commandement du général commandement', 30 June 1962; Gardet, 'Rapport de fin de commandement', 15 February 1960; Directorate of African and Malagasy Affairs, 'Note sur le budget 1959 de la Guinée', 30 April 195911; Intelligence Division, 'Fiche sur le potentiel militaire de la Guinée', 17 April 1959; Directorate for Africa-Levant, 'Fournitures d'armes tchécoslovaques à la Guinée', 11 April 1959, 51QO/3, CADC; Telegram, French Embassy Conakry, to Directorate of African and Malagasy Affairs, 7 November 1959, 51QO/3, CADC; Intelligence Division, 'Livraison d'armes à la Guinée', 11 April 1959, 51QO/34, CADC.

number of regular soldiers had risen to 3,500.[138] French officials estimated that the potential manpower of the Guinean military was significant, with a reserve close to 20,000, but noted that the loyalty of soldiers to Touré was not guaranteed. They also recognized that soldiers' loyalty to France would decrease over time, especially as family or ethnic ties of a 'quasi-national' nature gained importance.[139] Despite some continuity in terms of personnel and military bases, newly independent Guinea had clearly ruptured from the colonial period in terms of equipment and training. This helped legitimize its institutions of coercion and their use of force. Yet, colonial soldiers, still marked by their experiences fighting against nationalist movements in Indochina and Algeria, tended to be more dubious regarding the use of force. Building a national army out of colonial soldiers thus posed a double challenge: the loyalty of these soldiers to the state had to be assured, and these soldiers had to believe that institutions of coercion were credible.

To legitimize the national armed forces, the Guinean government emphasized differences between the colonial and national militaries. In an October 1963 speech, for example, Minister of Defence Keïta contrasted the colonial security system – which he said was based on the use of repressive force for the profit of the few – to the Guinean military, which contributed to economic development by building roads and producing food crops. He predicted that the national military would not only be able to pay for itself, but it would contribute to the state budget through economic activities. Both Keïta and Touré also noted publicly that relations had changed between the Guinean population and the armed forces after independence, as the colonial army had been characterized by racial discrimination. Postcolonial Guinean soldiers served instead in what Touré described in a radio speech as 'a popular army, issued by the people, in the service of the people.'[140] This rhetoric damaged Guinean relations with France, which were already tenuous. In late 1963, the French ambassador took offence to a parade of Guinean colonial and national troops in Guinea, because he thought the French military had been ridiculed by the way colonial forces were presented. He insisted that no further aid should be granted to Guinea.[141]

138 Ibid.
139 Gardet, 'Rapport de fin de commandement', 15 February 1960.
140 Touré, radio speech, 10 December 1958; *Expérience Guinéenne*, pp. 536 and 539; and *L'Afrique et la révolution*, pp. 300 and 302.
141 Telegram, French Ambassador in Guinea Jean-Louis Pons, to Paris, 1 November 1963, 5AGF/558, FFAN; Telegram, French Ambassador in Guinea Jean-Louis Pons to

The Malian government had made a similar choice to underline differences between its national military and the colonial forces in political speeches, especially by bringing attention to the changed role of soldiers, who were assigned non-military tasks in agricultural development.[142] Like Guinea, Mali had demanded the departure of all French troops, and its soldiers were equipped and trained by the communist bloc. In 1961, the government in Mali also ordered all Malian soldiers to come home, prompting a sudden mass return that posed a significant challenge.[143]

Of the 7,600 Malians who served in the French military in 1960, 4,500 were absorbed into the Malian national armed forces, which was a much higher percentage than those who were able to join Guinea's national forces. However, this also created economic and political problems for Mali, which had an equally poor economy and an inimical relation with France.

Even in francophone West African countries where they were fewer in number, colonial soldiers were the cause of political upheaval. In the case of Togo, for example, fewer than 900 Togolese soldiers were serving in the French military in 1960. Yet in 1963, colonial soldiers from the northern part of the country carried out a coup because they had not been included in the national military. According to French officials, the Togolese president, Sylvanus Olympio, had refused to increase the size of the armed forces and establish a second battalion, even if France was willing to furnish it.[144] By April 1962, Olympio was already distrustful of Togolese soldiers when he requested more French technical assistants,[145] and by November of that year, soldiers in the north of the country had organized protests demanding employment. French intelligence reports noted that Olympio could have quickly resolved the issue by providing jobs, but the president

---

the Directorate of African and Malagasy Affairs, 2 November 1963, 5AGF/558, FFAN; Lewin, *Sékou Touré (1922–1984)*, vol. 2, Chapter 53.

[142] US Embassy Bamako, 'Armed Forces of the Mali Republic', 2 August 1964, DEF 1964–1966, Box 1679, CGRDS, NARA, and 'Order of Battle of Malian army', 11 December 1966, DEF 1964–1966, Box 1679, CGRDS, NARA.

[143] General Secretary for African and Malagasy Affairs, 'Instruction pour le chargé d'affaires au Mali', 9 February 1961.

[144] General Secretary for African and Malagasy Affairs, 'Audience du President Nicolas Grunitzky', 4 July 1966, 5AGF/619, FFAN.

[145] Brigadier-General le Porz, Delegate for Overseas Defence Zone, to Minister of the Armed Forces, 'Commandement de la compagnie togolaise de Lomé', 18 April 1962, 5AGF/618, FFAN.

felt no responsibility to provide for 'former servants of colonialism'.[146] Much like Touré, Olympio believed it was France that was responsible for these soldiers' material wellbeing

This had fateful consequences, for Togolese colonial soldiers, assisted by officers of the Togolese armed forces, assassinated Olympio and arrested the Togolese government over the night of 12 January 1963.[147] Robert, the Head of French intelligence in Africa at the time, denied any French involvement in the coup, even if the incoming Togolese president happened to be more favourable to France. According to Robert, the seeds of the coup had been sown inside the country, allowing France to do nothing and still get what it wanted. It was a simple case of laissez-faire.[148] After the coup, the new Togolese government incorporated more colonial soldiers into the national army and requested French assistance in arming them.[149]

The coup in Togo led President Touré to deny entry to Guinean nationals repatriating from the French military.[150] He, like most African presidents, saw the 1963 coup as an indication that colonial soldiers were indeed a threat. But Touré had other reasons to view colonial soldiers as a threat, and even French officials deemed the Guinean president's decision to refuse them entry a rational one, considering the activities of these soldiers against Touré's regime. The French advised that colonial soldiers be repatriated in smaller groups, arguing that Guinean soldiers who had returned before 1963 had been well-received and were therefore not in need of alternative placement.[151] However, Touré was unwilling to allow any more former

---

146 Intelligence Exploitation Centre, Information Bulletin, 4 December 1962, GR11S159, SHD; Intelligence Exploitation Centre, 'République de Togo', 4 December 1962, GR11S159, SHD.

147 Intelligence Exploitation Centre, 'Le putsch militaire au Togo', 15 January 1963, GR9Q140, SHD.

148 Robert, '*Ministre' de l'Afrique*, pp. 74–5.

149 General Secretary for African and Malagasy Affairs, Special Staff, 'Possibilités d'intervention au Togo', 21 November 1966, 5AGF/618, FFAN; Goodwill Mission to Dahomey, 21–24 March 1963, 'Conclusion de la mission dahoméenne au Togo', 5 April 1963, 5AGF/618, FFAN.

150 Telegram, Ambassador Jean-Louis Pons to Directorate of African and Malagasy Affairs, 17 January 1963, 51ONT/41, CADC; Directorate of African and Malagasy Affairs, 'Démobilisation des militaires Guinéens en service dans l'armée française', 6 December 1963, 51QO/36, CADC; Ministry of the Armed Forces, Military Cabinet, 'Libération des militaires Guinéens dans les forces armées françaises', 30 April 1963, 5AGF/1643, FFAN.

151 Minister of Foreign Affairs to Minister of Armed Forces (Military Cabinet), 'Rapatriement de militaires Guinéens', 16 February 1963, 5QONT/36, CADC; Mr

colonial soldiers into the country, especially when France had refused to pay the pensions of those soldiers who had already returned.

For the French military, the loss of Guinean soldiers to repatriation, and also the approximately 1,000 Guinean soldiers who had remained in service, had been a challenge.[152] Some of those who remained, unhappy with their service conditions, were habitually disobedient.[153] When France decided to repatriate African soldiers in the early 1960s and Guinean soldiers could not return to their home country, these problems multiplied. France had promised Guinean colonial soldiers in 1958 that they could serve until their retirement and then return to Guinea, and these soldiers felt France had broken a moral contract owed to them.[154]

In 1963, there were still 247 Guineans serving in the French armed forces and another 255 former soldiers stuck abroad because Touré had refused their entry at the border. Most had taken up residence in either Senegal, Côte d'Ivoire, Niger or Dahomey.[155] However, the neighbouring Senegalese and Ivorian governments were hesitant to accept Guinean soldiers because they continued to act against Touré's regime.[156] Indeed, after the coup in Togo, Senegalese authorities signalled to the French ambassador that Senegal would no longer accept Guinean colonial soldiers on its territory.[157] Guinean

---

Rostain, 'Note à l'attention de monsieur le président de la république, président de la communauté ressortissants Guinéens en service dans l'armée française', 19 February 1961, 5AGF/1639, FFAN.

[152] Ibid.

[153] Captain Berthezene, Navy Signal Company, 'Rapport semestriel sur le moral des militaires de la 4o CIOM (Port-Bouët) et de transmission du Niger', 4 April 1962, GR5H32, SHD; Ministry of Land Armies, Department of Overseas Troops, 'Situation par état d'origine des personnels des troupes d'outre-mer en service en AFN situation au 1.2.1961' GR7T248, SHD; Gardet, 'Rapport de fin de commandement', 15 February 1960; Brebisson, 'Rapport annuel 1961'; Ministry of the Armed Forces, Military Cabinet, 'Libération des militaires Guinéens dans les forces armées françaises', 30 April 1963.

[154] Berthezene, Navy Signal Company, 'Rapport semestriel sur le moral des militaires de la 4o CIOM (Port-Bouët) et de transmission du Niger', 4 April 1962; Delegation for Overseas Defence Zone 4, 'Rapport sur la moral', 25 January 1965, GR5H32, SHD; Brebisson, 'Rapport annuel 1962'; Ministry of the Armed Forces, Military Cabinet, 'Libération des militaires Guinéens dans les forces armées françaises', 30 April 1963.

[155] Directorate of African and Malagasy Affairs, 'Démobilisation des Guinéens en service dans l'armée française', 6 December 1963.

[156] Ministry of Interior, Intelligence Directorate, to Ministry of Foreign Affairs, 19 January 1966, 5QONT/36, CADC; Ministry of Foreign Affairs to Minister of Interior, 'Demandes formulées par des ressortissants Guinéens en vue de quitter la France', 2 April 1968, 5QONT/36, CADC.

[157] Ambassador in Dakar, 2 August 1963, INVA321, CADC.

officials tied acceptance of the return of colonial soldiers to resolution of the pensions issue by France.[158] The dispute over how pensions should be paid to Guinean colonial soldiers increased tensions between France and Guinea, as the French were worried that pensions would end up in the coffers of Touré's PDG or go to individuals in the party.[159]

Financial questions pertaining to Guinean independence had complicated Franco-Guinean relations for some time, and the issue of pensions became part of a tangled set of problems. The two countries had managed to settle some outstanding disputes in May 1963, but both the interpretation and implementation of treaties were strained from the start. Guinea refused to recognize loans taken prior to independence, and France retaliated by ending pension payments to Guinean soldiers.[160] The sum that had paid each was close to FF 30 million.[161] A stalemate persisted, until talks were continued in 1965, but worsening relations excluded any chance of a negotiated solution.[162]

158 Lieutenant Laparra, Special Staff, Presidency of the Republic, 'Militaires Guinéens de l'armée française', 22 July 1965, 5AGF/558, FFAN; Vice-Admiral Descadre, Chief of the Special Staff, Presidency of the Republic, 'Sort des militaires Guinéens de l'armée française', 20 November 1965, 5AGF/561, FFAN; Laparra, Special Staff, Presidency of the Republic, 'Rapatriement des militaires Guinées stationnes en métropole', 1 October 1965, 5AGF/561, FFAN; Ministry of Interior, Intelligence Directorate, to Ministry of Foreign Affairs, 19 January1966.

159 Ministry of Foreign Affairs, 'Paiement des pensions en Guinée', 13 June 1959, 51QO/15, CADC.

160 Plantey, General Secretariat for African and Malagasy Affairs, to the Prime Minister, 17 June 1963, 5AGF/558, FFAN; Telegram, Ambassador Pons, to Paris, 'La situation en Guinée', 15 June 1963, 5AGF/558, FFAN; Secretary State of Foreign Affairs to Ambassador of France in Conakry, 'Contentieux franco-guinéenne: accords de 22 May 1963', 8 July 1964, 5AGF/558, FFAN; Directorate of African and Malagasy Affairs, Sub-directorate for Africa, 'Relations franco-guinéennes', 29 October 1965, 5AGF/558, FFAN; Directorate of African and Malagasy Affairs, 'Note contentieux financier franco-guinéen', 24 June 1970, 51QONT/29, CADC; Directorate of African and Malagasy Affairs, Sub-directorate for Africa, 'Évolution des relations franco-guinéennes', 22 June 1970, 51QONT/29, CADC.

161 Directorate of African and Malagasy Affairs, Sub-directorate for Africa, 'Schéma d'intervention concernant la Guinée', September 1967, 5QONT/27, CADC; Directorate of African and Malagasy Affairs, 'Note contentieux financier franco-guinéen', 24 June 1970.

162 Ministry of Interior, General Directorate for National Security, Intelligence Directorate, to Ministry of Foreign Affairs, 19 January 1966, 5QONT/36, CADC.

French officials began to suspect that even if the issues around pensions were solved, Touré would not accept the return of colonial soldiers.[163] In 1966, when President de Gaulle suggested that Guinean soldiers be reintegrated into the French armed forces.[164] The Guinean regime tried to leverage French economic interests in the country and, in 1967, threatened to sanction the partially French-owned bauxite mining company FRIA if the pensions of colonial soldiers were not paid.[165] In turn, French officials insisted pensions would only be paid if Guinea recognized loans taken prior to independence and the damages caused by nationalization.[166] By November 1970, the arrears for Guinean colonial pensions had grown to FF 160 million. A payment of FF 60 million had been made during the previous year, and though most of this French disbursement did not go directly to the Guinean government, some 20 to 40% was left to the disposition of the government to purchase French products.[167] French exports to Guinea had been diminishing since 1965, and it was hoped that unblocking pension payments would help reverse that trend.[168]

In August 1970, French officials noted that any small improvements in Franco-Guinean relations could be undermined by any Guinean opposition figures residing in France who were tempted to prevent any further improvement, and by force if necessary. Guineans who had taken refuge

---

163 Philippe Koenig, Ambassador of France in Guinea, to Minister of Foreign Affairs Maurice Couve de Murville, 'Rapatriement des militaires Guinéens démobilises de l'armée française', 18 February 1965, 51QO/36, CADC; Laparra, 'Militaires Guinéens de l'armée française', 22 July 1965.
164 General de Gaulle, note to Pompidou and Messmer dated 5 January 1966, 5AGF/561, FFAN.
165 René Journiac, General Secretariat for African and Malagasy Affairs, 'A l'attention du secrétaire général', 5 June 1967, 5AGF/561, FFAN.
166 Ministry of Foreign Affairs, 'Guinée, le problème des pensions', 25 January 1967, 5AGF/561, FFAN; Moussa Diakité, Minister of Foreign Trade and Banking of Guinea, to French Ministry of Foreign Affairs, 13 January 1967, 5AGF/561, FFAN.
167 General Secretariat for African and Malagasy Affairs, 'Note à la attention de monsieur le président: retour de Guinée d'une mission française', 17 November 1970, 5AGF/1648, FFAN; Richard, General Secretariat for African and Malagasy Affairs, 'Note à l'attention de monsieur secrétaire général', 18 November 1970, 5AGF/1648, FFAN; Directorate of African and Malagasy Affairs, 'Note contentieux financier franco-guinéen', 24 June 1970, 51QONT/29, CADC; Directorate of African and Malagasy Affairs, 'Fonctionnement des accords franco-guinéens: commerce franco-guinéen et intérêts française en Guinée', 31 August 1968, 51QONT/29, CADC; Ministry of Foreign Affairs, Sub-directorate for Africa, 'FRIA et le régime guinéen', 16 November 1971, 51QONT/34, CADC.
168 Ministry of Foreign Affairs, 'Relations économiques franco-guinéenne', 25 June 1970, 51QONT/29, CADC.

in France were thus reminded that accepting French hospitality entailed 'certain responsibilities.'[169] Two months later, Portuguese forces attacked the Guinean capital alongside Guineans who had served in the French military, which again caused significant damage to Franco-Guinean relations. French officials complained that France no longer had any retaliatory measures at its disposal in potential disputes with the Guinean government because of the way the pension issue had been handled, which had adverse effects on French economic interests in Guinea.[170]

Hence, the Guinean case aptly illustrates the conflicting roles of former colonial soldiers in building state institutions and contributing to instability in newly independent francophone West African states. While colonial soldiers had previously provided a positive link between the French and the Africans, in postcolonial Guinea, these same soldiers became both aggravating factors in Franco-Guinean disagreements and pawns in those same disputes. Colonial soldiers thus played an important dual part in the development of Franco-Guinean relations.

Relying on France: Continuity in Colonial Structures in Côte d'Ivoire

Colonial soldiers did not have the importance in Côte d'Ivoire that they had in Guinea, as they were smaller in number and Franco-Ivorian relations were also amicable. This is not to imply that they were politically insignificant, however. In fact, President Houphouët-Boigny had a distaste for the military and distrusted those Ivorian soldiers who had served in French forces. In 1964, Houphouët-Boigny noted to French Ambassador, Jacques Raphaël-Leygues, that 'the Ivorian army comes from Indochina and has not participated in national struggles. Trained abroad, it is easily mobilized for partisan causes. In that sense, the soldiers and the students here pose similar problems.' The Ivorian president was convinced that both soldiers and students wanted to implement 'foreign' ideologies in Côte d'Ivoire without understanding Ivorian realities.[171]

---

169 Ministry of Foreign Affairs, Sub-Directorate for Africa, 'Note pour le cabinet du ministre: activités de certaines militaires Guinéens en France', 28 August 1970, 51QONT/29, CADC.

170 Ministry of Foreign Affairs, Sub-directorate for Africa, 'FRIA et le régime guinéen', 16 November 1971.

171 Houphouët-Boigny, Message to Parliament, 3 August 1961; Telegram, Houphouët-Boigny to the French Ambassador, 27 February 1964, 324QONT/1, CADC; French Embassy Abidjan, 'Problèmes militaires', 15 November 1961.

The 1963 military coup in Togo served to increase Houphouët-Boigny's suspicions about colonial soldiers, who he was already concerned 'had acquired a taste for adventure' in the conflicts in Indochina and Algeria.[172] Uncertain about their loyalty, he established a party militia as a counterforce to the army. This did not surprise French officials, as the Ivorian president had never hidden his dislike of the military.[173] Prior to independence, the French had anticipated that he may prefer not to have one at all.[174] However, it soon became evident – even to Houphouët-Boigny – that a national military was necessary for the sake of national prestige. Discussing the formation of the national armed forces in 1961, he called them 'the armed forces of peace' and said they 'would be dismantled when a lasting peace in Africa was guaranteed.'[175]

Houphouët-Boigny also expressed publicly that the national military was not worth its price to the state, arguing that the country would be protected by the United Nations or France in the case of an external attack.[176] President Diori of Niger held similar views, recognizing the necessity of a national military as a symbol of independence, despite its cost and the threat it posed to the state.[177] In Niger, Côte d'Ivoire, and Senegal there was a degree of continuity from the colonial period, not only in military personnel but also in equipment, training, and the French presence. This made it more difficult to legitimize the national armed forces in these countries. While the Guinean government could justify defence spending by referencing external threats and the need to support anti-colonial movements, presidents who remained aligned with France could not make the same arguments.

In Côte d'Ivoire, Houphouët-Boigny argued that reduced defence spending justified a continued French military presence, which also ensured the stability of the Ivorian regime.[178] Even so, an ongoing continued French presence did not mean African governments were unwilling to break with

---

[172] Telegram, Raphaël-Leygues to Directorate of African and Malagasy Affairs, 13 December 1963.

[173] Raphaël-Leygues, 'La Côte d'Ivoire et l'Armée', 30 August 1974.

[174] Revol, 'Visite de Monsieur Houphouët-Boigny et problèmes Ivoiriennes en matière de sécurité et défense', 16 May 1960.

[175] Houphouët-Boigny, Message to Parliament, 3 August 1961.

[176] Raphaël-Leygues, 'La Côte d'Ivoire et l'Armée', 30 August 1974.

[177] Fouchet, Ambassador to Niger, 'Question sur l'évolution de l'assistance technique militaire au Niger', 30 January 1964.

[178] See documents in Files 324QONT/1, CADC; Files 5AGF/1806, 5AG5/1800, and 5AGF/535, FFAN.

French tradition, such as by using soldiers to carry out public works.[179] Unlike the military in Guinea and Mali, where alternative tasks were assigned to soldiers in order to emphasize the difference between colonial and national forces, the Ivorian government did so in order to justify why the military should exist at all. Houphouët-Boigny's view was that the state should allocate its limited resources only to institutions that directly contributed to the country's economic development. To this end, the Ivorian government focused on developing a civic service model, wherein soldiers would train Ivorian youth in agricultural techniques. Meanwhile, French officials criticized what they considered Ivorian negligence of its military.[180]

The French military presence in Côte d'Ivoire generated dissatisfaction among both Ivorian civilians and soldiers.[181] As far as the US was concerned, Côte d'Ivoire's reliance on France was so extensive that it had impacted the credibility of Houphouët-Boigny before domestic and African audiences. American officials recommended that Côte d'Ivoire diversify its sources of aid[182] and US Ambassador to Guinea James Loeb criticized the Ivorian president. He said that French policies in francophone Africa had 'created … islands of prosperity and modernism, where the European way of life could survive and flourish, where European commercial and financial interests could prosper, with only token regard for the development and participation of Africa's human resources and abilities.' Loeb added that the 'experiment' underway in some francophone West African states may represent an 'easy way for the Euro-African elites to solve their immediate problems. It is doubtful, however, these elites can perpetuate themselves as long as in Latin America.'[183]

Providing the Ivorian government succeeded in improving the material conditions of most Ivorians, it would face little opposition, and when the government did use force against its opponents, it was not widely discussed. Typically, the objective of Ivorian leaders was not to justify violence, but to deny it. Moreover, the regime framed opposition protests as the acts of

---

179 Brebisson, 'Rapport de fin de commandement du général commandement', 30 June 1962; French Embassy Abidjan, 'Problèmes militaires', 15 November 1961.
180 French Embassy Abidjan, 'Situation politique', 3 September 1963; Telegram, Abidjan to Paris, 31 August 1963.
181 Ambassador of France in Côte d'Ivoire to Ministry of Foreign Affairs, 'Situation politique du 22 au 28 septembre, 29 September 1962; Chafer, *The End of Empire in French West Africa*, p. 188; Brasseur, 'Crise politique en Côte d'Ivoire', 23 January 1963; Directorate of African and Malagasy Affairs, 'République de Côte d'Ivoire', 3 July 1963.
182 Wine, 'Ambassador's political-economic assessment', 12 February 1964.
183 Loeb, 'US policy assessment', 26 January 1966.

deranged individuals or blamed them on communist influences.[184] Whether Houphouët-Boigny actually saw communism as a threat is debatable,[185] however, as in 1967 he stated that 'the opposition in Africa is almost never global or doctrinal but tribal'.[186]

Ivorians were never numerous in the French military and the country only had to reabsorb a small number of colonial soldiers, who reintegrated into Ivorian society with relative ease. France had recruited 23,000 Ivorian soldiers during the First World War, but the long border with Liberia and the Gold Coast enabled many to escape recruitment. In fact, van Vollenhoven reported that by mid-1917, 50,000 Guinean and Ivorian youth had evaded conscription by leaving French territory.[187] These fugitive recruits were thought to have a negative impact on public perceptions of French colonialism and, in the post–war years, a yearly quota for Ivorian recruits was set at 2,000. French officials feared that if the quota was increased, more Ivorians 'would be tempted to seek refuge in the neighbouring colonies.'[188]

While Ivorian resistance to recruitment diminished over the years, the readiness of Ivorian recruits for military service was consistently considered poor.[189] However, between 1929 and 1932, the percentage of Ivorian absentees ranged from 6 to 13 %, whereas rates in Guinea were two to three times higher.[190] Following the end of the Second World War, more

[184] Brasseur, 'Crise politique en Côte d'Ivoire', 23 January 1963; US Embassy Abidjan, 'The Guerbie Problem and National Unity', 5 March 1971, POLIVCAST 1970–1973, Box 2399, CGRDS, NARA; Telegram, Raphaël-Leygues, Abidjan, to Directorate of African and Malagasy Affairs, 9 December 1967, 5AGF/1805, FFAN; General Secretariat for the Community, 'Audience du président Houphouët-Boigny auprès de Gaulle', 16 April 1969, 5AGF/535, FFAN; General Secretariat for National Defence, 'Incidents à Gagnoa', 30 October 1970, 5AGF/535, FFAN.

[185] This view was shared by French Ambassador Léon Brasseur. See Brasseur, 'Crise politique en Côte d'Ivoire', 23 January 1963.

[186] Telegram, Raphaël-Leygues, Abidjan, to Directorate of African and Malagasy Affairs, 9 December 1967.

[187] Governor-General van Vollenhoven, Military Cabinet, to Mr Maginot, Ministry of Colonies, July 1917; General Government of French West Africa, Colony of Côte d'Ivoire, 2nd Office of Military Affairs, 'Rapport à Monsieur le Gouverneur Général sur le recrutement 1926 des troupes indigènes à la Côte d'Ivoire', 28 May 1926, 4D3, AAOF.

[188] Lieutenant-Governor of Côte d'Ivoire to Governor-General of French West Africa, 'Rapport sur les opérations du recrutement indigène 1927–1928', 6 May 1928, 4D8, AAOF.

[189] Ibid.

[190] General Staff, French West Africa Group, 'Rapport annuel sur les opérations de recrutement indigène en 1929', 4 August 1929; Lieutenant-Governor of Côte d'ivoire

Ivorians sought to escape conscription, and by 1950, the rate of Ivorian absentees had risen to 35%. Nevertheless, more Ivorians volunteering for military service, at a rate of 59% in 1950.[191] Over the following seven years, more than 9,000 Ivorians joined the French armed forces – a few thousand less than from Upper Volta but only 20% of the number in Guinea.[192]

Ivorian recruits were amongst the best educated in FWA. In 1929, for example, of 1,880 Ivorian recruits, eighty-one spoke French and twenty-six could read and write.[193] Though this may not sound like a significant number, it was much higher than in most of the other colonies, reflecting the reach of the colonial administration and French presence in Côte d'Ivoire. According to French military officials, the language skills of Ivorian soldiers allowed them to acquire skills during their service that could be useful in civilian professions.[194] This was a clear advantage for these soldiers when it came to their postcolonial repatriation and reintegration.

After passage of the 1956 *loi-cadre* – which marked the first step in establishing the French Community – Houphouët-Boigny started an outreach campaign in Ivorian lycées to attract educated candidates for officer training in France. Former Commander of the Ivorian Gendarmerie Gaston Ouassénan Koné, said that he was inspired to join the French forces by the president's visit to his lycée in Bouaké as a part of this campaign. Koné began his training in France in 1958, and by 1964, when he was only 25 years old, had risen to command the gendarmerie. He had not hesitated to return to Côte d'Ivoire, he said, as his experiences during training in France had convinced him he could not advance in the French forces. French gendarmes would never accept command by an African.[195]

---

to Governor-General of French West Africa, 27 April 1929, 4D8, AAOF; Major-General Benoît, 'Rapport ... sur les opérations des recrutement indigène en 1929–1930', 21 August 1930; General Staff, French West Africa Group, 'Rapport sur le recrutement 1932'.

191 Ministry of the Overseas, Office of Defence Organization, 'Note sur les operations de recrutement concernant la classe 1948 de l'AOF', 23 March 1949.

192 Reports on recruitment in Guinea, Côte d'Ivoire, and Upper Volta, 1950–1958, SHD, Pau.

193 General Staff, French West Africa Group, 'Rapport annuel sur les opérations de recrutement indigène en 1929', 4 August 1929; Lieutenant-Governor of Côte d'Ivoire to Governor-General of French West Africa, 27 April 1929; Benoît, 'Rapport ... sur les opérations des recrutement indigène en 1929–1930', 21 August 1930; General Staff, French West Africa Group, 'Rapport sur le recrutement 1932'.

194 Berthezene, 'Rapport semestriel sur le moral des militaires de la 4o CIOM (Port-Bouët) et de transmission du Niger', 4 April 1962.

195 Kone, interview by author, 26 November 2015, Abidjan.

In an interview, Koné emphasized the personal role Houphouët-Boigny had played in filling command positions. This was certainly true for Thomas d'Aquin Ouattara, whom Houphouët-Boigny appointed Chief of Staff of the Armed Forces. D'Aquin Ouattara was loyal to the Ivorian president, but the French questioned his intellectual and leadership capacities.[196] Yet Koné noted that he and d'Aquin Ouattara had come from the same village and had no problems working together.[197]

Much like the Ivorians, the Senegalese government also started an outreach campaign in lycées, in 1958. Mamadou Seck, who later became Commander of the Senegalese Air Force, was among those selected to attend training in Strasbourg, where he completed a year-long preparatory course before entering Saint-Cyr Military Academy. There, he got off to a difficult start as some of his French peers were devout Catholics with racist prejudices. According to Seck, the difficult conditions shared by all the students at Saint-Cyr did foster unity among them over time.[198]

After graduating from Saint-Cyr, Seck completed a parachutist training course in Pau, in southern France, with the hopes of becoming a pilot and being one of the first Africans to do so. He explained in an interview that there were *tirailleurs* in every Senegalese family, but none had served in the colonial air force. Of course, the Senegalese air force first had to be established, but eventually he headed up this arm of the military. While he did not know Senegalese President Senghor personally, Seck said that he was known to enjoy the company of Senegalese officers. However, this did not mean the Senghor had no fear of coups or assassination, as Seck noted while reminiscing about how difficult it had been to convince Senghor to Africanize the flight crew of his personal plane.[199]

For the most part, Senghor had a different view of Senegalese officers, colonial soldiers, and the national military to Houphouët-Boigny. This was largely due to the different positions of Senegal and Côte d'Ivoire upon independence, when Senegal had the highest number of officers in the French forces (twenty-six) and Côte d'Ivoire relatively few (ten). French recruitment had been far less fruitful in Côte d'Ivoire because it offered better economic opportunities than Senegal, and because of issues related

---

196 French Embassy Abidjan, 'Malaise au sein de l'armée ivoirienne', 6 July 1965; Telegram, Abidjan to Ragunet, Paris, 6 July 1965; Telegram, Raphaël-Leygues, to Directorate of African and Malagasy Affairs, 13 August 1969.
197 Kone, interview by author, 26 November 2015, Abidjan.
198 Seck, interview by author, June 2018, Dakar.
199 Ibid.

to language and ethnicity. As none of the ethnic groups in Côte d'Ivoire formed a significant majority, it was harder for Ivorian soldiers to find support in their native language during their time in the military. Moreover, the French viewed members of these ethnic groups – including the Guéré, Bété, and Baoulé – as unfit for service. Hence, in 1960, there were only 1,486 Guéré, Bété, and Baoulé soldiers among the 22,670 African soldiers in FWA. None were officers and only eighty were non-commissioned officers. At independence, a total of 5,700 Ivorian soldiers served in the French military, of whom just ten were officers.[200] By January 1961, this number of Ivorian soldiers had dropped to around 3,000, and a year later, to under 2,000.[201]

Houphouët-Boigny was sensitive about Ivorian soldiers serving in the French military outside of Côte d'Ivoire, which the French attributed to the domestic political environment.[202] This notwithstanding, the concerns of the Ivorian president reflected the symbolic value of colonial soldiers and the national military to an independent Côte d'Ivoire. The country had gained independence in August 1960, but the creation of its national armed forces did not begin until the following year,[203] when the Ministry of Defence and Office of the Chief of Staff were established and three battalions were formed.[204] By the end of 1961, the Ivorian forces had almost 1,000 troops, including eighteen officers and 191 non-commissioned officers.[205]

French military authorities were quick to highlight deficiencies in the new Ivorian military, in stark contrast to how they described Senegalese forces. The Ivorians had reportedly failed to achieve a similar cohesion, and their insufficient technical skills meant they would likely rely on French assistance for years.[206] In many ways, the views of French observers on the potential of Ivorian soldiers represent a form of colonial continuity of their own, as they were clearly influenced by colonial-era biases about ethnic

---

200 Gardet, 'Rapport de fin de commandement', 15 February 1960.
201 Brebisson, 'Rapport annuel 1961'; Ministry of Land Armies, Department of Overseas Troops, 'Situation par état d'origine des personnels des troupes d'outre-mer en service en AFN situation au 1.2.1961'.
202 Secretary of State for Relations with the States of the Community, to the Minister of Armed Forces, 21 September 1960, 324QONT/23, CADC.
203 Arthur Banga, *La coopération militaire entre la France et la Côte d'Ivoire* (Universitares Européenne, 2014).
204 Brebisson, 'Rapport annuel 1961'.
205 Brebisson, 'Rapport de fin de commandement du général commandement', 30 June 1962 and 'Rapport annuel 1961'.
206 Ibid.

groups in Côte d'Ivoire. For example, in a 1963 report that referred to the 'mediocre' value of Ivorian forces and their lack of 'warrior qualities', a French official noted that Ivorian *tirailleurs* had 'never ... shone with military talent'. The official deemed the Ivorian military large but weak, and was critical of Ivorian officers and non-commissioned officers, whom he believed were incapable of supervising a young armed force.[207] French officials also had negative views of Nigerien soldiers, of whom there were comparatively few in the French army. In Niger, the general level of education was low, which had further limited the potential of its national military.[208]

Both Diori in Niger and Houphouët-Boigny in Côte d'Ivoire chose to establish party militias from members of their own ethnic groups, as a counterforce to the military. Indeed, as the Ivorian president grew increasingly insecure vis-à-vis his own army, the opinion of the French that his forces lacked strength became more and more of a reality, as Houphouët-Boigny had deliberately chosen to weaken them. In 1963, Ambassador Raphaël-Leygues said that, 'true to his idea of preventing any unified opposition against him, the president has adopted a new tactic.' Having found even his militias 'insufficient', the Ivorian president sought to 'split his small bloated and ineffective army' so that it would 'break in two or three in case of a ... coup.'[209]

Hence, after 1963, Houphouët-Boigny was content to rely on French assistance to confront both internal and external threats.[210] This generated dissatisfaction within the armed forces, particularly among young officers.[211] Signs of unease in the Ivorian military were noted by French officials,

[207] Directorate of African and Malagasy Affairs, 'Etudes de comportement des armées nationales en 1963'.

[208] Ambassador of France in Niger, 'L'armée retrouve sa place dans la nation', 29 June 1966, 478PO1–1, CADC; US Embassy Niamey, 'Nigerian military', 12 May 1965, POL Niger 64–66, Box 2516, CGRDS, NARA.

[209] Telegram, Raphaël-Leygues to Directorate of African and Malagasy Affairs, 13 December 1963.

[210] Raphaël-Leygues, 'La Côte d'Ivoire et l'Armée', 30 August 1974, and 'Rapport de la discussion avec le général délègue la défense de ZON 4', December 1963, 324QONT/10, CADC; Telegram, Raphaël-Leygues to Directorate of African and Malagasy Affairs, 13 December 1963; Military advisor, French Embassy Abidjan, 'Rapport mensuel September 1965', 4 October 1965, GR14S251, SHD.

[211] French Embassy Abidjan, 'Actualités politiques', 10 September 1963; Telegram, Abidjan to Paris, 31 August 1963; Military Advisor, French Embassy Abidjan, 'Rapport annuel pour 1965', 7 December 1965; Telegram, Raphaël-Leygues to Directorate of African and Malagasy Affairs, 13 December 1963; Intelligence Exploitation Centre, Section B, 'Les problèmes de défense en Côte d'Ivoire', 23 January 1968; Commander

who insisted that French personnel should be withdrawn from command positions.[212] This did not pacify officers who had foreseen a long military career and saw now their opportunities shrinking.[213] After a coup attempt in 1973, the Ivorian government moved to adapt the training offered to Ivorian soldiers in order to create job opportunities for them in the state administration.[214]

In lacking a clear rupture with the colonial past and the former colonial power, it had always been a challenge for Houphouët-Boigny to build legitimacy for institutions of coercion and the use of force. The integration of former colonial soldiers into the economic life of the state may not have created significant problems for the Ivorian president, as they were small in number and the Ivorian economy was relatively healthy, Houphouët-Boigny's own suspicion of soldiers saw him turned to France and, to some degree, embrace colonial continuity. The Senegalese government had taken a different approach, welcoming a French military presence, but less obviously than the Ivorians; as President Senghor was keenly aware of popular Senegalese opposition to French military bases.[215] Senghor emphasized the importance of a strong and independent military, telling French president Charles de Gaulle in 1961 that an excessive reliance on France would make Senegal susceptible to subversive movements.[216] However, as was the case in Côte d'Ivoire, Senegal's approach was related to the number of colonial soldiers and officers who returned to the country at independence. In Senegal, this number was much higher than in Côte d'Ivoire, but it was

---

Thenot, French Military Aid Office, 'Rapport sur le moral', 7 January 1964, 5H32, SHD; Telegram, Abidjan to Paris, 31 August 1963.

212 Thenot, 'Rapport sur le moral', 7 January 1964.

213 Raphaël-Leygues to Ministry of Foreign Affairs, 'Situation intérieure', 17 December 1968.

214 Raphaël-Leygues, to Minister of Foreign Affairs, Jean Sauvagnargues, 'Synthèse politique du 1 juin au 31 juillet 1974', 19 August 1974; Colonel André Gouri, interview by author, 23 November 2015, Abidjan.

215 French Embassy Dakar, 'Demande sénégalaise', 18 September 1964; General Secretary for African and Malagasy Affairs, 'Audience du president Leopold Senghor', 22 July 1965, 5AGF/608, FFAN; General Secretary for African and Malagasy Affairs, 'Attention president accords de défense franco-sénégalais', 17 December 1969, 5AGF/609, FFAN; Jean de Lagarde, Ambassador of France in Dakar, to Ministry of Foreign Affairs, 'Problèmes franco-sénégalais de déflation militaire, notamment la base de Thiès', 30 September 1964, INVA318, CADC.

216 General Secretary for African and Malagasy Affairs, 'Entretien avec le président Senghor', 21 April 1961, 5AGF/608, FFAN.

higher still in Upper Volta. This helps explain Voltaic decision-making, which is discussed in the next section.

A Reverence for Warriors: The Postcolonial Importance of Soldiers in Upper Volta

In his memoir, former Voltaic president Sangoulé Lamizana described his own conscription into French forces in 1936, noting how he had been labelled 'good for armed service' and had excited recruiters, who 'exclaimed: "I finally have someone who can read and write French".' Yet, as Lamizana explained, his 'incorporation looked like a kidnapping':

> My situation of voluntary engagement, I who was there only to know the answer to my request for employment as a veterinary nurse, was due to the fact that the commander who hated me cordially, wanted to see me away from him, as long as possible. Indeed, it had been reported to him that Sangoulé Lamizana was the tireless organizer of those noisy *gourmées* which lasted late into the night and disturbed his sleep. I was almost sad on the verge of tears.... Having no recourse, I pocketed a bonus of 150F granted for the additional year to the legal duration of military service which was three years. The dice were now cast. I had become a 2nd class rifleman.[217]

Lamizana's account accurately reflects French recruitment practices, which pushed many so-called 'volunteers' into military service through various non-voluntary means. The recruitment system allowed traditional chiefs and colonial administrators to send away anyone they disliked, and Lamizana believed this was part of why the commander who conscripted him had done so. However, Lamizana's language skills were another reason behind his forced 'volunteering'.[218] French reports referred almost habitually to problems recruiting Africans with sufficient knowledge of French.

After his conscription, Lamizana served the French in colonial conflicts in Indochina and Algeria. In 1961, when he was repatriated to Upper Volta, he was appointed Chief of Staff of the Voltaic Armed Forces. Then, in January 1966, he became the country's second president, in many ways symbolizing the ongoing significance of soldiers in Voltaic society. Indeed, in December 1965, when Upper Volta's first president, Maurice Yaméogo, had faced growing protests in the capital over austerity measures, protestors had

---

217 Lamizana, *Sous les drapeaux: Mémoires*, vol. 1 (Paris: Jaguar, 2000), p. 50.
218 Ibid.

called on the military to assume power.[219] This reflects what anthropologist and ambassador Elliott Skinner noted, namely, that a reverence for soldiers in Upper Volta, even prior to colonization, had long influenced Voltaic social values and perceptions.[220]

Of all the countries in FWA, Upper Volta provided the greatest number of recruits to the colonial French military, and for several reasons. Upper Volta was relatively populous but had a weak potential for agriculture, so Voltaic labour was used on plantations in other colonies, and in the French armed forces.[221] The hierarchical structure of Voltaic societies also made recruitment relatively easy, and was thought to produce the most obedient troops.[222] The role of the Mossi king, the *Moro Naba*, was key to the French, as his authority over the chiefs helped France manifest its authority and acquire the manpower it needed. Nevertheless, the French governor-general of FWA complained that the influence of France was limited by the insufficient language skills of the Mossi as well as their traditional beliefs. Hence, French authorities were eager to provide education to the children of chiefs and recruit them into the French military.[223] The importance of warfare and warriors in pre-colonial Mossi society, which had helped them avoid colonization until the end of the 19th century, led the French to believe the Mossi made exceptional soldiers.[224]

During the First World War, 70,217 soldiers from Haut-Senegal-Niger joined the French forces, despite a temporary pause in conscription when recruitment led to multiple revolts in 1915 and 1916. In the three years following the First World War, more than 12,000 more soldiers were conscripted from Upper Volta.[225] The youth in Upper Volta were not enthusiastic about joining the French military, which is reflected in the rate of

---

219 Levasseur, 'Crise politique en Haute-Volta', 4 January 1966; Military advisor, French Embassy Ouagadougou, 'Rapport mensuel mois de décembre', 6 January 1966.

220 Elliott Skinner, *The Mossi of the Upper Volta: The Political Development of the Sudanese People* (Stanford University Press, 1964). Also see French Embassy Ouagadougou, 'Compte-rendu hebdomadaire' 4 August 1961 and 'Compte-rendu hebdomadaire', 20 October 1961, 313QONT/4, CADC; Directorate of African and Malagasy Affairs, 'Questions militaires en Haute-Volta', 2 November 1961.

221 Palm, *Rassemblement Démocratique Africain*, p. 23.

222 Skinner, *The Mossi of the Upper Volta*.

223 Governor-General of French West Africa, 'La Haute-Volta exposition coloniale international de 1931', GR5H169, SHD.

224 Echenberg, *Les Tirailleurs sénégalais*, pp. 116–17 and *Paying the Blood Tax*, p. 190.

225 Governor-General of Indochina and French West Africa, 'Tableau des effectifs recrutes en Afrique occidentale française depuis 1910', 4D1, AAOF.

missing recruits, or *bons absents*, in the colony. Between 1926 and 1929, the rate of Voltaic absenteeism was between 20 to 25%, more than the average in FWA. Most of these absentees were thought to have sought refuge in the Gold Coast.[226] As the search for Voltaic *bons absent* became more effective, their number decreased slowly. Even so, in 1932, Upper Volta had the highest number in all of FWA.[227]

This high rate of absenteeism was matched by a lower number of volunteers in Upper Volta, especially when compared to countries like Guinea or even Côte d'Ivoire. In 1929, for example, of all those recruited for that year's quota, only 21% were volunteers, whereas in Guinea it was 79%. Voltaic recruits who could speak French were also rare. Throughout the 1930s, only a very small number of recruits from Upper Volta could speak French, or read and write. [228]

Between 1932 and 1947, the details of French recruitment in Upper Volta are less clear, as the territory was divided among its neighbouring colonies and most Voltaic conscripts were recorded in Ivorian data. Recruitment reports show, however, that the outbreak of the Second World War did not result in the Voltaic population being any more disposed to volunteer for the French military. In 1949, the percentage of Voltaic *bons absents* would again stand at 24%, and only 23% of the 1,560 recruits were volunteers.[229] Nevertheless, 16,000 conscripts from Upper Volta did join the French armed forces between 1950 and 1957.[230]

As a result of French colonial recruitment practices, soldiers from Upper Volta constituted the largest group of Africans in the French military and represented 28% of the 26,300 African soldiers in FWA. Altogether, there were more than 13,000 Voltaic soldiers serving in the colonial forces in 1960, and this large number made their reintegration into Voltaic postcolonial society difficult, 'as neither the national military nor the Voltaic fields

---

[226] Colony of Upper Volta, 'Rapport sur le recrutement 1927–1928', 12 April 1928, 4D8, AAOF; General Staff, French West Africa Group, 'Rapport sur le recrutement 1932', and 'Rapport annuel sur les opérations de recrutement indigène en 1929', 4 August 1929.

[227] General Staff, French West Africa Group, 'Rapport sur le recrutement 1932'.

[228] Ministry of the Overseas, Office of Defence Organization, 'Note sur les opérations de recrutement concernant la classe 1948 de l'AOF', 23 March 1949.

[229] Ibid.

[230] Reports on recruitment in Guinea, Côte d'Ivoire, and Upper Volta, 1950–1958, SHD, Pau.

could feed them all, after their military earnings would run out.'[231] There were also quite a few higher-ranking Voltaic soldiers, including nineteen officers and 645 non-commissioned officers, particularly from certain ethnic groups. The commander of the FWA reported, for example, that out of 3,900 Mossi soldiers, seven were officers and 201 were non-commissioned officers, and out of 2,500 Bambara soldiers, three were officers and 169 were non-commissioned officers.[232] Maintaining the material wellbeing of these high-ranking Voltaic officers would prove a particular challenge to the government. Only a small number of colonial soldiers could be integrated into the national armed forces, and the rest would need to return to civilian life, where they would have few options for employment.[233]

Not all Voltaic colonial soldiers were eager to return, particularly those nearing retirement. This was of concern to the Minister of Defence Bamina Nébié, who had ambitious plans to create a large armed force, and he thus demanded that colonial soldiers pledge allegiance to the Voltaic state.[234] In a speech in August 1961, during which he sought to convince colonial soldiers to leave the French military, Nébié appealed to their sense of nationalism, declaring they must 'serve unconditionally, serve without reluctance, serve simply because the country wants it, because your dignity and your honour demand it, because it is not possible for you to be mercenaries in the service of a country other than yours.'[235] However, Upper Volta could neither afford the immediate return of every colonial soldier, nor the cost of building the large military Nébié imagined, and the Voltaic president asked France not to repatriate all Voltaic soldiers at once. Thus, many Voltaic colonial soldiers continued to serve in the French armed forces well after independence. In February 1961, nearly 3,500 Voltaic colonial soldiers were active in West

231 French Embassy Ouagadougou, 'Compte-rendu hebdomadaire', 4 August 1961; See documents in Files 313QONT/20, 313QONT/4, and 313QONT/20, CADC.
232 General Gardet, 'Rapport de fin de commandement', 15 February 1960.
233 French Embassy Ouagadougou, 'Compte-rendu hebdomadaire', 18 February 1961, 313QONT/3, CADC, 'Compte-rendu hebdomadaire', 5 May 1961, 313QONT/3, CADC, 'Compte-rendu hebdomadaire', 4 February 1961; 'Compte-rendu hebdomadaire', 28 April 1961, and 'Compte-rendu hebdomadaire', 18 January 1961, 313QONT/3, CADC.
234 French Embassy Ouagadougou, 'Compte-rendu hebdomadaire', 4 August 1961, and 'Compte-rendu hebdomadaire', 18 August 1961; Directorate of African and Malagasy Affairs, 'Questions militaires en Haute-Volta', 2 November 1961.
235 French Embassy Ouagadougou, 'Compte-rendu hebdomadaire', 4 August 1961.

Africa, accounting for more than one-third of all troops.[236] The last of these colonial soldiers would only return to Upper Volta in early 1965.

The Voltaic military was established in November 1961, when approximately 750 Voltaic soldiers – including twenty-four officers – were officially transferred into Voltaic forces from the French.[237] In 1962, however, the Voltaic military comprised only 800 soldiers, making it the smallest in francophone Africa.[238] Nébié's ambitious plans had been throttled by President Yaméogo, who, for financial and political reasons, had decided not to increase the size of the army too quickly.[239] After Yaméogo rejected the formation of a second Voltaic battalion with support from the French, a US report noted that 'French policy (wisely, we believe) is not to encourage these states to build up forces faster than the states ask for them. Apparently, Yaméogo ... decided for domestic political reasons that he does not want the second battalion now.' According to American officials, the French were happy to comply, as they felt there were 'cheaper ways to reintegrate [colonial soldier] into a "normal" Voltaic life than setting up a new battalion.'[240]

Although the Voltaic military grew slowly, the inclusion of many experienced and high-ranking colonial soldiers resulted in significant costs. A considerable portion of military resources went to soldier salaries, at a time when the army had neither the most basic equipment, nor the means to purchase it.[241] Voltaic soldiers perceived their pay as inadequate and grew increasingly dissatisfied,[242] and numerous officers resigned in 1962, citing

---

236 Ministry of Land Armies, Department of Overseas Troops, 'Situation par état d'origine des personnels des troupes d'outre-mer en service en AFN situation au 1.2.1961'.

237 Brebisson, 'Rapport annuel 1961'.

238 Brebisson, 'Rapport de fin de commandement du général commandement', 30 June 1962.

239 US Embassy Ouagadougou 'Memorandum of conversation: participants Herni Bernard, French Chargé d'affaires; Major Demondiere, French military attaché; and Major Frank MTT Upper Volta', 18 May 1962; Frank, 'Military mission to Upper Volta', 12 June 1962.

240 Bovey, US Embassy Paris, to John Cunnigham, Office of African and Malagasy Affairs, 25 June 1962.

241 Ambassador Francis Levasseur to Minister of Foreign Affairs, Maurice Couve de Murville, 'Synthese XXXIX67', 13 October 1967, 313QONT/8 CADC; Ambassador Raoul Delaye to Minister of Foreign Affairs, Couve de Murville, 'Synthèse no VII68', 5 April 1968, 313QONT/8 CADC.

242 Estes, US Embassy in Ouagadougou, to Department of State, 'Speech by President Yaméogo', 23 October 1961, 770K 1960–1963, Box 1983, CGRDS, NARA.

insufficient remuneration.[243] This continued to be a source of dissatisfaction among Voltaic soldiers, and it is no coincidence that the 1966 military coup occurred just after the Voltaic government had tried to decrease soldier salaries.[244]

The integration of colonial soldiers into the national military was also difficult in Senegal and Niger. For financial reasons, the Senegalese government chose not to invite very many experienced non-commissioned officers into its armed forces, preferring younger (and cheaper) recruits instead. This policy meant that many Senegalese soldiers who had served in Algeria were disappointed to be excluded from the national military. Moreover, colonial soldiers who were included in the Senegalese armed forces were paid less than they had been by the French.[245] The Nigerien president had raised concerns about this same issue in discussions with French officials, complaining that the salaries of Nigerien soldiers serving on French military bases in Niger were higher than those of Nigeriens serving in the national armed forces. This created discontent among soldiers in the Nigerien military. As in Upper Volta, and for similar reasons, the governments in both Senegal and Niger also asked the French to postpone the repatriation of their colonial soldiers.[246] The last Senegalese soldiers serving with the French in North Africa were not repatriated until May 1964.[247]

Compared to Senegal or Niger – or Côte d'Ivoire, Dahomey, and Mauritania, for that matter – Upper Volta had taken a more independent approach to its defence by refusing to have any French military bases on its territory. French officials believed President Yaméogo had made this decision mostly due to Voltaic public opinion, and not because he was

243 Chief of Battalion Sangoulé, 'Note de Service No142/3M/3', 9 March 1962, 6V33, ANB.

244 Levasseur, 'Forces d'opposition et force de l'opposition en Haute-Volta', 10 July 1965; Francis Levasseur to Minister of Foreign Affairs, Couve de Murville, 'La Haute-Volta en 1964', 6 January 1965; Maurice Beaux, Chargé d'affaires, to Minister of Foreign Affairs, Couve de Murville, 'Synthèse no XVIII/65', 12 May 1965, 313QONT/4, CADC; Levasseur, 'Synthèse No XLVII/65', 1 December 1965, 313QONT/7, CADC and 'Synthèse XLVI/65', 24 November 1965, 313QONT/20, CADC.

245 Ambassador Lucien Paye to Ministry of Foreign Affairs, 1 August 1963, INVA321, CADC.

246 Ambassador Lucien Paye to Ministry of Foreign Affairs, 1 August 1963; General Secretary for African and Malagasy Affairs, 'Audience du président Diori Hamani', 23 January 1963, 5AGF/598, FFAN.

247 General Secretary for African and Malagasy Affairs, 'Note à l'attention de président de la république, April 1964, 5AGF/608, FFAN.

personally averse to a French security presence.[248] The manner in which the French military departed from Upper Volta in 1962 must have impacted the views of Voltaic soldiers regarding France. According to Lamizana, the French took everything they could and destroyed anything else, echoing the Guinean and Malian narratives.[249] Moreover, the departure of French troops and the transfer of a military base in Bobo-Dioulasso allowed Yaméogo to announce that Upper Volta was a truly independent and sovereign state.[250] Even if there was continuity from the colonial era in terms of personnel, equipment, and training, the absence of a French military base on Voltaic territory marked the end the colonial system of security.

Former Voltaic soldiers interviewed for this study who had been rank-and-file troops in the French military at the time of Voltaic independence all agreed that Upper Volta could not have been fully independent as long as the French maintained a base in the country.[251] However, Colonel Barthélémy Kombasre – who was an officer-in-training at the time of independence and was later responsible for army equipment – said the Voltaic government had made a mistake in denying the French a military base, arguing that this had severely hampered military development. He emphasized that the material conditions of colonial soldiers had significantly worsened after they transferred from French forces into the Voltaic military.[252] In contrast, Capitaine Didier Felicieu Compaore and Adjutant-Chef Major Macaire Yaméogo noted that Voltaic soldiers who were included in the Voltaic armed forces felt very fortunate, knowing that so many colonial soldiers had not been given the same opportunity. Compaore and Yaméogo had been eager to serve in the national military, although both said they had not previously

---

248 French Embassy Ouagadougou, 'Compte-rendu hebdomadaire', 4 February 1961, 'Compte-rendu Hebdomadaire', 28 April 1961 and 'Compte-rendu hebdomadaire, 4 August 1961'; Lamizana, *Sur la Brèche*, pp. 24–6 and 32; Ambassador of France to the President of Upper Volta, 27 December 1961; Estes, 'Defense Ministry Change', 24 May 1962.

249 Lamizana, *Sur la Brèche*, 32.

250 Service de documentation extérieure et de contre-espionnage (SDECE), 'Synthèse de renseignements: January 1962', 17 February 1962; French Embassy Ouagadougou, 'Compte-rendu hebdomadaire' 7 October 1961; Directorate of African and Malagasy Affairs, 'Questions militaires en Haute-Volta ' 2 November 1961.

251 Captain Didier Felicieu Compaore, Colonel Major Aly Paré, and Adjudant-chef Major Macaire Yaméogo, interviews by author, 15 January 2016, Ouagadougou.

252 Colonel Barthélémy Kombasre, interview by author, 18 January 2016, Ouagadougou.

entertained nationalist sentiment, 'as a soldier's duty was to follow orders not to engage in politics.'[253]

Even if Voltaic soldiers did not at first engage in politics, they did drive political decision-making. In fact, the Voltaic government opted to organize its defence more independently than many of its neighbours, partly due to the long-standing status of soldiers in Voltaic society. Both French and American reports from the early 1960s, for example, remarked on the importance Voltaic politicians placed on displays of Voltaic military might during Independence Day celebrations.[254] These politicians also frequently praised the qualities of Voltaic soldiers and referred to the important traditional – and non-political – role they had played in Upper Volta.[255]

However, both serving and retired Voltaic soldiers soon became important political forces in the country. The influence of retired colonial soldiers was evident when their dissatisfaction over their small pensions led to efforts by the Voltaic military government to increase the amounts.[256] In 1960, the pensions of all African soldiers had been harmonized with the current costs of living in each colony, but had not been increased thereafter. President Lamizana, who led the Voltaic military government, had discussed the insufficiency of military pensions with French officials on multiple occasions.[257] In 1966, he told the French that colonial soldiers in Upper Volta were profoundly discontent with the discriminatory practices to which they had been subject.[258] Lamizana brought the issue up again in 1969 and 1970, noting his concern that political parties would try to capitalize on the dissatisfaction of colonial soldiers in upcoming elections.[259]

253 Captain Compaore, Colonel Major Paré, and Adjudant-chef Major Yaméogo, interviews by author, 15 January 2016, Ouagadougou.
254 Dalsimer, 'Upper Volta Gains an Army', 20 October 1961; French Embassy Ouagadougou, 'Compte-rendu hebdomadaire', 4 August 1961.
255 Estes, 'Internal Security Assessment', 30 May 1962.
256 Levasseur, 'Forces d'opposition et force de l'opposition en Haute-Volta', 10 July 1965; Levasseur to Minister of Foreign Affairs, Couve de Murville, 'La Haute-Volta en 1964', 6 January 1965.
257 General Secretariat for African and Malagasy Affairs, 'Audience du général Lamizana', 26 August 1969.
258 French Embassy Ouagadougou to Minister of Foreign Affairs, Couve de Murville, 'Pensions des anciens combattants et militaires voltaïques', 26 October 1966, 5AGF/1849, FFAN.
259 Delaye to Maurice Schuman, 'Des pensions des anciens combattants voltaïques', 12 January 1970, 5AGF/1856, FFAN; General Secretariat for African and Malagasy Affairs, 'Audience du général Lamizana', 26 August 1969; Delaye, French Embassy

He was right to be concerned about losing the backing of former colonial soldiers, as French reports from the time suggest his support was waning and many of them would prefer a transfer to civilian rule.[260] These former soldiers were an influential constituency for any Voltaic government, military or civilian. During colonial rule, they had served as a link between the population and French authorities,[261] and after independence, they continued to be important actors in promoting pro-French policies. The French were aware of this, noting in 1961 that the country not only had large numbers of former soldiers but that they 'remain[ed] very deeply attached to the Community.'[262]

Conclusion

Across francophone West Africa, the transition from the colonial security system to national militaries and postcolonial African governments involved efforts to reintegrate colonial soldiers, and to reorganize and legitimize coercive institutions. While many African presidents held ambiguous views regarding soldiers who had served in French forces, their governments all faced the challenge of integrating them, building a national military from them, and legitimizing that national military and its use of force. Even if postcolonial governments could not always choose where French military bases were located, the number of colonial soldiers who were repatriated, or the training and education soldiers had received, these newly independent governments could choose how to deal with the problematic legacies of colonial structures. This included colonial recruitment practices and use of African soldiers in defending the French empire.

In 1912, France enacted universal conscription in West Africa in order to increase its military manpower and reinforce links between the metropole and the colonies. From the start, there were differences of opinion among

---

Ouagadougou, to Minister of Foreign Affairs, Michel Debré, 'Des pensions des anciens combattants voltaïque', 14 January 1969, 5AGF/1855, FFAN.

260 Military advisor, French Embassy Ouagadougou, 'Rapport mensuel mois d'avril', 30 April 1970, 'Rapport mensuel mois de mars 1970', 31 March 1970, 'Rapport mensuel, mois de fevrier, 28 February 1970, GR14262, SHD, and 'Rapport mensuel, mois de janvier' 31 January 1970.

261 Garbay, 'Effort entrepris concernant la remise en condition des forces terrestres de l'AOF' 23 March 1955.

262 Ministry of the Armed Forces, Overseas Office, Dakar, 'Notice sur Haute-Volta', 8 July 1960.

politicians in Paris, the colonial administration, and the French military on recruitment practices and objectives. French officials also disagreed on whether they should recruit more volunteers or continue setting a quota of conscripts for each region, so as to ensure African troops were sufficiently heterogeneous and so could not organize and rebel against their French superiors.

For the most part, the recruitment of African soldiers reflected the limits of colonial coercive control. Africans with some education and means generally succeeded in evading conscription, while disadvantaged rural youth were made to pay the colonial 'blood tax'. This meant that most colonial soldiers could not speak French, nor read and write, which limited the training France could provide them. In the 1950s, the French need for manpower led France to recruit increasing numbers of African volunteers, but upon their withdrawal from Indochina in 1954, the repercussions of 'short-sighted' recruitment policies became clear. African soldiers who had been promised career advancement in the French armed forces were being repatriated to colonies where nationalist movements were gaining momentum.

The conflict in Algeria appeared to solve a problem for the French, as African soldiers could serve in Algeria and be maintained on the French payroll. However, the growing popularity of nationalist movements caused French officials to question the loyalty of these soldiers, and attempts were made to provide advancement opportunities intended to entice them away from alternatives. Then, in 1960, the French decided to withdraw all African soldiers from Algeria, although this did not mean the immediate repatriation of colonial soldiers. Only Guinean soldiers had been repatriated by that point, with 11,000 having returned to Guinea in 1959, most of whom terminated their contracts early, thereby losing their rights to a pension.

By 1962, most African soldiers had been repatriated, and all had returned home by 1965. The integration of these former soldiers into newly independent states caused significant political, economic, and social problems. National armed forces and other state institutions could only employ a percentage of these soldiers, who were unskilled in any other profession. The challenge for African politicians, who had little experience and even fewer resources at their disposal, was considerable. As one would expect, the problems related to returning colonial soldiers were most severe in countries where their number was the highest, such as Guinea, Mali, and Upper Volta. The economic situation of each country and its relations with the former colonial power were also important factors that affected the reintegration of returning soldiers. Former colonial soldiers were assumed to maintain a certain affinity and loyalty towards France, which meant a pro-French regime like Côte d'Ivoire saw former soldiers as potential allies, whereas a revolutionary regime like Guinea saw them as potential threats. France did indeed use Guinean colonial soldiers in covert actions against President Touré and colonial soldiers also became pawns in Franco-Guinean disputes, such as when France suspended pension payments to Guinean soldiers and Touré responded by refusing to accept the return of Guinean soldiers repatriated from the French military. The Guinean case served as a warning to other African politicians and former soldiers that it was worth maintaining good relations with France.

Nevertheless, former colonial soldiers in Mali, Senegal, and Upper Volta played a part in the pressure exerted upon their governments to build strong and autonomous militaries . Both the Malian and Voltaic governments, for example, refused to host French military bases. In every francophone West African state, the manner in which the government interacted with colonial structures and legitimized institutions of coercion and the use of force was influenced by their relations with France. Revolutionary states like Guinea and Mali could most easily declare a rupture with the colonial past. Not only had the French troops departed, but the armed forces in these countries were equipped and trained primarily by the communist bloc. However, all national militaries included colonial soldiers, and even in Guinea and Mali they operated from military bases left empty by the French.

In countries where France did maintain a military presence, it was more difficult to mark the break between national and colonial forces. In fact, in Côte d'Ivoire, Senegal, Niger, Dahomey, and Mauritania, the transition to a national military was characterized by continuity, with France maintaining an important role in equipping and training soldiers. Despite this, French-occupied military bases were a source for criticism, as they marked ongoing 'neo-colonial' or 'imperialist' influence in the defence sphere, which was perceived to undermine independence. Indeed, this is why Voltaic leaders felt the departure of French troops was the only way to ensure an independent Upper Volta.

Independence was indeed complicated when former colonial soldiers retained an affinity for France that led presidents to distrust their loyalty. Many nationalist politicians already felt an unease towards colonial soldiers for their role in maintaining the French empire and fighting against anti-colonial movements, as well as their absence from nationalist struggles. In Guinea and Upper Volta, politicians had used the term 'mercenary' in reference to colonial soldiers, in an effort to emphasize the difference between national and colonial forces. This was difficult to do, as every francophone West African government built the national army out of colonial soldiers. However, legitimizing the state's use of force and its institutions of coercion required these new national forces to be presented as symbols of independence.

Hence, highlighting differences between colonial and national militaries became a common strategy for legitimizing these forces. In Guinea and Côte d'Ivoire, soldiers were also assigned non-military tasks in national development, undertaking agricultural, industrial, or road-building projects. For the Ivorian government, this decision was informed by the central question of why the state should spend so much on an institution that did not play a key role in its development. It made no sense to Houphouët-Boigny allocate resources to the military if it produced no economic benefit for the country, and he thus justified a French role in Ivorian defence. This allowed him to maintain a relatively small military that posed little threat to his power.

In Guinea, the regime sought to ensure the loyalty of soldiers by carefully selecting and ideologically training those who served in the national military. In Upper Volta, President Yaméogo took a more subtle approach, attempting to legitimize the national armed forces and assure their loyalty by frequently referencing the glorious historical role of Voltaic soldiers. Flattery was, in fact, a common tool used by governments seeking to influence soldiers. After a coup in a neighbouring country, presidents would often publicly declare, for instance, that 'military coups can happen elsewhere, but not in our country because our soldiers are devoted and loyal.'[263]

In this way, African leaders worked to capture the loyalty of soldiers through nationalist discourse, addressed directly to them. Yet, discourse alone did not prevent military coups. In 1963, the coup in Togo put many presidents in francophone West Africa on high alert and raised their suspicions of national armed forces and colonial soldiers. Some governments even purposely weakened their national military or created a new force to counter it. Others, like Côte d'Ivoire, turned to foreign protection. The strategies employed by francophone West African countries to control their national armed forces are discussed in the next chapter.

---

263 See, for example, Maurice Yaméogo's speech during the Independence Day celebrations of 2 November 1965. Yaméogo in Levasseur, 'Synthèse No XLIII/65', 3 November 1965.

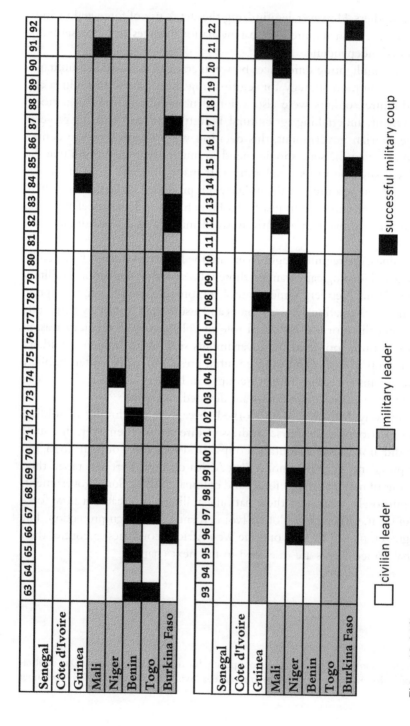

Figure 19. Military coups and rulers in francophone West Africa, 1963–2018 (Source: Coups database, https://www.jonathanm-powell.com/coup-detat-dataset.html, Published 2011, Accessed: 2021).

5

Governance: Control and Command
of the Armed Forces

The control and governance of armed forces in Africa have been widely discussed because the continent has experienced so many military coups and subsequent periods of military rule. This is particularly true of West Africa and former French colonies, which have seen more military coups and more military rule than elsewhere on the continent.[1] In fact, of the nine francophone West African countries analysed in this text, only Senegal has avoided a military takeover (see Figure 19). Given this, it is important to understand how the governments of these countries sought to control their militaries. This chapter explores the practices and tools used by these governments for that purpose, and the political environments in which they were applied.

Postcolonial political systems in sub-Saharan Africa tended to favour one-party rule, meaning that state institutions were controlled by a single party, and decision-making and resources were centralized to presidents and their close entourage. This aptly describes the experience of every country in francophone West Africa, all of which became de facto one-party states soon after independence, offering citizens few political or civil rights prior to the end of the Cold War (see Table 10). Generalizations about the capture of African political systems by patrimonialism, elevating the value of personal ties, also apply in francophone West Africa. This led to the allocation of resources to supporters or relatives of presidents, and was based on commonalities such as ethnicity, religion, or region. Thus, the patrimonial political system provided benefits for a select few, resulting in internal divisions and even conflict, in the long run. Nevertheless, Western countries justified support to authoritarian, centralized, one-party systems in Africa as essential to fostering unity, which was deemed necessary for

---

1   McGowan and Johnson, 'African Military Coups d'état and Underdevelopment'; McGowan, 'African Military coups d'état, 1956–2001'.

Table 10. Civil and political rights during and after the Cold War, 1973–2017 (1–2.5 Free; 3–5.5 Partly Free and 5.5–7 Not Free).

	1973	1974	1975	1976	1977	1978	1979	1980	1981	1982	1983	1984	1985	1986	1987
Benin	6	6	6.5	7	7	7	7	6.5	6.5	6.5	6.5	7	7	7	7
Burkina Faso	3.5	3.5	5	5	5	4.5	2.5	2.5	5.5	5.5	5.5	6	6.5	6.5	6.5
Côte d'Ivoire	6	6	6	5.5	5.5	5.5	5.5	5.5	5	5	5	5.5	5.5	5.5	5.5
Guinea	7	7	7	7	7	7	7	7	7	7	7	6	6	6	6.5
Mali	6.5	6.5	6.5	7	7	7	6.5	6.5	6.5	6.5	6.5	6.5	6.5	6.5	6.5
Mauritania	6	6	5.5	6	6	6	6	6.5	6.5	6.5	6.5	6.5	6.5	6.5	6
Niger	6	6	6.5	6.5	6.5	6.5	6.5	6.5	6.5	6.5	6.5	6.5	6.5	6.5	6.5
Senegal	6	6	5.5	5	5	4	3.5	4	4	4	4	3.5	3.5	3.5	3.5
Togo	6	6	6.5	6.5	6.5	6.5	6.5	7	6.5	6.5	6.5	6	6	6	6

	1988	1989	1990	1991	1992	1993	1994	1995	1996	1997	1998	1999	2000	2001	2002
Benin	7	7	5	2.5	2.5	2.5	2.5	2	2	2	2	2.5	2	2.5	2.5
Burkina Faso	6.5	5.5	5.5	5.5	5	4.5	4.5	4.5	4.5	4.5	4.5	4	4	4	4
Côte d'Ivoire	6	5.5	5	5	5	5.5	5.5	5.5	5.5	5	5	5.5	5.5	4.5	6
Guinea	6.5	6.5	5.5	5.5	5.5	5.5	5.5	5.5	5.5	5.5	5.5	5.5	5.5	5.5	5.5
Mali	6	6	5.5	5	2.5	2.5	3	2.5	2	3	3	3	2.5	2.5	2.5
Mauritania	6	6.5	6.5	6.5	6.5	6.5	7	6	6	6	6	5.5	5.5	5	5
Niger	6	6.5	5.5	5.5	4.5	3.5	4	4	4	4	6	5	4	4	4
Senegal	3.5	3.5	3.5	3.5	3.5	4.5	4.5	4.5	4	4	4	4	3.5	3.5	2.5
Togo	6	6	6	5.5	5.5	6	5.5	5.5	5.5	5.5	5.5	5	5	5	5.5

	2003	2004	2005	2006	2007	2008	2009	2010	2011	2012	2013	2014	2015	2016	2017
Benin	2	2	2	2	2	2	2	2	2	2	2	2	2	2	2
Burkina Faso	4	4.5	4	4	4	4	4	4	4	4	4	4.5	3.5	3.5	3.5
Côte d'Ivoire	5.5	6	6	6.5	6	5.5	5.5	6.5	6	5	4.5	4.5	4	4	4
Guinea	5.5	5.5	5.5	5.5	5.5	6	6.5	5	5	5	5	5	5	5	5
Mali	2	2	2	2	2.5	2.5	2.5	2.5	2.5	6	4.5	4.5	4.5	4.5	4.5
Mauritania	5.5	5.5	5	4.5	4	5.5	5.5	5.5	5.5	5.5	5.5	5.5	5.5	5.5	5.5
Niger	4	3	3	3	3.5	3.5	4.5	4.5	3.5	3.5	3.5	3.5	3.5	4	4
Senegal	2.5	2.5	2.5	2.5	2.5	3	3	3	3	2.5	2	2	2	2	2
Togo	5.5	5.5	5.5	5.5	5	5	4.5	4.5	4.5	4.5	4	4	4	4	4

Source: Freedom in the World Report, Washington DC; https://freedomhouse.org/report/freedom-world, accessed 2021.

building state institutions, generating economic development, and preventing ethnic competition, division, and conflict.[2]

As one might assume, patrimonialism in the political sphere impacted governance practices, which in turn impacted the military. This chapter examines how political systems developed in francophone West Africa after independence, and the effect these systems had on national armed forces, by asking the following questions: How were decisions about the armed forces made and by whom? How did the centralization of state structures affect national armed forces? What role did ethnicity play in the development of state political and military institutions? How were problems related to ethnicity dealt with in the military?

This chapter also focuses on the role of key executive and military actors, including presidents, chiefs and deputy chiefs of staff of the armed forces, and ministers of interior, defence, and finance. The roles of these political and military elites in francophone West Africa were accentuated by the centralization of power in postcolonial governments. Foreign military and economic assistance made it easier for African heads of states to monopolize the means of coercion without needing to make concessions to local actors. However, this narrowed the internal base of support for their governments, leaving only a handful of people with a stake and a say in how institutions were developed, which was a recipe for political instability.[3] If only a small group of people are granted proximity to power, it becomes vital to ensure their loyalty, lest they use their positions, knowledge, and connections to try and take that power. In francophone West Africa, this proximity put elites in a position to create both domestic and international contacts that allowed them to tap into the internal and external resources needed to monopolize the means of coercion.

In light of the military coup in Togo in January 1963, and the many more that followed in FWA, it is important to ask how francophone West African leaders responded to military coups and the imposition of military rule in other countries. The question is not *why* military coups took place in the region, but *how* these coups affected the decision-making of presidents

---

2   Robert, '*Ministre' de l'Afrique*, p. 119; Plantey, 'Note à l'attention de monsieur le président de la république', 7 August 1963; Raphaël-Leygues, 'Note: compte-rendu l'entretien avec Houphouët-Boigny', 5 August 1963; 'US/FRG talks on Africa', 13 February 1968.
3   Goody discusses the instability created by easily monopolized military technology in relation to precolonial military and political systems in Africa. See Goody, *Technology, Tradition and the State in Africa* (London: Hutchinson, 1980), pp. 53–5.

as they sought to control their national militaries. Only three of the first presidents of francophone West African countries – Léopold Senghor in Senegal, Félix Houphouët-Boigny in Côte d'Ivoire, and Sékou Touré in Guinea – successfully avoided military coups. In Niger, Hamani Diori lasted until 1974, and his Mauritanian counterpart, Moktar Ould Daddah, held on until 1978. This chapter analyses why some presidents endured while others did not, such as in Togo, Dahomey, Mali, and Upper Volta. It considers why soldiers in these four countries carried out coups, and why civilian governments were unable to stop them from so doing. Of equal importance is what a military takeover meant for the governance and capacities of the armed forces in these countries.

The analysis in this chapter begins with a focus on Guinea and Mali, two countries where the Soviet Union played an important role in providing military assistance and where control of the military became increasingly violent. This is followed by a comparison of the strategies of the president of Côte d'Ivoire, who relied on France to strengthen his authoritarian rule, with those of the president of Senegal, who embraced building a strong national army and slowly replaced mechanisms of personal rule with institutional checks and balances. It also analyses how both civilian and military governments sought to control society and the military in Upper Volta and Niger with limited resources. In all francophone West African countries government strategies to control the military depended on the resources at its disposal, the sources of aid, and the personal views of their presidents.

This chapter suggests that the legacy of these practices of the 1960s and 1970s persists to this day. According to the World Bank Good Governance Index (see Figure 6), indicators of stability were exceptionally poor in Guinea and Côte d'Ivoire from 1996 to 2019, and both countries also scored badly on indicators of accountability, effectiveness, and corruption. Conversely, Senegal and Burkina Faso (Upper Volta) have fared best, with Senegal exceeding the global average for accountability in those same years.

A Revolutionary Army Eats Itself: The Soviet Model in Guinea and Mali

The assistance provided by Czechoslovakia and the Soviet Union was key to building Guinean and Malian defence, security, and intelligence structures. This was even more true after the politicians and national soldiers who played the most important roles in developing their security apparatuses were eventually arrested in connection to alleged coup plots, of whom many were subsequently tortured or executed, or died in prison. The arrests of experienced officers with technical skills only increased the dependence of the Guinea and Malian governments on Soviet personnel to operate and maintain military equipment.

Military forces in Guinea and Mali were used against internal opposition, although the police and party militias took the initiative in suppressing protests. Militias had been formed in both countries as a counterforce to the army, but had different tasks and recruitment practices. Guinean militias constituted a force equal to the national army and were assigned almost identical tasks, whereas militias in Mali were used to exert political and economic control over the population, which was something the army did not want to do. However, the role of Malian militias made them unpopular among the population and they were dissolved after the 1968 military coup in 1968.

A key difference between Guinea and Mali was the fate of their first postcolonial presidents. Guinea's Sékou Touré held power until his death in 1984, while Modibo Keïta died in prison in 1977, after nearly a decade in detention. What explains the success of Touré and the failure of Keïta to control their national militaries? Both were suspicious of their national forces, which included colonial soldiers who had served with the French army, and thus both established networks of informants in the national army. Touré did not hesitate to use violence against both his opposition and soldiers, whereas Keïta wrongly calculated that he could retain the loyalty of his soldiers by assuring their material wealth.

The approach of Keïta's successor Moussa Traoré marked a departure, and was similar to that of Touré. Many of his allies would also be imprisoned, tortured, or executed, or died in prison. Yet, if violence as a strategy of control was effective at dispensing with opposition actors in the short run, it did not limit the political role of soldiers in the long run. Soldiers continue to have economic and political power in both countries, and in Guinea, this has clearly been to the detriment of good governance (see Figure 6).

Activists in uniform in Guinea

In February 1959, less than six months after Guinean independence and just one month after 11,000 Guinean colonial soldiers were repatriated from the French military, President Touré declared that these soldiers were now free to 'think and act solely to advance African liberation, which cannot be achieved without a full political and economic emancipation of Africa'. He promised that officers and soldiers alike would 'never again have to suffer' discrimination, as Guinea had been 'established on the basis of total equality and complete justice':

> There is no longer either white or black, or Susus, or Malinke; there are no longer any Guerze, nor Foula, nor Senegalese, nor Sudanese. Your army, the army of the Republic of Guinea is an army of order, an army that is a reflection of a whole country fulfilled by friendship between peoples, cooperation, real solidarity.[4]

The solidarity and singular purpose of Guinean forces was re-emphasized in 1963 by Guinea's first minister of defence, Fodéba Keïta. 'I would like it to be understood', he said, 'that, while elsewhere in Africa there are soldiers sordid enough to support outside plots, in the Republic of Guinea there can be no question of a coup d'état.' He described the national military as 'formed from the people' and constituting 'a specialized section of the PDG' (the ruling party), and claimed it would 'always ruthlessly sweep away psychological activity and attempts at division and diversion.'[5]

It may be tempting to view the twenty-six years Sékou Touré spent in office as an era during which the Guinean military was controlled and governed according to a constant set of principles. Changes did take place during those years, and practices to control the military evolved with time. Anti-colonial conflicts, military coups in neighbouring countries, and the fates of other pan-Africanist leaders affected the way Guinean forces were governed.[6]

In every francophone West African state, the president had an important hand in controlling the national military. Touré´s control was among the most repressive, although most of the soldiers who were condemned to death in Guinea received these sentences in 1969 and 1971. In other words, the repressive mechanisms of the state did not extensively target soldiers during the first decade of independence. There were, however, multiple practices to control the army at the time of independence, as Touré was already suspicious of former soldiers who had served the colonial power.[7]

---

4   Speech delivered on 25 February 1959 by President Sékou Touré at Camp Mangin in Conakry, quoted in Fode Momo Camara, *1 November 1958–1 November 2008: Cinquantenaire de la création l'armée Guinéenne* (unpublished memoir).
5   Telegram, Conakry to Paris, 29 October 1963, 51QO/36, CADC.
6   Lewin, *Ahmed Sékou Touré (1922–1984)*, vol. 5, pp. 177–90.
7   Touré, *Expérience Guinéenne*, pp. 536 and 539 and *L'Afrique et la révolution*, pp. 300 and 302; Hure, Chargé d'affaires of France in Guinée, 'Affaires militaires en Guinée', 19 March 1959, 51QO/15, CADC; Intelligence Exploitation Centre, 'Les événements de Guinée et leur développements diplomatiques', April 1971; Fodéba Keïta, Minister of

For example, with support from the Czechoslovakians, Touré created a rigorous intelligence service to detect possible threats to the regime.[8] These instruments of control were strengthened or adapted in response to both internal and external developments, such as the use of colonial soldiers in operations against Touré,[9] or the military coups that deposed his most important African allies.[10]

When Guinea gained independence after voting against membership of the French Community in 1958, French officials thought it was Touré who had persuaded the masses to support a 'no' vote,[11] but it has also been suggested that Touré's hand was forced by the Guinean anti-colonial movement.[12] Either way, Touré was very popular at the time of independence, especially among Guinean youth and labour unions. His popularity was further enhanced by the propaganda and local political structures of the PDG.[13] These structures enabled the state to extend power across its territory through the party organization, replacing previous community structures led by traditional chiefs.[14]

The Guinean state administration included both radical communists as well as Western-leaning figures who would have been happy to replace Touré.[15] It was therefore a priority for Touré to reinforce his domestic

---

Defence, presentation before the Chamber of Deputies, Delegation for the Defence of Overseas Zone 1, quoted in 'Bulletin de renseignements', 8 November 1963; General Secretariat for National Defence, Intelligence Exploitation Centre, 'La situation en République de Guinée à la suite du coup d'état militaire au Mali', 26 January 1969.

8   Fode Momo Camara, *1 November 1958–1 November 2008: Cinquantenaire de la création l'armée Guinéenne* (unpublished memoir); Robert *'Ministre' de l'Afrique*, pp. 103–4; see documents in File GR9Q5122, SHD.

9   Robert, *'Ministre' de l'Afrique*, pp. 103–9; Foccart, *Foccart Parle*, p. 175; US Embassy Conakry to Department of State, 13 May 1959.

10   See documents in File GR9Q5122, SHD; File 51QO/36, CADC, File USGUIN 1964–1966, Box 2259, and File DEFGUIN 1967–1967, Boxes 1550 and 2165, CGRDS, NARA.

11   For example, see Robert, *'Ministre' de l'Afrique*.

12   Schmidt, 'Cold War in Guinea: The Rassemblement Démocratique Africain and the Struggle over Communism, 1950–1958', *Journal of African History* 48, (2007), pp. 95–121, and 'Anticolonial Nationalism in French West Africa: What Made Guinea Unique?' *African Studies Review* 52, no. 2 (2009), pp. 1–34.

13   National Defence General Staff, Intelligence Division, 'Le problème Guinéen', 17 April 1959; James Loeb, 'US policy assessment', 26 January 1966.

14   See documents in File GRH151, SHD, Files 5AGF/1637 and 5AGF/561, FFAN and File POLGUIN 1964–1966, Box 2256, CGRDS, NARA.

15   French Intelligence Service, 'Problèmes de défense soulevés par l'indépendance de la Guinée', 18 January 1959; National Defence General Staff, Intelligence Division, 'Fiche

authority.[16] In this, he was fairly successful, as ethnic and regional divisions made organizing a unified opposition difficult. Touré himself was a Malinke, which was the second-largest ethnic group in Guinea and accounted for a little over half a million of the country's population of 3.5 million. The largest ethnic group was the Fula, numbering around one million, and they inhabited the Fouta-Djallon region in western Guinea. The cities of Labe in Fouta-Djallon and Kankan in the northeast were seen as hotbeds of the opposition. The three other major ethnic groups in Guinea were the Susu (250,000), the Kissi (175,000), and the Guerze (125,000).[17]

In addition to propaganda, the Guinean administration increasingly used its security apparatus – the police, gendarmerie, and intelligence service – to control the population. French officials noted that while these institutions seemed to become ever more effective, they also became ever more aggressive, especially in the capital.[18] Moreover, the Guinean constitution stipulated that the army could be requested to maintain domestic order, even though its primary purpose was to safeguard the country's territorial integrity and ensure security against external threats.[19] This had the potential to tarnish Touré's narrative of a national military that was one with the people and served only 'the common good'.[20]

In 1959, a core of 2,500 soldiers had been selected as the foundation of a new Guinean military, from the 11,000 colonial soldiers who chose to end their contracts with France and return to Guinea in January of that year.[21] The soldiers selected for national service were carefully screened and most were required to complete further training in the military academy in Conakry. The remaining colonial soldiers were obliged to find jobs in the

---

sur l'action communiste en Guinée', 24 April 1959, GR 9Q5122, SHD; Governor Bonfils, 'Note de renseignements: République de Guinée', 28 November 1958, 5QONT/11, CADC; The High Commissioner representing the President of the French Community in Dakar to President of the Community, General Secretariat, 25 May 1960.

16 SDECE, 'Guinée: durcissement du régime', 1 April 1959, 51QO/34, CADC.

17 See documents in Files 51QO/34 and 51QONT/33, CADC, and Files 5AGF/1637 and 5AGF/555, FFAN.

18 SDECE, 'Guinée: durcissement du régime', 1 April 1959; National Defence General Staff, Intelligence Division, 'Le problème Guinéen', 17 April 1959.

19 Ordonnance de création de l'armée Guinéenne (Ordinance for the creation of the Guinean army), No. 23/PG, 16 December 1958, 3N1, ANG.

20 See documents in File GR 9Q5122, SHD and File USGUIN 1963, Box 2254, File DEFGUIN 1964–1966, Box 1649, and File USGUIN 1964–1966, Box 1755, CGRDS, NARA.

21 See Chapter 4.

private sector, as administrative positions were prioritized for individuals who had participated in anti-colonial struggles.[22]

Guinean legislation on the armed forces had concentrated decision-making power to the president.[23] Touré sought to emphasize differences between the colonial and national forces, and the regime adopted the idea that soldiers were activists in uniform.[24] The concept was that Guinean soldiers were no longer separate from the population and no longer served 'imperialist interests' as colonial soldiers had done, and thus their rights and responsibilities were no different to those of civilians. As a consequence, the role of the armed forces was greatly expanded. In addition to military duties, soldiers were assigned tasks that ranged from the ideological to the agricultural to the industrial.[25] The Guinean military built roads, grew and harvested crops, and managed and worked in factories manufacturing shoes and clothing.[26] Soldiers also participated in ideological training. Despite this, all political participation was forbidden and they had no freedom of expression or association, although they naturally maintained the right to vote for the PDG.[27]

The Guinean security apparatus also included 1,200 Republican Guards, 1,200 gendarmes, and 850 police officers, almost all of whom were recruited from the ranks of former colonial soldiers. The gendarmerie controlled the borders and populations in rural areas, while police officers patrolled Conakry and other major towns. US Embassy reports from the early 1960s suggest that both forces were well-trained but had insufficient numbers and equipment for their missions. The Republican Guard, meanwhile, which was tasked with securing the president, had 'an overabundance of men and equipment, considering their limited functions'.[28]

---

[22] Camara, *1 November 1958–1 November 2008*.

[23] Ibid.

[24] Touré, *Expérience Guinéenne*, pp. 536 and 539 and *L'Afrique et la révolution*, pp. 300 and 302; Keïta, presentation before the Chamber of Deputies, quoted in 'Bulletin de renseignements', 8 November 1963.

[25] See documents in File GR9Q5122, SHD; File USGUIN 1963, Box 2254; File DEFGUIN 1964–1966, Box 1649; and File USGUIN 1964–1966, Box 1755, CGRDS, NARA.

[26] Camara, *1 November 1958–1 November 2008*; Fodéba Keïta, presentation before the Chamber of Deputies, quoted in 'Bulletin de renseignements', 8 November 1963.

[27] Guinean Ministry of National Defence and Security, 'Décret portant statut du personnel militaire', 28 December 1963, 3N1, ANG.

[28] US Embassy Conakry to Department of State, 'Capacities of Guinea Police Forces Adequate to Present Needs: no US aid recommended', 29 May 1963.

Given the threats he faced, Touré was especially focused on assuring the loyalty of the military elite and the government ministers responsible for internal security and defence. In these positions, individuals could develop domestic and international relationships that might facilitate their efforts to replace the president. In the eyes of domestic or foreign audiences, this meant that the popularity of a minister of defence or chief of staff of the armed forces could pose a credible danger to the head of state. Indeed, after French officials hinted in 1958 that General Noumandian Keïta, Chief of the Armed Forces General Staff, was very capable and could perhaps replace Touré,[29] it seems he was on borrowed time. The tragic fate of General Keïta, and that of Fodéba Keïta, signalled the threat Touré believed key officials posed.

Fodéba Keïta first served as the minister of interior, and then became the minister of defence in March 1960, when the post was first established. He was already popular at home and abroad, as a writer and composer, and founded *Les Ballets Africains*.[30] As defence minister, Keïta was responsible for building the Guinean security forces and constructing Camp Boiro, a prison near Conakry where many Guineans were jailed, tortured, and executed. It was where he would eventually be put to death.[31] French reports describe him as very ambitious and effective, and popular among the population, but less so with party leadership. He was thought to wield considerable influence among the armed forces and police.[32]

Keïta's efficiency and popularity put him at risk, however. According to the French, 'because he controlled the means to overthrow the government, the intent to do so was also attributed to him'.[33] French reports even suggested that Keïta's political ambitions had perhaps reached the point where he did want to replace Touré.[34] But American officials – who referred to the defence minister as 'the second most powerful man in Guinea'[35]

---

29 Fourquet, 'Au sujet de réunion de 9 October 1958 AMDN/PSY – Note sur la Politique française vis-à-vis de la Guinée,' 13 October 1958.

30 National Defence General Staff, Intelligence Division, 'Evolution politique de la république de Guinée', 17 March 1960, GR9Q5122, SHD.

31 Lewin, *Ahmed Sékou Touré (1922–1984)*, vol. 5, pp. 251–70.

32 Telegram, Conakry to Paris, 29 October 1963; The High-Commissioner representing the President of the French Community in Dakar to President of the Community, General Secretariat, 25 May 1960.

33 Ibid.

34 National Defence General Staff, Intelligence Division, 'Evolution politique de la république de Guinée', 17 March, 1960; Telegram, Conakry to Paris, 29 October 1963.

35 Loeb, 'Series of Annoyances', 20 May 1965.

– believed he was loyal to Touré.[36] Either way, Keïta's position was always precarious. Party members thought his role was unmerited because he had not participated in the anti-colonial movement and had only returned to Guinea in 1957.[37] However, Touré likely chose him because Keïta would then owe his position directly to the president, thus placing 'armed force[s] under the control of a man loyal to him personally rather than to the party'.[38] With time, Touré nevertheless grew suspicious of his hand-picked defence minister. By January 1963, a new interior security structure had been created, headed by a secretary of state whose mandate duplicated Keïta's.[39] Perhaps Minister Keïta was aware of his precarious position when, speaking before parliament in October of that year, he emphasized the fact that the national military would never carry out a coup because Guinean soldiers were aligned with the people and integral to the PDG.[40]

In 1965, when multiple allegations of American and French plots against Touré were made, Fodéba Keïta's friendly relations with American and West German officials became a liability.[41] In fact, his downfall has been linked to his refusal to arrest individuals accused of involvement in some of these plots.[42] He was demoted to the position of minister of rural economy in November 1965, and lost his seat in the government in 1968.[43] Upon Keïta's demotion, Lansana Diané, who was closely related to Touré, was

36 US Department of State, 'Memorandum of conversation: General situation in Guinea – Yves Eichenberger, President of Bauxites du Midi; Tom Covel, Washington representative of Aluminum limited Canada; Henry Tasca, Deputy Assistant Secretary', 6 February 1963; Loeb, 'Guinean request for military assistance', 10 March 1964.
37 Lewin, *Ahmed Sékou Touré (1922–1984)*, vol. 1, Chapter 10; Loeb, US Embassy Conakry, to Department of State, 26 March 1965, POLGUIN 1964–1966, Box 2260, CGRDS, NARA.
38 Fredericks, US Department of State Bureau of African Affairs, to Secretary of State, 6 December 1963, POLGUIN 1963, Box 3922, CGRDS, NARA.
39 Lewin, *Ahmed Sékou Touré (1922–1984)*, vol. 5, pp. 251–70.
40 Telegram, Conakry to Paris, 29 October 1963.
41 McIlvaine, US Embassy Conakry, to Department of State, 10 March 1965, POLGUIN 1964–1966, Box 2260, CGRDS, NARA; Graham to Department of state, 12 March 1965; Loeb to Department of State, 26 March 1965.
42 Lewin, *Ahmed Sékou Touré (1922–1984)*, vol. 5, Chapter 58; Kaa Camara, *Dans la Guinée de Sékou Touré: Cela a bien eu lieu* (Paris: Harmattan, 1998); US Embassy Conakry to Department of State, 'Bi-weekly no 38', 2 December 1965, POLGUIN 1964–1966, Box 2256, CGRDS, NARA.
43 Lewin, *Ahmed Sékou Touré (1922–1984)*, vol. 5, pp. 251–70; US Embassy in Conakry to Department of State, 'Bi-weekly no 38', 2 December 1965; Graham, US Embassy Conakry, to Department of State, 19 November 1965, USGUIN 1964–1966, Box 2258, CGRDS, NARA.

named minister of defence.[44] His appointment reflected Touré's need to install someone absolutely loyal to him in that post.

Months before the 1965 cabinet shuffle that saw Diané being appointed minister of defence, US officials had noted the importance of the military in the sphere of Guinean politics, estimating that 'a change of government could not be effected in Guinea without the support of the armed forces.'[45] Earlier reports out of the US Embassy had suggested that Guinean soldiers received preferential treatment from the government, and demonstrated their loyalty in return by dealing 'quickly and ruthlessly with turbulent elements' of the population.[46] However, army operations against civilians did reduce the public popularity of the military, which increased the potential for a coup.[47]

Following the 1966 military coup in Ghana, Touré took steps to limit soldiers' access to munitions.[48] Soon after, in April 1966, *Front de Libération Nationale de la Guinée* (FLNG) addressed an open letter to Guinean forces calling on them to follow the example of Ghanaian soldiers: 'Officers and soldiers, if you will, you can. See how the Ghanaian colossus had feet of clay. Sékou fears you.'[49] Nevertheless, US officials were confident that Touré could deter any possible coup through his extensive intelligence network, which included informants in the FLNG and the military.[50] Several years later, they noted that Touré 'frequently boasts that it would be impossible

44 Lewin, *Ahmed Sékou Touré (1922–1984)*, vol. 5, pp. 251–70.

45 Loeb, 'Another Guinean crisis', 15 June 1965.

46 Graham, US Embassy Conakry, to Department of State 'Political instability in Guinea', 2 March 1965, POLGUIN 1964–1966, Box 2256, CGRDS, NARA.

47 Loeb, 'US policy assessment', 26 January 1966; Graham, 'Guinean military strength: Personnel and weapons', 19 April 1966 and 'Current position and future prospects of the Touré regime', 14 April 1966.

48 McIlvaine, US Embassy Conakry, to Donald Rusk, 13 December 1966, DEFGUIN 1964–1966, Box 1649, CGRDS, NARA; Graham to Rusk, 'Guinean military preparedness', 18 March 1966; Hughes, 'Guinea: Touré Demilitarizes the Military', 16 January 1969.

49 Directorate of African and Malagasy Affairs, Sub-directorate for Africa, 'Note pour le sécretaire general – activités du front national de liberation de la Guinée', 8 April 1966, 51QONT/27, CADC. The letter was published in foreign newspapers such as the *New York Herald Tribune*.

50 Graham, 'Current position and future prospects of the Touré regime', 14 April 1966; Rusk to US Mission in Geneva, 'Guinean National Liberation Front', 22 November 1967; Haverkamp, 'Guinea: Guidelines for Policy', 3 February 1970.

for any group of plotters to get together to overthrow him as his agents would know about it immediately and take action.'[51]

In October 1967, Touré established popular militias as a further measure to ensure control of the military. The move was seen as a vote of no confidence in the armed forces.[52] Publicly, the militias were characterized by the government as a sort of go-between, and a way of creating stronger links between the people and the People's Armed Forces.[53] In some places, though, these militias counted as many members as there were soldiers in the army, which made this official explanation unconvincing. The militias were also placed under the direct control of the president, as the gendarmerie had been since 1965.[54]

Militia members were recruited from among Guineans between the ages of twenty and thirty who were farmers, industrialists, civil servants, or university students. The unemployed and idle were systematically excluded. Training for the militias took place over a two-year period and included ideological training from the PDG along with military training from the gendarmerie. The militias were given a multitude of tasks, including border surveillance, the implementation of major economic projects, and providing security in towns and strategically important regions to fighting against smuggling and other crimes.[55] According to US officials, this was part of a years-long strategy by Touré to reduce 'army authority by parceling out security responsibilities to competing services: the gendarmerie, the police and the republican guard'.[56] The militias were seen as a continuation of this strategy, and Touré had clearly chosen them as the basis of his power.[57]

51 Haverkamp, 'Guinea: Guidelines for Policy', 3 February 1970.
52 Lewin, *Ahmed Sékou Touré (1922–1984)*, vol. 5, pp. 251–70; US Embassy Conakry to Department of State, 'Formation of armed popular militia', 15 August 1966, DEFGUIN 1964–1966, Box 1649, CGRDS, NARA.
53 General Secretariat for National Defence, Intelligence Exploitation Centre, 'Organisation de la milice populaire et du service civique en République de Guinée', 13 May 1968.
54 See documents in File USGUIN 1964–1966, Boxes 2258 and 2256; File DEFGUIN 1964–1966, Box 1649, CGRDS, NARA; and File GR9Q5122, SHD.
55 General Secretariat for National Defence, Intelligence Exploitation Centre, 'Organisation de la milice populaire et du service civique en République de Guinée', 13 May 1968, 'Les forces armées guinéennes', 17 April 1970, and 'La situation en République de Guinée à la suite du coup d'état militaire au Mali', 26 January 1969.
56 Hughes, Assistant Secretary of State for Intelligence and Research, 'Guinea: Has crisis peaked?', 28 March 1969, DEFGUIN 1967–1967, Box 1550, CGRDS, NARA.
57 Hughes, 'Guinea: Touré Demilitarizes the Military', 16 January 1969.

In an emergency, it was the militias who were expected to take charge.[58] By April 1970, there were an estimated 8,000 militia members, while the military consisted of approximately 4,800 soldiers.[59]

The establishment and growth of the militias did not greatly reduce Touré's suspicions of the military, and by early 1969, Guinean soldiers were hostile towards the militias.[60] In January of that year, French intelligence suggested that Touré had almost completely reassigned the defence duties of the army to the militias, and had re-tasked soldiers to mainly agricultural and industrial projects.[61] Then, in February 1969, just two months after the ousting of Modibo Keïta in Mali, a coup against Touré by Guinean parachutists was announced.[62] The French assessed that the plot was real and had been aimed at overthrowing the regime, and not just another 'prefabricated story created by Touré as a pretext for further strengthening his authority over the country.'[63] Deputy Army Chief of Staff Colonel Kaman Diaby was implicated, as well as former Minister of Defence Fodéba Keïta. Both men were executed in May 1969.[64]

In the view of US officials, the 1969 coup plot was linked to the government's decision to establish Military Committees (*comités d'unités militaire*, or CUM) that ideologically moulded the army. Soldiers opposed the changes, arguing that committees 'drawing their political power from outside the army can only weaken the army through the destruction of discipline and the military chain of command'.[65] In December 1968,

---

58   Charles Whitehouse, US Embassy Conakry, to Department of State, 15 November 1966, DEFGUIN 1964–1966, Box 1649, CGRDS, NARA.

59   General Secretariat for National Defence, Intelligence Exploitation Centre, 'Les forces Armées Guinéennes', 17 April 1970, and 'Évolution de la situation en Guinée et développement diplomatique', 3 February 1971.

60   See documents in File GR9Q5122, SHD; File DEFGUIN 1964–1966, Box 1649; File DEFGUIN 1967–1969, Box 1550; and File POLGUIN 1970–1973, Box 2341, CGRDS, NARA.

61   General Secretariat for National Defence, Intelligence Exploitation Centre, 'La situation en République de Guinée à la suite du coup d'état militaire au Mali', 26 January 1969, and 'Les forces armées guinéennes', 17 April 1970.

62   McIlvaine, US Embassy Conakry, to Department of State, 'Flight to freedom in Bamako Aborts', 2 March 1969, DEFGUIN 1967–1969, Box 1550, CGRDS, NARA.

63   Military Bulletin, General Secretariat for National Defence, 'Découverte d'un complot militaire en République de Guinée', 23 March 1969, GR9Q5122, SHD.

64   Lewin, *Ahmed Sékou Touré (1922–1984)*, vol. 5, pp. 251–70.

65   Bob Melone, 'Stirrings in the Guinean army', 17 December 1968. Also see US Embassy Conakry to Department of State, 'Bi-weekly no. 2', 24 December 1968, POLGUIN 1967–1967, Box 2163, CGRDS, NARA.

Deputy Chief of Staff Diaby is believed to have spoken with Touré about the soldiers' misgivings regarding the CUM, their agricultural duties, and the withholding of munitions. Touré arrested Diaby and brought other officers in for questioning.[66]

Prior to the 1969 plot against Touré, the US had warned that actions of the Guinean president to control the military might well provoke the events he was seeking to avoid.[67] Afterwards, they acknowledged that Touré had probably calculated correctly that 'the risk of inaction was bigger than a military action against him.'[68] There is also some reason to believe that Diaby was indeed eager to oust Touré. French officials assumed that soldiers who had served in the French forces continued to maintain an allegiance to France, and both General Noumandian Keïta and Colonel Diaby were thought to have been particularly marked by their French training and service.[69] French intelligence reported in 1966 that Diaby had declared himself favourable to regime change, and had stated that General Keïta would welcome it as well.[70] However, the US judged the general beyond reproach and described him as a 'genial figurehead about whose basic loyalty even a man as suspicious as Sékou Touré should have little doubt.'[71] They saw Diaby as a leading military figure with whom they were keen to establish good relations, and noted that Guinean soldiers would never carry out a coup without his consent, but saw no proof of Diaby's disloyalty to Touré. However, American officials knew that Touré had been keeping a close eye on his deputy chief of staff from at least the mid-1960s onwards.[72]

66 Ibid.; Hughes, 'Guinea: Touré demilitarizes the military', 16 January 1969; Lewin, *Ahmed Sékou Touré (1922–1984)*, vol. 5, pp. 251–70.
67 Melone, 'Stirrings in the Guinean army', 17 December 1968; Hughes 'Guinea: Touré demilitarizes the military', 16 January 1969.
68 Hughes, Director of the Bureau of Intelligence and Research, US Department of State, 'Guinea: Sékou Touré's formula for staying in power', 13 March 1969, POLGUIN 1967–1969, Box 2165, CGRDS, NARA. Also see Hughes, 'Guinea: Has crisis peaked?', 28 March 1969.
69 Koenig, Ambassador of France in Guinea, to Minister of Foreign Affairs, Couve de Murville, 20 July 1965, 51QO/36, CADC.
70 Ministry of Armed Forces, SDECE, 'Guinée–Sénégal–Côte d'Ivoire', 29 July 1966.
71 Melone, 'Stirrings in the Guinean army', 17 December 1968.
72 Graham, 'Current position and future prospects of the Touré regime', 14 April 1966; Graham, US Embassy Conakry, to Department of State, 'US visits for distinguished African military leaders', 24 June 1966, DEFGUIN 1964–1966, Box 1649, CGRDS, NARA.

There is, in fact, little information that connects Fodéba Keïta to the 1969 coup plot, and his role has largely been rewritten in Guinean historical narratives that present him as equally a perpetrator and a victim of state repression. For example, the story is repeated that Minister Keïta eventually expressed regret for his role in Touré's repressive regime, allegedly writing on the wall of his prison cell before his death: 'I have always worked for injustice. I have always served this unjust cause. To serve this unjust cause, I invented plots to be able to liquidate all those who were likely to express the will of the martyred people of Guinea.'[73] This is widely read as an apology to all Guineans.

There were of course real plots against Touré, and not all plotters were expressing 'the will of the people'. Opposition to Touré represented a wide variety of interests, including those of foreign powers.[74] Yet it had been Fodéba Keïta, along with Czechoslovakian assistants, who organized Guinean security structures in a way that had effectively prevented most attempts to depose Touré.[75] Nonetheless, he, Diaby, and thirteen soldiers were sentenced to death for playing a role in plotting the failed 1969 coup, and twenty-eight others were sentenced to long periods of forced labour.[76] In the aftermath, the armed forces were further diverted to agricultural tasks, while military training and exercises became rare, and purges and reorganizations frequent. The cohesion of forces weakened to the point of significantly reducing the operational value of the military.[77]

Military effectiveness also decreased at this time as the result of equipment being poorly maintained. This was largely due to a lack of technical skills, technicians and insufficient logistical support. Fuel, tanks, and artillery were

---

73 Ousmane Ardo Bâ, *Camp Boiro: Sinistre geôle de Sékou Touré* (Paris: Harmattan, 1986). Slightly different versions of this parting sentiment appear in Camara, *Dans la Guinée de Sékou Touré* and Lewin, *Ahmed Sékou Touré (1922–1984)*, vol. 5.

74 National Defence General Staff, Intelligence Division, 'Le problème Guinéen', 17 April 1959; Robert, *'Ministre' de l'Afrique*, pp. 103–9; Foccart, *Foccart Parle*, pp. 175 and 214.

75 Camara, *1 November 1958–1 November 2008*. See also documents in File POLGUIN 1970–1973, Box 2340, and File FNGUIN 1970–1973, Box 891, CGRDS, NARA.

76 Lewin, *Ahmed Sékou Touré (1922–1984)*, vol. 5, pp. 251–70; Military Bulletin, General Secretariat for National Defence, 'Découverte d'un complot militaire en République de Guinée', 23 March 1969; US Embassy Conakry to Department of State, 'Bi-weekly no. 7', 15 April 1969; McIlvaine, 'The plotters are sentenced', 19 May 1969.

77 General Secretariat for National Defence, Intelligence Exploitation Centre, 'Les forces armées guinéennes', 17 April 1970; General Secretariat for National Defence, 'Évolution de la situation en Guinée et développement diplomatique', 3 February 1971; Camara, *1 November 1958–1 November 2008*.

also stored in unsuitable conditions, leading to their rapid deterioration. Additionally, military vehicles were often requisitioned for the transport of agricultural products or needed extensive repairs.[78] To the French, these were all signs that Touré was fulfilling his intention to transform the army into a docile instrument in service of his regime, even at the price of efficiency.[79] In his memoirs, one Guinean soldier described how the ideological indoctrination to which soldiers were subjected hurt military discipline, especially because regular soldiers served as the presidents of revolutionary military committees and provided their superiors with ideological training. These committees would also discuss and question the orders of officers before they were carried out. This climate of distrust together with a mandate that increasingly involved ineffectual activities in the economic sphere led to considerable dissatisfaction among soldiers.[80] Even though ideological training in the military was a main reason for this dissatisfaction, such training only increased after the Portuguese attack in Conakry in 1970.[81]

The Portuguese attack was motivated by Guinean support to the anti-colonial movement in neighbouring Guinea-Bissau, and its purpose was to liberate Portuguese prisoners detained in Conakry. The Guinean dissident group FLNG also participated in the attack, and French intelligence reports indicate that half of the 300 assailants were Guineans trained by the Portuguese.[82] It was the assessment of US intelligence that the attackers most likely benefitted from inside collaboration.[83] This aligned with previous claims of the FLNG that they had several collaborators in the Guinean army, gendarmerie, and police.[84] Whether this was bluster or fact, American officials concluded in 1971 that 'the ease with which the attackers

---

[78] General Secretariat for National Defence, Intelligence Exploitation Centre, 'Les forces Armées Guinéennes', 17 April 1970; National Defence General Staff, Intelligence Division, 'Le problème Guinéen', 17 April 1959. A Guinean report that discusses the influence of the French fifth column on the Guinean armed forces and notes that improving the technical skills of soldiers would be one effective way to fight against imperialist forces. See Mamadi Keïta, 'Rapport sur les méfaits de agents de la 5eme colonne', 18 November 1971.

[79] General Secretariat for National Defence, Intelligence Exploitation Centre, 'Les forces armées guinéennes', 17 April 1970.

[80] Camara, *1 November 1958–1 November 2008.*

[81] Intelligence Exploitation Centre, 'Les événements de Guinée et leur développements diplomatiques', April 1971.

[82] Ibid.; 'Un rescapé des geôles de Sékou Touré', *Jeune Afrique*, 18 May1971.

[83] Ray C. Cline, 'Guinea Touré's opponents strike by sea', 24 November 1970.

[84] Williams, 'Purported plans for coup in Guinea', 17 July 1967.

penetrated Conakry's defenses and the lethargic response of Guinean armed forces confirmed in Touré's mind the inadequacies, unpreparedness – and perhaps disloyalty – of his military.'[85] It was the militias that had played they key role in defeating the attackers.[86]

The Portuguese-led attack marked the start of a dark period in Guinean history. One French intelligence report noted that 'the winds of madness were blowing again', as raids and arrests increased across the country.[87] In 1971, over sixty Guineans were arrested, tried, and condemned to death or forced labour for allegedly acting against the regime, with twelve soldiers among those sentenced to capital punishment.[88] As an American official put it, the attack in 1970 had led to the 'elimination of a very large portion of the politically, administratively and technically experienced Guineans' that the country had invested in developing since independence. This loss came at an especially heavy price for a 'poor developing country' like Guinea.[89] In the wake of the attack, the US estimated that seventeen out of twenty-four Guinean ministers had been arrested, as well as 90% of the highest-ranking military officers, including the commanders of all principal garrisons and a third of the officer corps.[90]

In 1971, soldiers' salaries were increased, but all officer promotions were suspended for ten years.[91] At the same time, Guinean soldiers were accused of damaging and stealing vehicles and equipment, inciting discontent among the troops, informing the enemy about Guinean defences, sabotaging the economic activities of the army, and inciting conflict between the militias and the military.[92] Most of these problems were attributed to malign foreign influences, and French and West German agents were accused of having

---

85 US Embassy Conakry to Department of State, 'Policy Planning Paper', 6 July 1971.

86 See documents in File POLGUIN 1970–1973, Box 2340, and File FNGUIN 1970–1973, Box 891. US reports suggested that the Guinean population had likewise been passive during previous upheavals. See documents in File POLGUIN 1964–1966, Box 2256, and File POLGUIN 1970–1973, Box 2340, CGRDS, NARA.

87 Intelligence Exploitation Centre, 'Guinée: Le grand procès populaire de la Cinquième Colonne', 24 August 1971.

88 Lewin, *Ahmed Sékou Touré (1922–1984)*, vol. 6, Chapter 65.

89 Albert Sherer, 'Prospects of Sékou Touré's regime', 11 October 1971.

90 Ibid.

91 Intelligence Exploitation Centre, 'Guinée: Le grand procès populaire de la Cinquième Colonne', 24 August 1971. Non-commissioned officers and regular soldiers were still allowed to advance. See Decrees No 618/PRG of 29 December 1971 and No 103/PRG of 4 March 1982 in Camara, *1 November 1958–1 November 2008*.

92 'Rapport sur les méfaits de agents de la 5eme colonne', 18 November 1971, 3N1, ANG.

participated in the Portuguese aggression.[93] West Germany had, since 1963, played an important role in assisting the Guinean military in building roads and operating military factories, but in 1971, Guinea imprisoned three West German technical assistants and deported the rest.[94] The failures of military factories were also said to be the result of West German sabotage.[95] However, US diplomats thought the Guineans were exaggerating the role of foreigners in the 1970 attack as a means of hiding domestic issues related to the increasing dissatisfaction of indigenous groups, particularly the Fulani. A report from the US Embassy pointed out that some of the arrested plotters were even Malinke, the same ethnic group as the president.[96]

An american diplomatic report suggested that Touré took a personal role in supervising arrests and identifying suspects in the attack, up to 'the final editing of the self-confessions'.[97] General Noumandian Keïta was at first dismissed, then arrested and executed in July 1971. Similar questions surround the fate of Fodéba Keïta and General Keïta, as it is unclear whether the general had conspired against Touré or why he was executed. American officials felt the former chief of staff was targeted because he had married a French woman and been associated with West German military assistance projects.[98] The theory of Guineans who have published their narratives of these events is that General Keïta was killed because he 'knew too much'. Several authors have suggested that he and several other officers ran to Touré and requested the key to the ammunition storage when the Portuguese attacked, but Touré thought they were attempting to seize power and pleaded, 'Kill me, but don't hand me over to the people. Don't put me to shame.'[99] Supposedly, a friend of the general told him later that he and his fellow officers had made a grave mistake by not taking power and killing

93   Ibid; Presidency of the Republic of Guinea, State Secretariat for National Defence, 'Élément de renseignement sur la production agricole dans l'armée' 17 November 1971.
94   Lewin, *Ahmed Sékou Touré (1922–1984)*, vol. 6, Chapter 65.
95   Lewin, 'La Guinée et les deux Allemagnes'.
96   US Embassy Conakry to Department of State, 'Fifth column in Guinea', 20 July 1970.
97   Sherer, 'Prospects of Sékou Touré's regime', 11 October 1971.
98   US Embassy Conakry to Department of State, 'Fifth column in Guinea', 20 July 1970.
99   Alpha-Abdoulaye Diallo, *La vérité du ministre: dix ans dans les geôles de Sékou Touré* (Paris: Calman-Lévy, 1985); Ibrahima Baba Kaké, *Sékou Touré: le héros et le tyran* (Paris: Groupe Jeune Afrique, 1987); Camara, *Dans la Guinée de Sékou Touré*.

Touré when they had the chance. Given the weakness they had witnessed, he said, Touré would have them all killed.[100]

There is no concrete evidence to substantiate this story, but it includes some interesting elements. First, it implies that limits on the access of soldiers to munition hampered the Guinean response to the attack. Second, it suggests that Touré believed he was so unpopular in 1970 that he knew if he were delivered to the people, they had reason to put him 'to shame'. In earlier years, Touré's popularity had been an obstacle to subversive action,[101] but his popularity had diminished by 1970, mostly due to the economic problems and repressive nature of his regime.[102] In fact, over the nearly three decades that Touré was in power, two million Guineans – approximately one-third of the population – left the country,[103] voting with their feet when voting at the ballot box was not an option.

Incidents of desertion in the army also became commonplace as conditions for soldiers deteriorated. A US official observed in 1973, for example, that living conditions 'in most border installations … were deplorable due to lack of food and clothing' and that food supplies often fell into the hands of corrupt civilian administrators, who sold it at 'exorbitant prices for their own personal gain'.[104] In these same years, challenges of subsistence also extended to the civilian population, as former rice-producing areas became reliant on imports.[105] Herein lies the contradiction of Touré's regime: at a time when the regime was dependent on foreign assistance and investments, all popular dissatisfaction was attributed to the influence of foreign actors.[106] Many Guineans also believed that foreign plots were the cause of their misfortune.

---

100 Ibid.
101 Intelligence Exploitation Centre, 'Evolution de la situation en Guinée et développements diplomatiques', 24 January 1971.
102 See documents in File DEFGUIN 1963, Box 3724; File POLGUIN 1963, Box 2257; File 770b 1960–1963, Box 1944; and File POLGUIN 1964–1966, Boxes 2256 and 2259, CGRDS, NARA.
103 The Regional Delegate in West Africa, Dakar, 'Situation des Guinées (Conakry) qui vivent en dehors de leur pays', 21 June 1977, and 'La sitation des Guinées vivant à l'étranger', 26 November 1976; 'Deux million d'exiles', *Jeune Afrique*, 14 October 1977.
104 Terence Todman, 'Report on fifteen-day inspection tour of border military installations by Guinea chiefs of staff (army and airforce)', 1 November 1973.
105 Ibid.
106 See documents in File POLGUIN 1963, Box 2257; File POLGUIN 1967–1969; Box 2165, File USGUIN 1964–1966, Boxes 2259 and 2258; and File POLGUIN 1970–1973, Box 2340, CGRDS, NARA.

Following independence, the Guinean regime had worked to build the means by which the messages of the president could be broadcast, whether through direct emissions of propaganda, or party structures, labour unions, and youth organizations.[107] Touré wisely paired his accusations of foreign influence with an emphasis on the role of Guinea in African struggles of liberation.[108] This gave the population a sense that it was part of something important, and something that was larger than any individual. This discourse was also directed towards soldiers, as it was their participation in anti-colonial struggles elsewhere that strengthened the claim that Guinea was fighting against imperialism on both a national and international level. Guinea sent troops to Congo and Guinea-Bissau and trained members of anti-colonial movements from Congo, Guinea-Bissau, Angola, Namibia, South Africa, Mozambique, and Rhodesia (Zimbabwe).[109] The Portuguese attack had provided evidence about the reality of the threat posed by 'imperialist' powers, and it lent credibility to Touré's claims that Guinean institutions of coercion were mostly used against regressive colonialist forces inside and outside the country.

Unity was another issue at the centre of Touré's discourse, though this did not always reflect facts on the ground. After independence, he made serious efforts to eradicate colonial patronage systems, specifically the power of traditional chiefs, but his administration had not succeeded in developing ethnically balanced state institutions. In the absence of opposition parties, this meant that dissidence was organized along ethnic lines. By 1959, French officials suggested that ethnic tensions were already on the rise in Guinea, particularly in the Susu and Fulani regions.[110] Throughout his time in office,

---

107 National Defence General Staff, Intelligence Division, 'Le problème Guinéen', 17 April 1959, and 'Prestige africaine de la Guinée', 12 October 1959.

108 For example, during a trip to the USSR in November 1959, Touré emphasised that '*the main significance we attach to our independence is that our independence serves as a launching pad for African liberation struggles.*' See National Defence General Staff, Intelligence Division, 'Note d'information: Voyage à Moscou de M. Sékou Touré, Discours prononce le 19 novembre 1959 à l'aérodrome de VNOWKOVO', 26 November 1959 GR9Q5122, SHD.

109 Camara, *1 November 1958–1 November 2008.*

110 SDECE, 'Guinée: La situation intérieure en Guinée vue par un membre d'opposition', 31 March 1959, 51QO/34, CADC; Governor Bonfils, 'Note de renseignements: république de Guinée', 28 November 1958; SDECE, 'Malaise politique en Guinée', 7 March 1959, 51QO/34, CADC.

Touré's administration would be accused of persecuting the Fulani and favouring Touré's own ethnic group, the Malinke.[111]

However, the issue of ethnic favouritism in Guinea was more complex than policies that simply benefitted one ethnic group over others. The Fulani were located in a mountainous region along the border with Senegal, making it difficult for both colonial and postcolonial administrations to submit them to state authority.[112] The French had also used the Fulani in efforts to overthrow Touré. Meanwhile, as Touré faced growing internal and external threats, he assigned the most important tasks to people he considered absolutely loyal to him, and these were often members of his extended family.[113] The president's half-brother, Ismaël Touré, was given an important decision-making role in ensuring regime security, for example.[114] Even so, many Malinke suffered as a result of Touré's politics, and foreign observers noted that the president was careful to assign any blame for the population's grievances to the plotting of different ethnic groups. Unsurprisingly, this strategy hardly inspired national unity.

Although most members of the military elite at the time of Touré's death were Malinke, Deputy Army Chief of Staff Lansana Conté was Susu. From the mid-1960s onwards, Conté had played an important role in the surveillance of soldiers, and his actions are said to have increased favouritism, distrust, and denunciations within the military. Conté reportedly orchestrated promotions for his friends, and convinced many soldiers to become informers. When Touré died in 1984, it was Conté who seized power. Thereafter he not only executed the Guinean political elite, including Ismaël Touré, but awarded the highest military posts to members of his ethnic group, the Susu.[115] He also set about destroying the political system Sékou Touré had spent his life building.

Mali's socialist leader, Modibo Keïta, was not as successful as Touré in building an effective party structure. As the next section shows, this made it harder for the Malian president to convince his domestic audience of the need to endure economic hardship in exchange for a socialist society.

111 Graham, 'Political instability in Guinea', 2 March 1965; Sherer, 'Prospects of Sékou Touré's regime', 11 October 1971.

112 Bonfils, 'Note de renseignements: république de Guinée', 28 November 1958; SDECE, 'Malaise politique en Guinée', 7 March 1959.

113 Lewin, *Ahmed Sékou Touré (1922–1984)*, vol. 5, pp. 251–70.

114 Hughes, 'Guinea: Has crisis peaked?', 28 March 1969; Sherer, 'Prospects of Sékou Touré's regime', 11 October 1971.

115 Camara, *1 November 1958–1 November 2008.*

He relied more on cooptation than he did on coercion in controlling the Malian military, although his successor, Lieutenant-Colonel Moussa Traoré, had no misgivings about arresting and killing opponents of the regime and their collaborators.

The death march of Malian officers to Taoudenni

The socialist policies of Mali's first president Modibo Keïta reduced the country's wealth and bred popular dissatisfaction.[116] By 1964, when the GDP PPP had decreased by more than 20% from the previous year (see Figure 15), food shortages were frequent. The main challenge for the government was assuring a sufficient supply of cereal to the cities, as the pre-set price offered to peasants was no incentive to increase the size of their harvests.[117] From 1964 to 1968, the economic situation improved slightly, but the Malian citizens who suffered the most as a result of the government's economic policies had few opportunities to be heard, as the president's Sudanese Union-African Democratic Rally party (*Union soudanaise-Rassemblement démocratique africain*, or US-RDA) was the country's only legal political organization.[118]

Despite these economic gains, the military's share of GDP spending did not increase. In 1968, Malian soldiers staged a military coup, on the pretext that the poor economic policies of the socialist government had to be corrected. That year, however, Mali's GDP PPP had grown by 10% from the previous year, which suggests that economic hardships were not the motivating factor. In fact, members of the armed forces enjoyed material comforts that made it all but impossible for them to relate to the poverty in which most of the Malian population lived.[119]

Keïta made sure that soldiers remained satisfied with their salaries, benefits, and equipment, even as the civilian population struggled. This was consistent with the fact that during most of Mali's history, a large portion of the country's wealth has been allocated to the military, and more than

[116] Ambassador Wibeaux to the General Secretary for African and Malagasy Affairs, 28 April 1962.
[117] US Embassy Bamako, 'An insider's view of Mali', 15 December 1965, POL 1964–1966, Box 2461, CGRDS, NARA; Wibeaux to Foccart, 21 April 1965, 5AGF/583, FFAN.
[118] Ibid.
[119] Advisor to the Squadron Battalion Commander, 'Rapport fin de mission août 1962–juillet 1965', 29 June 1965; Ambassador Pelen, 'Inquiétudes maliennes: problèmes de sécurité intérieure', 14 February 1966, 62PO1–15, CADN.

in other francophone West African countries.[120] In the opinion of Western observers, the material privileges afforded to Malian soldiers, combined with Soviet military equipment, were enough to keep the armed forces loyal to Keïta.[121] Conversely, their material wellbeing also made them a political threat.[122] As members of the Malian security apparatus tended to be more moderate and conservative than the leftist government, they were increasingly politicized and controlled by the US-RDA.

Even though the material conditions of soldiers set them apart from the rest of the population, the country's economic situation did prompt some loyal soldiers to express doubt about Mali's socialist policies.[123] The government's efforts to force peasants to sell their produce to the state at low prices had only convinced them to produce less. In 1963, Keïta's land appropriation scheme in the north had provoked an armed rebellion by the Tuareg. The army had crushed the rebellion by the end of 1964, in an operation that gave soldiers a sense of unity and common purpose.[124]

Nevertheless, there were divisions within the military between soldiers who had served in the French forces and were nostalgic about the past, and those who had not and were not, and were thus considered loyal to the socialist government.[125] In October 1964, when Army Chief of Staff General Abdoulaye Soumaré was replaced by Lieutenant Sékou Traoré, a French military attaché anticipated that this would have a negative impact on the forces, as Soumaré was liked by old officers and new recruits alike, and his role in creating cohesion was important. Traoré was described instead as someone who could 'control the turbulent elements, especially as he had for some time profited from the sickness of his boss to increase

120 Military advisor, French Embassy Bamako, 'Rapport de renseignements des deux premiers trimestres de 1964', 9 June 1964, GR14S267, SHD; Wibeaux to Foccart, 21 April 1965; Lieutenant-Colonel Lebe, 'Rapport fin de mission octobre 1965–November 1967', 27 October 1967.

121 Advisor to the Squadron Battalion Commander, 'Rapport fin de mission août 1962–juillet 1965', 29 June 1965; Pelen, 'Inquiétudes maliennes: problèmes de sécurité intérieure', 14 February 1966; US Embassy Bamako, 'Order of Battle of Malian army', 11 December 1966, DEF 1964–1966, Box 1679, CGRDS, NARA.

122 Pelen, 'Quelques reflétions sur l'armée malienne', 2 December 1966.

123 Advisor to the Squadron Battalion Commander, 'Rapport fin de mission août 1962–juillet 1965', 29 June 1965; Pelen, 'Inquiétudes maliennes: problèmes de sécurité intérieure', 14 February 1966.

124 Military advisor, 'Rapport de renseignements des deux premiers trimestres de 1964', 9 June 1964.

125 Pelen, 'Inquiétudes maliennes: problèmes de sécurité intérieure', 14 February 1966.

his authoritarian influence.'[126] Promotions were indeed based on political calculations rather than the display of any leadership capacity.[127]

Within little more than a year, the Malian army lost two more important figures. Captain Leon Sankharé, whom the US Embassy referred to as 'the most capable officer of the Malian army', resigned after he did not receive a promotion due to tensions with leadership. It had not helped that his French wife disliked Mali.[128] Another high-ranking officer, Mohamed Ould Issa, died accidentally in early 1966. The loss of both Sankharé and Issa negatively impacted the army, not least because the positions they vacated became the subject of internal rivalries.[129]

The Malian government was aware of problems in the military, and its concern deepened after military coups took place in Upper Volta, and then in Ghana, in 1966. Following the coup in Upper Volta, Keïta's administration declared the Voltaic government corrupt and said that nothing similar could happen in Mali. The US Embassy characterized the Malian regime as 'distrustful of the army', despite its control 'through surveillance and informers, and having the officers become members of the party.'[130] That the coup in Ghana had ousted a socialist regime made Keïta even more distrustful. He promoted Army Chief of Staff Sékou Traoré and made him a member of the National Committee for the Defence of the Revolution (*Comité National de Défense de la Révolution*, or CNDR). Traoré's promotion meant he was the only colonel above five lieutenant-colonels, which intensified the rivalries among these officers. In hindsight, the actions of President Keïta in 1966 – which also included promoting the commander of the Presidential Guard[131] – did nothing to reduce the likelihood of a coup,

---

126 Advisor to the Squadron Battalion Commander, 'Rapport fin de mission août 1962–juillet 1965', 29 June 1965.

127 US Embassy Bamako, 'Discontent among the provincial gendarmerie', 8 February 1966.

128 US Embassy Bamako, 'Weekly summary', 4 January 1966, DEF 1964–1966, Box 1679, CGRDS, NARA.

129 US Embassy Bamako, 18 January 1966, DEF 1964–1966, Box 1679, CGRDS, NARA.

130 Ibid.

131 Wibeaux to Foccart, 21 April 1965; Lebe, 'Rapport fin de mission octobre 1965–novembre 1967 ', 27 October 1967; Pelen, 'Quelques reflétions sur l'armée malienne, 2 December 1966; US Embassy Bamako, 'Weekly summary', 4 January 1966; Pelen, 'Inquiétudes maliennes: problèmes de sécurité intérieure', 14 February 1966.

and Malian troops looked upon the political entanglements of the military elite with scorn .[132]

By 1968, only a few weeks before the military did carry out a coup in Mali, the French ambassador noted that Malian forces had avoided participating in operations against political protests, estimating that soldiers may take the side of demonstrators in any future protests.[133] The Malian government, aware that soldiers were hesitant to engage in political policing, had used mostly party militias to deal with opposition actors, both inside and outside the party. The tasks of these militias varied, from reinforcing national unity to spying on party members to detecting economic crimes.[134]

The militias were established in 1962, after the short-lived federation between Mali and Senegal came abruptly to an end, largely because the Malian government did not fully trust colonial soldiers who had served in the French military and now constituted the armed forces. The militias were recruited from among the illiterate and unemployed youth, which it was hoped would reinforce their obedience to the party.[135] President Keïta's son-in-law played an important role in organizing the militias, which were trained by Czechoslovakian, Soviet, and Chinese advisors. Members were given personal weapons that they stored after hours at the local gendarmerie. Western officials regarded the militias as disciplined, and French and American reports also described militia members as 'the most faithful supporters of the regime', even if they rated their capacities as mediocre.[136]

Before the military coup in 1968, there were around 1,200 militia members in Kati and Bamako and 2,800 elsewhere in the country. They were immensely unpopular among the population and were seen as a major cause of dissatisfaction with the government. They were unpopular among soldiers as well, but the militias enabled these forces to avoid undesirable tasks that would have diminished their public image.[137] The gendarmes were not so lucky and could not escape the work of political surveillance. In

---

132 US Embassy Bamako, 'Order of battle of Malian army', 11 December 1966.

133 Pelen to Ministry of Foreign Affairs, 'Rapport fin de mission 25 septembre 1964 à 1 novembre 1968', 5AGF/2708, FFAN.

134 General Secretariat for National Defence, Intelligence Exploitation Centre, 'L'armée malienne', 23 October 1962; US Embassy Bamako, 'Security forces of the government of Mali', 24 May 1962, 770E Mali, MAL61–63, Box 1951, CGRDS, NARA.

135 Pelen to Ministry of Foreign Affairs, 'Rapport fin de mission 25 septembre 1964 à 1 novembre 1968'; US Embassy Bamako, 'French view of Mali's paramilitary forces', 12 September 1966, POL 1964–1966, Box 2463, CGRDS, NARA.

136 Ibid.

137 Ibid.

February 1966, for example, when gendarmes in northern Mali reportedly refused to act as 'party policemen to harass party members attend party meetings', underlining that their responsibility was the safety of Malian citizens, Commandant Bale Koné travelled to discipline them in person.[138]

In 1967, worried about soldiers' increasing power, the Malian government increased the resources allocated to internal security forces and militias and slightly reduced the allocation to the military.[139] This did nothing to help stave off the military coup that came in November 1968. In fact, Malian soldiers interviewed for this study noted that popular discontent with the militias was a major driver of the coup, and in the weeks leading up to it, the French ambassador had observed growing conflict between the military and the militias.[140] When the militias were dissolved immediately thereafter, it was a relief for most of population.[141]

According to French and American officials, traders, business owners, and peasants supported the coup in Mali, while young people and trade unions did not.[142] It was carried out by junior officers in the Malian army, who formed the Military Committee for National Liberation (*Comité Militaire de Libération National*, or CMLN) for the purposes of ruling the country, and then sent soldiers into the interior to explain the rationale for the coup to the population.[143] The French contended the coup had been planned by four officers who worked at the Kati Military Academy, including Captain Yoro Diakité, director of the academy since 1963, and Lieutenant Moussa Traoré, an instructor who had been there since 1964.[144] Two senior military officers, Pinana Drabo and Charles Sissoko, were named the new chief of staff and minister of defence and interior to ease the concerns of senior

---

[138] US Embassy Bamako, 'Discontent among the provincial gendarmerie', 8 February 1966, and 'The secret militia in Mali', 26 January 1965, DEF 1964–1966, Box 1679, CGRDS, NARA.

[139] Pelen, 'Budget de la république du Mali', 8 December 1966, 62PO1–15, CADN.

[140] Pelen to Ministry of Foreign Affairs, 'Rapport fin de mission 25 septembre 1964 à 1 novembre 1968'.

[141] US Embassy Bamako, 'Malian developments', 23 December 1968, POLMALI 67–69, Box 2331, CGRDS, NARA.

[142] General Secretary for African and Malagasy Affairs, 'Audience du lieutenant Moussa Traore', 3 November 1970; US Embassy Bamako, 'Malian developments', 23 December 1968.

[143] US Embassy Bamako, 'Mali's senior military officers and the coup d'état', 17 December 1968, POLMALI 67–69, Box 2332, CGRDS, NARA.

[144] Ambassador Dallier, 'Le capitaine Yoro Diakite', 25 February 1969, 62PO1–56, CADN.

officers. In an effort to keep 'the discontent of upper ranks in manageable portions', military officers were also named governors of different regions in Mali.[145] Nevertheless, when some officers protested the arrest of the previous Chief of Staff, they too were arrested.[146]

In January 1969, the CMLN made the decision to retire the fourteen most senior officers in the armed forces to make room for younger officers. These higher-ranking officers were also thought to have profited from the previous regime's opulence.[147] By May 1969, more officers had been moved into administrative positions,[148] and in August, Captains Diby Silas Diarra and Alassane Diarra, together with eleven other officers, were arrested for plotting against the military government. All of the accused were said to have 'socialist opinions' and all were from the northern part of the country. The French ambassador reported that they had not received promotions and were unhappy with their material conditions after having been deployed to the Sahel. Indeed, the CMLN's decision to exclude anyone who had not completed a secondary education from attending officer school angered some former colonial soldiers, who thus lost any prospects of promotion.[149]

The two captains who allegedly led the planning of the 1969 coup had networks in northern Mali and were in contact with supporters of the former president in that region, having both worked there. Diby Silas Diarra had played an important role in repressing the Tuareg rebellion and was named Governor of Gao following the coup, and Alassane Diarra had commanded the Saharan Company in Kidal until 1968.[150] They were sent to a labour camp in Taoudenni that had been established by the CMLN. Diby Diarra died there three years later.[151] In many ways, the 1969 arrests of these officers foretold what was to come in Mali, as internal divisions in

145 US Embassy Bamako, 'Mali's senior military officers and the coup d'état', 17 December 1968, and 'Malian army and Gendarmerie Officer Roster', 31 May 1969, POL 1964–1966, Box 2463, CGRDS, NARA.

146 US Embassy Bamako, 'Malian developments', 23 December 1968, and 'Mali's senior military officers and the coup d'état', 17 December 1968.

147 US Embassy Bamako, 'MCNL most senior army officers', 10 February 1969, POL 1964–1966, Box 2463, CGRDS, NARA; Ambassador Dallier, 'Mise à la retraite d'officers superieurs', 28 January 1969, 62PO1–56, GR6Q44, SHD.

148 US Embassy Bamako, 'Malian army and Gendarmerie Officer Roster', 31 May 1969.

149 Dallier, 'La nuit du 12 août, 24 August 1969, 62PO1–72, CADN.

150 Ibid.

151 Maurice Gourage, Chargé d'affaires, 'Procès des capitaines Yoro Diakite et Malik Diallo', 2 August 1972, 61PO160, CADN.

the military deepened throughout the 1970s and countless Malian soldiers were sent to Taoudenni.

The arrests of Malian soldiers were directed at bolstering the personal power of Moussa Traoré, who had ousted Modibo Keïta in November 1968. The main challenger to Traoré's power, his one-time collaborator Yoro Diakité, was arrested in April 1971. It was no help to Diakité that the international press had been reporting on the rivalry between himself and Traoré for quite some time,[152] nor that he was several years older, more experienced, and better educated. Both men were from military families, had attended military school in their youth, had volunteered to serve in the French army, and served in Indochina and Algeria. However, Diakité had attended officer school in Fréjus (France) in 1956, while Traoré – who started his training in Fréjus in October 1960 – had been forced to return to Mali when it ended its military assistance agreement with France, before he had graduated. The two men were also of different ethnic origins: Diakité was Fula and Traoré Malinke.[153] The real threat Diakité posed to Traoré also came from the fact that he had his own base of support within the military.

According to the French ambassador, two other key members of the CMLN had taken the lead in getting rid of Diakité. Tiécoro Bagayoko and Kissima Doukara – who, together, largely controlled the Malian security apparatus – both had a personal feud with Diakité because he had opposed their promotions when he was director of the military academy in Kati. In January 1970, animosity among the three escalated to an armed altercation in which Bagayoko and Doukara drew their guns. President Traoré held Diakité responsible for 'provoking' the other two men. It was surely clear to Diakité by that point that he was in a precarious position.[154]

Beyond his personal grievances with Diakité, Bagayoko was also concerned about Diakité's ongoing influence, as well as that of fellow CMLN member Malik Diallo, on soldiers at the Kati base. Diakité and Diallo were the most liberal, pro-French members of the CMLN, and were critical of increasing

---

152 Dallier, 'Physionomie du comité militaire de libération nationale à la veille de l'arrestation de deux de ses membres', 1 April 1971, 61PO160, CADN.

153 US Embassy Bamako, 'Malian army and Gendarmerie Officer Roster', 31 May 1969.

154 Dallier, 'Arrestation de deux membres du CMLN', 5 April 1971, and 'Physionomie du comité militaire de libération nationale à la veille de l'arrestation de deux de ses membres', 1 April 1971; Courage, 'Procès des capitaines Yoro Diakité et Malik Diallo', 2 August 1972.

Chinese influence in Mali. Bagayoko and Doukara had nearly polar opposite views. The arrests of Diakité and Diallo were thus intended to end their influence on soldiers, and despite the popularity of these officers among older Malians, peasants, and business owners, there was no public reaction when they were taken into custody in July 1970. In the end, Bagayoko was undoubtedly the victor. However, his cannibalism of the CMLN meant the Committee was left with just one senior officer, Minister of Foreign Affairs Charles Sissoko.[155]

Diakité and Diallo were brought to trial in the same month they were arrested, and they were condemned to a life of forced labour in Taoudenni Whilst this did little to boost the popularity of the military government,[156] it did dissuade any further opposition.[157] In some ways, the fate of Diakité, who died in prison in 1977, paralleled that of Fodéba Keïta, the Guinean minister of defence. Both men died at the hands of an organization, and in a prison, they had been instrumental in building. In other words, they were consumed by the very beasts they had created. Fate would not look kindly upon Bagayoko either, as he would be executed in Taoudenni in 1983.

By 1971, the CMLN was facing rising indebtedness, looming budget deficits, difficulties enforcing discipline in the military, and declining public popularity.[158] Despite expectations to the contrary, the military government in Mali had not succeeded in managing the economy any better than the civilian administration of Modibo Keïta. In fact, the policies of the CMLN differed little from those of the socialist government. At the same time, Traoré was becoming increasingly authoritarian and repressive, and his government more corrupt. Limits placed by the government on the distribution of cereals, for example, allowed for the personal enrichment of those who were politically well-connected through state companies.[159]

In 1973, the CMLN took the step of using force in the countryside in order to assure the availability of food crops in the most politically important cities. Even by this point, there was no organized opposition in Mali, and internal fighting among the remaining fourteen members of the

---

155 Ibid.
156 Courage, 'Procès des capitaine Yoro Diakite et Malik Diallo', 2 August 1972.
157 General Secretary for African and Malagasy Affairs, 'Entretien en tête à tête avec le colonel Moussa Traoré', 28 April 1972, 5AGF/582, FFAN.
158 Blake, US Embassy Bamako, 'Memorandum of conversation: Ambassador Louis Dallier, French Ambassador', 14 December 1971, POLMALI 70–73, Box 2466, CGRDS, NARA; Dallier, 'Arrestation de deux membres du CMLN', 5 April 1971; Courage, 'Procès des capitaine Yoro Diakite et Malik Diallo', 2 August 1972.
159 Dallier, 'Arrestation de deux membres du CMLN', 5 April 1971.

CMLN was threatening its stability.[160] That year, another member of the Committee, Foreign Minister Baba Diarra, was imprisoned. He had been in poor standing with President Traoré since Diakité's arrest in 1971, when Diarra himself had only avoided arrest due to his strong support within the army.[161]

The Malian military government was aware it had to do more than arrest soldiers to consolidate its power. Cooptation was important, too, which continued to make it imperative to assure soldiers' material wellbeing.[162] Military spending had risen to 3.2% of GDP by 1975, after hovering between 2.2% and 2.9% under the socialist government. In fact, until the 1980s, Malian spending on the military as a percentage of GDP was the highest in francophone West Africa. This only measured official spending, of course, and did not account for the many economic benefits granted to military ruling elites due to their political power.[163]

The excesses of these elites served as a cause of dissatisfaction among the population and envy among other soldiers.[164] French reports suggest that by the early 1970s that higher-ranking Malian officers who had governmental positions were out of touch with the lower ranks and younger forces, who were growing more politicized and were increasingly driven by personal grievance, political ambition, and material inducements.[165] To calm tensions, in 1978, President Traoré arrested his long-time collaborators Kissima Doukara, Karim Dembélé, Tiécoro Bagayoko, and Charles Sissoko on charges of corruption. The following year, Traoré was re-elected with 99.9% of the vote (and no opposition), despite the country's catastrophic economic situation. Government debt was six times the annual budget, and even though the arrests of figures in Traoré's own inner circle were part of a series of supposed anti-corruption measures, corruption had been normalized. A mere twenty-seven state-owned enterprises accounted for 70% of Mali's economic activity.[166]

---

[160] Intelligence Exploitation Centre, 'Évolution récente et situation actuelle du Mali', 8 March 1973, GR9Q5128, SHD.

[161] Dallier, Bamako, 'Remaniement ministériel', 18 May 1973, 61PO160, CADN.

[162] General Secretary for African and Malagasy Affairs, 'L'armée malienne et l'aide militaire française', 28 April 1972.

[163] Lieutenant-Colonel Chenevoy, 'Rapport fin de mission 25 October 1973–31 August 1976'.

[164] Ibid.

[165] Dallier, 'Arrestation de deux membres du CMLN', 5 April 1971.

[166] General Secretariat for National Defence, Sub-department for Africa and the Middle East, 'Évaluation de la situation au Mali des risques de crise grave', 28 April 1980, GR9Q5128, SHD.

Moussa Traoré managed to stay in power until the end of the Cold War, even with a very poor economy. In the 1980s, his primary opposition came from a student movement that demanded a multiparty democracy in the country, and which finally led indirectly to his downfall in 1991. In March of that year, when student protests were violently repressed and over one hundred students were reportedly killed, Lieutenant-Colonel Amadou Toumani Touré responded by staging a coup. Several days after the protests were repressed, Touré imprisoned Traoré and organized a committee to assure a transition to democracy. Touré would serve as the Malian president from 2002 to 2012, when he himself was ousted by yet another coup, this time carried out by Captain Amadou Sanogo. The 2012 coup was motivated by the displeasure of soldiers regarding a lack of support from the government for the military's fight against a rebellion in northern Mali. On this occasion, however, the soldiers who took power almost immediately transferred it to a civilian president, bowing to both domestic and foreign pressure. Nevertheless, Malian soldiers continue to play important economic and political roles in the development of their country, as is true of soldiers in Guinea. The same cannot be said of Côte d'Ivoire or Senegal, and the next section will discuss why.

Economic Liberalism vs Multiparty Democracy: Ivorian and Senegalese Decision-making

Soldiers in Côte d'Ivoire and Senegal enjoyed more security than in Guinea and Mali. Far fewer were arrested and apparently none were executed, partly because the Ivorian and Senegalese presidents had no need to control their forces through coercion, as the French military presence in both countries assured regime security. French officials were also able to apply pressure on the Ivorian and Senegalese governments to avoid excessive use of force, especially against civilians.

Of those presidents in francophone West Africa, Félix Houphouët-Boigny of Côte d'Ivoire and Léopold Senghor of Senegal were exceptional for successfully exerting civilian control over their militaries. They did this in different ways, however, as Houphouët-Boigny turned externally to France and foreign investment, while Senghor engaged internally with the Senegalese political, religious, and economic elite as well as with students, labour unions, and soldiers. The fact was, Senghor did not possess the resources, nor perhaps the will, to ignore domestic interest groups. Houphouët-Boigny, on the other hand, was able to coopt most individuals who challenged his rule. In this sense, Ivorian economic success was also its curse.

The ideological posture of these two presidents also set them apart. Houphouët-Boigny leaned towards a liberal economic model under his authoritarian, and increasingly corrupt, control. In contrast, Senghor slowly replaced mechanisms of personal control with institutional checks and balances. The most significant step in this process came in 1980, when Senghor resigned at the end of his fifth term and handed power to his prime minister Abdou Diouf. In turn, Diouf conceded when he lost an election in 2000, carrying on the example Senghor had set – one that has built the trust of Senegalese citizens in democracy. Houphouët-Boigny instead ruled for thirty-three years, and died in power in 1993. After his demise, an ensuing power struggle led to the first successful coup in Côte d'Ivoire and a lengthy civil war. In 2011, the country experienced further political crisis when former president Laurent Gbagbo refused to stand down after his electoral defeat, reflecting the illiberal legacy of earlier Ivorian governance practices.

Indeed, in terms of various measures of good governance, the Ivorian government has regularly been among the worst-ranked in francophone West Africa, especially since 1996. The Senegalese government, on the other hand, is consistently rated as the freest, most effective, and least corrupt in the region (see Figure 6). Despite this, Senegal has fared worse than Côte d'Ivoire in terms of its economy. Nonetheless, the Senegalese military continues to be known for its strength and professionalism, which cannot be said of Ivorian forces. This extends from the fact that Senghor emphasized the training and professionalism of soldiers, whereas Houphouët-Boigny – who relied on the French for security and was indifferent, if not resistant, to building military capacity – transferred soldiers into the civilian administration. The contrasting approaches of Senghor and Houphouët-Boigny to governing their national armed forces are discussed below.

The personal control of Houphouët-Boigny –
'l'homme au totem caïman'

In some ways, Houphouët-Boigny was less like Senghor and more like Guinea's Sékou Touré. The Ivorian and Guinean presidents both remained in power until their deaths, while most of their colleagues were overthrown in military coups. That these countries only experienced a military coup only after their deaths highlights the personal role Houphouët-Boigny and Touré had in controlling their militaries. Although the two presidents took almost opposite positions regarding their economic policies, relations with the former colonial power, and Cold War alignment, they both succeeded in controlling their national forces for several decades. However, the practices and mechanisms they used to control these forces were neither sustainable nor sufficiently institutionalized to outlive the Ivorian and Guinean presidents themselves.

Houphouët-Boigny exerted control over the Ivorian military by less violent means than Touré did in Guinea. This was one reason why Côte d'Ivoire was among the few countries in francophone West Africa where most soldiers served until their retirement.[167] For the most part, Houphouët-Boigny favoured cooptation and imprisonment to executions, but he was not averse to employing repressive tactics. Like Touré, Houphouët-Boigny was apt to do away with anyone who could be considered a threat to his rule by announcing a coup plot.[168] The accused would be imprisoned and sentenced to death or many years of forced labour, and, as in Guinea, there were allegations of torture. However, where the Guinean government executed almost all the people it sentenced to death, the Ivorian regime later pardoned most of these individuals.[169]

It is worth asking how francophone African leaders like Touré, who was openly coercive, offered a certain relativity to the autocratic tendencies of a 'soft authoritarian' like Houphouët-Boigny. Ivorian writer Ahmadou Kourouma tackled this question in his satirical novel of 1998, *Waiting for*

---

167 Guy-André Kieffer, 'Armée ivoirienne: le refus du déclassement', *Politique africaine* 78, no. 2 (2000), pp. 30–1.

168 Directorate of African and Malagasy Affairs, 'République de Côte d'Ivoire', 3 July 1963.

169 There were a few exceptions. For example, Ernest Boka, the former Ivorian Minister of Education and Public Service and President of the Supreme Court, died in prison under suspicious circumstances in April 1964. It was rumoured that Boka had been murdered. See US Embassy Abidjan to Department of State, 'The Boka affair', 23 April 1964, POLIVCAST 1964–1966, Box 2370, CGRDS, NARA.

the Wild Beasts to Vote [*En attendant le vote de bêtes sauvages*], in which he wrote of a character based on Houphouët-Boigny:

> You wanted to know how the man with the caiman totem managed to conceal, to forget all his practices – torture, corruption, arbitrary imprisonment. How had he managed to pass himself off as the sage of Africa? How had he managed to maintain such respectability …. He told you it was because he was an African head of state. You did not understand immediately. So, he added … My practices may seem reprehensible in other circles, in other skies, in other contexts; but not in Africa. During your initiatory journey you will have to compare me to other heads of state and you will quickly conclude that I am an angel, a sage who deserves the recognition of humanity.[170]

If Houphouët-Boigny was indeed able to pass himself off as the angel and sage of francophone West Africa, it was largely due to the nature of the internal and external threats he faced. This had much to do with why the Ivorian and Guinean presidents made different decisions regarding the strength of their militaries and the degree to which they used coercion to control their forces. External threats to Guinea made it more of a necessity for Touré to establish a strong armed force, for example. By contrast, Côte d'Ivoire faced few external threats, and because Houphouët-Boigny relied on France to defend Ivorian territory, he could intentionally weaken his military.[171] His priority was building the Ivorian gendarmerie, which he ensured was better trained and equipped than other security forces (see Chapter 3).[172]

Some of the practices Houphouët-Boigny and Touré used to control their armed forces were similar, though. Both believed that by fragmenting the military and creating a strong counterforce in the form of party militias, they could avoid a coup. Both presidents also established extensive networks of informants within the armed forces,[173] which greatly assisted with the identification and detention of individuals who might pose potential threats.[174]

---

170 Ahmadou Kourouma, *En attendant le vote de bêtes sauvage* (Seuil, Paris, 1998), p. 203
171 Directorate of African and Malagasy Affairs, 'Problèmes militaires franco-ivoiriens', 3 June 1961; Raphaël-Leygues, 'La Côte d'Ivoire et l'armée', 30 August 1974.
172 Rood, 'Ivorian internal security forces', 19 February 1964.
173 Ministry of Armed Forces, SDECE, 'Sécurité: mesures prises par le président Houphouët-Boigny', 9 February 1966, 5AGF/1795, FFAN; US Embassy Abidjan 'Assessment of Internal Situation in Ivory Coast', 22 January 1966; Rood, 'Ivorian internal security forces' 19 February 1964.
174 Directorate of African and Malagasy Affairs, 'République de Côte d'Ivoire', 3 July 1963.

Houphouët-Boigny strongly rejected comparisons between himself and Touré, declaring in 1965 that he would 'never spill the blood of an Ivorian regardless of the crime committed.' He called this 'a belief of faith' and insisted that he knew 'how to forget and forgive'. Addressing Touré, he asked, 'Since independence how many men have you had murdered?' He noted that Guineans themselves had weighed in on which leader they preferred, claiming, 'at least two hundred thousand Guineans live in Côte d'Ivoire, most of whom have come since their country gained independence.' Further, Houphouët-Boigny charged, any plots against Touré were the fault of Touré's own poor economic mismanagement and totalitarian tendencies.[175]

Even if the proceedings in which Guineans were condemned to death were undeniably deficient, and judgements from them dubious, there is no doubt that both internal and external plots to oust Touré were very real. This was not the case in Côte d'Ivoire, where Houphouët-Boigny himself later acknowledged that the regime had fabricated plots against him.[176] In 1969, addressing student protests, Houphouët-Boigny admitted that in the earlier part of the decade, Ivorians had been arrested and imprisoned without regular procedure and on poorly established grounds, based solely on the fears of their compatriots. He assured the crowd he would not repeat the mistakes of the past.[177] In May 1971, the state even apologized to individuals who had been sentenced in connection to alleged plots in 1963 and 1964.[178]

When talking to Ivorians today, it is quite clear that their opinions of Houphouët-Boigny are split. He is both loved and hated, seen as a traitor and a father of the nation. Some Ivorians praise him but disparage France, having adopted the narrative that the French forced Houphouët-Boigny to

175 'Déclaration de HB sur le prétendu complot dénoncé par Monsieur Sékou Touré', 17 November 1965, ADCI.
176 At the time of the alleged 1963 plot, Houphouët-Boigny had announced that the government had received thousands of letters criticizing the president for having been too lenient toward plotters, as he had not executed anyone. He emphasized that only who were proven guilty would be punished. See 'Conférence de presse du président Félix Houphouët-Boigny sur la politique intérieure', 10 September 1963, ADCI.
177 Ministry of Interior, Director of International Police Technical Cooperation Services, to Foccart, 'Concernant la réunion étudiants à Yamoussoukro', 22 August 1969, 5AGF/1805, FFAN; Director of International Police Technical Cooperation Services to Foccart, 'Note concernant le règlement de la crise estudiantine et sur la situation politique en Côte d'Ivoire', 3 June 1969, 5AGF/1805, FFAN.
178 Samba Diarra, *Les faux complots d'Houphouët-Boigny: Fracture dans le destin d'une nation (1959–1970)* (Paris: Karthala, 1997), p. 215.

implement policies that compounded Ivorian dependence on the former colonial power. However, archival evidence paints a different picture of the power dynamics at play in relations between the Ivorian president and French officials. In fact, Houphouët-Boigny was so important to French objectives that they went to great lengths to comply with his wishes and demands. Some Ivorians even argue that Houphouët-Boigny was the only leader capable of governing Côte d'Ivoire. It is true, of course, that the country became unstable after his death, but the situation was little different to a the sudden departure of a CEO who had run a company in such a way that it could not survive without them. Certainly, compared to Touré, Modibo Keïta or Moussa Traoré, the presidency of Houphouët-Boigny was less violent and created greater prosperity, but what legacy did it leave?

At the centre of Ivorian policy under Houphouët-Boigny were the goals of peace and economic development. His scepticism as to whether the military could contribute to either largely informed Houphouët-Boigny's negative view of the Ivorian national armed forces, his disdain for which was evident in public speeches and his policies. In fact, at independence, the French speculated that the Ivorian president may not even form an army and could establish only a small gendarmerie.[179] Establishing and running a military was not only expensive, but at a time when military coups were taking place across the continent, its role in ensuring national security had to be balanced against the risk soldiers were seen to pose to the Ivorian political elite. Côte d'Ivoire faced few external threats during the thirty-three-year presidency of Houphouët-Boigny,[180] which certainly made a national military less of an imperative.[181] Furthermore, the military cooperation agreement between Côte d'Ivoire and France guaranteed Ivorian security against both external and internal threats.[182]

This alignment with France, together with Houphouët-Boigny's liberal economic policies, did give rise to domestic opposition, particularly among students and educated elites who were drawn to the socialist

---

179 Revol, 'Visite de monsieur Houphouët-Boigny et problèmes ivoiriens en matière de sécurité et défense', 16 May 1960.

180 Telegram, Abidjan to Directorate of African and Malagasy Affairs, 27 February 1964; Directorate of African and Malagasy Affairs, 'Problèmes militaires franco-ivoiriens', 3 June 1961.

181 Speech by Houphouët-Boigny to the National Assembly, 15 January 1962, ADCI; Directorate of African and Malagasy Affairs, 'Problèmes militaires franco-ivoiriens', 3 June 1961.

182 L'accord d'assistance militaire technique entre la République française et la République de Côte d'Ivoire, 24 April 1961.

and pan-Africanist ideas of Kwame Nkrumah and Sékou Touré. Ivorian opposition actors believed their president's decision-making was driven by French interests and dictated by the French advisors who surrounded him.[183] They were especially displeased by his decision to accept a French military base on Ivorian territory.[184] For Houphouët-Boigny, this was an easy price to pay for French protection, and for the freedom to weaken his own national forces.

After independence, the Ivorian political system had quickly steered itself towards one-party rule by the Democratic Party of Côte d'Ivoire (*Parti Démocratique de Côte d'Ivoire*, or PDCI), with power centralized to Houphouët-Boigny.[185] In 1963, although the French described his administration as 'a one-party presidential regime' with 'habits inherited perhaps unconsciously from the traditional chieftaincy', [186] this authoritarian rule did not stop them from offering significant economic and military aid. As far as the French were concerned, authoritarian leadership was necessary in its former colonies in order to forge national unity and avoid potentially destructive ethnic conflicts.[187]

Houphouët-Boigny did tend to emphasize national unity in his speeches,[188] although he did not manage to alleviate ethnic divisions in the country. In the political sphere, the Ivorian president used cooptation to retain power, which was based on personal ties and reciprocal obligations between Houphouët-Boigny and his supporters.[189] According to the French, his rule relied on, and often favoured, members of his own

---

183 Chafer, *The end of the Empire in French West Africa*, p. 188; Brasseur, 'Crise politique en Côte d'Ivoire', 23 January 1963; Directorate of African and Malagasy Affairs, 'République de Côte d'Ivoire', 3 July 1963.

184 Directorate of African and Malagasy Affairs, 'Problèmes militaires franco-ivoiriens', 3 June 1961.

185 Catherine Boone, *Political Topographies of the African State: Territorial Authority and Institutional Choice* (Cambridge University Press, 2005), pp. 177–220; Telegram, Abidjan to Paris, 'Résultats des Election en Côte d'Ivoire', 2 December 1970, 5AGF/1806, FFAN; Ministry of Armed Forces, SDECE, 'Côte d'Ivoire: la situation intérieure au début de l'année', 18 January 1968, 5AGF/1803, FFAN; Telegram, Abidjan to the Directorate of African and Malagasy Affairs, 16 December 1967, 5AGF/1802, FFAN.

186 French Embassy Abidjan, 'Fiches documentaires', 1963, 1PO/1/5, CADN.

187 Robert, *'Ministre' de l'Afrique*, p. 119.

188 For example, see President Houphouët-Boigny, Message to Parliament, 3 August 1961, and 'L'armée et l'école doivent creuser de l'unité', 3 January 1970.

189 Weber, *The Theory of Social and Economic Organization*, pp. 325–66.

ethnic group, the Baoulé.[190] Nevertheless, Houphouët–Boigny felt it was important that recruitment in the armed forces be based on ethnic quotas, because 'a mixture of races' in the military would reduce the likelihood of a military coup.[191]

We now know that Houphouët–Boigny may have exaggerated the threat of a military coup. For example, Ivorian historian Pierre Nandjui maintains that the two plots announced by the Ivorian government in 1963, allegedly planned in January and in August, were cynical inventions designed to validate the arrest of opposition actors.[192] It was mostly the educated elites who were accused of the January plot, but soldiers were implicated in August.[193] Even if these allegations were fabricated, events in other African countries – namely, military coups in Togo in January 1963 and in Congo in August 1963 – had alerted Houphouët-Boigny to the danger soldiers could represent and had made him more uneasy about the prospect of a coup.[194] According to French reports, the Ivorian president seemed truly unnerved about this possibility when he sought assurances, in multiple communications over months, that France would intervene if similar events took place in Côte d'Ivoire.[195]

In any case, arrests made by the Ivorian government in response to coup allegations served as a warning to any potential challengers. They silenced

190 General Secretariat for the Community, 'Audience du président Houphouët-Boigny', 8 April 1970, 5AGF/535, FFAN; Diefenbacher, Ministry of Interior Director of International Police Technical Cooperation Services, to Foccart, 'Note sur les réactions provoquées par le récent remaniement ministériel', 26 January 1970, 5AGF/1806, FFAN; State Minister in charge of National Defence, SDECE, 'Note d'information sur Côte d'Ivoire: les rivalités ethniques dans le contexte politique actuel', 3 October 1969, 5AGF/1805, FFAN.

191 Ministry of Armed Forces, SDECE, 'Sécurité: mesures prises par le président Houphouët-Boigny', 9 February 1966.

192 Pierre Nandjui, *Houphouët-Boigny: L'homme de la France en Afrique* (Paris: Harmattan, 2000).

193 Robert, *'Ministre' de l'Afrique*, pp. 216–22.

194 Marcel Amondji, 'Assabou et Marcoussis: deux tragédies ivoiriennes', *Outre-Terre* 11, no. 2 (2005), pp. 215–22.

195 Letter, Houphouët-Boigny to Charles de Gaulle, 2 March 1963; General Secretariat for African and Malagasy Affairs, 'Projet d'instruction pour m. Raphaël-Leygues', 5 March 1963, 5AGF/535, FFAN, and 'Audience du président Houphouët-Boigny', 29 July 1963, 5AGF/535, FFAN; Plantey, 'Note à l'attention de monsieur le président de la république', 7 August 1963, and 'Compte-rendu l'entretien avec Houphouët-Boigny', 5 August 1963; Courage, 'Procès des capitaine Yoro Diakite et Malik Diallo', 2 August 1972.

dissenting voices and prevented the formation of a unified opposition. As internal dissatisfaction with his policies was mounting, the Ivorian president thus used coercion but avoided outright violence.[196] Of the eighty people accused of involvement in the January 1963 plot, eight were given death sentences from the Special Court of State Security that was established to adjudicate their alleged crimes.[197] For the military, the impact of these proceedings was limited, as the January plot had been attributed to civilians. In August, however, the accused included a number of high-ranking soldiers, as well as the ministers of interior and defence.[198] Officers and non-commissioned officers with links to Defence Minister Jean Konan Banny were especially targeted.[199]

Houphouët-Boigny used the August allegations to justify disarming the Ivorian military and the creation of a parallel organization of party militias. He had been out of the country for over four months when the alleged coup plot was announced and worried that his opponents might stage protests in the capital upon his return, prompting the military to assume power. French observers felt that some of Houphouët-Boigny's closest allies took advantage of his absence to exaggerate the purported threat to his regime in order to cast suspicion on their own competitors.[200] From where he sat in Paris, all the Ivorian president knew was that there had already been clear signs of dissatisfaction within the armed forces.[201] As the news from Abidjan became more distressing, Houphouët-Boigny explained to the French ambassador that Côte d'Ivoire was as susceptible to military coups as any other former French colony, because politicians had yet to consolidate their position vis-à-vis the masses. 'In a country as unstructured as mine,' he said, 'it only takes about twenty men to make a conspiracy and an assassination.'[202]

196 Telegram, Abidjan to Directorate of African and Malagasy Affairs, 27 February 1964.

197 French Embassy Abidjan, 'Situation Politique du 5 avril au 12 avril 1963'.

198 'Conférence de presse du président Félix Houphouët-Boigny sur la politique intérieure', 10 September 1963.

199 French Embassy Abidjan, 'Fiches documentaires', 1963.

200 His brother-in-law Casimir Brou, who was the head of the Police, was deeply implicated. See French Embassy Abidjan, 'Tension en Côte d'Ivoire', 25 August 1963, 1PO/1/14, CADN; Raphaël-Leygues, 'Compte-rendu l'entretien avec Houphouët-Boigny,' 5 August 1963.

201 Directorate of African and Malagasy Affairs, 'République de Côte d'Ivoire', 3 July 1963.

202 Raphaël-Leygues, 'Compte-rendu l'entretien avec Houphouët-Boigny', 5 August 1963. Also see Letter, Houphouët-Boigny to Charles de Gaulle, 2 March 1963.

French officials estimated that while it was politically unwise for French forces to engage in an internal police operation in Côte d'Ivoire, Houphouët-Boigny was vital to French influence efforts in Africa. Hence, there was concern that if he was ousted the country could fall into ethnic conflict, and then fragment.[203] Hence, on 13 August 1963, at Houphouët-Boigny's request, Ivorian soldiers were asked to submit their arms to French troops for inspection.[204] Before departing for Côte d'Ivoire, the Ivorian president detailed his further plans to respond to the plot, explaining to the French ambassador that he would 'send the least important elements of subversion to the villages', where they would 'no longer be dangerous' and would also undertake 'a serious purge' of the army and police. 'The entire Ivorian army will have to be consigned for three days in its barracks', Houphouët-Boigny told him, asking that the French military 'put its tanks in places that we decide together.'[205]

When Houphouët-Boigny returned to Côte d'Ivoire on 18 August 1963, most of the weapons that had been handed in from soldiers were returned. The rest were used to arm over 3,500 party militia members,[206] all of whom were either party adherents, former combatants, or the Baoulé (the president's ethnic group).[207] It was hoped that ethnic solidarity would ensure the safety of the regime, as the main objective of the militias was to protect the political elite.[208] Houphouët-Boigny acknowledged that the militias were intended to function as a counterforce to the armed forces,

---

[203] Plantey, 'Note à l'attention de monsieur le président de la république', 7 August 1963; Raphaël-Leygues, 'Compte-rendu l'entretien avec Houphouët-Boigny', 5 August 1963.

[204] Telegram, Abidjan to Paris, 14 August 1963; Directorate of African and Malagasy Affairs, 'Situation politique en Côte d'Ivoire', 29 August 1963.

[205] Raphaël-Leygues, 'Compte-rendu l'entretien avec Houphouët-Boigny,' 5 August 1963.

[206] Directorate of African and Malagasy Affairs, 'Situation politique en Côte d'Ivoire', 29 August 1963.

[207] General Secretariat for the Community, 'Audience du président Houphouët-Boigny', 8 April 1970; Ministry of Armed Forces, SDECE, 'Politique intérieure', 4 March 1966, 5AGF/1795, FFAN, and 'Sécurité: mesures prises par le président Houphouët-Boigny', 9 February 1966; Rood, 'Ivorian internal security forces', 19 February 1964; US Embassy Abidjan, 'Assessment of Internal Situation in Ivory Coast', 22 January 1966.

[208] Raphaël-Leygues, 'Retour de Houphouët-Boigny à Côte d'Ivoire', 28 August 1963; French Embassy Abidjan, 'Actualités politiques', 10 September 1963, and 'Extrait du bulletin de renseignements hebdomadaires, 19–25 August 1963'; Raphaël-Leygues, 'Situation politique 26 October au 8 November 1963,' 9 November 1963, and 'Situation politique 13 au 20 December 1963', 24 December 1963; Directorate of African and

discouraging any plans to assassinate or otherwise depose him.[209] For this reason, his most loyal supporters were appointed militia leaders. French reports noted that the militias were primarily deployed to the Senoufo and Bété regions, where they were also the most heavily armed.[210]

The creation of party militias had a negative effect on morale in the armed forces, as it reflected how little the regime trusted the military. This was especially evident given that Houphouët-Boigny had once disarmed the national forces, which had further diminished their effectiveness.[211] The question of effectiveness already plagued the Ivorian military, with the French having described Ivorian troops as lethargic, mediocre, and inefficient.[212] In fact, a French military attaché speculated that the establishment of the militias might have a positive impact on the military by allowing it to concentrate on its primary duty of defending the territory against external threats.[213] However, France and the US assessed that the militias were not particularly well-trained either. By 1965, their number had been reduced and they were enjoined to the Presidential Guard, working exclusively in Yamoussoukro and Abidjan.[214]

In this way, the August 1963 coup allegations led to long-term changes in the Ivorian security forces. They also impacted the governance of

---

Malagasy Affairs, 'Situation politique en Côte d'Ivoire', 29 August 1963; Military Advisor, French Embassy Abidjan, 'Rapport mensuel September 1965', 4 October 1965.

209 'Conférence de presse du président Félix Houphouët-Boigny sur la politique intérieure', 10 September 1963; Telegram, Abidjan to Directorate of African and Malagasy Affairs, 27 February 1964; Raphaël-Leygues, 'Retour de Houphouët-Boigny à Côte d'Ivoire', 28 August 1963.

210 Directorate of African and Malagasy Affairs, 'Situation politique en Côte d'Ivoire', 29 August 1963; Military Advisor, French Embassy Abidjan, 'Rapport mensuel mois d'octobre 1965', 5 November 1965, GR14S251, SHD.

211 French Embassy Abidjan, 'Actualités politiques', 10 September 1963; Telegram, Abidjan to Paris, 31 August 1963.

212 Military advisor, French Embassy Abidjan, 'Rapport annuel pour 1965', 7 December 1965; Intelligence Exploitation Centre, Section B, 'Les problèmes de défense en Côte d'Ivoire', 23 January 1968; Telegram, Raphaël-Leygues to Directorate of African and Malagasy Affairs, 13 December 1963.

213 Military advisor, French Embassy Abidjan, 'Rapport mensuel septembre 1965', 4 October 1965.

214 Ministry of Armed Forces, SDECE, 'Sécurité: mesures prises par le président Houphouët-Boigny', 9 February 1966; Commander-in-chief Central Africa, 'Rapport du général commandant en chef désigné en Afrique centrale sur la mission qu'il a effectué en Afrique centrale du 12 au 21 mars 1970', 3 April 1970, 5AGF/1806, FFAN; US Embassy Abidjan, 'Assessment of Internal Situation in Ivory Coast', 22 January 1966; Rood, 'Ivorian internal security forces', 19 February 1964.

Ivorian security structures, as both Minister of Interior Germain Coffi Gadeau and Minister of Defence Jean Konan Banny were among those arrested.[215] Gadeau, who agreed to testify against other defendants, was acquitted.[216] Banny and five others received death sentences, although they were never executed.[217] It is believed that Gadeau and Banny were accused of involvement in the plot because they had protested against the harsh sentences levied against the alleged coup-plotters in January. It is also possible that Houphouët-Boigny felt a need to balance the ethnic composition of the accused plotters, as both ministers were Baoulé, and few Baoulé had been accused or convicted of being involved in the January plot.[218] The Bété, Malinké, and Senoufo were reportedly bitter about the fact that the crackdown in January had further centralized power into Baoulé hands.[219]

Targeting Baoulé ministers in August 1963 could thus have been intended as a way of easing ethnic tensions, although this does not explain why Gadeau was acquitted and Banny condemned to death. French officials had never hidden their negative views of Banny.[220] They were sensitive to public speeches Banny had made in which he mentioned the suffering of Ivorians during colonial rule and the need to turn the page.[221] Banny's admiration for socialism and his praise of the Guinean military and police had also irritated French authorities.[222] They viewed him as a problematic

---

[215] Directorate of African and Malagasy Affairs, 'Situation politique en Côte d'Ivoire', 29 August 1963.

[216] Perrier, 'Audience du Président Houphouët-Boigny', 25 June 1965; General Secretariat for African and Malagasy Affairs, 'Audience du cabinet du président de la république de Côte d'Ivoire', 8 June 1971, 5AGF/1783, FFAN.

[217] The verdict was delivered on 30 December 1964. Didier Ragunet to Ministry of Foreign Affairs, 'Mesures de clémence', 26 November 1965, 5AGF/1794, FFAN; Raphaël-Leygues, French Embassy Abidjan, to Ministry of Foreign Affairs, 'Libération des derniers détenus politiques', 26 May 1967, 5AGF/1800, FFAN.

[218] Diarra, *Les faux complots*, pp. 174–9 and 212–13.

[219] Raphaël-Leygues, 'Retour du Président Houphouët-Boigny en Côte d'Ivoire', 28 August 1963; French Embassy Abidjan, 'Fiches documentaires', 1963; Telegram, Abidjan to Paris, 17 August 1963, 324QONT/10, CADC.

[220] Ambassador of France in Côte d'Ivoire to Minister of Foreign Affairs, 'Situation politique du 30 juin au 6 juillet 1962', 7 July 1962; Brasseur to Minister of Cooperation, 'Organisation de l'armée ivoirienne et l'assistance militaire technique', 8 February 1963.

[221] French Embassy Abidjan, 'Rapport concernant Monsieur Banny Jean, Ministre de la Défense de Côte d'Ivoire', 15 November 1961; 'Problèmes militaires', 15 November 1961; Telegram, Abidjan to Paris, 12 September 1963.

[222] French Embassy Abidjan, 'Mission de M. Banny en Guinée', 15 November 1961, 1PO/1/1, CADN.

figure not only in Franco-Ivorian relations, but also domestically, and they were wary of Banny's political ambitions. He enjoyed considerable support among Ivorian youth, particularly young Baoulé.[223] However, the long-term fate of Banny exemplified the idiosyncrasy of Houphouët-Boigny's rule, as the minister's downfall was far from permanent. Banny was pardoned in 1967 and was eventually reinstated as minister of defence in 1981. His alleged co-conspirator Gadeau was also pardoned and appointed Secretary of State in 1971.[224]

It is fair to say that Houphouët-Boigny used a carrot-and-stick approach to controlling the armed forces, and Ivorian society more generally, offering economic benefits and cooptation with one hand while ordering arrests and coercion with the other. In fact, following the arrests of so many soldiers in August 1963, Houphouët-Boigny had taken a pause, directing economic rewards to forces he considered loyal before he risked carrying out further detentions. They re-started in January 1964, when nineteen officers and non-commissioned officers were arrested, ten of whom were Bété.[225] This was despite the fact that the Bété had little political power at the time, as they had been eliminated from the Ivorian government in early 1963 and would only re-enter it in 1966, when Bissouma Tapé was named minister of youth and sports.[226]

Despite several reshufflings of the Ivorian administration in 1963, there was a striking continuity in the key personnel who governed the Ivorian military from 1960 to 1973. Banny's successor Kouadio M'Bahia Blé served as minister of defence for eighteen years, before Banny was reinstated. Similarly, the first Chief of Staff of the Armed Forces, General Thomas d'Aquin Ouattara, held his post until 1974. The French did not consider this continuity in a positive light. They saw d'Aquin Ouattara as incompetent

---

223 French Embassy Abidjan, 'Rapport concernant Monsieur Banny Jean, Ministre de la Défense de Côte d'Ivoire', 15 November 1961.

224 Diarra, *Les faux complots*, p. 245. Perrier, 'Audience du Président Houphouët-Boigny', 25 June 1965; General Secretariat for African and Malagasy Affairs, 'Audience du cabinet du président de la république de Côte d'Ivoire', 8 June 1971; Ragunet, 'Mesures de clémence', 26 November 1965; Raphaël-Leygues, 'Libération des derniers détenus politiques', 26 May 1967.

225 French Embassy Abidjan, 'Fiches documentaires', 1963; Telegram, Abidjan to Paris, 21 February 1964, 324QONT/10, CADC; Telegram, French Embassy Abidjan to Directorate of African and Malagasy Affairs, 27 February 1964.

226 Plantey, General Secretariat for African and Malagasy Affairs, 'Affaire Tape', 6 February 1966, 5AGF/1795, FFAN; Perrier, General Secretariat for the Community, 'Note à l'attention de monsieur Journiac,' 12 December 1967, 5AGF/1805, FFAN.

and incapable of managing the armed forces, citing his temper, limited intelligence, and lack of leadership skills.[227] A French official complained in 1963, for example, that problems related to the disloyalty of Ivorian soldiers could be easily solved if the chief of staff would simply do his job rather than leaving it to his French advisor.[228] It must be said, though, that this offered the Ivorian president a certain degree of security, as it was unlikely that French officials or Ivorian soldiers would ever seek to replace him with d'Aquin Ouattara.

The French were not particularly fond of Minister of Defence Kouadio M'Bahia Blé, either. In 1966, he had objected to the visit of a French inspector to a military base in Bouaké,[229] and criticized the fact that France were maintaining a military base on Ivorian territory.[230] There were also tensions between M'Bahia Blé and General d'Aquin Ouattara, which did nothing to improve the popularity of M'Bahia Blé among Ivorian soldiers.[231] Indeed, by the late 1960s, a number of Ivorian officers were unhappy that their superior officers had not been disciplined for their corruption and dishonesty.[232] M'Bahia Blé's appointment also created jealousy among the Ivorian political elite.[233] In 1965, Director of National Security Pierre Goba suggested that the gendarmerie should be transferred from the defence minister's purview to that of the minister of security and interior, arguing that it was dangerous to leave both the army and the gendarmerie under the direction of a single individual.[234] This did not come to fruition, and

227 French Embassy Abidjan, 'Malaise au sein de l'armée ivoirienne', 6 July 1965; Telegram, Abidjan to Ragunet, Paris, 6 July 1965; Telegram, Raphaël-Leygues to Directorate of African and Malagasy Affairs, 13 August 1969.
228 Telegram, Abidjan to Paris, 31 August 1963.
229 Ministry of Armed Forces, SDECE, 'Attitude antifrançaise du ministre ivoirien des forces armées', 17 February 1966, 5AGF/1795, FFAN.
230 Ibid; Perrier, Technical Advisor, Intelligence Exploitation Centre, Section B, 'Attitude du ministre ivoirien des forces armées', 1 March 1966.
231 Telegram, Raphaël-Leygues, Abidjan, to Paris, 7 January 1966, 5AGF/1795, FFAN.
232 French Embassy Abidjan, 'Rapport mensuel mois de juillet 1969', 6 August 1969, GR14S252, SHD; Diefenbacher, Ministry of Interior Director of International Police Technical Cooperation Services, to Foccart, 'Note sur le mécontentement chez les jeunes officiers de l'armée ivoirienne', 4 July 1969, 5AGF/1805, FFAN.
233 Plantey, 'Affaire tape', 6 February 1966.
234 Ragunet, Chargé d'affaires, to Ministry of Foreign Affairs, 'Perspective d'un remaniement ministériel éventuel', 8 December 1965, 5AGF/1794, FFAN.

while M'Bahia Blé remained in his post, it was Goba who was forced to step down in 1969, accused of misuse of public funds.[235]

Though M'Bahia Blé questioned the French military presence in Côte d'Ivoire, Houphouët-Boigny still felt that the arrangement decreased the likelihood of a military coup.[236] It was at his request that France maintained a military base, with some 300 French soldiers, adjacent to the airport in Abidjan.[237] Notably, the US concurred with Houphouët-Boigny that the presence of these troops deterred any potential coups in Côte d'Ivoire due to 'the general belief that the French would intervene.'[238] This was another hangover from colonialism that served as a source of criticism among the population and among Ivorian soldiers, as the French military was not only present, but French technical assistants also continued to play key roles in the decision-making and governance of the Ivorian armed forces, long after independence. The Africanization of Ivorian security structures had simply never been a priority for Houphouët-Boigny.[239] In fact, in the instances when he had ostensibly done so, the Ivorian president was still accused of having more confidence in the French than in his fellow countrymen.[240] For example, in 1962, Houphouët-Boigny had appointed his brother-in-law Casimir Brou as Director of National Security, but he nevertheless retained the French commissioner Brou had replaced to serve as his advisor.[241]

American officials speculated whether the reassurances of the French technical assistants in the Ivorian military that soldiers would carry out

235 State Minister in charge of National Defence, SDECE 'Note d'information sur Côte d'Ivoire: les rivalités ethniques dans le contexte politique actuel', 3 October 1969; Diefenbacher, Ministry of Interior Director of International Police Technical Cooperation Services, to Foccart, 'Enquête sur l'ancien directeur de la sûreté nationale de Côte d'Ivoire', 17 July 1969, 5AGF/1805, FFAN.

236 Telegram, Abidjan to Directorate of African and Malagasy Affairs, 27 February 1964.

237 Presidency of the Republic, Naval Vice-Admiral of the Special Staff, 'Les forces française en Côte d'Ivoire', 17 December 1966; General Secretariat for the Community, 'Audience du président Houphouët-Boigny', 8 April 1970.

238 US Embassy Abidjan, 'Assessment of Internal Situation in Ivory Coast', 22 January 1966. Also see US Embassy Abidjan, 'Assessment of military coup possibilities', 9 April 1964.

239 Houphouët-Boigny, 'L'armée et l'école doivent creuser de l'unité', 3 January 1970; Giraudon, 'l'ivoirisation de cadres', 11 September 1973; Courage, 'Procès des capitaines Yoro Diakite et Malik Diallo', 2 August 1972.

240 Rood, 'Ivorian internal security forces', 19 February 1964; US Embassy Abidjan, 'Assessment of military coup possibilities', 9 April 1964.

241 Ambassador of France in Côte d'Ivoire to Minister of Foreign Affairs, 'Situation politique du 30 juin au 6 juillet 1962' 7 July 1962.

the orders of the Ivorian government actually held any weight.[242] Indeed, French diplomat Alain Plantey contended that the hasty formation of the Ivorian armed forces had created conditions ripe for subversion. While Plantey deemed the Ivorian military to be of 'zero value', he noted that its ethnic heterogeneity had fostered a sense of unity, as a function of the shared identity of soldiers as part of a national force. In his opinion, the country's prognosis was poor, as its stability relied on the personal role of Houphouët-Boigny in controlling the military. 'Sooner than later', he predicted, 'this useless force, unsuited for its role of defending the borders, will ... end up being a danger to Côte d'Ivoire.'[243]

In 1970, a decade after independence, French technical assistants were still in command of the Ivorian navy and air force, and instructed in Ivorian military schools.[244] The French base was politically problematic for Houphouët-Boigny by this time, generating both popular discontent and criticism within the armed forces.[245] In 1973, a French intelligence report warned about the dissatisfaction of Ivorian soldiers with the ongoing French military presence, noting that some soldiers believed French troops were being used to keep the Ivorian president in power.[246] Nonetheless, it was not until 1974 that most French assistants had been transferred from command posts, although they still continued to serve in important technical and advisory roles.[247] Moreover, to domestic audiences, the Ivorian government framed French military aid as an altruistic gesture, free of any ulterior motive. According to Houphouët-Boigny, the French gained nothing from maintaining a military base in Côte d'Ivoire and would be relieved when the Ivorians could take responsibility for their own defence.[248] He implied that French assistance was an unavoidable necessity due to the capacity of Ivorian forces, and even a burden on France. It was, of course, the Ivorian

---

[242] Rood, 'Ivorian internal security forces', 19 February 1964; US Embassy Abidjan, 'Assessment of military coup possibilities', 9 April 1964.

[243] Plantey, 'Affaire tape', 6 February 1966.

[244] Couetdic, 'Note sur les forces armées ivoiriennes et sur notre assistance technique en Côte d'ivoire', 17 March 1970.

[245] Ambassador of France in Côte d'Ivoire to Ministry of Foreign Affairs, 'Situation politique du 22 au 28 septembre, 29 September 1962; General Secretariat for the Community, 'Audience du président Houphouët-Boigny', 15 July 1969.

[246] Minister of the Armed Forces, SDECE, 'Côte d'Ivoire: les progrès de opposition', 14 May 1973.

[247] Raphaël-Leygues, 'La Côte d'Ivoire et l'armée', 30 August 1974.

[248] Speech by Houphouët-Boigny to the National Assembly, 15 January 1962; President Houphouët-Boigny, Message to parliament, 3 August 1961.

president himself who had systematically undermined the capacity of his own military.

Publicly, Houphouët-Boigny had long underscored that Ivorian national forces were forces of peace. He insisted they would never attack another country, creating the impression that Ivorian soldiers had no meaningful role in providing security. France's continued military presence had reportedly led to dissatisfaction within the military as early as 1963, particularly among young officers, who could see their opportunities shrinking.[249] The situation did not improve over time, as Houphouët-Boigny intentionally fostered division among Ivorian forces.[250] Young officers thus remained apprehensive about their future prospects, increasingly criticized their superiors for being dishonest and incapable, and resented the role of French assistants in the Ivorian military.[251] Aware of this discontent among soldiers, the Ivorian government made the cooptive decision in the late 1960s to change how it trained its forces, so that military capacity building corresponded to the needs of the civilian administration.[252]

Although the strategies Houphouët-Boigny employed to control the Ivorian armed forces and Ivorian society were certainly less violent than those used by Touré in Guinea, the Ivorian president's rule was neither politically liberal nor non-violent.[253] Houphouët-Boigny himself admitted as much when he explained his response to alleged coup plots in 1963 by quoting Goethe in a speech: 'I prefer injustice to disorder: one can die of disorder, one cannot die of injustice. An injustice can be repaired.' Even so, in the same speech, he downplayed his own role in punishing the plotters, emphasizing that it had been the PDCI that had made the ultimate decisions.[254]

The Ivorian military certainly played its part in manifesting Houphouët-Boigny's Goethian preference for injustice over disorder. In 1968, the French ambassador described the Ivorian armed forces as a discreet but effective auxiliary to the civilian government that had not hesitated to suppress the

---

249 Telegram, Abidjan to Paris, 31 August 1963.
250 Telegram, Raphaël-Leygues to Directorate of African and Malagasy Affairs, 13 December 1963.
251 See documents in Files 5AGF/1803, 5AGF/1805, 5AGF/1813, 5AGF/1795, 5AGF/1793, and 5AGF/1812, FFAN.
252 Raphaël-Leygues to Ministry of Foreign Affairs, 'Situation intérieure', 17 December 1968.
253 Diarra, *Les faux complots*, p. 238.
254 'Conférence de presse du président Félix Houphouët-Boigny sur la politique intérieure', 10 September 1963.

protests that had erupted in response to unpopular Ivorian foreign policy decisions, a high rate of unemployment, and the large number of foreign workers in the country.[255] The military had participated in operations against student protests in 1969,[256] and against regional popular protests in Aboisso in 1969 and Gagnoa in 1970.[257] According to General Koné, commandant of the Ivorian gendarmerie from 1964 to 1974, Houphouët-Boigny played a personal role in deciding on the use of force in these cases.[258]

These internal operations negatively impacted the armed forces and left soldiers with a lingering sense of professional unease. Following the repression of student protests in 1969, the US Embassy noted that 'the first battalion's "action" against the university has hardly covered it with glory ... nor does it seem likely that running an oversize reformatory for recalcitrant students meets the army's own notion of its mission.'[259] General d'Aquin Ouattara was particularly displeased about having to use force against students. According to American officials, he was 'put in the doghouse' for his open criticism, but was 'the type of man to stay loyal even when kicked.'[260]

Regional protests in 1969 and 1970 involved the opposition, which was organized along ethnic lines. The Bété in particular sought to confront what they saw as their exclusion from Ivorian economic and political life.[261]

255 Raphaël-Leygues to Ministry of Foreign Affairs, 'Situation intérieure', 17 December 1968.
256 US Embassy Abidjan to Department of State, 'The Ivory Coast Student Strike: A preliminary assessment', 29 May 1969, POLIVCAST 1967–1969, Box 2240, CGRDS, NARA.
257 Diefenbacher, Ministry of Interior Director of International Police Technical Cooperation Services, to Foccart, 'Note sur l'affaire du Sanwi en Côte d'Ivoire', 9 January 1970, 5AGF/1806, FFAN; Military advisor, French Embassy Abidjan, to Paris, 'Le Sanwi', 29 October 1970, 5AGF/1806, FFAN; SDECE, 'Côte d'Ivoire situation dans la région de Gagnoa', 1 December 1970, 5AGF/1806, FFAN; General Secretariat for the Community, 'Audience du président Houphouët-Boigny auprès de Gaulle', 16 April 1969.
258 Koné, interview by author, 26 November 2015, Abidjan.
259 US Embassy Abidjan, 'The Ivory Coast Student Strike: A preliminary assessment', 29 May 1969.
260 Ibid.
261 Perrier, General Secretariat for the Community, 'Note à l'attention de monsieur Journiac,' 12 December 1967; State Minister in charge of National Defence, SDECE, 'Note d'information sur Côte d'Ivoire: les rivalités ethniques dans le contexte politique actuel', 3 October 1969; Dubois, Chargé d'affaires, French Embassy Abidjan, to Ministry of Foreign Affairs, 'Chômage et désœuvrement chez les jeunes appelés du service militaires en Côte d'Ivoire', 4 September 1969, 5AGF/1805, FFAN.

When their discontent took the form of mass protest, the government did not hesitate to use armed force in response. In October 1970, the Ivorian military was deployed against approximately 200 Bété demonstrators in Gagnoa, who were protesting their lack of representation in the state administration. The operation was criticized by both French and US officials for an excessive use of force and slow deployment. The French reported that four Ivorian army infantry companies and one mobile gendarmerie unit had been sent to the region to re-establish order after local gendarmes had been attacked by protestors. Estimates of civilian deaths ranged from one hundred to five hundred, whereas the armed forces suffered only a few casualties.[262]

Even after the leader had been arrested, Ivorian troops remained deployed in Gagnoa, in what the US Embassy described as a military occupation,[263] even though French officials insisted that further violence would erupt between local Bété and Baoulé if Ivorian soldiers left the region.[264] In December 1969, Ivorian soldiers and gendarmes were deployed against the Sanwi separatist movement in Aboisso, near the Ghanaian border. The movement had been campaigning since 1960 to establish the independent Kingdom of Sanwi, a territory of the Agni people. During 1969, 200 Agni were arrested by Ivorian forces.[265]

262 Colonel Charles, 'L'armée en Côte d'Ivoire', 27 November 1970, 5AGF/1806, FFAN; General Secretariat for National Defence, 'Incidents à Gagnoa', 30 October 1970; French Embassy Abidjan, 'Cérémonie de réconciliation à Gagnoa après les incidents du moins d'October', 17 December 1970, 5AGF/1806, FFAN; SDECE, 'Côte d'Ivoire situation dans la région de Gagnoa', 1 December 1970; Military advisor, French Embassy Abidjan, to Paris, 29 October 1970; Rood, US Embassy Abidjan, 'Events at Gagnoa: The informational aspect', 11 December 1970, POLIVCAST 1970–1973, Box 2399, CGRDS, NARA; US Embassy Abidjan to Department of State, 'Localized dissident group draws prompt suppression', 3 December 1970, POLIVCAST 1970–1973, Box 2399, CGRDS, NARA.
263 US Embassy Abidjan, 'The Guerbie Problem and National Unity', 5 March 1971; Rood, 'Events at Gagnoa: The informational aspect', 11 December 1970.
264 SDECE, 'Côte d'Ivoire situation dans la region de Gagnoa', 1 December 1970; Telegram, Raphaël-Leygues, Abidjan, to Directorate of African and Malagasy Affairs, 9 December 1967; General Secretariat for the Community, 'Audience du président Houphouët-Boigny auprès de Gaulle', 16 April 1969; US Embassy Abidjan, 'The Guerbie Problem and National Unity', 5 March 1971.
265 Diefenbacher to Foccart, 'Note sur l'affaire du Sanwi en Côte d'Ivoire', 9 January 1970; Diefenbacher, Ministry of Interior Director of International Police Technical Cooperation Services, to Foccart, 'Note sur une reprise des activités du mouvement séparatiste du Sanwi en Côte d'Ivoire', 11 December 1969, 5AGF/1805, FFAN; Telegram, Raphaël-Leygues to General Secretary for African and Malagasy Affairs, 'Renaissance

While the Ivorian government belittled the Sanwi movement and attributed the protests in Gagnoa to a single individual, French and American observers agreed that events in 1969 and 1970 were more significant than Ivorian officials were willing to admit and were linked to broader issues of uneven development and the ethnic polarization of state institutions.[266] French reports alluded to long-running animosities between the Bété and Baoulé, for example, and noted the deterioration of economic and political opportunity for the Bété – whose land ownership rights had been undermined by the policies of Houphouët-Boigny.[267] French and US officials also highlighted what they saw as 'over-management' of the media on the part of Ivorian authorities, in order to maintain a public silence about what had taken place in Aboisso and Gagnoa. This silence left space for rumours and may even have raised popular interest, leading the population to seek information through unofficial channels.[268]

The French director of police technical cooperation reported to Jacques Foccart that Ivorians tended to get their information by listening to Guinean or Voltaic radio.[269] He argued that 'within one week of the Gagnoa disturbances, there could have been few people in Abidjan who were unaware that something had happened and was happening', but said 'the government news media ignore[d] the developments completely.' He described this lack of state media coverage as 'one of the most striking aspects of the Gagnoa episode'. In fact, the US reported that Ivorian state media made no mention

---

du mouvement Sanwi', 4 December 1969, 5AGF/1805, FFAN, and 'Résurgence du mouvement autonomiste "Sanwi"', 3 December 1969, 5AGF/1805, FFAN.

266 US Embassy Abidjan, 'The Guerbie Problem and National Unity', 5 March 1971; Rood, 'Events at Gagnoa: The informational aspect', 11 December 1970; Minister of Armed Forces, SDECE, 'Côte d'Ivoire les progrès de opposition', 14 May 1973; General Secretariat for National Defence, 'Incidents à Gagnoa', 30 October 1970; SDECE, 'Côte d'Ivoire situation dans la région de Gagnoa', 1 December 1970; Diefenbacher to Foccart, 'Note sur une reprise des activités du mouvement séparatiste du Sanwi en Côte d'Ivoire', 11 December 1969.

267 SDECE, 'Côte d'ivoire situation dans la région de Gagnoa', 1 December 1970; General Secretariat for the Community, 'Audience du président Houphouët-Boigny auprès de Gaulle', 16 April 1969.

268 SDECE, 'Côte d'Ivoire situation dans la région de Gagnoa', 1 December 1970 ; Diefenbacher to Foccart, 'Note sur une reprise des activités du mouvement séparatiste du Sanwi en Côte d'Ivoire', 11 December 1969.

269 Ministry of Interior, Director of International Police Technical Cooperation Services, to Jacques Foccart, 'Note sur des critiques formulées en Côte d'Ivoire contre la politique gouvernmentale dans le domaine de l'information', 27 January 1970, 5AGF/1806, FFAN; Rood, 'Events at Gagnoa: The informational aspect', December 11, 1970.

of any casualties in Gagnoa until one month after the events. According to the editor of the state newspaper, this was driven by the Ivorian president's desire to show the best face of Côte d'Ivoire to the world.[270] To that end, Houphouët-Boigny had complained to the French ambassador when *Le Monde* reported in real time that the Sanwi operation had resulted in numerous causalities in the Aboisso region. Houphouët-Boigny found it unacceptable that the world be informed about the Ivorian regime killing its own citizens.[271]

However, the reverberations of these operations, especially their negative impact on the military, were far deeper at home than they were on the international stage. In June 1973, when thirteen young Ivorian officers – mainly from the Guéré, Bété, and Yacouba minority ethnic groups – stood accused of plotting to assassinate the president, they cited a fear of potential ethnic conflict as their motivation. French reports indicated that these young conspirators believed they could 'prevent a crisis' by establishing a military regime and that the army was the only institution capable of ensuring national unity.[272] According to French officials, the organizers of the plot had been traumatized by military operations against the Beté in Gagnoa.[273] Their plot was condemned by the public and, unlike in 1963, no special court was established and their adjudication was left to the military court, in order that the Ivorian government could not be implicated in the affair. The judgements were severe. Seven officers were condemned to death and four received long sentences of forced labour.[274]

In the aftermath of the 1973 coup allegations, Houphouët-Boigny created more civilian opportunities for young soldiers. Two young officers were even given ministerial positions, and fifteen soldiers were named sub-prefects.

---

270 Rood, 'Events at Gagnoa: The informational Aspect' December 11, 1970.

271 Telegram, Raphaël-Leygues to General Secretary for African and Malagasy Affairs, 31 December 1969, 5AGF/1805, FFAN.

272 Giraudon, Chargé d'affaires, to Minister of Foreign Affairs, Jobert, 'Synthèse Politique 1 au 31 août 1973', 15 September 1973, 1PO/1/4, CADN; General Secretariat for the Community, 'Audience du président Houphouët-Boigny', 14 October 1973, 5AGF/535, FFAN.

273 Raphaël-Leygues to Minister of Foreign Affairs, Jobert, 'Complot des jeunes officiers contre le régime ivoirien', 13 September 1973.

274 Giraudon to Minister of Foreign Affairs, Jobert, 'Synthèse Politique 1 au 31 août 1973', 15 September, 1973; General Secretariat for the Community, 'Audience du président Houphouët-Boigny', 14 October 1973; Raphaël-Leygues to Minister of Foreign Affairs, Jobert, 'Complot des jeunes officiers contre le régime ivoirien', 13 September 1973.

Soon thereafter, the training for army soldiers and civilian administrators was combined, so that both would attain the general competence for state administration. While Ivorian navy and air force officers were still being trained in France, the hope was that the skills of the army would better reflect the needs of Ivorian society.[275] According to the French, these developments were received favourably by young officers, who took some satisfaction in 'the prospect of being integrated into the working life of the country.'[276] There were also changes to the leadership of the Ivorian armed forces in 1974, when Chief of Staff d'Aquin Ouattara – who was not particularly popular – was replaced by his deputy, General Ibrahima Coulibaly. This could be seen as a concession to younger officers, and an attempt to address the grievances of soldiers in general.[277]

Although Coulibaly was better trained than d'Aquin Ouattara, Houphouët-Boigny nonetheless remained sceptical of the value of the Ivorian military, telling the French ambassador in 1974 that 'the Ivorian armed force costs more than it is worth to the state.'[278] The Ivorian president thus saw no reason to increase the capacities of the national military. This policy of neglect was later connected to the poor performance of Ivorian troops in 2002, almost a decade after Houphouët-Boigny's death, when rebels from the north launched an attack towards the capital. By then, years of disregard for the military had left Côte d'Ivoire with a force unprepared for combat.[279]

Interestingly, the policies and legacies of Houphouët-Boigny are often viewed as having contributed to the Ivorian military's weakness in 2002, but less so to the military coup in 1999. The 2002 rebellion is seen to extend directly from the legacy of his patrimonial system, which led to uneven

[275] Officers school and the school for state administration were united into a single polytechnic school with three branches: administration, military, and public works. See Ambassador Jacques Raphaël-Leygues, to Minister of Foreign Affairs Jean Sauvagnargues, 'Synthèse politique du 1 June au 31 July 1974', 19 August 1974.

[276] Raphaël-Leygues, to Minister of Foreign Affairs, Jean Sauvagnargues, 'Synthèse politique du 1 juin au 31 juillet 1974', 19 August 1974.

[277] Ibid; French Embassy Abidjan, 'Malaise au sein de l'armée ivoirienne', 6 July 1965; Telegram, Abidjan to Ragunet, Paris, 6 July 1965; Telegram, Raphaël-Leygues, Abidjan, to Paris, 7 January 1966; Telegram, Raphaël-Leygues to Directorate of African and Malagasy Affairs, 13 August 1969.

[278] Houphouët-Boigny quoted in Ambassadeur de la France en Côte d'Ivoire, Ambassador Jacques Raphaël-Leygues, 'La Côte d'Ivoire et l'armée', 30 August 1974.

[279] Azoumana Ouattara, 'Le coup d'état de décembre 1999 ou la fin de l'exception militaire ivoirienne: les mutations de l'armée ivoirienne depuis 1960' in Côte d'Ivoire: la réinvention de soi dans la violence, edited by Francis Akindès (Dakar: CODESRIA, 2011), pp. 169–212; Kieffer, 'Armée ivoirienne : le refus du déclassement', pp. 30–6.

development of the northern and southern parts of the country, unresolved problems related to citizenship and land-owning rights, and in the 1980s, a deteriorating economic situation and a power vacuum in the wake of Houphouët-Boigny's death. The 1999 military coup, on the other hand, is thought to be connected mostly to events and conditions that occurred after his death, rather than to policy decisions the Ivorian president during his rule. Studies have suggested that the coup was caused by discontent among soldiers due to the decreasing military budget, worsening conditions for soldiers and the increasing corruption of their superiors, fewer opportunities for soldiers to obtain administrative positions, the use of soldiers to establish and maintain domestic security, and ethnic favouritism in promotions and recruitment.[280] Even so, these factors and problems cannot be disentangled from the strategies Houphouët-Boigny used to control the armed forces – which left Ivorian soldiers lacking a shared strategic purpose[281]

From personal to institutional control under Senghor

To all intents and purposes, the approach of President Senghor in Senegal was the opposite of that taken by Houphouët-Boigny. Senghor made efforts to share responsibility for control of the military, and to guarantee the existence of feedback channels between himself and young officers. The structure of Senegal's government also differed from other francophone West African states. Power was shared between the president and prime minister (at least, initially), and the responses of the government to opposition and various pressure groups were more permissive and less violent than in other countries in the region.[282] However, Senegal's economic policies were not strictly liberal, and its economic potential was limited. Additionally, the country's public administration was quickly undermined by apathy and corruption. Not long after independence, French officials were already claiming that 'French technical assistants assured the functioning of the state apparatus' in Senegal, as 'the highest state officials were only interested in

---

280 Ibid.
281 Azoumana Ouattara, 'L'armée dans la construction de la nation ivoirienne' in *Frontières de la citoyenneté et violence politique en Côte d'Ivoire*, edited by Jean-Bernard Ouédraogo and Ebrima Sall (Dakar: CODESRIA, 2008), p. 150.
282 State Secretariat for Relations with the States of the Community, 'Relative à l'évolution de la situation politiques intérieure au Sénégal', 3 May1961, 5AGF/607, FFAN.

their personal benefits'.[283] – or the fact that this control relied on a single individual.

Incompetence and dishonesty in the civil administration generated dissatisfaction among Senegalese soldiers. This compounded problems for the Chief of the Defence Staff, Colonel Idrissa Fall, who faced challenges to his authority because many young officers had little respect for him due to his lack of combat experience.[284] US officials estimated that a potential threat to President Senghor could come from inside his government, for example, Minister of Interior Valdiodio N'diaye, who controlled the security forces and was considered to be ambitious. In 1962, the US Embassy concluded that the significant number of French assistants within the Senegalese armed and security forces had contributed to 'an excellent intelligence network which would doubtless immediately alert the French to any serious internal security threat.'[285]

The main challenge to Senghor did not come from N'diaye or other security actors, though, but from the country's first prime minister, Mamadou Dia, whose socialist policies had inspired domestic opposition by threatening the economic interests of politically powerful religious leaders. According to the French ambassador, Dia's insistence on carrying out economic reforms created conflict within the Senegalese government that exacerbated existing personal rivalries.[286] Further, the army became entangled in these political tensions when it received two conflicting orders from the prime minister and the president. When Fall refused to take sides and Senghor replaced him with Jean-Alfred Diallo.[287] Fall was not imprisoned, but he had trouble finding employment after his dismissal from the army because companies feared potential political repercussions were they to offer him a job.[288]

These internal struggles culminated in Dia's arrest at the end of 1962, when he and three other ministers were accused of planning a coup d'état. All received prison sentences but were amnestied in 1976. The details of events surrounding their arrests as well as the army's role in the affair remain disputed to this day. One former soldier who was interviewed for this study

283 Ibid.
284 Ibid.
285 US Embassy Dakar, 'Senegal Internal Security', 6 June 1962.
286 Paye, 'La crise gouvernementale au Sénégal', 28 December 1962, 184PO1–400, CADN.
287 Interview by author, July 2019, Dakar.
288 Lieutenant-Colonel Labarra, 'Visite du General Fall', 3 November 1964, AG/5F/2683, FFAN.

emphasized that it was politicians, not soldiers, who were the source of conflict in 1962.[289] Nevertheless, the coup allegations negatively impacted the Senegalese security apparatus, driving a wedge between the army and gendarmerie and creating divisions within the security forces, especially between officers from different ethnic backgrounds. It only complicated matters that Chief of Staff Diallo was initially quite unpopular.[290]

Diallo was close to Senghor and to French officials, reflecting his dual nationality as an '*originaire*' – the term used to denote Africans born in Dakar, to whom French citizenship had been granted during the colonial period. Diallo's dual nationality also extended from his parentage, as his father was a French and his mother a local. The French ambassador claimed that Diallo was unable to command Senegalese officers because his status as an *originaire* meant he did not understand how to treat the '*broussards*' (bushmen).[291] When President Senghor undertook efforts to ensure his control of the military by reorganizing it, Diallo's popularity suffered further, as officers were transferred to the interior until it was assured that they did not hold anti-government views. Diallo stated publicly that the transfers had not been decided by him, but by members of the president's entourage.[292]

In 1963, two of Diallo's rivals were sent abroad, including Lieutenant-Colonel Claude Mademba-Sy, who was dispatched to Paris. According to French reports, Senegalese soldiers would have preferred to have Mademba-Sy as Chief of Staff. Perhaps aware of this, Mademba-Sy told friends that 'he was young enough to wait' and that he found his post in Paris fulfilling, 'especially on a material level'.[293] It was part of Senghor's strategy to manage conflicts within the military by sending soldiers abroad, to diplomatic postings or for training, leading the French ambassador to note with some sarcasm that the Senegalese president seemed likely to send his whole army to France.[294] Yet, all joking aside, these efforts by Senghor to control the Senegalese armed forces did not permanently compromise

289 Interview by author, July 2019, Dakar.
290 General Secretary for African and Malagasy Affairs, 'Situation politique au Sénégal', 21 August 1963, 5AGF/607, FFAN; Paye to Ministry of Foreign Affairs, 1 August 1963; Military Advisor, Dakar, 'état d'esprit de l'armée et de la gendarmerie vue par la sureté nationale', 11 October 1963, 184P01–325, CADN.
291 French Embassy Dakar, 'Dans l'armée sénégalaise', 19 March 1963, 184P01–325, CADN.
292 French Embassy Dakar, 'Malaise dans l'armée sénégalaise', 1 August 1963, INVA321, CADC; Paye to Ministry of Foreign Affairs, 1 August 1963.
293 Ibid.
294 French Embassy Dakar, 23 March 1964, 184PO1–394, CADN.

national military capacities, as in Côte d'Ivoire, and were clearly less violent than in Guinea and Mali.

The political situation in Senegal was tense in 1963, and a presidential election in which Senghor ran as the sole candidate triggered protests. The government responded by asking France to provide tear gas, grenades, and barbed wire to ensure crowd control. French authorities questioned whether this would be enough to manage the situation, and further speculated whether the Senegalese military forces and gendarmes would remain loyal to the government in the event of large-scale popular demonstrations.[295] The successful military coup in Congo in August 1963 undoubtedly led Senghor to view the situation in his own country as even more grave. He soon had four parliamentarians in the southern and eastern parts of the country arrested, but silence from the government about these arrests encouraged harmful rumours.[296] In September, when the Senegalese army and gendarmerie were commanded to quell continuing protests, the French military attaché reported that 'the president witnessed the almost total defection of both services.'[297] However, in December 1963, forces from the army and gendarmerie were again ordered to intervene, and this time they complied. Apparently, they opened fire against protestors, killing somewhere between ten and forty people.[298]

Continuing protests, problems in the organization of Senegalese security forces, and Senghor's precarious political position increased the political power of the military. In May 1964, when Diallo asked to be included in political decision-making, the president hesitantly agreed.[299] Senegalese officers remained concerned about government corruption,[300] and Diallo himself expressed disdain about the inefficiency and incompetence of the civilian administration, condemning both their political bickering and the

---

[295] Ministry of Foreign Affairs, 'L'état d'esprit dans l'armée sénégalaise', 1963, 184P01–325, CADN.

[296] SDECE, 'Note d'information situation au Sénégal', 20 August 1963, 5AGF/607, FFAN.

[297] Military advisor, Dakar, 'État d'esprit de l'armée et de la gendarmerie vue par la sûreté nationale', 11 October 1963.

[298] French Embassy Dakar, 'Situation politique', 23 May 1964, 184PO1–394, CADN, and 'Affaires administratives', 22 May 1964, 184PO1–394, CADN.

[299] Ibid.

[300] French Embassy Dakar, 'L'état d'esprit dans l'armée sénégalaise', 18 September 1964, 184PO/1/325, AND.

government's tendency to engage 'with various pressure groups whose real power is greatly exaggerated'.[301]

In August of that year, Senghor recognized the need to reorganize the gendarmerie and police. In an interview, a former Senegalese soldier noted that these forces had sided with Prime Minister Dia during the 1962 constitutional crisis.[302] In 1964, it was suspected that the gendarmerie still harboured sympathies for Dia, and the police were plagued by systemic corruption. Senghor replaced Ahmed Fall, the commandant of the gendarmerie, for failing to ensure discipline and for meeting with Dia in Kedougou. Senghor did this discreetly by sending Fall to France for training. Senghor put Tamsir Ba at the head of the gendarmerie, but Ba also had problems securing his command of the forces, and he also succeeded in making a personal enemy of the French technical assistant responsible for gendarmerie equipment.[303]

Police reform proved even more of a challenge. By 1962, a US Embassy security assessment had noted that Senegalese police were prone to corruption and political influences.[304] When Senghor tried to address the problem of corrupt officers in 1964, those involved found new ways to continue their illicit activities. The president was forced to enact stiffer measures when this corruption became increasingly visible, as officers were investing their illegal gains in houses, taxis, and trucks.[305] Senghor reorganized the police in such a way that the army was given a larger role in assuring public security and border control. He also recruited non-commissioned officers who had been released from the French army into the police forces. Senghor believed that problems in the police were the result of Africanizing the agency with too much haste.[306] Although the president generally emphasized training over

[301] US Embassy Dakar, 'General Diallo stresses need for work and discipline in Senegal', 10 August 1965, DEF 1964–66, Box 1694, CGRDS, NARA.
[302] Interview by author, June 2019, Dakar.
[303] Plantey to M. Mouriradian, 17 June 1964, AG/5F/2683, FFAN; French Embassy Dakar, 'Informations militaires', 27 August 1964, 184P01–325, CADN.
[304] US Embassy Dakar, 'Senegal Internal Security', 6 June 1962.
[305] Ambassador Jean de Lagarde, 'Les forces de l'ordre au Sénégal', 29 August 1964, 184P01–325, CADN.
[306] French Embassy Dakar, 'Réorganisation des services de sécurité', 14 November 1964, 184P01–325, CADN, 'L'affaire de police', 10 October 1964, 184P01–325, CADN, and 'Les coups d'état en Afrique', 7 January 1966, 184PO1–517, CADN; de Lagarde, 'Les forces de l'ordre au Sénégal', 29 August 1964.

a reliance on French technical assistance, his defence minister asked the French to increase the number of technical assistants, but they refused.[307]

Senghor's was in a stronger position by 1965, even though he still had to lean on the military to bolster his legitimacy.[308] In a New Year address, Senghor praised Senegalese soldiers in a discourse described by French officials as a form of 'moral blackmail' that was intended to convince the armed forces to the side with him, as he knew he would need their help again soon. According to the French, some soldiers were displeased that Diallo had been promoted to general, which they saw as political favouritism.[309] While Diallo's personal loyalty to Senghor was assured, but French observers doubted whether Diallo's own men would follow him in case of popular protests.[310] The view of American officials, however, was that Diallo could step in to assure stability if Senghor was assassinated, but that the military may not be loyal to Senghor if Diallo was assassinated.[311] Perhaps Senghor suspected this himself, as his personal plane was piloted by a French crew.[312]

As both the unemployment rate and the price of goods rose between 1967 and 1969, the resulting economic difficulties generated political contestations that once again forced Senghor to rely on the military.[313] In May 1968, when the army was used against student and labour union protests, young Senegalese officers grew keenly aware of their political power. The Senegalese government had little choice but to take their opinions into consideration. In June 1968, these officers communicated through Diallo that the corruption of government officials needed to be put to a stop, leading Senghor to make ministerial changes and to personally assume the role of minister of defence. He continued to have doubts about the loyalty of the armed forces, and sought to limit their power by re-establishing a

[307] De Lagarde, Dakar, to Paris, 6 October 1964, AG/5F/2683, FFAN.

[308] General Secretary for African and Malagasy Affairs, 'Audience du président Leopold Senghor', 22 July 1965.

[309] International Police Technical Cooperation Service, 'Etat d'esprit de l'armée Sénégalaise' 2 January 1965, AG/5F/2683, FFAN.

[310] French Embassy Dakar, 'Les coups d'état en Afrique', 7 January 1966; Courage, 'Procès des capitaines Yoro Diakite et Malik Diallo', 2 August 1972.

[311] US Embassy Dakar, 'Politico-Economic Assessment', 26 March 1967, SENPOL 1967–69, Box 2477, CGRDS, NARA.

[312] Interview by author, July 2019, Dakar.

[313] General Secretary for African and Malagasy Affairs, 'Audience du président Senghor', 16 April 1968, 5AGF/609, FFAN.

balance between labour unions, politicians, and the administration. He also reorganized the Republican Guard.[314]

The intervention of the military in the political protests had increased the personal power of Chief of Staff Diallo. Several months later, a French military attaché reported that he had become the most important man in Senegal. Diallo continued to be a controversial figure nonetheless, due to his mixed origins, his isolation at the top of the army hierarchy, and his clear exploitation of the position to ensure himself a profitable retirement.[315] In an interview, one officer also said that Diallo was seen by many soldiers as too French, having served in the French army, and that some soldiers doubted Diallo could even speak Wolof.[316] Both his daughters had also married French men. Despite this, French intelligence indicated that Diallo somehow managed to wall himself off from growing disputes within the military and seemed to be the only person capable of holding the forces together in early 1969. [317]

French intelligence warned that the Senegalese military was becoming increasingly politicized and internally divided, and that soldiers had learned two lessons from domestic protests: authority and discipline were necessary for the country's development, and the civilian administration was both incapable and corrupt. The politicization of soldiers created personal rivalries within the military, which were accentuated by religious and ethnic differences. Diallo had kept himself separate from brewing tensions, and was supported by a personal network of informants that kept him aware of what was happening within various units and to take countermeasures, if needed. Yet, Diallo's power within the military did have limits, and he sought to consider the opinions of young officers.[318]

---

314 Army Historical Service, 'L'agitation estudiantine et syndicale à Dakar et ses conséquences au sein des forces armées', 23 June 1969, GR9Q5134, SHD, and 'évolution de la situation au Sénégal', 22 June 1969, GR9Q5134, SHD; General Secretary for African and Malagasy Affairs, 'Audience de monsieur Léopold Senghor', 16 December 1969; US Embassy Dakar, 'The mysterious General Diallo', 18 June 1970, SENEGAL DEF 1970–1973, Box 1794, CGRDS, NARA; Intelligence Exploitation Centre, 'L'armée sénégalaise face au problème du maintien de l'ordre', 10 April 1969, GR9Q5134, SHD.
315 Colonel le Coniac, Military advisor, 'Éléments d'appréciation', 22 October 1968, GR6Q44, SHD.
316 Interview by author, July 2019, Dakar.
317 Intelligence Exploitation Centre, 'L'armée sénégalaise face au problème du maintien de l'ordre', 10 April 1969.
318 Ibid.

After the May 1968 protests, Diallo had demanded the removal of any intermediaries between him and the president. He also continued to criticize the government. Senghor thought that if Diallo were more closely involved in certain governmental responsibilities he would 'better understand the complexity of managing the affairs of the state.'[319] According to the US Embassy, French technical assistant Marc Bonnel – who had primary responsibility for operating the defence ministry, as the defence minister was also the president – cautioned Senghor about giving too much power to Diallo. Diallo, who did not like Bonnel, asked that he be removed, and shortly thereafter that French military attaché Colonel Le Coniac also be removed.[320]

Le Coniac had become a target as a by-product of Diallo's conflict with another Senegalese officer, Major Pereira. Diallo had accused Pereira of plotting a coup, and Senghor agreed at first to arrest Pereira. According to the US Embassy, however, Diallo was trying to cover for having directed military contracts to his French son-in-law and taking other measures to assure his 'own financial wellbeing' and 'profitable retirement'.[321] The Embassy reported that 'Diallo accused Pereira of plotting a coup because he was talking about Diallo's shady financial dealings to everyone.'[322] Diallo's desire to remove the French attaché stemmed from the fact that 'at the time of the trial of Major Pereira, [Le] Coniac made the mistake of running around town like a super detective trying to find out what was happening'.[323]

American officials believed that the president would not punish Diallo, because it would 'pose a threat to Senghor' if the Chief of the Defence Staff lost respect among young officers. Whilst Diallo was clearly becoming more problematic as the 1960s came to a close, but he was due to retire in 1972.[324] Hence, the challenge for Senghor was not only to find a replacement who

---

319 French Embassy Dakar, 'Situation au Sénégal', 13 May 1969; Army Historical Service, 'évolution de la situation au Sénégal', 22 June 1969; General Secretary for African and Malagasy Affairs, 'Audience de monsieur Léopold Senghor', 16 December 1969; US Embassy Dakar, 'The mysterious General Diallo', 18 June 1970; General Secretary for African and Malagasy Affairs, Special Staff, 'Visite du président Senghor', 30 July 1968.
320 US Embassy Dakar, 'The mysterious General Diallo', 18 June 1970.
321 Ibid.; US Embassy Dakar, '_Le monde_ correspondent Pierre Biarnes' views on alleged military plot', 29 January 1969.
322 US Embassy Dakar, '_Le monde_ correspondent Pierre Biarnes' views on alleged military plot', 29 January 1969.
323 US Embassy Dakar, 'The mysterious General Diallo', 18 June 1970.
324 US Embassy Dakar, 'Malaise in Senegal' 26 April 1969, POL 1967–1969, Box 2477, CGRDS, NARA.

young officers would accept, but who would also have the experience and capacities to manage the armed forces.[325] Senghor needed someone he could trust to the same degree as Diallo, and in June 1972, the president appointed his former aide-de-camp, and former Minister of Defence, Idrissa Fall. At the same time, the centralized command of the Senegalese armed forces was brought to end, and Diallo's previous responsibilities were subdivided. Here, the purpose was to replace Diallo's personal control with a system of institutional checks and balances.[326]

As explained in an American report, until June 1972, 'Diallo [had] made all the decisions affecting the readiness and capacities of all the various military forces. He carefully and personally selected subordinates to command key units and pursued a policy of choosing commanding officers even down to the platoon level.' According to US officials, Diallo's success in controlling the army hinged on the fact that he was 'meticulous in selecting officer candidates and in keeping an even balance at all command levels with respect to their tribal origins and religion. He also kept the armed forces preoccupied with a rigorous training schedule which he insisted be maintained.'[327] Soldiers interviewed for this research similarly noted that Diallo had emphasized discipline, right down to the smallest detail.[328]

French officials predicted that decentralizing the command of the military would reduce the likelihood of soldiers intervening in politics. Until 1972, President Senghor's reliance on Diallo and on his authority over soldiers to settle social unrest had made Diallo increasingly powerful. Close cooperation between the President and the Chief of Staff had also assured functional feedback channels between Senegalese officers, the President, and the political elite. Diallo had insisted on keeping the armed forces separate from politics, however, emphasizing that Senegalese officers only have official relations with members of the government. Upon his departure, Diallo pledged that the military was devoted to the government as long as the government was up to the task, but also said that soldiers would do what was necessary if the country slid into disorder.[329]

325 US Embassy Dakar, 'The mysterious General Diallo', 18 June 1970; General Secretary for African and Malagasy Affairs, Special Staff, 'Visite du président Senghor', 30 July 1968, and 'Audience du président Senghor', 16 April 1968.
326 US Embassy Dakar, 'A look in depth at the GOS at the end of 1971–1972 political year', 5 August 1972, SEN POL 1970–73, Box 2588, CGRDS, NARA.
327 Ibid.
328 Interview by author, July 2019, Dakar.
329 Army Historical Service, 'Sénégal', 31 July 1973, GR9Q5134, SHD.

Diallo's departure and the division of his previous responsibilities was an occasion for other actors to increase their personal power. Fall, the new Chief of Staff, would have liked to replace Diallo in all his tasks and capacities, and he challenged the authority of the defence minister.[330] Along with a number of young officers, Fall also questioned the need for such an extensive French military presence. Under Diallo, there was a significant number of French technical assistants in Senegal throughout the 1960s (see Table 7).[331] As Fall sought to decrease the importance of the French assistants, a French military attaché complained that technical assistants in Senegal were no longer being used effectively, noting that the Senegalese military wanted to 'fly on its own wings, but needs a push, especially with its military equipment.'[332] In interviews, soldiers made the point that Fall was not anti-French, just more of a nationalist than Diallo. According to one soldier, Fall's mentality was evident in the emphasis he put on developing Senegalese military schools and training more Senegalese soldiers locally.[333]

Fall maintained his post for twelve years, during which time Senegalese forces participated in multiple UN peacekeeping missions. Despite slow economic growth over these years, by the 1980s, Senegal was one of Africa's most politically liberal countries. When Senghor voluntarily relinquished his power in 1980 – one of the few African presidents to so – he set an important example. This is a key reason that Senegal has never experienced a military coup. Senegalese historians have also noted that his emphasis on military training and recruitment were particularly important to assuring civilian control of the armed forces.[334] Senghor's policies go a long way towards explaining why Senegal was relatively successful in developing a strong and professional military. Chief of Staff Diallo played an important role in this process during the challenging early years of independence, but

---

[330] General Secretary for African and Malagasy Affairs, 'Déjeuner à l'Élysée', 5 June 1973, 5AGF/610, FFAN; French Embassy Dakar, 'Complots', 9 May 1973, 184PO1–517, CADN.

[331] US Embassy Dakar, 'A look in depth at the GOS at the end of 1971–1972 political year', 5 August 1972.

[332] Laparra, French Embassy Dakar, 'Rapport annuel juillet 1973–juillet 1974', 7 August 1974, GR9Q5134, SHD.

[333] Interviews by author, July 2019, Dakar.

[334] Moussa Paye and Momar Diop, 'The army and political power in Senegal' in *The Military and Militarism in Africa*, edited by Eboe Hutchful and Abdoulaye Bathily (Dakar: CODESRIA, 1998), pp. 315–54.

Senghor's decision to establish institutional checks and balances at Diallo's departure was equally important.[335]

The high esteem in which soldiers in Senegalese society were held also facilitated civilian control of the military, as soldiers were viewed as guardians of the nation's moral values.[336] The military was also a popular employer, in part due to Senegal's weak economic development, which meant it could select the best talent from a large pool of candidates. French military attaché Colonel Bourgeon commented in 1972 that when recruitment campaigns began, 'the lines are long before the start of the day.' Bourgeon also noted the ubiquity of the military in Senegal, reporting that 'the army is present everywhere and participates in road building and providing health care services.'[337] The importance given to the armed forces was reflected in high levels of military spending by the Senegalese government (see Figure 17).

The success of Senegal in developing its military is also due to the fact that its leadership did not rely exclusively on French military assistance and the French military presence during crises in the 1960s. President Senghor was obliged to consider the opinions of Senegalese soldiers, as well as their complaints about the corruption of political elites or the French presence. This dialogue was only possible due to the close relationship between Diallo and Senghor, and, as US officials noted, because Diallo guarded his independence vis-à-vis the French and respected the opinions of younger Senegalese soldiers.[338]

Clearly, the Senegalese government's approach to controlling its national forces diverged considerably from that of the Ivorian and Guinean governments, both of which deliberately weakened their militaries and also created strong counterforces to them. All three countries avoided coups during the turbulent 1960s and 1970s, however, making them exceptions in francophone West Africa. The next section discusses why coups occur, and what happened after the coups in Upper Volta and Niger. The strategies of the unsuccessful civilian governments in these countries differed, particularly in the extent to which they resorted to coercion or cooptation, but what

---

335 Tiquet Romain, 'Service civique et développement au Sénégal. Une utopie au cœur des relations entre l'armée et pouvoir politique (1960–1968)', *Afrique contemporaine*, 260, no. 4 (2016), p. 45–59.
336 Ibid.
337 Colonel Bourgeon, Military advisor, French Embassy Dakar, 'Rapport de mission au Sénégal période de septembre 1969 à juillet 1972', GR9Q5134, SHD.
338 Ibid.

Upper Volta and Niger had in common were resource limitations that influenced the control strategies they were able to adopt.

Nigerien and Voltaic Soldiers: Guardians of the Treasury?

The first presidents of Niger and Upper Volta, Hamani Diori and Maurice Yaméogo, were part of a small, educated elite in countries with very limited resources. The two had a common interest in international affairs and spent a lot of time abroad, but their long absences and lavish spending created political problems in the domestic arena. To French observers, the focus of the Nigerien and Voltaic presidents on international relations also seemed impractical. Both Diori and Yaméogo were accused of corruption, and their states accumulated recurring large budget deficits that were usually offset by France. The visible wealth of these presidents and their entourages was a source of widespread dissatisfaction among their citizens, who struggled to meet their most basic needs. As Niger and Upper Volta were the poorest countries in francophone West Africa, their presidents lacked the resources to coopt the entire population, and so the Nigerian and Voltaic governments focused instead on satisfying the demands of key interest groups and the political elite.

Diori and Yaméogo did have different attitudes about their national armed forces. Yaméogo, who refused to host a French military base, was not openly suspicious of his national military but sought to assure his control of these forces by fragmentating the Voltaic security apparatus. Diori preferred to rely on a French military presence, along with the Nigerien gendarmerie, police, and party militias, rather than on the national army. The means by which the Nigerien government exerted control of the military, and of society, was also more violent than in Upper Volta. President Diori imprisoned and tortured opponents, both within and outside the military. An army mutiny in 1963 and armed rebellion by the exiled opposition in 1964 were representative of the increasing internal threats to Diori's position. After he was ousted in a coup in 1974, the military ruler who took his place, Seyni Kountché, continued to control Nigerien soldiers and society through coercion. Upper Volta took a very different path. In 1966, in the midst of labour union protests, Voltaic president Yaméogo asked Chief of the General Staff, Sangoulé Lamizana, to take power rather than asking him to use force against the demonstrators. In keeping with this, Lamizana's subsequent military rule was also relatively non-violent.

In both Niger and Upper Volta, the ethnicity of the president and the ethnic composition of the population played a role in determining strategies of control. As a member of a minority ethnic group, Diori had more of a challenge controlling his armed forces than Yaméogo, who like most of the Voltaic military and broader population, was Mossi. In Upper Volta, there were also many former colonial soldiers who held both social prestige and political lobbying power. The opinions of these soldiers might explain why Voltaic presidents sought to avoid the use of force by the military and within it.

There has been some degree of long-term continuity in the control strategies of Niger and Upper Volta, as various indexes on governance reveal, which rate Upper Volta as relatively free between 1974 and 2018, and Niger as less so (see Figures 19 and 20). The history of these two countries also illustrates that when soldiers take on political roles, they often resist returning to strictly military duties. In Niger, military rule did not end until 2010, and Burkina Faso (formerly Upper Volta) had a military leader until 2015.

Soldiers in both Niger and Upper Volta framed the coups they undertook as necessary to save their countries from economic crises attributed to corrupt politicians. This did not mean that soldiers were more effective than politicians when it came to improving the economic conditions of the population, although Voltaic soldiers were more successful than their Nigerien counterparts, at least in terms of the countries' GDP. In fact, by 1985, the Burkinabe (Voltaic) GDP had surpassed that of Niger, even though the country lacked similar mineral resources. In addition, despite spending more on its military than Niger, Burkinabe indicators related to the education and health of its population are still superior.[339]

During military rule, there was no organized opposition in Niger or Upper Volta, and thus no counter to presidential power. Nigerien and Voltaic soldiers justified the continuation of their rule by citing the corrupt practices of civilian politicians that had driven their countries into crisis. However, were soldiers actually better guardians of the treasury? In Upper Volta, it seems they were, but the same cannot be said of Niger. By the 1970s, Niger was more heavily in debt than Upper Volta. And at the end of the Cold War, GGIs rated Burkina Faso (Upper Volta) as the least corrupt of all the francophone West African countries, and Niger the most corrupt and also the least accountable (see Figure 6). The policies of the civilian and military

---

[339] Data on child malnutrition, life expectancy, and literacy from the World Bank DataBank.

governments in Niger and Upper Volta are discussed below, including why violence played a lesser role in Voltaic strategies of control.

From civilian to military rule in Upper Volta

In November 1965, on the fourth anniversary of the establishment of the Voltaic armed forces, , President Yaméogo acknowledged that 'when we asked to have an autonomous national army, it was very difficult at the time to be able to predict the future.' Yet Upper Volta had succeeded in developing an independent military, and the president lauded that fact that:

> ... at a time when, everywhere, soldiers ... are getting involved in destroying what politicians have so painfully built, on the contrary, here in Upper Volta ... officers, non-commissioned officers, gendarmes, and soldiers have understood that a country can prosper in independence and truly enjoy genuine freedom only if the military, which is responsible for protecting all that is dear ... knows how to play its role.[340]

However, just two months later, Yaméogo was forced to transfer power to the Voltaic military in order to quell rising popular discontent. Yaméogo had always refrained from taking strong action against the military and had maintained apparently cordial relations with Voltaic soldiers. He had thus emphasized in his November 1965 speech that, despite military coups in many African countries, Voltaic soldiers would never do the same because of their discipline, loyalty to the government, and calling to serve their country as guardians of peace and order.[341] Yaméogo had specifically praised the loyalty of Chief of the General Staff Sangoulé Lamizana, who would replace him as president by early January 1966, at Yaméogo's request.

Lamizana's rule was meant to be temporary, but he became convinced that it was naïve to expect politicians who were preoccupied with their personal ambitions and interpersonal feuds to implement any real change.[342] In 1968, on the eighth anniversary of Voltaic independence, Lamizana addressed the fact that he had remained in power long after his 'provisional' rule should have come to an end and admitted that the military government had no confidence in civilian politicians to enact necessary but 'unpopular and thankless measures'. According to him, the Supreme Council of the Armed Forces had therefore chosen to remain in power as 'the simple consequence

---

340 Levasseur, 'Synthèse No XLIII/65', 3 November 1965.
341 Ibid.
342 Lamizana, quoted in Levasseur to Minister of Foreign Affairs, Couve de Murville, 'Synthèse no XLVIII/66', 16 December 1966, 313QONT/22, CADC.

of an objective analysis of the country's financial situation', because it was 'unrealistic to think that politicians, obliged to serve their electoral clientele and care for their popularity, could implement the austerity measures we were forced to implement.'[343]

In 1961, Yaméogo had tasked Lamizana with organizing the national armed forces of Upper Volta.[344] His decision to grant this responsibility to a soldier and not a civilian was linked to both historical and political factors. Soldiers had long played a central role in Voltaic society, even prior to the country's colonisation, whereafter the French military recruited a significant number of Voltaic men.[345] As a result, there were 100,000 former colonial soldiers in Upper Volta at independence, and they were economically and politically influential.[346] The traditional role of the Voltaic soldier was often celebrated in political speeches and the Voltaic military was seen as a symbol of independence.[347]

Compared to other military coups in Africa, the start of military rule in Upper Volta in 1966 was barely a coup at all. In fact, the civilian government actually asked the military to assume power.[348] Lamizana himself emphasized that he had never expected to become president and only accepted the position out of a sense of patriotism, after politicians proved themselves incapable of governing. He had a negative view of politicians and politics and

343 Lamizana, radio speech, 4 August 1968, quoted in Mathivet, Chargé d'affaires, to Minister of Foreign Affairs, Debré, 'Synthèse no XVI/68', 9 August 1968, 313QONT/8, CADC.

344 Lamizana, *Sur la Brèche* and *Sous les drapeaux*.

345 Burkinabe historian Jean March Palm suggests that, for France, Africa was nothing but a reservoir of manpower and raw materials. See Palm, *Rassemblement Démocratique Africain*, p. 23.

346 Ministry of the Armed Forces, Overseas Office, 'Notice sur Haute-Volta', 8 July 1960; US Embassy Ouagadougou 'Potential Opposition Elements: Upper Volta', 23 April 1964, POLUVOLTA 1964–1966, Box 2908, CGRDS, NARA; US Embassy Ouagadougou to State Department, 'US Overseas Internal Defense Policy in Upper Volta', 23 November 1962.

347 Director-General G. Berard-Quelin, Envoy of the French Republic and the Community, to Secretary of State of Relations with the States of the Community, 18 August 1960, 313QONT/20, CADC; French Embassy Ouagadougou, 'Compte-rendu hebdomadaire', 4 August 1961, and 'Compte-rendu hebdomadaire', 20 October 1961; Directorate of African and Malagasy Affairs, 'Questions militaires en Haute-Volta', 2 November 1961; Levasseur, 'Synthèse No XLIII/65', 3 November 1965; Political Advisor, French Embassy Ouagadougou, 'Synthèse générale March 1961', 313QONT/3, CADC.

348 Levasseur, 'Crise politique en Haute-Volta', 4 January 1966; Military adviser, French Embassy Ouagadougou, 'Rapport mensuel mois de décembre', 6 January 1966.

had little hope that either could escape the grip of clientelism and prioritize the needs of the country.[349] Notably, the Voltaic military government was also unique for engaging in significantly less violence than many civilian African governments, and French reports went so far as to describe Lamizana's regime as liberal.[350] It could even be argued that Lamizana was more liberal than Yaméogo.

Lamizana's perspective was shaped by his experience of corruption and centralized power within the government of President Yaméogo. While he may not have resorted to the extreme measures of the Guinean and Ivorian presidents of announcing coup plots in order to dispose of opponents, Yaméogo could hardly be described as liberal. Prior to independence, for example, Yaméogo had outlawed his political opponents.[351] Then, in 1960, when Upper Volta became a one-party state led by Yaméogo's Voltaic Democratic Union (Union démocratique voltaïque, or UDV), his main opponents were either imprisoned or exiled. Yaméogo used the police and gendarmes to detain his opposition,[352] as soldiers were more politically influential and he worried they would resist using force against civilians. He had been alerted to the danger that soldiers could pose by a 1958 coup attempt undertaken by Moro Naba, a Mossi, who was purportedly encouraged by a French colonel to establish a constitutional monarchy.[353] This may explain why Yaméogo did not rely on the French for regime security.

The large number of colonial soldiers who returned to Upper Volta led to political pressure to reject French guarantees and create a strong independent Voltaic armed force. In 1961, there were still 10,000 Voltaic soldiers serving in the French military, although most had returned by 1964 or early 1965. This created a problem for the government, as it was

---

349 Lamizana, radio speech, 4 August 1968, quoted in Mathivet, Chargé d'affaires, to Minister of Foreign Affairs, Debré, 'Synthèse no XVI/68', 9 August 1968.
350 Directorate for African and Malagasy Affairs, 'La situation politique en Haute-Volta', 25 March 1968, 313QONT/10, CADC; Telegram, Ouagadougou to Paris, 8 July 1968, 313QONT/10, CADC.
351 Ministry of the Armed Forces, Overseas Office, 'Notice sur Haute-Volta', 8 July 1960.
352 French Embassy Ouagadougou, 'Compte-rendu hebdomadaire', 12 May 1962; Levasseur, 'Forces d'opposition et force de l'opposition en Haute-Volta', 10 July 1965.
353 Paul Masson to Foccart, 'Position actuelle de Moro Naba', 10 June 1959, 5AGF/563, FFAN; Henri Bernard, French Embassy Ouagadougou, to Foccart, 10 February 1958, 5AGF/564, FFAN; Palm, *Rassemblement Démocratique Africain*, p. 147; French Embassy Ouagadougou, 'Moro Naba', 1966, 313QONT/11, CADC and 'Compte-rendu hebdomadaire', 6 January 1962, 313QONT/4, CADC.

impossible to incorporate all of them into the national forces.[354] Nonetheless, given their number, Yaméogo made it a priority to rapidly Africanize the Voltaic military.[355]

Upper Volta's first Minister of Defence Bamina Nébié had laid out ambitious plans for the development and growth of the national military in the early days of independence, but in 1962, Yaméogo decided against increasing the size of the Voltaic force for political and economic reasons.[356] The cost of building a prestigious and effective military would be a heavy burden on an arid, land-locked country. Voltaic political elites had hoped that French generosity would finance their armed forces,[357] but the president's refusal to allow a French military base in Upper Volta had jeopardized this assistance.[358] Nébié also antagonized the French,[359] whom they described as 'authoritarian'.[360] When the Voltaic government failed to secure sufficient assistance from the US or Israel, finding a new defence minister was seen as the only way to win back French favour.[361] According to French reports, Yaméogo sent Nébié to Israel in April 1962 to ensure that he was not left alone in charge of the country while the president was abroad,[362] before

[354] French Embassy Ouagadougou, 'Compte-rendu hebdomadaire', 18 February 1961, 'Compte-rendu hebdomadaire', 5 May 1961, 'Compte-rendu hebdomadaire', 4 February 1961, 'Compte-rendu hebdomadaire', 28 April 1961, and 'Compte-rendu hebdomadaire', 18 January 1961; Directorate of African and Malagasy Affairs, 'République de Côte d'Ivoire', 3 July 1963.

[355] French Embassy Ouagadougou, 'Compte-rendu hebdomadaire', 18 January 1961, 'Compte-rendu hebdomadaire', 19 May 1961, 'Compte-rendu hebdomadaire', 10 November 1961; Directorate of African and Malagasy Affairs, 'Questions militaires en Haute-Volta', 2 November 1961, and 'République de Haute-Volta', 3 July 1963.

[356] US Embassy Ouagadougou 'Memorandum of conversation: participants Henri Bernard, French Chargé d'affaires; Major Demondiere, French military attaché; and Major Frank, MTT Upper Volta', 18 May 1962; Frank, 'Military mission to Upper Volta', 12 June 1962; Bovey, US Embassy Paris, to Cunnigham, Office of African and Malagasy Affairs, 25 June 1962.

[357] French Embassy Ouagadougou, 'Compte-rendu hebdomadaire', 4 August 1961, and 'Compte-rendu hebdomadaire', 18 August 1961.

[358] French Embassy Ouagadougou, 'Compte-rendu hebdomadaire', 4 February 1961, 'Compte-rendu hebdomadaire', 28 April 1961, and 'Compte-rendu hebdomadaire', 4 August 1961.

[359] Lamizana, *Sur la Brèche*, pp. 24–6 and 32; Ambassador of France to the President of Upper Volta, 27 December 1961.

[360] French Embassy Ouagadougou, 'Compte-rendu hebdomadaire', 7 April 1962 CADC, 313QONT/4, CADC.

[361] Lamizana, *Sur la Brèche*, p. 33.

[362] French Embassy Ouagadougou, 'Compte-rendu hebdomadaire', 7 April 1962.

replacing him with Michel Tougouma in May.[363] The interpretation of the US, however, was that Nébié had been made 'the scape-goat for Yaméogo's personal independence policy – no foreign troops or bases in Upper Volta'. [364] Indeed, Tougouma was quick to express his gratitude to France and even finished his first speech as minister by declaring, '*vive l'amitié franco-voltaique!*' ('long live the Franco-Voltaic friendship!').[365] Even if Tougouma did manage to form a better relationship with France, this in no way guaranteed his position.[366]

In 1963, Yaméogo received a threat that led him to increase the number of Republican Guards responsible for his personal security.[367] He took no steps to neutralize the military, but he did purposely fragment the Voltaic security forces by giving different units parallel tasks, which resulted in duplication, competition, and rivalries. US officials recommended that various security agencies be merged but noted that it was practically impossible due to political considerations and the differences between pay scales in these agencies. These officials also criticized Voltaic recruitment practices, which were based on personal connections rather than merit.[368] The heads of the security forces selected their subordinates, 'creating a certain amount of personal following' that the US predicted could be problematic if the government sought to transfer or discipline members of the military elite. Even so, the material benefits, promotions, and social esteem afforded to soldiers were thought to increase their morale and discipline, and therefore reduce the likelihood of a coup.[369]

By 1964, American officials could no longer ignore the fact that Yaméogo's regime had become problematically authoritarian.[370] The US

---

363 Lamizana, *Sur la Brèche*, pp. 33–5; French Embassy Ouagadougou, 'Compte-rendu hebdomadaire', 12 May 1962.

364 Estes, 'Defense Ministry Change', 24 May 1962.

365 French Embassy Ouagadougou, 'Compte-rendu hebdomadaire', 26 May 1962.

366 Maurice Beaux, 'Synthèse XVIII/65', 12 May 1965.

367 Cordocan, US Embassy Ouagadougou, 'Propaganda and subversive activities in Upper Volta', 23 April 1964, POLUVOLTA 1964–1966, Box 2909, CGRDS, NARA.

368 Estes, 'Improving Police Forces Capabilities', 23 May 1962, and 'Internal Security Assessment', 30 May 1962; Estes, US Embassy Ouagadougou, to Department of State, 'Internal Security Forces', 13 February 1964, POLUVOLTA 1964–1966, Box 2909, CGRDS, NARA; Estes, 'Special program for Foreign Government Civilian officials', 23 February 1964.

369 Estes, 'Internal Security Assessment', 30 May 1962.

370 US Embassy Ouagadougou, 'Vulnerabilities of the Government of Upper Volta', 18 March 1964.

found the government's excessive control of media troubling,[371] and warned that Yaméogo's 'free use of police and security services against cabinet members causes nervousness and anger in high places and may give men in uniform dangerous ideas'.[372] Though they did not believe there was an immediate threat of a coup,[373] a US Embassy report nonetheless characterized a visit by Yaméogo to an army barracks as akin to 'Daniel in the Lion's Den'.[374] By contrast, interviews with former Voltaic soldiers suggest that even though Yaméogo became more paranoid over time, he was never particularly suspicious of the military.[375]

In centralizing power, Yaméogo had made Upper Volta increasingly reliant on French assistance. The French ambassador noted that Yaméogo, conscious of his country's financial position, behaved like 'a good student waiting for his reward'. It was the ambassador's opinion that 'if the goodwill of the outside world – and particularly that of France – were to cease, the foundations of [Yaméogo's] authority would be shaken and serious consequences would ensue, on the economic level as well as in the social and political arenas.'[376] It did not help his position that he spent more time out of the country than in it during periods of economic crisis, especially given that he was accused of using public funds to cover his personal expenses.[377] In fact, in 1964, amid efforts to understand the cause of the Voltaic deficit of CFA 600 million, French officials concluded that CFA 400 million of this had been attributed to the president's personal expenses but had not been accounted for in any way.[378] In 1966, the American ambassador reported that, 'as Yaméogo had no private income and his expenses were well above

---

371 Cordocan, 'Propaganda and subversive activities in Upper Volta', 23 April 1964.

372 US Embassy Ouagadougou to Department of State, 10 July 1963, POLUVOLTA 1963, Box 4133, CGRDS, NARA.

373 US Embassy Ouagadougou, 'Potential Opposition Elements: Upper Volta', 23 April 1964.

374 US Embassy Ouagadougou, 'Bi-weekly situation report', 11 March 1964, POLUVOLTA 1964–1966, Box 2907, CGRDS, NARA.

375 Captain Didier Felicieu Compaore, Colonel Major Aly Paré, and Adjudant-chef Major Macaire Yaméogo, interview by author, 15 January 2016, Ouagadougou; Colonel Barthélémy Kombasre, interview by author, 18 January 2016, Ouagadougou.

376 Levasseur, 'La Haute-Volta en 1964', 6 January 1965.

377 Levasseur, 'Synthèse XLV/65', 17 November 1965, 313QONT/7, CADC, 'Synthèse XLVII/65', 1 December 1965, and 'Synthèse XLIL/65', 15 December 1965, 313QONT/7, CADC.

378 Perrier, General Secretariat for the Community, 'Note à l'attention de monsieur le secrétaire général: Evénements survenus en Haute-Volta en novembre 1964', 5 November 1964, 5AGF/1847, FFAN.

his salary, it was generally assumed that the money had been taken from the national treasury.'[379]

The Voltaic political elite did not look kindly on Yaméogo's use of public money for private expenses, nor on his habit of appointing his family members to political posts.[380] It was, however, the announcement of austerity measures in December 1965, which included wage cuts of up to 20% state employees, that prompted widespread public outrage.[381] Yaméogo's hope was that this would secure more French assistance, which, with the exception of military aid, had been decreasing.[382] The military was particularly affected by the cuts, though.[383] Voltaic officers had already communicated concerns about their diminishing salaries months earlier, in a May 1965 meeting between Yaméogo, Tougouma, and Lamizana.[384]

In November 1965, rumours were swirling that Yaméogo, upon returning from abroad, would dismiss Tougouma.[385] French officials warned that this could spur a violent reaction, even if most gendarmes and soldiers were assumed to be loyal to the regime.[386] However, the French ambassador saw Tougouma as dishonest and said he had previously stirred up trouble during Yaméogo's long absences. Two weeks before Lamizana was installed via the military coup, Yaméogo dismissed Sibiri Salembéré as his minister of interior, and relieved Tougouma of his post as minister of defence.[387]

---

[379] Roberts, 'Upper Volta coup', 26 February 1966. Also see US Embassy Ouagadougou, 'Criticism of President Yaméogo', 25 March 1964, POLUVOLTA 1964–1966, Box 2908, CGRDS, NARA.

[380] Palm, *Rassemblement Démocratique Africain*, pp. 204–6, and 208–11; French Embassy Ouagadougou to the Directorate for African and Malagasy Affairs, 'Les forces politiques', 31 December 1964; Telegram, Ouagadougou to Paris, 23 November 1965, 313QONT/10, CADC.

[381] Levasseur, 'Crise politique en Haute-Volta', 4 January 1966.

[382] Beaux, 'Synthèse XVIII/65', 12 May 1965.

[383] Levasseur, 'Synthèse XLVI/65', 24 November 1965; Military advisor, French Embassy Ouagadougou, 'Rapport trimestriel, mois de janvier–fevrier–mars 1965', 5 April 1965, GR14S261, SHD, and 'Rapport annuel, année 1965', 30 November 1965, GR14S261, SHD.

[384] Levasseur, 'Synthèse XLVII/65', 1 December 1965, and 'Synthèse XLVI/65', 24 November 1965.

[385] Levasseur, 'Synthèse no XLVI/65', 24 November 1965; Levasseur to Minister of Foreign Affairs, Couve de Murville, 'Remaniement ministériel', 14 December 1965, 313QONT/11, CADC.

[386] Levasseur, 'Synthèse no XLVI/65', 24 November 1965, and Telegram, Ouagadougou to Paris, 23 November 1965.

[387] Levasseur, 'Synthèse no XIL/65', 15 December 1965, and 'Remaniement ministériel', 14 December 1965.

Yaméogo assumed this post himself and assigned the post of minister of interior to a cousin, Denis Yaméogo.[388] He also appointed his nephew, Édouard Yaméogo, minister of finance and commerce.[389] Tougouma was imprisoned on charges of mismanaging public funds[390] – an accusation the French ambassador supported,[391] but Lamizana deemed unfounded.[392] Lamizana's government would later confiscate Tougouma's property, as it did the that of most members of the Yaméogo government.[393]

Over the course of Yaméogo's five years in power, he managed to antagonize every group that could have supported him, namely, the political elite, labour unions, traditional chiefs, and the Catholic Church.[394] His nepotism and centralization of power frustrated the political elite, who were dissatisfied that ministerial positions depended entirely on relations with the president.[395] As the list of individuals Yaméogo dismissed from these positions, so did the number of opponents to his regime. In 1965, the French ambassador cautioned that Yaméogo's ministers felt no loyalty to the president and were either trying to maximize profits from the positions they held or were impatiently waiting for Yaméogo to take a wrong step so they could replace him.[396] Student groups and labour unions, which were under surveillance by Yaméogo's government, were also dissatisfied with his politics. Even the interests of traditional chiefs were threatened by Yaméogo, who had attempted to extend the authority of the state to the countryside and strip chiefs of their traditional power. On top of this, the Catholic Church disapproved of Yaméogo's divorce. Nevertheless, not even

---

388 Ibid.; Roberts, 'Upper Volta coup', 26 February 1966.

389 Telegram, Levasseur, Ouagadougou, to Paris, 10 December 1965, 313QONT/11, CADC.

390 Levasseur, 'Synthèse L/65', 22 December 1965, 313QONT/7, CADC.

391 Telegram, Ouagadougou to Paris, 23 November 1965; Levasseur, 'Remaniement ministériel', 14 December 1965.

392 Lamizana, *Sur la Brèche*, pp. 55–6.

393 Levasseur, 'Synthèse XLVI67', 15 December 1965; French Embassy Ouagadougou, 'Rapport mensuel, mois de mars 1971', 31 March 1971, GR14S262, SHD.

394 Frédéric Guirma, *Comment perdre le pouvoir?: le cas de Maurice Yaméogo* (Paris: Boradard et Taupin, 1991); Palm, *Rassemblement Démocratique Africain*; Roberts, 'Upper Volta coup', 26 February 1966.

395 French Embassy Ouagadougou, 'Compte-rendu hebdomadaire', 5 May 1961; Telegram, Ouagadougou to Paris, 23 November 1965; French Embassy Ouagadougou to the Directorate for African and Malagasy Affairs, 'Les forces politiques', 31 December 1964.

396 Levasseur, 'Forces d'opposition et force de l'opposition en Haute-Volta', 10 July 1965.

this number of discontented groups could form a coherent opposition, and as late as mid-1965, French observers dismissed the idea that the president faced any immediate threat.[397]

Voltaic decision-making was not only concentrated in the hands of the president and his close allies, but it was also geographically centralized in the capital.[398] This meant it was possible for educated interest groups in the cities to overthrow the government even if most of the population remained passive. This became clear in January 1966, when protests organized by labour unions forced Yaméogo to hand over power to the military. At the time, the majority of the population lived in rural areas and worked in agriculture, and there were only 33,000 salaried workers in the country, of whom merely 4,000 belonged to a labour union.[399] The coup demonstrated the outsized power of these unions and the importance of the capital in determining the fate of the country. The exclusion, indifference, and passivity of much of the rural population, who were largely illiterate, would be a continuing trend in Voltaic politics, and military governments would do little to change this.[400]

Yaméogo also created regional antagonisms by centralizing power to the capital. For example, the population around Bobo-Dioulasso felt neglected in favour of Ouagadougou.[401] Bobo-Dioulasso had once been considered the country's economic capital, but the closure of a French military base there had negatively impacted the livelihoods of the local population.[402] Regional divisions were entwined with ethnic divisions as well, and the French ambassador reported in early 1965 that various minority ethnic groups, particularly in the western part of the country, felt overlooked by

---

[397] Ibid; Levasseur, 'La Haute-Volta en 1964', 6 January 1965.

[398] Palm, *Rassemblement Démocratique Africain*, pp. 204–6 and 208–11; French Embassy Ouagadougou to the Directorate for African and Malagasy Affairs, 'Les forces politiques', 31 December 1964; Roberts, 'Upper Volta coup', 26 February 1966.

[399] Levasseur, 'Synthèse No XLVI/65', 24 November 1965; Roberts, 'Upper Volta coup', 26 February 1966.

[400] Palm, *Rassemblement Démocratique Africain*, pp. 204–6 and 208; Le Cannellier, 'Fin de Mission (24 June 1977–31 August 1981)'; Levasseur, French Embassy Ouagadougou, to Minister of Foreign Affairs, Couve de Murville, 'Situation en Haute-Volta', 8 February 1966, 313QONT/10, CADC; Levasseur, 'Forces d'opposition et force de l'opposition en Haute-Volta', 10 July 1965, and 'Rapport fin de mission 16 June 1963–18 décembre 1967', 18 December 1967.

[401] Ministry of the Armed Forces, Overseas Office, 'Notice sur Haute-Volta', 8 July 1960; French Embassy Ouagadougou, 'Compte-rendu hebdomadaire', 20 October 1961; Levasseur, 'La Haute-Volta en 1964', 6 January 1965.

[402] French Embassy Ouagadougou, 'Compte-rendu hebdomadaire' 20 October 1961.

what they saw as the 'Mossi government' in Ouagadougou.[403] The fact that Yaméogo and most of the soldiers in the national forces were Mossi likely helped facilitate the president's civilian control of the military, however,[404] and may explain why both civilian and military strategies to control the army were relatively peaceful.

In his memoir, Lamizana wrote that on 3 January 1966, Yaméogo opted to transfer power to him rather than give an order to use force against protestors.[405] The government and the constitution were suspended, and Lamizana assumed the presidency. Initially, the military was meant to hold power on a provisional basis, but negotiations with politicians left Lamizana disillusioned. He came to believe it was a fantasy that any significant change would ever be implemented by politicians who, in his view, were driven solely by personal ambitions.[406] As a result, a military council was formed, and in December 1966, Lamizana announced that the military would remain in power for four more years and that all political activity would be suspended.[407]

Lamizana's government included only four civilian ministers. The rest were all Voltaic soldiers who had served in the French military. Nonetheless, French officials viewed Lamizana's government positively and believed it would be more fiscally responsible than Yaméogo's civilian government.[408] The French ambassador noted that Voltaic soldiers had taken power not in search of honours or riches and that the military government was focused

403 Levasseur, 'La Haute-Volta en 1964', 6 January 1965, and 'Forces d'opposition et force de l'opposition en Haute-Volta', 10 July 1965; US Embassy Ouagadougou to Department of State, 'US Overseas Internal Defense Policy in Upper Volta', 23 November 1962; Estes, 'Internal Security Assessment', 30 May 1962.

404 US Embassy Ouagadougou, 'Potential Opposition Elements: Upper Volta', 23 April 1964; US Embassy Ouagadougou to Department of State, 'US Overseas Internal Defense Policy in Upper Volta', 23 November 1962; Colonel Barthélemy Kombasre and Sergent Laurent Ouedraogo, interview by author, 18 January 2016, Ouagadougou.

405 Lamizana, *Sur la Brèche*, pp. 55–6; Levasseur, 'La Haute-Volta en 1965', 22 March 1966; Richard, 'Note à l'attention de monsieur le secrétaire général: la situation en Haute-Volta', 4 February 1966, 5AGF/3705, FFAN.

406 Lamizana quoted in Levasseur, 'Synthèse no XLVIII/66', 16 December 1966.

407 Levasseur, 'Synthèse no XLVIII/66', 16 December 1966; General Secretariat for the Community, 'Proclamation de Lieutenant-Colonel Lamizana au peuple voltaïque', 13 December 1966, 5AG/1850, FFAN; M. Kirch, General Secretariat for African and Malagasy Affairs, 'Note de synthèse sur la situation politique et sociale en Haute-Volta', 31 December 1966, 5AG/1850, FFAN.

408 Levasseur, 'Situation politique en Haute-Volta', 5 February 1965, 'Situation en Haute-Volta', 8 February 1966, and 'Rapport fin de mission 16 juin 1963–18 décembre 1967'.

on advancing the country through realistic approaches learned in French military schools, rather than travelling to and from conferences and congresses as Yaméogo had done.[409] The new Minister of Defence, Lieutenant-Colonel Arzouma Ouédraogo, also received the blessing of France, which looked rather favourably on all the new military ministers.[410]

Despite the formation of a government, the military council continued to play an important role in Voltaic decision-making. It consisted of the chief of the general staff, every military minister, and the commanders of every military and gendarmerie unit, and Lamizana called it into session whenever there were difficult questions he wanted to discuss.[411] According to American officials, the Voltaic population only accepted the situation because they saw no other option, and not because the armed forces had any particular appeal. Even though President Lamizana was 'not a magnetic figure and arouse[d] no enthusiasm', US diplomats did indeed observe a 'popular belief' by 1967 that 'no better alternative' existed. This allowed the military to rule without having to 'exercise force or even make any show of it.'[412]

The American forecast for Upper Volta became gloomier as concerns increased that military rule could lead to fragmentation within the Voltaic armed forces and an internal coup, in part due to the apathy of the population. In April 1967, a US Embassy report noted:

> The Voltaic army governs in a political vacuum. Its leaders have no close civic attachments. Any group within the army that seized control would at this time be passively accepted by the country. The ease with which national power can be acquired may prove an irresistible temptation to some officers.[413]

The internal unity of the Voltaic military and its public image suffered during these years of military rule. Labour unions accused the military

[409] Levasseur, 'Situation en Haute-Volta', 8 February 1966.

[410] Delaye, Ambassador of France in Upper Volta, to Minister of Foreign Affairs, Debre, 'Synthèse no XIII68', 28 June 1968, 313QONT/8 CADC; General Secretariat for the Community, 'Note à l'attention de Monsieur le Président de la République: Remanieraient ministériel en Haute-Volta', 6 April 1967, 5AGF/1852, FFAN.

[411] Elliot Skinner, US Embassy Ouagadougou, 'Memorandum of conversation: Colonel Darchy and O.W. Roberts', 7 January 1967, DEFUVOLTA 1967–1969, Box 1714, CGRDS, NARA.

[412] US Embassy Ouagadougou, 'Political situation', 30 January 1967, POLUVOLTA 1967–1969, Box 2696, CGRDS, NARA.

[413] US Embassy Ouagadougou, 'Tenuous Stability of Military Regime', 19 April 1967, POLUVOLTA 1967–1969, Box 2696, CGRDS, NARA.

government of corruption and insisted that the national armed forces were no longer the 'armed forces of the people' but had become 'armed forces for the soldiers.'[414] According to the French, however, Lamizana's government was relatively liberal and ruled without resorting to force or propaganda. Divisions within Voltaic political parties and the passivity of most of the population meant the military did not face popular protests. Labour unions, which represented only a small fraction of the population, were in fact the only organized counterforce to the government.[415] When Lamizana introduced a policy of austerity – which he characterized as a set of 'unpopular and thankless measures' that his government was 'forced to implement'[416] – the government neglected to inform labour unions, other state officials, or the population about the decision he had made.[417] An observable increase in absenteeism among state civilian employees thereafter was interpreted by some French officials as a form of silent protest against military rule.[418]

The military government was sometimes confronted in bolder ways by actors seeking to return to civilian rule, and it was haunted by the fate of former president Yaméogo. For example, in 1967, several individuals close to Yaméogo were arrested for planning to reinstate the former president.[419] In 1968, French officials reported rumours of another plot in which Voltaic politician Gérard Ouédraogo and his brother, Minister of Defence Arzouma Ouédraogo, were plotting to restore a civilian government.[420] Towards the end of 1970, as soldiers were scheduled to transfer power back to civilians

---

414 Geraud de la Batut, 'Synthèse XVII69', 19 August 1969; US Embassy Ouagadougou, 'Political situation', 30 January 1967; Hughes, Director of the Bureau of Intelligence and Research, US Department of State, 'Upper Volta: Lamizana faces flare-up', 11 August 1967, POLUVOLTA 1967–1969, Box 2696, CGRDS, NARA.

415 Delaye, 'Synthèse no XX69', 30 September 1969.

416 Lamizana, radio speech, 4 August 1968, quoted in Mathivet, Chargé d'affaires, to Minister of Foreign Affairs, Michel Debré, 'Synthèse no XVI/68', 9 August 1968.

417 Telegram, Ouagadougou to Paris, 8 July 1968; Mathivet, 'Synthèse no XIV/67', 14 April 1967.

418 Mathivet, 'Synthèse no XIV/67', 14 April 1967; Parisot, 'Rapport de fin de mission', 25 June 1975.

419 Mathivet, Chargé d'affaires, to Ministry of Foreign Affairs, 'Synthèse XXXV67', 15 September 1967. 313QONT/8, CADC.

420 Mathivet, Chargé d'affaires, to Minister of Foreign Affairs, Michel Debre, 'Synthèse no XVI68', 9 August 1968, 313QONT/8, CADC, and 'Synthèse no XVII68', 23 August 1968, 313QONT/8, CADC.

imminently, criticism directed at the military government grew and divisions within the forces became more evident.[421]

The opinion of French officials was that the Voltiac military had been corrupted by its years in power and that soldiers had become incompetent and power-hungry.[422] The discipline and effectiveness of the forces had suffered because its most competent officers were involved in governing the country.[423] Due to the administrative responsibilities of many soldiers, military exercises had become rare and training was insufficient.[424] This had lasting impacts: in 1973, for example, the French ambassador noted that soldiers had lost interest in their military duties, absenteeism was common, and officers were no longer ensuring their orders were obeyed.[425] Former Voltaic soldiers who were interviewed for this research agreed that military rule had negatively affected the armed forces in ways that continue to echo through the Voltaic military.[426] These soldiers also agreed that Lamizana had avoided disciplining officers partly because he feared a countercoup.[427]

[421] Military advisor, French Embassy Ouagadougou, 'Rapport mensuel mois de mars 1970', 31 March 1970, and 'Rapport mois d'avril', 30 April 1970.

[422] Military dvisor, French Embassy Ouagadougou, 'Rapport annuel 1970', 31 January 1971, GR14 S262, SHD; Parisot, 'Rapport de fin de mission', 25 June 1975; Azais, 'Rapport de fin de mission', 30 June 1972; Battalion Commander Debacker, 'Fiche d'analyse du rapport annuel de l'Ambassade de la France en Haute-Volta', June 1974; National Defence General Staff, Intelligence Division, 'Le différend frontalier Malo-Voltaïque', 27 November 1974.

[423] Military advisor, French Embassy Ouagadougou, 'Rapport mensuel mois de mars 1970', 31 March 1970, 'Rapport annuel 1970', 31 January 1971, and 'Rapport mensuel fevrier 1971', 27 February 1971; Debacker, 'Fiche d'analyse du rapport annuel de l'Ambassade de la France en Haute-Volta', June 1974; National Defence General Staff, Intelligence Division, 'Le différend frontalier Malo-Voltaïque', 27 November 1974.

[424] Azais, 'Rapport de fin de mission', 30 June 1972; Battalion Commander Debacker, 'Fiche d'analyse du rapport annuel de l'Ambassade de la France en Haute-Volta', June 1974; National Defence General Staff, Intelligence Division, 'Le différend frontalier Malo-Voltaïque', 27 November 1974; Parisot, 'Rapport de fin de mission', 25 June 1975.

[425] Parisot, 'Rapport annuel', 15 June 1973.

[426] Captain Didier Felicieu Compaore, Colonel Major Aly Paré, and Adjudant-chef Major Macaire Yaméogo, interview by author, 15 January 2016; Colonel Barthélémy Kombasre and Sergeant Laurent Ouédraogo, interview by author, 18 January 2016, Ouagadougou; Lieutenant Gariko Yaya and Commandant Paul Tonde, interview by author, 22 January 2016, Ouagadougou.

[427] Colonel Barthélémy Kombasre, interview by author, 18 January 2016; Lieutenant Gariko Yaya and Commandant Paul Tonde, interview by author, 22 January 2016.

Lamizana also had to contend with growing generational divides in the military. By the late 1960s, older officers were expressing dissatisfaction with the economic rewards they received for performing important duties for their country.[428] Chief of Staff of the Armed Forces Vadogo Ouédraogo suggested that the remuneration for soldiers was inadequate given their position in society. In a March 1968 report, he acknowledged that the military government had 'been given a mission to redress the country's economic and financial situation' but argued that 'it should not neglect itself', especially as a stable armed force 'is the sole guarantor of national sovereignty'.[429]

The austerity measures that the military government had to implement made it impossible to grant direct financial rewards to soldiers, promotions were the only way to reward their good work. Hence, in February 1968, several government ministers and other Voltaic officers were promoted. The minister of defence, chief of staff, and commandant of the first battalion were all promoted to lieutenant-colonel. Other ministers were promoted to the rank of battalion chief. The retirement of other officers was announced at the same time as these promotions, in the hope that this would keep younger officers satisfied with their professional prospects.[430]

Younger officers remained frustrated, particularly those who had graduated from French military schools and found the material situation in their home country lamentable.[431] The promotions of older officers would not resolve the more pressing problems facing the military, such as a lack of funding for equipment. Typically, almost 90% of the Voltaic military budget was allocated to soldiers' salaries (see Table 6), leaving little

---

428 Battalion Commander Vadogo Ouédraogo, 'Rapport annuel du 1 janvier 1966 au 31 décembre 1967 sur le morale, le fonctionnement et les activités des forces armées nationales', 21 March 1968.

429 Ibid. According to Ouédraogo, one of the main problems in the armed forces was that high-ranking officers did not have better cars, as 'other social strata should not be privileged over the officer'.

430 Delaye, 'Synthèse IV/68', 23 February 1968; Delaye, Ambassador of France in Upper Volta, to Minister of Foreign Affairs, Maurice Schumann, 'Synthese no XXV68', 9 December 1968, 313QONT/9 CADC; US Embassy Ouagadougou to Department of State, 'New Voltan Chief of Staff Baba Sy', 8 January 1969, DEFVOLTA 1967–1969, Box 1714, CGRDS, NARA.

431 Delaye, 'Synthèse no VII68', 5 April 1968, and 'Synthèse no XXVI69', 23 December 1969; Intelligence Exploitation Centre, 'Eléments destines à l'élaboration d'une directive pour le conseiller militaire à Ouagadougou', 17 October 1969.

for equipment and other costs (see Chapter 2).[432] . In an interview, former officer Colonel Barthélémy Kombasre noted that the finance minister, quartermaster Tiémoko Garango, had been disliked by soldiers due to his role in carrying out austerity measures. According to Kombasre, it was impossible to get Garango to sign off on the acquisition of even the most basic military equipment.[433] However, French and American officials had nothing but praise for Garango's efficiency and professionalism, as he did manage to balance the budget.[434] The French also argued that their military aid had helped to satisfy younger Voltaic officers during this time, allowing Lamizana to maintain some degree of order within the forces.[435]

This became more difficult when Lamizana began to prepare for the transition to civilian power. In November 1969, when Lamizana announced that political parties were again allowed to organize, officers pushed back and made it clear that they were reluctant to transfer power by taking it upon themselves to write a new constitution.[436] According to the French, they presented a draft constitution that allowed the military to maintain key governmental positions for an indefinite period, 'without asking the opinion of anyone', not even the consultative constitutional committee. A French advisor attributed this 'imprudence' to pressure from younger officers.[437]

[432] Levasseur, 'Synthese XXXIX67', 13 October 1967; Delaye, 'Synthèse no VII68', 5 April 1968.

[433] Interview by author, 18 January 2016.

[434] Parisot, 'Rapport de fin de mission', 25 June 1975; French Embassy Ouagadougou, 'Rapport mensuel, mois de mars 1971', 31 March 1971; General Secretariat for African and Malagasy Affairs, 'Note à l'attention de monsieur le secrétaire general: Situation de l'armée voltaïque', 17 April 1971, 5AGF/2719, FFAN; Telegram, French Embassy Ouagadougou to Directorate of African and Malagasy Affairs, 'Crise gouvernementale', 15 January 1972, 5AGF/1857, FFAN.

[435] Military advisor, French Embassy Ouagadougou, 'Rapport annuel de l'année 1965', 30 November 1965, GR14S261, SHD; Delaye, 'Synthèse no XXVI69', 23 December 1969; Intelligence Exploitation Centre, 'Eléments destines à l'élaboration d'une directive pour le conseiller militaire à Ouagadougou', 17 October 1969.

[436] Delaye, 'Synthese no XXIV69', 26 November 1969; Diefenbacher, Ministry of Interior Director of International Police Technical Cooperation Services, to Foccart, 'Note sur la situation politique en Haute-Volta', 2 December 1969, 5AGF/1855, FFAN.

[437] Military advisor, French Embassy Ouagadougou, 'Rapport mensuel, mois d'avril', 30 April 1970, 'Rapport mensuel mois de mars 1970', 31 March 1970, 'Rapport mensuel mois de février', 28 February 1970, and 'Rapport mensuel, mois de janvier, 31 January 1970.

This effort to avoid relinquishing power proved fruitless, as 'all important elements in the country loudly protested against their plans'.[438] In keeping with the non-coercive, and even liberal, approach of the Voltaic military government, it responded to popular pressure by making changes to the draft constitution. A soldier would only be able to hold a ministerial position for the subsequent four years, and if they chose to remain in politics after that, they would be required to resign from the armed forces.[439] In June 1970, the new constitution was accepted in a referendum, and soldiers maintained their government positions during a transitional phase, with elections in December of that year.[440]

In the months prior to the elections, the military government took measures to assure 'sufficient' resources for the armed forces, and an increase in force size.[441] A French military advisor reported that discussions among soldiers in September 1970 on reorganizing the armed forces were 'confused', and 'proposed plans were subject to numerous critiques and mockery'. Even Lamizana was personally attacked by young officers.[442] The president took no forceful action to silence dissenting views, though, and arguably made too great an effort to incorporate all perspectives. As a consequence, he adopted a plan that was 'very ambitious', to the point of failing to account for what the French advisor called 'the country's realities'.[443] When the reorganization plan that was adopted proved impossible to implement in 1971, this only created further conflict within the military.[444]

Elections held in December 1970 inspired a low turnout, at barely 50%, largely because there had been limited resources and time with which political parties could prepare. Yaméogo's party, the UDV, won the vast

---

438 Ibid.

439 Military advisor, French Embassy Ouagadougou, 'Rapport mensuel mois d'avril', 30 April 1970, 'Rapport mensuel mois de juin 1970', 30 June 1970, GR14S262, SHD; 'Rapport mensuel mois de mars 1970', 31 March 1970, and 'Rapport annuel 1970', 31 January 1971.

440 Directorate of African and Malagasy Affairs, 'Haute-Volta: Situation intérieure', 19 October 1970, 5AGF/1856, FFAN.

441 Military advisor, French Embassy Ouagadougou, 'Rapport mensuel mois de décembre 1970', 31 December 1970, GR14S262, SHD.

442 Military advisor, French Embassy Ouagadougou, 'Rapport mensuel, mois de septembre 1970', 29 September 1970, GR14S262, SHD.

443 Ibid.

444 Military advisor, French Embassy Ouagadougou, 'Rapport mensuel mois d'août', 31 August 1971, GR14S262, SHD.

majority of seats.[445] In February 1971, a new government consisting of both civilians and soldiers was formed.[446] Gérard Ouédraogo was named the (civilian) prime minister and Lamizana maintained his role as president. The most important ministerial positions remained in the hands of soldiers, however, including the ministries of finance, interior, information, and youth and agriculture.[447]

Conflicts between civilian and military ministers made the functioning of the new Voltaic government difficult from the start.[448] French reports indicated that civilian ministers criticized Minister of Finance Garango for his 'dictatorship' over the budget, and extended their criticism to Voltaic officers 'who had not earned their stripes in the service of Upper Volta and had assigned themselves as judges of those elected by the people.' For their part, Voltaic officers accused civilian politicians of an 'embezzlement of public funds that only soldiers' intransigence prevents from taking catastrophic proportions.'[449] They described the UDV political elite as 'more interested in their own affairs than the affairs of the state.'[450]

According to French observers, the rift between the civilian and military leaders was so deep that it was difficult to imagine how the Voltaic government could function effectively.[451] Lamizana's relationship with Prime Minister Ouédraogo was particularly tense. There were also rumours that the president, as well as some leading officers, supported a key opposition

[445] Telegram, Delaye to Paris, 'Elections en Haute-Volta', 22 December 1970; Military advisor, French Embassy Ouagadougou, 'Rapport mensuel mois de décembre 1970', 31 December 1970, and 'Rapport mensuel, mois de septembre 1970', 29 September 1970.

[446] Palm, *Rassemblement Démocratique Africain*, pp. 224–5; General Secretariat for African and Malagasy Affairs, 'Haute-Volta', 23 February 1971; Telegram, Delaye to Paris, 'Elections en Haute-Volta', 22 December 1970.

[447] Azais, 'Rapport de fin de mission', 30 June 1972.

[448] Telegram, Delaye to Paris, 'Élections en Haute-Volta', 22 December 1970; Telegram, French Embassy Ouagadougou to Directorate of African and Malagasy Affairs, 'Crise gouvernementale', 15 January 1972; Military advisor, French Embassy Ouagadougou, 'Rapport mensuel fevrier 1971', 27 February 1971.

[449] Ibid.

[450] Military advisor, French Embassy Ouagadougou, 'Rapport mensuel', 1 June 1973, GR14S262, SHD.

[451] Telegram, French Embassy Ouagadougou to Directorate of African and Malagasy Affairs, 'Crise gouvernementale' 15 January 1972.

party.[452] It did not take long for the new government to become unpopular,[453] and by early 1973, mass protests were organized. For the first time, French reports decried the excessive use of force by Voltaic soldiers, which was said to reflect their 'weak level of training and preparation.'[454] Lamizana also faced criticism for his passivity during the protests. He commented to the French that it was the prime minister's 'brutal methods' and 'threats to unleash the army against the population' that had restored 'tranquillity'. However, soldiers were becoming increasingly unhappy that Lamizana was deferring to the UDV, leaving the military was left to do the dirty work.[455]

After their violent response to protests in 1973, the popularity of the armed forces declined in Upper Volta.[456] Ambitious young officers were eager to take Lamizana's place and grew bolder in challenging him.[457] When Voltaic officers met in May 1973, shortly after the protests, French officials were of the opinion that the military council had reassumed power.[458] A French intelligence report of May 1973 suggested the political situation was so precarious that this was indeed possible.[459] Although Lamizana made public assurances that soldiers would return to their garrisons in 1974 and that those wanting to remain in politics 'would need to leave their uniform',[460] it was clear to a French military advisor that Voltaic soldiers were too politicized to return to purely military duties.[461] He was correct, as the Voltaic military retook power in February 1974, forming a new government that consisted of ten soldiers and four civilians.[462]

452 Military advisor, French Embassy Ouagadougou, 'Rapport mensuel', 1 June 1973.

453 General Secretariat for National Defence, Intelligence Exploitation Centre, 'Éléments destinés à l'élaboration d'une directive pour le conseiller militaire à Ouagadougou', 8 June 1972.

454 Military advisor, French Embassy Ouagadougou, 'Rapport de mai', 2 May 1973.

455 Military advisor, French Embassy Ouagadougou, 'Rapport mensuel', 1 June 1973.

456 Ibid.

457 Parisot, 'Rapport de fin de mission', 25 June 1975; Military advisor, French Embassy Ouagadougou, 'Rapport mensuel', 1 June 1973.

458 Military advisor, French Embassy Ouagadougou, 'Rapport mensuel', 1 June 1973.

459 Diefenbacher, Ministry of Interior Director of International Police Technical Cooperation Services, to Foccart, 'Note sur la situation générale de Haute-Volta', 9 May 1973, 5AGF/1858, FFAN.

460 Military advisor, French Embassy Ouagadougou, 'Rapport mensuel', 30 November 1973.

461 Military advisor, French Embassy Ouagadougou, 'Rapport mensuel', 1 June 1973.

462 Palm, *Rassemblement Démocratique Africain*, p. 235; General Secretariat for National Defence, Intelligence Exploitation Centre, 'Éléments destinés à l'élaboration d'une

The composition of the new government led to disputes among soldiers. Younger soldiers were dissatisfied that they had been left out of the government, as many had already seen themselves becoming ministers. Officers in Bobo-Dioulasso were also disgruntled because none of them had been included. Furthermore, the civilian ministers who were appointed were figureheads of opposition parties and labour unions, not the UDV. Given all of these reasons, it was difficult for the military to present itself as an impartial mediator.[463]

The governing role of the armed forces also continued to create problems in the military command, as most officers were now engaged in civilian administration. These problems came into full view in December 1974, when conflict broke out between Mali and Upper Volta. For France, the poor performance of Voltaic armed forces in the conflict was proof that the Voltaic military could not run the country and ensure sufficient organization and training for its forces at the same time. Despite generating a slight upsurge in nationalism, the conflict also did little to improve popular opinions of the military, as the country's economic situation remained a source of discontent.[464] Nevertheless, the military continued to play an important role in the governance of Upper Volta. In fact, Lamizana maintained his presidency for a further six years, and without resorting to coercive measures against his opponents. This did leave him vulnerable to an internal coup, however, and he was eventually ousted in 1980.

Former soldiers who were interviewed for this study considered the coup of 1980 to be the first military coup in Upper Volta, as the earlier transfer of power from Yaméogo to Lamizana and the political role of the military had, in their view, been dictated by necessity.[465] So many years in power had also politicized the Voltaic military, with soldiers reluctant to lose personal benefits linked to governmental posts.[466] In fact, the military

directive pour le conseiller militaire à Ouagadougou', 8 June 1972; Parisot, 'Rapport de fin de mission', 25 June 1975.

463 Parisot, Military Advisor, French Embassy Ouagadougou, 'Rapport mensuel de February 1974', 2 March 1974, GR14S263, SHD; Intelligence Exploitation Centre, 'Eléments destinés à l'élaboration d'une directive pour le conseiller militaire à Ouagadougou', 17 October 1969; Parisot, 'Rapport annuel', 15 June 1973, and 'Rapport de fin de mission', 25 June 1975.

464 Parisot, 'Rapport de fin de mission', 25 June 1975.

465 Captain Didier Felicieu Compaore, Colonel Major Aly Paré, and Adjudant-chef Major Macaire Yaméogo, interview by author, 15 January 2016; Colonel Barthélémy Kombasre, interview by author, 18 January 2016.

466 Parisot, 'Rapport de fin de mission', 25 June 1975.

was eventually seen as a pathway to politics, and former soldiers noted in interviews that, in the later years of military rule, politically-minded youth began joining the armed forces for this very reason.[467]

In 1983, another military coup delivered power to a group of young revolutionary soldiers who criticized the reliance of Upper Volta on France. The new leaders renamed the country Burkina Faso and capitalized on the anti-French sentiment that had been growing for years.[468] They were part of a sequence of military leaders who would play a continuous political role in the country until 2015, when the president was finally changed through an election. In Niger, the armed forces also played a political role for decades, although Nigerien strategies of control were more violent, partly as a consequence of the domestic and external threats faced by the first civilian government.

The violent threat response of Nigerien governments

Two distinct events, the first in November 1963 and the second in October 1964, had a significant impact on how the Nigerien armed forces were governed. In 1963, a mutiny led by Captain Hassan Diallo resulted in the government questioning the loyalty of the national forces. Then, an armed incursion of the Sawaba rebel movement in 1964 was met with such brutality by the Nigerien security apparatus that the affair profoundly impacted relations between the government, security forces, and citizens. When Captain Diallo undertook what would end as a failed mutiny, the power of President Diori was already fragile. His position was threatened by external pressure from Algeria and Nigeria, as well as by internal subversion, with the Sawaba movement carrying out small-scale attacks from neighbouring countries and spreading anti-government propaganda.[469] The government did itself no favours either, as it was widely seen as corrupt, and the luxurious business dealings of Diori's wife only added to this impression.

---

467 Captain Didier Felicieu Compaore, Colonel Major Aly Paré, and Adjudant-chef Major Macaire Yaméogo, interview by author, 15 January 2016; Colonel Barthélémy Kombasre, interview by author, 18 January 2016.
468 French Embassy Ouagadougou, 'Situation politique', 21 April 1972; Diefenbacher, Ministry of Interior Director of International Police Technical Cooperation Services, to Foccart, 'Note sur situation en Haute-Volta', 17 May 1972, 5AGF/1857, FFAN; Delaye 'La Haute-Volta et la révision des accords de coopération', 12 August 1972.
469 General Secretary for African and Malagasy Affairs, 'Audience du président Diori Hamani', 2 May 1963, 5AGF/598, FFAN.

Though previous studies have suggested that Captain Diallo was connected to the Sawaba movement,[470] there is little evidence to confirm this. Both US and French officials reported Diallo's mutiny as just that, not a conspiracy to carry out a larger coup d'état. According to archival reports, it would seem that President Diori may have linked him to the Sawaba movement in order to make it difficult for Nigerien officers to defend the captain and other mutineers as they would be punished. The US Embassy also emphasized that Diallo was an apolitical actor, noting 'he could have taken over the government, and the fact that he did not, tells that his intentions were not political, and he only wanted to get better salaries and benefits for the soldiers.'[471] After discussing the events with President Diori in February 1964, Jacques Foccart was also the similar view that Diallo's actions did not seem to have been premeditated. However, Foccart also cautioned that the incident had clarified the extent to which African presidents were at the mercy of their armed forces. According to him, the mutiny revealed 'the indiscipline of certain officers', who he described as 'inapt for a life in the garrisons … and whose inaction leads them to plotting.'[472] Hence, the president knew that if he did not act against Diallo, it would set a dangerous precedent.

The events that led to the mutiny began on 9 November 1963, when Captain Diallo expressed his dissatisfaction with the material wellbeing of Nigerien soldiers in the company of the president and other officers. On 30 November, Diallo was reproached by members of the government about his lack of discipline. Rather than accepting this admonishment, Diallo accused the government of inefficiency and corruption. Several days later, on the evening of 2 December, President Diori relieved him of his duties and replaced him with Sani Souna Siddo, Diori's aide-de-camp. When Siddo presented himself at Diallo's military base that night and informed the captain that he had been ordered to take charge, Diallo refused to give up his command and also put the whole company on full alert.[473] He gathered up the 300 soldiers and explained that the government wished

---

[470] Van Walraven, *The Yearning for Relief: A History of the Sawaba Movement in Niger* (Leiden: Brill, 2013).

[471] US Embassy Niamey, 'Preliminary assessment of Niger's first major crisis', 16 December 1963, POLNIGER 1963, CGRDS, NARA.

[472] General Secretary for African and Malagasy Affairs, 'Audience du président Diori Hamani', 17 February 1964, 5AGF/598, FFAN.

[473] French Embassy Niamey, 'Situation intérieure', 3 December 1963, 478PO1–13, CADC.

to remove him because he was seeking better conditions for the military. The US Embassy reported that Diallo had the support of his troops, and sent a messenger to inform the government that he had refused to give up his command and had closed all entries to the base.[474]

The events generated much confusion within the Nigerien government, as President Diori and the defence minister were both in the dark as to the number of men involved, their exact location, and the weapons they had in their possession.[475] French sources conveyed that Diori wanted to enter the base by force the next day, but that this would be difficult. The captain had the most well-trained soldiers at his disposal, along with 80% of the weapons and munitions in Niamey, whereas the government only had some 150 badly organized gendarmes and police officers.[476] According to American officials, Diori thus asked that French forces break into the camp and subdue Diallo, but the French refused.[477] The French ambassador reported that Diori was informed that French troops could only be used to guarantee the president's personal safety and protect the radio station.[478]

Diori had little choice but to send Minister of Defence Yacouba Djibo (whose sister was Diallo's wife) to negotiate with Diallo. An agreement was reached on 3 December.[479] Soldiers would get better salaries and Diallo could maintain his position until 10 December, after which he would be transferred elsewhere.[480] After pressure from the French to respond, the government issued a public statement that minimized Diallo's actions as a misunderstanding.[481] The French ambassador credited French technical assistants with playing an important role in negotiating a peaceful settlement.[482] The agreement was not to Diori's satisfaction; he still wanted to take action against Diallo but knew that other Nigerien officers were

474 US Embassy Niamey, 'Preliminary assessment of Niger's first major crisis', 16 December 1963.
475 Ibid.
476 Ibid.; French Embassy Niamey, 'Situation intérieure', 3 December 1963.
477 US Embassy Niamey, 'Preliminary assessment of Niger's first major crisis', 16 December 1963.
478 French Embassy Niamey, 'Situation intérieure', 3 December 1963.
479 Ibid.
480 US Embassy Niamey, 'Preliminary assessment of Niger's first major crisis', 16 December 1963.
481 US Embassy Niamey, 'Preliminary assessment of Niger's first major crisis', 16 December 1963.
482 Fouchet, 'Question sur l'évolution de l'assistance technique militaire au Niger', 30 January 1964.

likely to protest. All seemed to have returned to normal, nevertheless, when rumours started circulating on 4 December that Diallo was conspiring with the Sawaba to prepare a coup.

The US Embassy levelled considerable criticism at the Nigerien government regarding its management of the Diallo affair from start to finish:

> Total confusion reigned within Niger's government for two or three days after Diallo's refusal to give up command. President Diori could not be made to believe that the French would not use their troops at his bidding and became distrustful of every member of his government. Minister of African Affairs Zodi Ikhia, Minister of Defense Yacouba Djibo and Minister for Foreign Affairs Issoufou Djermakoye Mayaki were the chief object[s] of Diori's suspicion, and he placed them under the surveillance of his French security advisor's men.[483]

The US assessment was that Diori did not trust 'most of the members of his cabinet' – who were expected to be 'even more unreliable' after having been banished by the president – and that his regime would become increasingly more fragile. The military, including officers, were not thought to be loyal to Diori, 'and having successfully defied the government once', the US predicted that soldiers could 'be considered more susceptible to disaffection in the future.' It was also clear to the US that France would not 'bail out the [Nigerien] government by using their troops to put down internal revolt unless their vital interests are threatened.'[484] Given this, it was foreseeable that Diori felt he could not afford to let Diallo go unpunished.

On 5 December 1963, Diallo was arrested along with eight-four others, twenty-four of whom were soldiers. Minister of African Affairs Zodi Ikhia, was also detained. Diori sought to demonstrate that the captain's actions were part of a larger plot linked to the Sawaba movement and carried out by enemies of the Nigerien government. A French police cooperation report noted that Diallo's assistant died during interrogation, and that Diallo himself was in a 'piteous state' after police questioning.[485] The French ambassador explained away such violence, arguing that it played an important role in Niger because, in primitive societies, 'force rather than argumentation

---

483 Ibid.
484 Ibid.
485 Director of International Police Technical Cooperation Services, 'Demande de renseignements', 6 February 1964, 478PO1–1, CADC.

reigns supreme ... to use force is sufficient to be the Chief'.[486] Historian Klaas van Walraven has underlined the racism of such statements, but did emphasize Diori's widespread use of torture, particularly against the Sawaba movement.[487] Samuel Decalo suggests that ethnic tensions also played a key role in Nigerien politics, including the Diallo affair. Diori and other members of the government were mainly from the Djerma minority (who constituted around 23% of the population), while Sawaba members and supporters were mainly Hausa (who made up 50% of the population). Captain Diallo was Fulani (10% of the population) and Minister Ikhia was Tuareg (10% of the population).[488]

In response to the mutiny and the continuing Sawaba threat, the leadership of the army and the gendarmerie were changed. In early 1964, the management of the gendarmerie was also transferred from the minister of defence to the minister of interior.[489] The Army Chief of Staff, Lieutenant-Colonel Bemba, whom the French described as practically illiterate and primarily interested in sustaining his material advantage for as long as possible, was also replaced. His successor, Colonel Balla Arabé, was characterized instead as a well-educated patriot who was personally attached to Diori. He also happened to be Hausa, like most Sawaba members.[490] In interviews, Nigerien soldiers described Balla Arabé as someone who valued discipline, perhaps slightly too much.[491]

Even with all these changes, Diori continued to worry about his personal security and lacked confidence in Nigerien security forces. In the spring of 1964, he ordered the wall surrounding the presidential palace to be fortified and decided to create a small Presidential Guard comprising sixty troops, all of whom were Djerma. Diori would have liked to grant exceptionally high salaries to the guard, but the defence minister convinced him that this would dramatically lower the morale of military forces, who earned much

486 Fouchet, 'Question sur l'évolution de l'assistance technique militaire au Niger', 30 January 1964.

487 Van Walraven, *The Yearning for Relief*.

488 General Secretariat for National Defence, Intelligence Division, 26 May 1977, GR9Q5131, SHD.

489 Fouchet, 'Question sur l'évolution de l'assistance technique militaire au Niger', 30 January 1964.

490 Ambassador of France in Niger, 'L'armée retrouve sa place dans la nation', 29 June 1966.

491 Interview by author, 20 May 2019, Niamey.

less.[492] In countering the Sawaba threat, the president preferred to rely on the guard, and on those gendarmes who had remained loyal in the midst of Diallo's mutiny.[493]

An armed incursion by Sawaba rebels in October 1964 – led by the president's old political opponent, Djibo Bakary – forced Diori to reinvest in Niger's security apparatus. Since independence, the Sawaba movement had operated clandestinely in Niger from neighbouring Ghana and Mali, where it had supporters among the Hausa population. The movement was eventually crushed inside Niger by the gendarmerie and militias, who used torture and public executions to leave those Nigeriens who did not support the government too frightened to help the Sawaba rebels.[494] Foccart's office noted that public executions, the loyalty of militias and some citizens, and aid from friendly states did help the Nigerien government counter the Sawaba movement.[495]

Nigerien soldiers suggested in interviews that the conflict with Sawaba rebels also brought the military and the population closer together, but they noted that the army had not played the main role in confronting the rebels.[496] The viciousness of the police also created many political problems. In December 1964, for instance, the French Embassy described how some 200 policemen, searching for around forty Sawaba 'terrorists' near the Voltaic border, had forced members of the public to watch as they executed these 'terrorists' because the police suspected that locals had helped the rebels. French officials observed that such atrocities might be counterproductive, as they could increase the popularity and legitimacy of the rebel movement, which already had the support of about half the population in that region.[497] Nevertheless, by the end of 1964, the Nigerien government had succeeded in killing or capturing most of the rebels.[498]

---

[492] French Embassy Niamey, 'Création d'une "garde présidentielle"', 16 April 1964, 478PO1–5, CADC.

[493] Fouchet, 'Question sur l'évolution de l'assistance technique militaire au Niger', 30 January 1964.

[494] Van Walraven, *The Yearning for Relief*.

[495] General Secretary for African and Malagasy Affairs, 'Audience du président Diori Hamani', 25 February 1965, 5AGF/598, FFAN.

[496] Interview by author, June 2019, Niamey.

[497] French Embassy Niamey, 'Activités du Sawaba', 11 December 1964, 478PO1–1, CADN.

[498] Lieutenant-Colonel Serat, Military advisor, French Embassy Niamey, 'Relatif à l'action de la gendarmerie nigérienne à l'occasion de l'attentat du 13 May 1965', 478PO1–1, CADC.

In 1965, a lone Sawaba member tried to assassinate President Diori. The president ordered a violent response, led by the gendarmerie, but without the participation of French technical assistants within the gendarmerie or army, who were not even consulted.[499] Captain Garba Badié, who had the command of the gendarmerie – he had been hurriedly appointed to replace the French technical assistant in command in 1962 – was known for his brutality, especially against prisoners.[500] Badié was close to Minister of Interior Diamballa Maïga, Diori's brother-in-law, who was similarly known for his cruelty.[501] Under pressure from the Nigerien population, and the French, the gendarmerie was transferred from the control of Minister Maïga back to that of the minister of defence in 1966. At the same time, Badié was arrested for allegedly advocating a military coup while drunk,[502] and was widely denounced.[503] He was replaced by Lieutenant Boulama Manga, who the French had recommended, describing him as 'young, energetic and honest'.[504] Manga was also from the minority Kanouri ethnic group.[505] His task was difficult, as the gendarmerie had been badly led for years, and its recruitment had been determined by ethnic or political favouritism.[506]

In 1966, Diori also increased the size of the Presidential Guard to 160, even though his confidence in the military was starting to grow.[507] This may have been due to his personal trust in his Chief of Staff, Balla Arabé, who had played an important role in guiding the army through the Sawaba crisis.[508] Nevertheless, French and American observers warned that Nigerien forces might still carry out a coup.[509] When the French encouraged Arabé

---

499 Ibid.
500 French Embassy Niamey, 'Activités du Sawaba', 11 December 1964.
501 US Embassy Niamey, 'Departure of gendarmerie captain Badie Garba', 15 January 1966, POLNIGER 64–66, Box 2516, CGRDS, NARA.
502 Ibid; Ambassador of France in Niger, 'L'armée retrouve sa place dans la nation' 29 June 1966.
503 Interview by author, June 2015, Niamey.
504 Ambassador of France in Niger, 'L'armée retrouve sa place dans la nation', 29 June 1966.
505 US Embassy Niamey, 'Departure of gendarmerie captain Badie Garba', 15 January 1966.
506 Ambassador of France in Niger, 'L'armée retrouve sa place dans la nation', 29 June 1966.
507 Ibid.
508 US Embassy Niamey, 'Niger's security forces', 27 May 1967, NIGERPOL 67–69, Box 2370c, CGRDS, NARA.
509 Ambassador of France in Niger, 'L'armée retrouve sa place dans la nation', 29 June 1966.

to invest in developing military intelligence structures, he refused. The Sawaba movement had shaped Nigerien intelligence-gathering, which was focused on the border areas and carried out by militias and the gendarmerie. These two agencies had the most frequent contact with the population and were also responsible for surveilling the state administration and party leadership.[510]

Assuming a coup was possible, French and US officials set out to determine which Nigerien officers were most influential and whether any of them were likely to try and unseat the president.[511] The second most experienced officer in the ranks, after the former chief of staff, was Lieutenant-Colonel Depuis, but he was not thought to pose a threat to Diori because his origins (a French father and Voltaic mother) prevented him from playing an important role in the military.[512] Among the remaining twenty Nigerien officers, the French viewed Captain Moussa Bayéré as the most intelligent and ambitious. However, after completing his engineer training in France, Bayéré had run into problems with his superiors and was subsequently deployed far outside Niamey.[513] Given the centralized nature of state control in Niger, this significantly reduced his ability to carry out a coup. However, a French intelligence report also mentioned Deputy Chief of Staff Captain Seyni Kountché as a possible threat. He was Djerma, like the president, and from a military family. Kountché had volunteered for the French military in 1949 and had served in Algeria and Indochina between 1957 and 1959.[514] The French ambassador thought him intelligent, hardworking, and among the best officers in the Nigerien forces.[515] As far as the US was concerned, Kountché was the only officer capable of carrying out a coup.[516]

By the spring of 1969, problems inside the Nigerien armed forces had escalated to such a degree that a French general recommended French troop

[510] Lieutenant-Colonel Chabriais, Military Advisor, French Embassy Abidjan, 'Étude sur l'organisation et le fonctionnement de renseignement en république du Niger', 6 July 1967, 478PO1–13, CADN.
[511] Ambassador of France in Niger, 'L'armée retrouve sa place dans la nation', 29 June 1966.
[512] US Embassy Niamey, 'Niger's security forces', 27 May 1967.
[513] Ambassador of France in Niger, 'L'armée retrouve sa place dans la nation', 29 June 1966.
[514] Intelligence Exploitation Centre, 'La république du Niger', 17 June 1975, GR9Q5131, SHD.
[515] Ambassador of France in Niger, 'L'armée retrouve sa place dans la nation', 29 June 1966.
[516] US Embassy Niamey, 'Niger's security forces', 27 May 1967.

numbers be increased to ensure the security of President Diori.[517] Later that year, conflict arose within the air force when a Nigerien officer tried to replace the French technical assistant in command and refused to obey his orders. Young Nigerien officers were becoming increasingly dissatisfied with their lack of advancement and with the material conditions of the military.[518] Then, in 1970, economic circumstances in Niger worsened, and budget deficits and trade imbalances grew. On top of this, French intelligence sources indicated that the security situation in the northern part of the country had deteriorated as 'the Tuareg population, left to its own devices after the French departure', had engaged in unremitting political agitation against the government. Nigerien forces were thought capable of re-establishing order, but not prolonged operations.[519]

Conditions in northern Niger degraded further through 1973 and 1974 due to drought and famine, forcing the population to migrate south and into the capital. Interviews with former Nigerien soldiers suggest that the armed forces were moved by the suffering they witnessed during this time. Many soldiers had relatives in the affected areas, and because of their frequent travel to these places, they had seen the severity of the drought and the misery of the general population.[520] Indeed, the inability of the Nigerien government to adequately respond to the famine was the main justification for the 1974 military coup.[521]

In 1973, President Diori had promoted Kountché to Chief of Staff of the Armed Forces, despite warnings that he could not be trusted. Indeed, on 15 April 1974, Kountché successfully carried out a coup, displacing Diori with almost no resistance. Diori's wife was one of the few people killed and Diori was arrested, as were with his government ministers. Nigerien soldiers interviewed for this research said they had been given twenty-four hours advanced notice and that soldiers from Agadez and Zander were discreetly transferred to the capital in that time. They also claimed that Commander Manga had good relations with Kountché and had known about the coup even earlier. Gendarmes had only been informed on the evening of the

---

517 Air Force General Fourquet, 'Implantation à Niamey', 22 April 1969.

518 General Secretary for African and Malagasy Affairs, 'Audience du président Diori Hamani', 3 September 1971, 5AGF/598, FFAN.

519 Intelligence Exploitation Centre, 'Éléments destinés à l'élaboration d'une directive pour le conseiller militaire à Niamey', 15 May 1970, GR9Q5131, SHD.

520 Interviews by author, May 2019, Niamey.

521 Richard Higgott and Finn Fuglestad, 'The 1974 Coup d'État in Niger: Towards an Explanation', *Journal of Modern African Studies* 13, no. 3 (1975), pp. 383–98.

coup, when they were gathered in barracks, and the most experienced among them were selected to participate. The rest were ordered to remain on base and were carefully monitored throughout. In interviews, soldiers and gendarmes alike characterized their role during the coup as a matter of having to obey orders.[522]

French intervention could have been an obstacle to the coup, but Kountché wisely chose to undertake the operation on Easter weekend, after the death of President Pompidou, thereby avoiding any response. Nigerien soldiers also noted that many French technical assistants were away that weekend for the holiday.[523] Even though the combination of drought, famine, and the government's inefficacy had made Diori's regime increasingly unpopular, the coup seemed to take the French by surprise.[524] According to Nigerien soldiers and gendarmes, the government's unpopularity was the primary reason the coup was successful. As one gendarme put it, 'everyone was tired of Diori, even his ministers. Even Sani Siddo, who was one of Diori's *fidèles*, was among the plotters.'[525]

After the coup, security structures designed to provide security for the president and the party – the Presidential Guard and party militias – were dismantled. Nigerien soldiers formed a Supreme Military Council (*Comité Militaire Supreme*, or CMS) and Kountché took a firm hold of the country's administration.[526] His grip was indeed so firm that a French intervention intended to reinstate Diori was called off.[527] French intelligence assessed that Kountché, marked by his experience in the French military, would prove favourable for France.[528]

One of the first tasks of the military government was administrative reform, which improved the functioning of some ministries but weakened others. In some cases, civil servants believed themselves intellectually superior to soldiers and had problems working with military ministers. Much as

[522] Interviews by author, May 2019, Niamey.
[523] Ibid.
[524] General Secretariat for National Defence, Intelligence Division, 'Le coup d'état de Niamey', 1 April 1974 GR9Q5131, SHD; Military attaché, French Embassy Niamey, 'Rapport annuel années 73–74', 1 August 1974, GR9Q5131, SHD.
[525] Interview by author, May 2019, Niamey.
[526] General Secretariat for National Defence, Intelligence Division, 'Le coup d'état de Niamey', 1 April 1974; Military attaché, French Embassy Niamey, 'Rapport annuel années 73–74', 1 August 1974.
[527] Van Walraven, '"Opération Somme": *La French Connection et* le coup d'État de Seyni Kountché au Niger en avril 1974', p.133–54.
[528] Intelligence Exploitation Centre, 'La république du Niger', 17 June 1975.

in Upper Volta, absenteeism increased among the Nigerien civil corps, which resented being under greater surveillance, especially when it came to their financial dealings.[529] Kountché's government was also somewhat paralyzed by his insistence on having the final say. Within months, he had centralized power to himself and had taken charge of the country's security apparatus (police, gendarmerie, and armed forces). Sani Siddo, who was at first Kountché's number two, was given a role in Nigerien economic development because the president was fearful of his influence. Siddo's new role meant he was often absent from the capital, travelling abroad and around the country.[530]

However, in August 1975, Siddo was arrested, along with Sawaba leader Djibo Bakary, for allegedly plotting another coup. Kountché had only allowed Bakary to return from exile in Ghana a few months earlier. The arrests consolidated Kountché's personal power as well as Djerma control of the country. Over the previous year, conflict between the president and Siddo had grown so evident that Nigerien soldiers were guessing who key officers would support in their eventual confrontation.[531] The French ambassador and military attaché had also noted the growing chasm between the two Nigerien leaders. The CMS had announced that it would punish the economic crimes of the Diori government, and Siddo was marked by his closeness to the former president and other members of the previous regime. Moreover, when Diori had been interrogated about his wife's financial dealings, he indicated he knew less about the matter than Siddo,[532] who was Diori's aide-de-camp and commander of the Presidential Guard. If Kountché was seen as domineering, reserved, and blunt, Siddo was known for his oratory skills and warm demeanour. In other words, Siddo had the skills of a politician. Had Kountché not seen him as a threat, Siddo could have been a valuable complement to the president, and even helped him be more appealing to the population and important interest groups.[533]

By early 1975, those Nigeriens who had initially praised the military coup had become disillusioned with the military government for being too authoritarian and too close to France.[534] Instead of addressing the concerns

529 Gaschignard, 'Situation intérieure', 3 July 1974.
530 Ibid; Gaschignard, 'Situation intérieure', 24 September 1974.
531 Ibid; Military attaché, French Embassy Niamey, 'Rapport annuel années 73–74', 1 August 1974.
532 Ibid.
533 Ibid.
534 French Embassy Niamey, 2 August 1975, 478PO1–94, CADN.

of the disaffected, Kountché sought to improve the image of the military by arresting Minister of Public Works Captain Cyrille Gabriel. He had led the attack on the presidential palace during the 1974 coup and, with his brother, was assumed responsible for multiple deaths, including that of Madame Diori. According to French reports, Gabriel was known for his unpredictable cruelty and is said to have stolen as much as CFA 150 million from Diori's office on the night of his ousting. The captain's propensity for flaunting his newfound riches automatically made him a liability for the military government.[535]

In March 1976, seven months after the August 1975 arrests of Siddo and Bakary, another coup was said to be in the making. Supposedly, the plotters had intended to instigate ethnic antagonism in the armed forces by pitting Hausas and Tuaregs against Djermas. Commenting on the arrests that followed, Kountché declared that anyone who attempted an ethnic rebellion would be shot. He also emphasized his own impartiality, noting that even though he was from a specific ethnic group, he was the president for all Nigeriens.[536] Soldiers, however, described Kountché as an authoritarian who valued discipline more than inclusion.[537]

The Nigerien president's use of force may have had more success in helping him avoid coups than Lamizana's relatively peaceful strategy in Upper Volta, but in terms of good governance metrics, Niger rated much worse. Ultimately, it is governance factors that tend to matter most to citizens. Nonetheless, Kountché's coercive control strategies kept him in power until his death in 1987, after which his cousin, the army chief of staff, assumed power. In 1993, domestic and foreign pressure resulted in a civilian being elected to office. Nevertheless, the country's instability and the military's participation in politics continued when a Tuareg rebellion started in the north that same year. There were further military coups in 1996, 1999, and 2010, and former soldiers said in interviews that the younger generation of Nigerien soldiers now in service has a tendency to question orders rather than following them without hesitation or protest.[538] This marks a notable contrast to the discipline Kountché demanded and enforced.

535 Gashinard, 'Arrestation du capitaine Gabriel membre du conseil militaire suprême et ministre des travaux', 19 February 1975, 478PO1–94, CADN.
536 Ibid.
537 Interviews by author, May 2019, Niamey.
538 Ibid.

Conclusion

In every postcolonial francophone West African country, presidents played the most important role in controlling the national armed forces, as the fate of ministers and military elites depended on their relationship with the president. However, it was only in Guinea, Côte d'Ivoire, and Senegal that first civilian presidents succeeded in avoiding a coup. The strategies each of their governments used to control the military differed, a fact that is reflected in the fate of key individuals responsible for the governance of national forces in these countries.

In Guinea, where Sékou Touré ruled through repression and was suspicious of members of the national military, the first minister of defence and the first chief of staff of the armed forces were both executed for supposedly planning a coup. Touré particularly targeted individuals who had connections abroad, despite the fact that external actors played an important role in training and equipping the Guinean army. Although the presence of foreign actors from both sides of the Iron Curtain created instability in Guinea, it did offer Touré an excuse on which to hang all the country's misfortunes, which he claimed were caused by foreign powers. This alleged ever-present external threat helped Touré successfully avoid a coup, but after his death in 1984, the Guinean military assumed power and ruled for decades.

While the first minister of defence in Côte d'Ivoire was condemned to death, but later pardoned, the first Ivorian chief of staff maintained his position for fourteen years, even though French officials considered him incapable and unpopular. Indeed, none the soldiers who served under him, nor the French, would have tried to install him in place of the Ivorian president. Houphouët-Boigny remained in power until his death in 1993, thanks to the French military presence and his purposeful weakening of the armed forces and creation of militias. Houphouët-Boigny also allocated civilian posts to soldiers as part of his strategy of controlling the military. After his death however, a power struggle ensued that led to the country's first successful military coup in 1999.

Senegal is the only francophone West African country that has never experienced a successful coup, despite enduring years of considerable instability in the 1960s. In 1962, in the midst of disputes about the country's economic policies, both the prime minister and chief of staff were dismissed and accused of attempting a coup. The new chief of staff, Alfred Diallo, succeeded in strengthening the armed forces through rigorous training and highly selective recruitment, and communicated the concerns of younger officers to President Senghor. As of 1972, the personal control of these forces that had been based on the mutual confidence of Diallo and Senghor was replaced by slow process of institutionalization that divided Diallo's responsibilities between several individuals. The peaceful transfer of power by Senghor to his prime minister in 1980 also established a principle that has made this practice a part of Senegalese political culture.

In every country in francophone West Africa, the first post-colonial president was ousted by the national military. In Togo and Dahomey, this had taken place by 1963; in Upper Volta and Mali this occurred in 1966 and 1968 respectively; and in Niger and Mauritania, this happened far later, in 1974 and 1978. After the coups in each of these countries, civilian presidents and ministers were often imprisoned, and in Togo and Mali, the former presidents died in the hands of their captors. In most cases, the army or the armed forces chief of staff, or his deputy, became the new president. As the coups in all six of these countries were carried out by colonial soldiers who had transferred into their national forces from the French military after independence, postcolonial presidents in francophone West Africa had good reason to fear their militaries. The large number of colonial soldiers in Upper Volta and Mali were thus politically influential. Arguably, their smaller number in Niger and Mauritania helps explain why these countries experienced coups much later, although the very first coups in the region occurred in Dahomey and Togo, both of had relatively few colonial soldiers.

The decision-making of the governments in Niger and Upper Volta was also strongly influenced by French opinion. In Upper Volta, for example, the first defence minister was dismissed in 1962 because President Yaméogo sought to please the French – who found the minister objectionable – in an effort to obtain more economic aid. The next Voltaic defence minister may have built a better relationship with France but he was imprisoned in 1965 for mismanaging public funds. Soon after, Army Chief of Staff Sangoulé Lamizana assumed power, at the behest of Yaméogo, largely to try and alleviate pervasive mismanagement and corruption in the civilian government.

The Nigerien civilian government was plagued by similar problems, but the military did not take power until 1974. President Diori managed to control the armed forces for longer than Yaméogo through a combination of coercive tactics and the French military presence. As Nigerien soldiers did not have the lobbying power of Voltaic soldiers, Diori was also able to weaken the army and rely on other security agencies. Thus, it was the gendarmerie that played a key role in crushing the incursion of the Sawaba movement in 1964. The commander of the gendarmerie, who had a reputation for brutality, was imprisoned in 1966 in an effort to improve its public image, but Diori's government became increasingly unpopular, nonetheless. His regime was viewed as corrupt and, worse still, had responded ineffectually to widespread famine. This laid the ground for Chief of Staff Seyni Kountché to take power in a coup in 1974. The Diori government had been warned about the potential for Kountché to do just that, and had thus been encouraged to establish a functioning military intelligence system, but to no avail. Once he gained power, Kountché held on to it until his death.

Malian military ruler Moussa Traoré was forced to transfer power before his death, in 1991. Like Kountché, Traoré had arrested and imprisoned most of his co-conspirators and had centralized power to himself. The rule of Voltaic military leader Sangoulé Lamizana was much more peaceful, but in 1980, he was ousted by fellow officers seeking to reduce the role of France in Upper Volta's defence.

A desire to modify defence relationships similarly led the Nigerien military government to seek new sources of military assistance after the 1974 coup. For the Malian military, the Soviet Union was the main provider of assistance, before and after the 1968 coup. Modibo Keïta, Mali's first president, relied on cooptation rather than coercion, and this was reflected in the country's military spending. Keïta also sought to ensure the loyalty of the army chief of staff by engaging him in politics, but after the military coup that was carried out by his deputy, Moussa Traoré, the chief of staff was imprisoned along with Keïta. Traoré then eliminated almost all of his fellow plotters, one by one. Not unlike Touré in Guinea, the control strategies used by Traoré in Mali became increasingly violent, and the country grew more dependent on Soviet military assistance.

Most postcolonial presidents in francophone West Africa, civil or military, were suspicious of their national forces and at times managed perceived or real threats by eliminating certain military figures. Civilian presidents in Guinea, Côte d'Ivoire, Niger, and Mali intentionally fragmented their militaries and worked to create counterforces in the form of party militias or Presidential Guards. In Niger and Côte d'Ivoire, these forces were recruited on ethnic grounds, and in Guinea and Mali, on ideological grounds. The Guinean, Malian, and Ivorian governments also widened the traditional role of the military to non-military tasks, such as agriculture, administration, and industry, even though these duties reduced their effectiveness.

Presidents across francophone West Africa also made efforts to assure the economic wellbeing of soldiers, but they needed to do more than control, weaken, or induce their forces to avoid coups. Ultimately, they needed some degree of popular support. It is often assumed that ethnicity is at the heart of consolidating support in African politics, but other factors come into play. It is true that these presidents frequently allocated a disproportionate amount of benefits to members of their own ethnic group, but remaining in power required them to take a wider view of their constituency. This was easier for presidents in relatively wealthy countries, such as Côte d'Ivoire, as they had greater resources to distribute among supporters and thereby coopt the opposition. Presidents in poor countries such as Niger and Upper Volta, on the other hand, had very limited resources at their disposal and their own visible wealth disaffected the populations they ruled.

Ethnic favouritism was at play in almost every country in francophone West Africa. In most cases, this resulted from an assumed loyalty that was seen to help ensure the president's security. Hence, the ministers of interior and defence – who typically control a country's security apparatus – were always individuals considered absolutely loyal to the president. They were frequently family members, or individuals otherwise dependent on them. For example, at the time of President Touré's death in 1984, a disproportionate number of individuals in the highest echelons of the Guinean military were also Malinke. Power had also been centralized to Touré's half-brother Ismaël and another close relative, Lansana Diané, who had an important role in controlling the armed forces. Shared ethnicity was not always seen as necessary, though, when other ties inferred an assumption of loyalty. In Côte d'Ivoire, for instance, the commander of the gendarmerie and the chief of staff of the armed forces came from the same village.

There were ethnic imbalances in every francophone West African country, but their presidents did make an effort to avoid being seen to favour one group over another and would commonly emphasize national unity in public speeches. However, all too often, these presidents tried to achieve this 'unity' by silencing dissenting voices rather than applying policies of inclusion. Importantly, as this chapter has shown, the governance practices established from independence up until 1974 had long-term impacts on national development. It is certainly true that the more peaceful strategies of Senegal and Upper Volta allowed the military to offer feedback to the government and seem to have created the least corrupt and least violent societies in the region and the most accountable and effective governance.

6

Conclusion: Legacies of Control

The analysis in this book, which is based on the defence-related decision-making of francophone West African governments from 1958 to 1974, has sought to reframe decolonization and state-building in Africa by focusing on the agentive role of African leaders. The nine countries examined were all part of the same French colonial unit but took different paths at independence regarding their international alignments and economic policies. In Guinea, Mali, and Upper Volta, the governments demanded a withdrawal of the French military, for example, while presidents of Côte d'Ivoire, Niger, Senegal, and Mauritania all insisted French troops stay. Every francophone West African country did, however, request foreign training, equipment, and technical assistance in building its national military.

As has been shown, foreign interest in providing military assistance to newly independent West African states cannot be decoupled from Cold War competition, which intensified during the period of decolonization. Military assistance and personal relations with African political and military elites were seen as the most effective ways of maintaining or gaining influence and allies in the region. For African governments, foreign military assistance provided an opportunity to obtain significant external resources for state-building efforts or to increase their personal power. Guinea and Mali received the bulk of their military assistance from the Soviet Union, whereas other francophone West African countries maintained their alliance with the former colonial power. Even so, by the end of the Cold War, five out of these had accepted military aid from the Soviets, and all of them had acquired military equipment from the US.

These decisions, and the evolution of defence policies over time in francophone West Africa, reflect the autonomy of governments in the region to choose the sources of their military assistance and how it would be used. In other words, France was not the all-powerful puppeteer as is sometimes depicted in the literature. Indeed, by choosing to rely on a French military presence, the Ivorian and Nigerien presidents were able to weaken their national militaries, as national soldiers were thought to pose a greater threat to the regime than any outside enemy. French technical assistance also provided countries with free foreign experts who were unlikely to plan a coup. Conversely, the Senegalese president used French assistance to train national forces, in part to strengthen and legitimize his military.

To appreciate how military forces have represented an obstacle to the stability and development of francophone West Africa, it is necessary to understand the history of state formation and the impact of foreign military assistance on this process. Conceptions of what constitutes a state tend to centre on the monopolization of the means of coercion, as this is what enables control of the population and land within a given territory. Previous studies have determined that, along with the availability of military technology, whoever owns the means of coercion shapes the kind of political systems created and the degree to which they are centralized.[1] State formation has also been described in the European context as a function of war-making, as the efforts of regimes to obtain the resources for warfare led them to create state administrative structures needed to tax their populations, thereby creating reciprocal responsibilities between those regimes and the civilians who contributed either men or money to the war effort.[2] However, in African states formed as the consequence of decolonization, at least in countries where independence was not attained through armed struggle, the means of coercion did not play this role. In fact, the important part played by foreign actors and resources in building the national militaries of many African countries were believed to weaken the links between national forces, populations, and governments.

The approach of this book, which has highlighted four key aspects of statehood – autonomy, sovereignty, legitimacy, and governance – has intended to reflect the transformation of colonies into independent states. Decolonization not only changed the status of these states, but it also generated very concrete expectations about independence, including that new states could enact policies of their own choosing and would be able to create state institutions to govern their populations and territories effectively. Moreover, the principle of self-determination that paved the way to independence presupposed that these new states would form a relationship with their subjects, offering legitimacy to leaders and institutions as well as a participatory role for citizens through political institutions and processes. It has often been alleged that postcolonial African states were not fully

---

1   Goody, *Technology, Tradition and the State in Africa*.
2   Tilly, *Coercion, capital, and European states, AD 990–1992* (Oxford: Blackwell, 1997).

autonomous, that is, not fully self-determined, because external actors and resources played such important roles in policy decision-making and the development of state institutions. Some have even questioned whether these states were fully sovereign, as their independence did not lead to the development of effective state administrations and infrastructure across their entire territories.[3]

As we have seen, the capacity of newly independent states in francophone West Africa to control and govern their territories was indeed deficient, especially if the authority of the state was challenged by non-state armed groups. The monopoly of the states over their means of coercion also lacked legitimacy. This was due to the colonial roots of these institutions, and to the way authoritarian rulers used security apparatuses to silence dissent in what often became one-party states. Above all, this monopoly was in question because the entire region experienced so many military coups and frequent periods of military rule in the decades after independence. Hence, the focus of the research was on the decision-making of African governments and presidents in building their national militaries, and how that decision-making influenced the formation of postcolonial states vis-à-vis their autonomy, sovereignty, legitimacy, and governance.

Despite appearances to the contrary, governments in francophone West Africa did have a significant degree of autonomy in making defence decisions. The competition of the Cold War increased the availability of foreign military and economic aid, which contributed to the use of strategies of extraversion by African political and military elites to mobilize resources from the external sources rather than relying their own citizens for support. However, in order to benefit from these strategies of extraversion, African leaders had to have something to offer, or be able to turn to multiple credible sources of aid that could be pitted against each other. For example, Sékou Touré knew that if military assistants from the communist bloc withdrew from Guinea, Western aid would be reduced.[4] Félix Houphouët-Boigny often fed French fears of increasing US or Israeli involvement in Côte d'Ivoire to acquire more aid from France.

Even if Touré's and Houphouët-Boigny's approaches differed in many respects, both presidents tried to mobilize as many external resources as possible. However, the case of Upper Volta demonstrates that there were

---

3   Jackson, *Quasi-States Sovereignty, International Relations and the Third World* (Vancouver: University of British Columbia, 1993).

4   Cassidy, 'Sino-Soviet Bloc Political-Economic Relationships with Guinea', 18 July 1963.

limits to a strategy of extraversion. Moreover, policy decisions in postcolonial states were not only driven by a desire to maximize external assistance, but also by nationalist and pan-Africanist ideals. This motivated Touré to maintain a certain degree of independence from the Soviets in order to preserve his image as a pan-Africanist, which would have suffered had Guinea became completely reliant on Soviet aid. The Voltaic decision to reject a French military base on its territory was also an expression of nationalism – that of Voltaic politicians and their constituencies.

Notably, even though every government in francophone West Africa relied heavily on foreign assistance, this assistance posed risks to African presidents. The centralization of resources and power, or a reliance on foreign aid, tended to generate public dissatisfaction. This sometimes led to a military coup, even though the same economic and military assistance was often (and easily) transferred to the next government. In this context, it is important to note that the main objective of foreign powers in granting military aid was not to build states but to ensure stability, gain influence, and develop allies. Foreign powers were also motivated to provide various forms of assistance to African countries by the belief that successful assistance schemes would ultimately reflect the superiority of Western economic models, culture, and technology.

This did not preclude some grantors of aid from feeling a sense of responsibility towards former colonies, or towards nascent capitalist or socialist economies, depending on that country's alignment during the Cold War. While, for example, French officials in particular felt a responsibility towards their former colonial subjects, this did not mean that assistance from France came without strings attached or that recipients did not have to show a sufficient degree of gratitude. This was certainly on display in French relations with Guinea, and also in the sensitivities of French officials regarding nationalistic discourse from any West African politician, which they saw as a rejection of the French colonial legacy, which it often was.

These examples, and the cases presented in this book, make it clear that providing military assistance did not give foreign powers any control over the national defence policies of postcolonial francophone West African states. In fact, the decision-making of these governments frequently diverged from the interests or desires of their former colonial power, as well as other Cold War players. In Côte d'Ivoire, for example, President Houphouët-Boigny temporarily disarmed Ivorian security forces and established armed party militias to function in their place, despite French objections. Voltaic President Yaméogo refused to host a French military base, which resulted in him receiving only minimal assistance from France. Guinea's President Touré decided to played both sides of the East–West divide, depending on what each had to offer at the time.

Independent decision-making by African leaders increased the foreign pressure and antagonism they faced. Touré was met by violent external threats due to his defiance of France, his conditional Cold War alignments, and his broad support for anti-colonial movements. Houphouët-Boigny was pressured by the French to reduce both the role of party militias and the influence of Israel, and to separate Ivorian civic service from the military. After Upper Volta gained independence, French troops displayed considerable hostility when they withdrew in response to the announcement of the Yaméogo government that it would not host a French military base in the country.

Initially, the Voltaic military government that took power in 1966 was given a positive reception by France and the US. Over time, however, both of these Western powers increasingly pushed Voltaic soldiers to step away from politics and return to their military duties. French officials were particularly insistent, convinced that the political role of soldiers had corrupted and degraded a once effective and respected Voltaic armed force, which had been trained and structured according to the French model. Clearly, relations between African decision-makers and foreign powers were not mono-directional, and foreign powers were not dictating the terms.

Although assessments of internal and external threats obviously influenced decision-making when it came to building national military capacities, much can also be attributed to the personal views of the presidents in postcolonial West African states. Even so, the shape of the states that emerged after independence was most impacted by the internal and external resources available to each government. In countries with more abundant economic resources, the government could provide opportunities, services, and benefits to the population. Senegal and Côte d'Ivoire, for example, relied primarily on cooptation to control their societies and armed forces, and could do so because of their relative economic success. In states where the economy was weak but coercive resources were strong, the government maintained power through intimidation, ideology, and violence. Mali and Guinea both fell into this category, as they received significant Soviet military assistance but lacked the economic resources to easily coopt important social groups or large parts of the population.

In some francophone West African countries with limited economic or military resources, civilian governments concentrated all available resources in the capital. This centralization of power and resources into a few hands, coupled with a reliance on foreign assistance, left these governments vulnerable to coups. Yet even when military rulers replaced civilian governments and increased spending on defence, the national military capacities of these states did not improve. This was partly due to the fact that the bulk of the defence budget was absorbed by salaries and benefits. Moreover, as most experienced military officers were focused on governing the country, discipline, training, and logistics suffered. The lack of any overall supervision, and politicization and internal conflict among the ranks, meant it was less likely that orders would be followed and that those abusing power or misusing public funds would be taken to task. This reduced both the effectiveness and cohesion of national militaries.

Some of the conflicts that emerged within and among national forces were the result of the legacies of colonialism and the degree to which national militaries Africanized after independence. Colonial structures influenced the building of national militaries in various ways, determining things such as where military bases were located, and how soldiers were trained and educated. Changing these structures often required resources that newly independent countries simply did not have. The colonial recruitment of African soldiers by the French also had a significant impact on the development of national armed forces in francophone West Africa. Not only did the number of colonial soldiers that returned to postcolonial states from service in the French military influence the way political actors viewed their national forces, but the colonial role of African soldiers in maintaining order locally and against anticolonial movements led many to view them with suspicion.

Relations between soldiers and civilian governments were also complicated by the fact that the overwhelming majority of African soldiers typically came from very different social backgrounds to the political elite. French colonial recruitment had always been polarized along social lines, with poor and illiterate youth from rural areas being forced to sign up while educated city-dwellers escaped recruitment. Due the large numbers of soldiers that had been recruited to the French Army, Upper Volta, Mali, and Guinea were unable to incorporate every returning colonial soldier into their national security or armed forces, which left many having to reintegrate into civilian society.

The vast number of returning colonial soldiers in these countries also impacted the defence decisions of their governments. For example, the Senegalese, Voltaic, Guinean, and Malian civilian governments were all pressured by former colonial soldiers to invest heavily in their national armed forces. However, their poor education and their limited training not only made it difficult to reintegrate those soldiers who had not been able to transfer into the national military, but also presented challenges to building national military capacities. Soldiers lacked the necessary technical skills, and armed forces the necessary financial resources, to ensure proper maintenance of military equipment. This made national forces dependent on external technical assistance long after independence. Differences between the training delivered to younger officers who enlisted after independence, and that provided to former colonial soldiers by the French, also created generational conflicts within the militaries of postcolonial francophone West Africa.

The 1963 military coup in Togo was a wake-up call for presidents in West Africa. In the aftermath, they increasingly operated as though a potential threat emanated from every former colonial soldier and from their national armed forces more broadly. The surge of coups that followed may have increased the interest of foreign countries in building relations with African military elites through military assistance, but it also led some African governments to intentionally weaken their national forces. A military coup in a neighbouring country often had an immediate effect on the strategies employed by a government to control its own military. In some cases, soldiers were assigned non-military tasks, while in others the access to weapons and ammunition was restricted. Furthermore, networks of informers were created, and individuals identified as a threat to regimes were either arrested or 'sent abroad'. In some countries, institutions with parallel tasks were also created as a counterforce to the military.

These strategies enabled Guinea's Sékou Touré and Côte d'Ivoire's Félix Houphouët-Boigny to remain in power until their deaths, but they did not institutionalize civilian control of their militaries. Only Léopold Senghor of Senegal was able to replace a system based on centralized personal rule with institutional checks and balances. Successful civilian control of the military was rare across the continent, in part because both domestic and international actors had initially believed that soldiers would make better leaders than corrupt politicians. Hence, six of the francophone countries in West Africa would experience at least one military coup by 1980. When the time came for these soldiers to relinquish their political roles, their return to strictly military duties proved a difficult transition.

In general, rule that was personalized and centralized was the principal reason for instability in the region. That said, the degree of that centralization and how key alliances were managed were important in determining just how unstable a government was. With limited resources, it was more difficult for a government to spread them widely enough to maintain the alliances needed to stay in power. As a result, members of a president's own ethnic group were often recruited to undertake key tasks or fill important posts, largely as a means of ensuring security.

The presidents of every francophone West African country also played personal roles in controlling the armed forces. Each one handpicked the most important civilian and military officials, especially those responsible for managing the security apparatuses. These officials often had family, regional, or other close ties to the president, and their appointment usually depended on their personal relationship with him, and sometimes superseded ethnicity. The importance of foreign economic and military assistance made it vital for presidents to control individuals who were influential within the military and had the connections to tap into foreign resources if necessary. In the case of governments that exerted coercive control, such as in Guinea, the lives of ministers responsible for the security of the state could easily come to a violent end. Touré executed many key individuals involved in controlling his national armed forces for allegedly plotting with foreign powers. Authoritarian rule such as his left little space for developing feedback systems, whether between the government and the military, or between the government and the population.

It was only in Senegal that soldiers were able to influence their service conditions and criticize government policies. The legacy of President Senghor's more liberal and eventually institutionalized approach to controlling his military, as well as his own peaceful transfer of power to a successor in 1980, immediately made Senegal an outlier in francophone West Africa. In other states in the region, economic factors, the urgency of internal and external threats, and the personal views of their leaders combined in myriad and changing ways to set each one on a different course. All these countries navigated state- and military-building in unique if sometimes similar ways, and with a degree of agency that, as we have seen, should be more readily recognized. The development of francophone West Africa's national armed forces had a significant impact on state formation, not only because these forces were essential to keeping presidents in power, but because they were a threat to that power. National militaries were also important symbols of independence in postcolonial states, even if foreign actors and resources were crucial to their development, and they were built from colonial structures and colonial soldiers.

Bibliography

I. French Archives

A. Diplomatic Archives, Ministry for Europe and Foreign Affairs

1. Centre des Archives diplomatiques de La Courneuve (CADC)

Direction des affaires politiques, Sous-direction d'Afrique – Afrique Levant, Guinée 1953–1965: 51QO/3, 11, 15, 24, 26, 27, 28, 29, 32, 33, 34, 35, 36, 41, 52, 59; and Afrique Levant, Guinée 1966–1972: 5QONT/26, 27, 28, 29, 33, 34, 36, 52.

Direction des affaires africaines et malgaches – Haute-Volta 1959–1969: 313QONT/1, 2, 3, 4, 7, 8, 9, 10, 11, 13, 20, 22; Côte d'Ivoire 1959–1969: 324QONT/1, 2, 3, 4, 6, 7, 8, 9, 10, 11, 12, 23; and Assistance militaire: INVA/15, 16, 17, 18, 19, 180, 203, 298, 299, 313, 316, 318, 320.

2. Centre des Archives Diplomatiques de Nantes (CADN)

Abidjan: 1PO/1 /1, 3, 4, 5, 10, 14, 15, 16; Ouagadougou: 499PPO/1/1, 15, 386; Bamako: 62PO1–15, 28, 30, 51, 56, 57, 60, 72; Niger: 478PO1–5/13, 14, 15, 94, 96, 104, 105, 112, 118; and Dakar: 184PO1–325, 394, 400, 517, 632, 635, 1043.

B. National Archives, Fonds Foccart, Pierrefitte-sur-Seine (FFAN)

1. Papiers Foccart (Fonds Scribe: 5AGF/1–5AGF/1085)

Conseiller pour les affaires de renseignement et de sécurité – Guinée: 5AGF/330.
Conseiller pour les affaires africaines et malgaches – Côte d'Ivoire: 5AGF/531, 535; Guinée: 5AGF/555, 558, 561; and Haute-Volta: 5AGF/563, 564.

2. Secrétariat général des Affaires africaines et malgaches et de la Communauté (Fond Elysée: 5AGF/1086–5AGF/4155)

Affaires politiques – Côte d'Ivoire: 5AGF/1787, 1783, 1787, 1792, 1793, 1794, 1795, 1797, 1800, 1802, 1803, 1805, 1806, 1810, 1812, 1813; Guinée: 5AGF/1637, 1638, 1639, 1640, 1643, 1644, 1646, 1647, 1648; and Haute-Volta: 5AGF/1846, 1847, 1848, 1849, 1850, 1852, 1854, 1856, 1855, 1856, 1857, 1858.

Affaires militaires – Côte d'Ivoire: 5AGF/2661, 2717; and Haute Volta: 5AGF/2719.

Services du Secrétariat General, Protocol – Côte d'Ivoire: 5AGF/3702; and Haute-Volta: 5AGF3705.

C. Defence Historical Service (SHD)

1. Centre historique des archives, Vincennes

Série H (GR5H Outre-mer) – Afrique occidentale française: GR5H27, 28, 29, 32, 37, 40, 51, 61, 92, 150, 151, 169, 170, 470.

Série S – État–major des armées et organismes rattachés 1948–1980: GR11S84, 85, 153, 159, 251, 252, 253, 254, 261, 262, 263, 267, 268, 382.

Série T – GR7T248

Série Q – Secrétariat général de la défense nationale et organismes rattachés: GR5Q22; GR6Q42, 44; and GR9Q118, 140, 510, 5107, 5111, 5113, 5114, 5122, 5128, 5131, 5134.

2. Centre des archives du personnel militaire, Pau

Les rapports de recrutement en Guinée, Côte d'Ivoire, et Haute-Volta 1950–1958.

II. African Archives

A. Archives d'Afrique Occidentale Française, Dakar, Sénégal (AAOF)

Affaires militaires, Rapports de recrutement: 4D1, 2, 3, 8, 9, 11, 12, 15, 16.

B. Archives Diplomatiques, Côte d'Ivoire (ADCI)

C. Centre National des Archives du Burkina Faso (ANB)

Files 2V18, 3V54, 4V37, 6V8, 13, 33, 7V429, 35V117–129, 43V262, and 44V721.

D. Archives Nationales de Guinée (ANG)

Affaires militaires: 3N.

E. Archives Nationales du Niger (ANN)

III. US Archives

A. Department of State, Foreign Relations of the United States (FRUS)

FRUS 1961–1963, Volume XXI, Africa; FRUS 1964–1968, Volume XXIV, Africa; and FRUS 1969–1976, Volume E–5, Part 1, Documents on Sub–Saharan Africa.

B. National Archives and Records Administration (NARA)

1. Record Group 59: Central General Records of the Department of State (CGRDS)

Central Decimal File 1910–1963 – Guinea 1955–1959, Box 3651; Guinea 1960–1963, Box 1944; POLGUIN 1963, Box 3922; Upper Volta 1960–1963, Box 1983; Mali 1960–1963, Box 1951; and Senegal 1960–1963, Box 1989.

Subject-Numeric File 1963–1973 – Côte d'Ivoire: DEFIVCAST 1964–1966, Box 1663; POLIVCAST 1964–1966, Boxes 2370 and 2371; POLIVCAST 1967–1969, Box 2240; POLIVCAST 1970–1973, Box 2399; Guinea: POLGUIN 1963, Boxes 2240 and 2257; USGUIN 1963, Box 2254; DEFGUIN 1963, Box 3724; DEFGUIN 1964–1966, Box 1649; USGUIN 1964–1966, Box 1755; POLGUIN 1964–1966, Boxes 2256, 2258, 2259, 2260, and 2261; FNGUIN 1967–1969, Box 763, DEFGUIN 1967–1969, Box 1550; POLGUIN 1967–1969, Boxes 2163, 2164, and 2165; FNGUIN 1970–1973, Box 891; DEFGUIN 1970–1973, Box 1740; POLGUIN 1970–1973, Boxes 2340 and 2341; Upper Volta: POLUVOLTA 1963, Box 4133; POLUVOLTA 1964–1966, Boxes 2907, 2908, and 2909; DEFUVOLTA 1967–1969, Box 1714; POLUVOLTA 1967–1969, Box 2696; POLUVOLTA 1970–1973, Box 2766; Mali: POLMALI 1964–1966, Box 2463; DEFMALI 1964–1966, Box 1679; POLMALI 67–69, Box 2331; POLMALI 67–69, Box 2332; Senegal: POLSEN 67–69, Box 2477; DEFSEN 1964–66, Box 1694; DEFSEN 1970–73, Box 1794; POLSEN 1970–73, Box 2588; Niger: POLNIGER 1963, Box 1693; POLNIGER 1964–66, Box 2514; POLNIGER 1964–66, Box 2516; NIGERPOL 1967–69, Box 2370; and DEFNIGER 1967–69, Box 1613.

IV. Other Archives and Data Sources

A. Archives of the United Nations High-Commissioner of Refugees

100.GEN.GUI Refugees from Guinea, General 1967/1984, 11.02.BOX.0023; and 100.ICO.GUI Refugees from Guinea in Ivory Coast [Volume 1] 1966/1971, 11.02.BOX.0095.

B. Online sources

Arrested Dictatorship Coup Database: https://www.arresteddictatorship.com/global-instances-of-coups.html (From: Powell, Jonathan and Clayton Thyne. 'Global instances of coups from 1950 to 2010: A new dataset.' *Journal of Peace Research* 48, no. 2 (2011), pp. 249–59.)

Frankema-Jerven African Population Database 1850-1960, version 1.0: https://www.aehnetwork.org/data-research/african-population-database-1850-1960/ (From: Frankema, E. and Jerven, M. 'Writing history backwards or sideways: towards a consensus on African population, 1850–2010.' *Economic History Review* 67, no. 4 (2014), pp. 907–31).

Freedom Index: https://freedomhouse.org/report/freedom-world

Human Development Index: http://hdr.undp.org/en/content/human-development-index-hdi

International Monetary Fund Macroeconomic and Financial Data: https://data.imf.org

Penn World Table: https://www.rug.nl/ggdc/productivity/pwt/ (From: Feenstra, Robert C., Robert Inklaar and Marcel P. Timmer. 'The Next Generation of the Penn World Table.' *American Economic Review* 105, no. 10 (2015), pp. 3150–82).

SIPRI Arms Transfers Database: https://www.sipri.org/databases/armstransfers

United Nations Digital Library: https://digitallibrary.un.org

World Bank DataBank: https://databank.worldbank.org/source/world-development-indicators#

V. Memoirs and Contemporary Texts

Camara, Fode Momo. *1 Novembre 1958–1 Novembre 2008: Cinquantenaire de la création l'armée Guinéenne* (unpublished memoir).

Foccart, Jacques. *Foccart Parle: Entretiens avec Philippe Gaillard*. Paris: Fayard, 1997.

Lamizana, Sangoulé. *Sous les drapeaux: Mémoires*. Paris: Jaguar, 2000.

— *Sur la Brèche trente années durant: Mémoires*. Paris: Jaguar, 1999.

Morrow, John Howard. *First American Ambassador to Guinea, 1959-1961*. New Brunswick, NJ: Rutgers University, 1968.

Robert, Maurice. '*Ministre' de l'Afrique; Entretiens avec André Renault*. Paris: Seuil, 2004.

Touré, Sékou. *Expérience Guinéenne et l'Unité Africaine*. Paris: Présence Africaine, 1961.

— *L'action politique du parti démocratique de Guinée pour l'émancipation africaine*. Conakry: Imprimerie nationale, 1959.

— *L'Afrique et la revolution*. Paris: Présence Africaine, 1977.

VI. Literature

Amondji, Marcel. 'Assabou et Marcoussis: deux tragédies ivoiriennes.' *Outre-Terre* 11, no. 2 (2005), pp. 215–22.

Banga, Arthur. *La coopération militaire entre la France et la Côte d'Ivoire.* Universitares Européenne, 2014.

Bangoura, Dominique. 'L'état et la sécurité'. *Politique Africaine* 61 (1996), pp. 39–53.

Bat, Jean-Pierre. *Le syndrome Foccart: la politique française en Afrique, de 1959 à nos jours.* Paris: Gallimard, 2012.

Bates, Robert. *Essays on the Political Economy of Rural Africa.* Cambridge University Press, 1983.

Bayart, Jean-Francois. 'Africa in the World: A History of Extraversion'. *African Affairs* 99 (2000), pp. 217–67.

— *The State in Africa: The Politics of the Belly.* New York: Longman, 1993.

Beck, Curt F. 'Czechoslovakia's Penetration of Africa, 1955–1962'. *World Politics* 15, no. 3 (1963), pp. 403–16.

Blessing-Miles, Tendi. 'Transnationalism, Contingency and Loyalty in African Liberation Armies: The Case of ZANU's 1974–1975 Nhari Mutiny'. *Journal of Southern African Studies* 43, no. 1 (2017), pp. 143–159.

Blum, Françoise. 'Sénégal 1968: révolte étudiante et grève générale'. *Revue d'histoire moderne et contemporaine* 59-2, no. 2 (2012), p. 144.

Bodin, Michel. *Les Africains dans la guerre d'Indochine, 1947–1954.* Paris: Harmattan, 2000.

Boone, Catherine. *Political Topographies of the African State: Territorial Authority and Institutional Choice.* Cambridge University Press, 2005.

Chabal, Patrick and Jean-Pascal Daloz. *Africa Works: Disorder as Political Instrument.* Oxford: James Currey, 1999.

Chafer, Tony. *The End of Empire in French West Africa: France's successful decolonization?* Oxford: Berg, 2002.

Clapham, Christopher. *Africa and the International System.* Cambridge University Press, 1996.

Cogneau, Denis, Yannick Dupraz, and Sandrine Mesplé-Somps. 'African states and development in historical perspective: Colonial public finances in British and French West Africa'. *PSE Working Papers*, No. 2018–27, 2018.

Connelly, Matthew. *A Diplomatic Revolution: Algeria's Fight for Independence and the Origins of the Post-Cold War Era.* New York: Oxford University Press, 2002.

Cooper, Frederick. *Africa since 1940: The Past of the Present.* Cambridge University Press, 2002.

— *Colonialism in Question: Theory, Knowledge, History.* Berkeley: University of California Press, 2005.

— 'Possibility and Constraint: African Independence in Historical Perspective'. *Journal of African History* 49, no. 2 (2008), pp. 167–96.

Crawford, James. *The Creation of States in International Law.* Oxford: Clarendon Press, 2006.

Crowder, Michael. *West Africa under Colonial Rule.* London: Hutchinson, 1982.

Decalo, Samuel. *Coups and Army Rule in Africa*. London: Yale University Press, 1976.

Deroche, Andy. 'Asserting African Agency: Kenneth Kaunda and the USA, 1964–1980'. *Diplomatic History* 40, no. 5 (2016).

Diallo, Abdoulaye. *Sékou Touré 1957–1961: Mythe et réalités d'un héros*. Paris: Harmattan, 2008.

Diallo, Alpha-Abdoulaye. *La vérité du minister: dix ans dans les geôles de Sékou Touré*. Paris: Calman-Lévy, 1985.

Diallo, Boubacar Yacine. *La Guinée un demi-siècle de politique (1945-2008)*. Paris: Harmattan, 2011.

Diarra, Samba. *Les faux complots d'Houphouët-Boigny: Fracture dans le destin d'une nation*. Paris: Karthala, 1997.

Echenberg, Myron. *Les tirailleurs sénégalais en Afrique occidentale française, 1857–1960*. Paris: Karthala, 2009.

— 'Paying the Blood Tax: Military Conscription in French West Africa, 1914–1929'. *Canadian Journal of African Studies* 9, no. 2 (1975), pp. 171–92.

Englebert, Pierre. *La Révolution Burkinabè*. Paris: Harmattan, 1986.

— *Burkina Faso: Unsteady Statehood in West Africa*. Boulder, CO: Westview, 1996.

Evrard, Camille. 'Quelle transmission du "pouvoir militaire" en Afrique? L'indépendance mauritanienne vue par l'armée française'. *Afrique contemporaine* 235, no. 3 (2010), pp. 27–42.

— 'Retour sur la construction des relations militaires franco-africaines'. *Relations internationals* 165, no. 1 (2016), pp. 23–42.

Frankema, Ewout and Marlous van Waijenburg. 'Metropolitan Blueprints of Colonial Taxation: Lessons from Fiscal Capacity Building in British and French Africa, c.1880–1940'. *Journal of African History* 55, no. 3 (2014), pp. 317–400.

Gardner, Leigh. *Taxing Colonial Africa: The Political Economy of British Imperialism*. Oxford University Press, 2012.

Gerits, Frank. '"When the Bull Elephants Fight": Kwame Nkrumah, Non-Alignment, and Pan-Africanism as an Interventionist Ideology in the Global Cold War (1957–66)'. *International History Review* 37, no. 5 (2015), pp. 951–69.

Gleijeses, Piero. *Conflicting Missions: Havana, Washington, and Africa, 1959–1976*. University of North Carolina Press, 2002.

Goody, Jack. *Technology, Tradition and the State in Africa*. London: Hutchinson, 1980.

Guirma, Frédéric. *Comment perdre le pouvoir?: le cas de Maurice Yaméogo*. Paris: Boradard et Taupin, 1991.

Hecht, Gabrielle. *Being Nuclear: Africans and the Global Uranium Trade*. MIT Press, 2012.

Herbst, Jeffrey. *States and Power in Africa: Comparative Lessons in Authority and Control*. Princeton University Press, 2000.

Hien, Pierre Claver. 'Les frontières du Burkina Faso: genèse, typologie et conflits (1885–1985)'. In *Burkina Faso cent ans d'histoire 1985–1995*, edited by Yenouyabe Georges Madiega et Oumarou Na, pp. 695–720. Paris: Khartala, 2003.

Higgott, Richard, and Finn Fuglestad. 'The 1974 Coup d'État in Niger: Towards an Explanation'. *Journal of Modern African Studies* 13, no. 3 (1975), pp. 383–98.

Hodzi, Obert. 'China and Africa: economic growth and a non-transformative political elite'. *Journal of Contemporary African Studies* 36, no. 2 (2018), pp. 191–206.

Jackson, Robert. H. *Quasi-States: Sovereignty, International Relations, and the Third World.* Cambridge University Press, 1990.

Jacob, Abel. 'Israel's Military Aid to Africa, 1960–66'. *Journal of Modern African Studies* 9, no. 2 (1971), pp. 165–87.

Jerven, Morten. *Poor Numbers: How We Are Misled by African Development Statistics and What to Do about It.* Cornell University Press, 2013.

Kaba, Camara. *Dans la Guinée de Sékou Touré: cela a bien eu lieu.* Paris: Harmattan, 1998.

Kaké, Ibrahima Baba. *Sékou Touré: le héros et le tyran.* Paris: Jeune Afrique, 1987.

Kieffer, Guy-André. 'Armée ivoirienne: le refus du déclassement'. *Politique africaine* 78, no. 2 (2000), pp. 26–44.

Kourouma, Ahmadou. *En attendant le vote de bêtes sauvage.* Paris: Seuil, 1998.

Krasner, Stephen D. *Sovereignty: Organized Hypocrisy.* Princeton University Press, 1999.

Lefèvre, Marine. *Le soutien Américain à la Francophonie: Enjeux africains, 1960–1970.* Paris: Presses de la Fondation Nationale des Sciences Politiques, 2010.

Levey, Zach. 'Israel's Strategy in Africa, 1961–67'. *International Journal of Middle East Studies* 36, no. 1 (2004), pp. 71–87.

— 'Israel's Exit from Africa, 1973: The Road to Diplomatic Isolation'. *British Journal of Middle Eastern Studies* 35, no. 2 (2008), pp. 205–26.

Lewin, André. *Ahmed Sékou Touré (1922-1984): Président de la Guinée de 1958 à 1984.* Paris: Harmattan, 2010.

— 'La Guinée et les deux Allemagnes'. *Guerres mondiales et conflits contemporains* 210, no. 2 (2003), pp. 77–99.

Luckham, Robin. 'French Militarism in Africa'. *Review of African Political Economy* 2, no. 5 (1982), pp. 55–84.

— 'The Military, Militarization and Democratization in Africa: A Survey of Literature'. *African Studies Review* 37, no. 2 (1994), pp. 13–75.

Mak, Dayton and Charles Stuart Kennedy. *American Ambassadors in a Troubled World: Interviews with Senior Diplomats.* Praeger, 1992.

Mangin, Charles. *La force noire.* Paris: Harmattan, 2011.

Manning, Patrick. *Francophone Sub–Saharan Africa, 1880–1985.* Cambridge University Press, 1988.

Martin, Guy. 'Continuity and Change in Franco-African Relations'. *Journal of Modern African Studies* 33, no. 1 (1995), pp. 1–20.

— 'The Historical, Economic, and Political Bases of France's African Policy'. *The Journal of Modern African Studies* 23, no. 2 (1985), pp. 189–208.

McGowan, Pat and Thomas H. Johnson. 'African Military Coups d'état and Underdevelopment: A Quantitative Historical Analysis'. *Journal of Modern African Studies* 22, no. 4 (1984), pp. 633–66.

McGowan, Patrick J. 'African military coups d'état, 1956–2001: frequency, trends and distribution'. *Journal of Modern African Studies* 41, no. 3 (2003), pp. 339–70.

Migani, Guia. 'Sekou Touré et la contestation de l'ordre colonial en Afrique sub–Saharienne, 1958–1963'. *Monde(s)* 2, no. 2 (2012), pp. 257–73.

Mitrokhin, Vasili and Christopher Andrew. *The World Was Going Our Way: The KGB and the Battle for the Third World*. Basic Books, 2005.

Muehlenbeck, Philip E. *Betting on the Africans: John F. Kennedy's Courting of African Nationalist Leaders*. New York: Oxford University Press, 2012.

— 'Kennedy and Touré: A Success in Personal Diplomacy'. *Diplomacy and Statecraft* 19, no. 1 (2008), pp. 69–95.

Nandjui, Pierre. *Houphouët-Boigny: L'homme de la France en Afrique*. Paris: Harmattan, 2000.

Nugent, Paul. *Africa Since Independence*. New York: Palgrave Macmillan, 2004.

— *Smugglers, Secessionists and Loyal Citizens on the Ghana-Togo Frontier*. Oxford: James Currey, 2002.

Osborn, Emily. '"Circle of Iron": African colonial employees and the interpretation of colonial rule in French West Africa'. *Journal of African History* 44, no. 1 (2003), pp. 29–50.

Ouattara, Azoumana. 'L'armée dans la construction de la nation ivoirienne'. In *Frontières de la citoyenneté et violence politique en Côte d'Ivoire*, edited by Jean-Bernard Ouédraogo and Ebrima Sall, pp. 149–68. Dakar: CODESRIA, 2008.

— 'Le coup d'État de décembre 1999 ou la fin de l'exception militaire ivoirienne: les mutations de l'armée ivoirienne depuis 1960'. In *Côte d'Ivoire: la réinvention de soi dans la violence*, edited by Francis Akindès, pp. 169–212. Dakar: CODESRIA, 2011.

Palm, Jean Marc. *Rassemblement Démocratique Africain (RDA) en Haute-Volta (1947–1980)*. Burkina Faso: DIST/CNRST, 2011.

Posner, Daniel and Daniel Young. 'The Institutionalization of Political Power in Africa'. *Journal of Democracy* 18, no. 3 (2007), pp. 126–40.

Rakove, Robert B. *Kennedy, Johnson, and the Nonaligned World*. Cambridge University Press, 2012.

Reid, Richard. *Warfare in African History*. Cambridge University Press, 2012.

Reno, William. *Warlord Politics and African States*. London: Lynne Rienner Publishers, 1998.

Romain, Tiquet. 'Service civique et développement au Sénégal. Une utopie au cœur des relations entre armée et pouvoir politique (1960–1968)'. *Afrique contemporaine* 260, no. 4 (2016), pp. 45–59.

Schmidt, Elizabeth. 'Anticolonial Nationalism in French West Africa: What Made Guinea Unique?' *African Studies Review* 52, no. 2 (2009), pp. 1–34.

— 'Cold War in Guinea: The Rassemblement Démocratique Africain and the Struggle over Communism, 1950–1958'. *Journal of African History* 48, no. 1 (2007), pp. 95–121.

— *Foreign Intervention in Africa: From the Cold War to the War on Terror*. Cambridge University Press, 2013.

Skinner, Elliot. *The Mossi of the Upper Volta: The Political Development of the Sudanese People*. Stanford University Press, 1964.

Thomas, Martin. *Violence and Colonial Order: Police, Workers and Protest in the European Colonial Empires, 1918–1940*. Cambridge University Press, 2012.

Tilly, Charles. *Coercion, Capital, and European States, AD 990–1992*. Oxford: Blackwell, 1997.

van de Walle, Nicolas. *African Economies and the Politics of Permanent Crisis, 1979–1999*. Edinburgh: Cambridge University Press, 2001.

van Walraven, Klaas. '"Opération Somme": La *French Connection* et le coup d'État de Seyni Kountché au Niger en avril 1974'. *Politique africaine* 134, no. 2 (2014), pp. 133–54.

—— *The Yearning for Relief: A History of the Sawaba Movement in Niger*. Leiden: Brill, 2013.

Verschave, François-Xavier. *La Françafrique: le plus long scandale de la République*. Paris: Stock, 1998.

Weber, Max. *Theory of Social and Economic Organization*. New York: Free Press, 1964.

Westad, Odd Arne. *The Global Cold War: Third World Interventions and the Making of Our Times*. Cambridge University Press, 2006.

Winrow, Gareth M. *The foreign policy of the GDR in Africa*. Cambridge University Press, 2009.

Youla, Nabi Ibrahima. *Grande figure africaine de Guinée: Entretiens avec Djibril Kassomba Camara*. Guinea: Harmattan, 2012.

Young, Crawford. *The African Colonial State in Comparative Perspective*. London: Yale University Press, 1994.

Index

Printed and bound by CPI Group (UK) Ltd, Croydon, CR0 4YY

09/06/2025

14685691-0001